The Queen's Knight

www.**booksattransworld**.co.uk

Also by Martyn Downer

NELSON'S PURSE

The Queen's Knight

The extraordinary life of Queen Victoria's
most trusted confidant

Martyn Downer

BANTAM PRESS

LONDON · TORONTO · SYDNEY · AUCKLAND · JOHANNESBURG

TRANSWORLD PUBLISHERS
61–63 Uxbridge Road, London W5 5SA
a division of The Random House Group Ltd
www.booksattransworld.co.uk

First published in Great Britain
in 2007 by Bantam Press
a division of Transworld Publishers

A CIP catalogue record for this book
is available from the British Library.

ISBN 9780593054857

Addresses for Random House Group Ltd companies outside
the UK can be found at: www.randomhouse.co.uk
The Random House Group Ltd Reg. No. 954009

The Random House Group Ltd makes every effort to ensure that the papers used
in its books are made from trees that have been legally sourced from well-managed
and credibly certified forests. Our paper procurement policy can be found at:
www.randomhouse.co.uk/paper.htm

Typeset in 13.25/15pt Perpetua by
Falcon Oast Graphic Art Ltd.

Printed and bound in Great Britain
by CPI Mackays, Chatham, ME5 8TD

2 4 6 8 10 9 7 5 3 1

For Tabitha, Bill and Mary:
the story of your great-great-great-grandfather

Contents

Wilhelm I
King of Prussia
and Kaiser of Germany
1797–1888

m

Augusta
Princess of
Saxe-Weimar
1811–1890

Victoria
Princess Royal of
Great Britain
(*Vicky*)
1840–1901

m
1858

Friedrich III
Kaiser of Germany
(*Fritz*)
1831–1888

Edward VII
King of England
(*Bertie*)
1841–1910

m
1863

Alexandra
Princess of Denmark
(*Alix*)
1844–1925

Alice
1843–1878

m
1862

Ludwig
Grand Duke of
Hesse and by Rhine
1837–1892

Alfred
Duke of Edinburgh and
of Saxe-Coburg-Gotha
(*Affie*)
1844–1900

m
1874

Marie
Grand Duchess of Russia
1853–1920

Wilhelm II
Kaiser of Germany
1859–1941

m
(1)
1881

Augusta
Princess of Schleswig-Holstein
1858–1921

m
(2)
1922

Hermine
Princess of Schönaich-Carolath
1887–1946

Victoria
(*Moretta*)
1866–1929

m
(1)
1890

Adolf
of Schaumburg-Lippe
1859–1916

m
(2)
1927

Alexander Zubkuv
1900–1936

3 other sons
and
3 other daughters

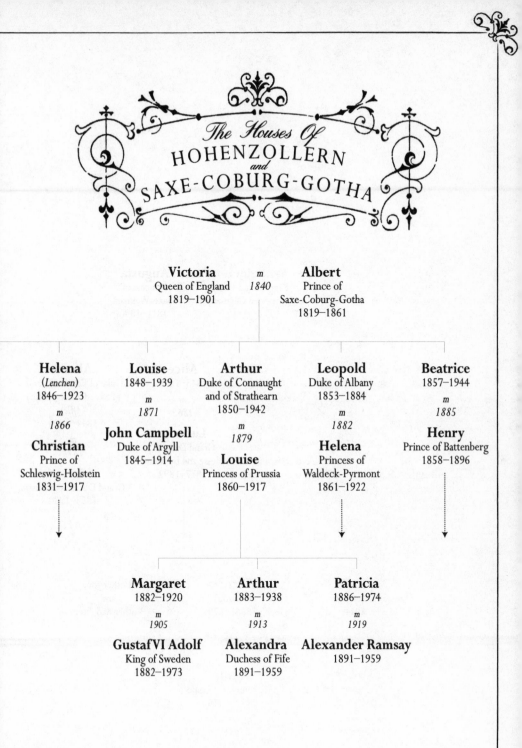

The Houses Of
HOHENZOLLERN
and
SAXE-COBURG-GOTHA

Victoria
Queen of England
1819–1901

m
1840

Albert
Prince of
Saxe-Coburg-Gotha
1819–1861

Helena
(*Lenchen*)
1846–1923

m
1866

Christian
Prince of
Schleswig-Holstein
1831–1917

Louise
1848–1939

m
1871

John Campbell
Duke of Argyll
1845–1914

Arthur
Duke of Connaught
and of Strathearn
1850–1942

m
1879

Louise
Princess of Prussia
1860–1917

Leopold
Duke of Albany
1853–1884

m
1882

Helena
Princess of
Waldeck-Pyrmont
1861–1922

Beatrice
1857–1944

m
1885

Henry
Prince of Battenberg
1858–1896

Margaret
1882–1920

m
1905

Gustaf VI Adolf
King of Sweden
1882–1973

Arthur
1883–1938

m
1913

Alexandra
Duchess of Fife
1891–1959

Patricia
1886–1974

m
1919

Alexander Ramsay
1891–1959

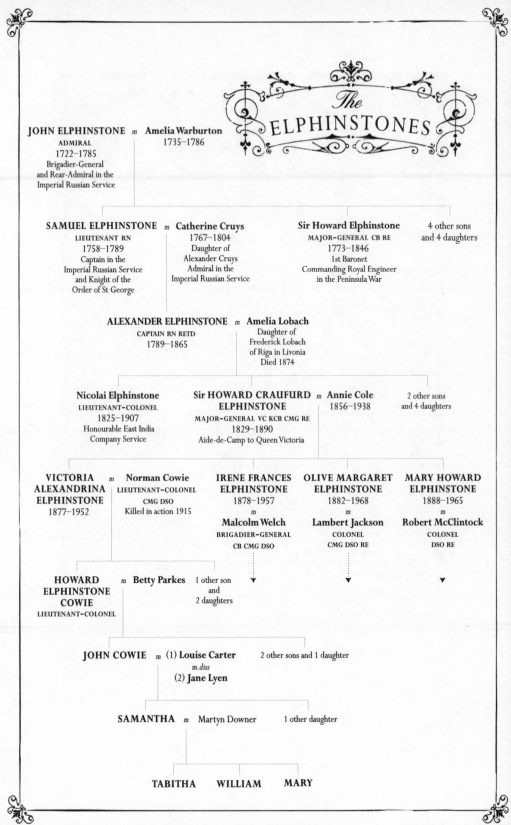

The ELPHINSTONES

JOHN ELPHINSTONE _m_ **Amelia Warburton**
ADMIRAL
1722–1785
Brigadier-General
and Rear-Admiral in the
Imperial Russian Service
1735–1786

SAMUEL ELPHINSTONE _m_ **Catherine Cruys**
LIEUTENANT RN
1758–1789
Captain in the
Imperial Russian Service
and Knight of the
Order of St George
1767–1804
Daughter of
Alexander Cruys
Admiral in the
Imperial Russian Service

Sir Howard Elphinstone
MAJOR-GENERAL CB RE
1773–1846
1st Baronet
Commanding Royal Engineer
in the Peninsula War

4 other sons
and 4 daughters

ALEXANDER ELPHINSTONE _m_ **Amelia Lobach**
CAPTAIN RN RETD
1789–1865
Daughter of
Frederick Lobach
of Riga in Livonia
Died 1874

Nicolai Elphinstone
LIEUTENANT-COLONEL
1825–1907
Honourable East India
Company Service

Sir HOWARD CRAUFURD ELPHINSTONE _m_ **Annie Cole**
MAJOR-GENERAL VC KCB CMG RE
1829–1890
Aide-de-Camp to Queen Victoria
1856–1938

2 other sons
and 4 daughters

VICTORIA ALEXANDRINA ELPHINSTONE _m_ **Norman Cowie**
1877–1952
LIEUTENANT-COLONEL
CMG DSO
Killed in action 1915

IRENE FRANCES ELPHINSTONE
1878–1957
_m_
Malcolm Welch
BRIGADIER-GENERAL
CB CMG DSO

OLIVE MARGARET ELPHINSTONE
1882–1968
_m_
Lambert Jackson
COLONEL
CMG DSO RE

MARY HOWARD ELPHINSTONE
1888–1965
_m_
Robert McClintock
COLONEL
DSO RE

HOWARD ELPHINSTONE COWIE _m_ **Betty Parkes**
LIEUTENANT-COLONEL

1 other son
and
2 daughters

JOHN COWIE _m_ **(1) Louise Carter**
m.diss
(2) Jane Lyen

2 other sons and 1 daughter

SAMANTHA _m_ **Martyn Downer**

1 other daughter

TABITHA   WILLIAM   MARY

Bookplate designed by Princess Louise, later Duchess of Argyll, for Howard Elphinstone after he was knighted in 1871.

PROLOGUE
London, 1890

Buckingham Palace

Thursday 13 March 1890

IT WAS GOING TO BE an uneventful day. The Queen planned to see the Prime Minister for an audience at three before going for a drive with Beatrice. Her country was at peace, enjoying the fruits of its hard-won empire. Looking for news, the papers reported a colliery disaster in Wales; the plans for a tunnel under the Thames at Blackwall; and excitement at the forthcoming University Boat Race.

But Reid was waiting for her when she reached London from Windsor at twelve-fifteen, which unsettled her. The unexpected appearance of the doctor, she wrote later, 'always alarms me'.[1] In his hand, Reid held a telegram which the palace had received at precisely five minutes past eleven that morning. He tried to break the news gently, keen not to frighten the elderly Queen as he murmured Sir Howard's name. Was he ill? she asked anxiously. No, the doctor replied quietly, he was dead.

Despite Reid's caution, Victoria, he recalled, was 'much upset and cried' at the news.[2] In fact, she was shocked beyond belief: first Albert; then Disraeli and Brown, now Howard Elphinstone. He had been Albert's friend – indeed, he had held her hand on the night her husband died, promising her his devotion. Then, as a father-figure to her children, he had been her constant, rock-like support, through happy times and sad: a shoulder to cry on, a friend to turn to. Now he, too, was gone – and in such a way!

After dining quietly with Alix, hurriedly summoned from Marlborough House to console her, the Queen sought solace in her private journal, as she had every day now for nearly sixty years. 'Dear Sir Howard is an awful loss,' she wrote; 'he was such a confidential devoted friend, and has been a father to Arthur, with whom he has been since 1859, having been chosen by beloved Albert. I am quite in despair. The whole thing haunts me.'[3]

Unusually, Victoria composed the court circular announcing the death herself, brushing aside the objections of her private secretary Henry Ponsonby. 'The Queen', she began with tears in her eyes, 'received . . . with profound grief the terrible news of the untimely death of Sir Howard Elphinstone. Sir Howard possessed' – here Victoria paused, scratching out the last word before continuing – '*enjoyed* Her Majesty's entire confidence, esteem, and friendship for 31 years . . . All the Royal Family unite with the Queen in deeply deploring Sir Howard Elphinstone's loss.'[4]

The Master of the Household, Sir John Cowell, who 'cried bitterly' when he heard that his old friend was dead,[5] was sent to meet Lady Elphinstone at Plymouth. He carried a letter from the Queen. 'Words cannot be found to express all I feel!' Victoria wrote to Annie, 'except to repeat how dear *He* was to me and my children. What a beloved and invaluable friend he was. My tears flow fast while I write in thinking of you *both*! My poor Arthur loses a second father and he owes his success in life to *Him*!'[6]

All the children had reason to mourn. Bertie, who had always looked to Elphinstone for advice, told his mother that 'Old friends like Sir Howard can be ill spared, as they are not to be replaced.'[7] Princess Helena, who was holidaying at Wiesbaden in Germany, felt 'sick with horror and grief. I cannot, cannot believe it is really true that we have indeed lost that dear devoted valued friend!! And in such a terrible way too! Christian and I always consulted dear Sir Howard about our ways & went to him in so many cases, when we wanted advice. We are awfully distressed.'[8] Helena's younger sister Louise equally struggled to comprehend the appalling news. 'It is really too terrible and has given me quite a shock,' she wrote from Rome. 'He was so good, clever, kind, devoted, one of the oldest, truest friends. Dear Papa was so fond of him and thought so highly of him.'[9] But it was the Queen's eldest daughter Victoria, known to the family as Vicky, who sent the most affecting letter. She had been very close to Elphinstone and, having recently lost her own husband, she felt this new tragedy especially keenly. 'You know that Fritz and I were devoted to him,' she wrote to her mother, 'and what a loss to you! You had not a truer and a more devoted servant and how profoundly attached to dear Arthur.'[10]

In fact, Vicky's brother, currently in India with his regiment, was among the last to learn the news. 'I don't know how to begin,' the Queen wrote carefully to her son, 'oh; this is *sad, sad,* dreadful. Our dear beloved devoted friend . . . to think he is gone and in *so* awful a manner. What I too have lost I cannot say! Few if *any* gentlemen . . . ever were on such confidential terms with me as dear excellent Sir Howard.'[11]

PART ONE
War

Trenches before Sevastopol, the Crimea

7 JUNE 1855

LIEUTENANT HOWARD ELPHINSTONE crouched down low beneath the parapet. He felt the blood pumping in his ears and the sweat prickling on his back. The trench was wrapped in folds of acrid black smoke, which pricked his eyes and invaded his mouth, gagging him. He gripped his sword more tightly, counting down the seconds to the attack. Shells burst overhead, spraying red-hot splinters across the torn ground. Then, with a distant yell from Colonel Tylden and a roar from the men, they were over and running towards the Quarries, a trench system protecting the Russian front line. Howard heard his breath rasping across his lips as he ducked into the storm of grapeshot, his boots slipping over the stony ground. As he broke through the smoke into the moonlight he was assailed by the sweet smell of crushed grass and death. Men crumpled soundlessly beside him. The Russian trenches were already thick with the dead and the dying. He fell in among them, stabbing, jabbing and slicing with his sword. When there was no-one left to kill, he called hoarsely for his men to start reversing the trench parapet, his voice sounding distant and unfamiliar. Sandbags and gabions – wicker baskets – were filled with the warm, bloodied earth to build the defences; the men tore their hands as they scratched and scraped at the soil. Even the soft, wet corpses of the Russians were bundled onto the ledge of the trench for protection, their bodies popping beneath the bullets. To his right, Howard could see Captain Wolseley's men sapping back to the British lines, their picks ringing above the thumping of the guns.

All night the enemy forces tried to recover their position, launching repeated assaults on their lost trenches. 'More than once there was a fierce hand-to-hand fight in the position itself,' wrote William Russell, *The Times*'s celebrated war correspondent, who watched the bloody action from the British front line. The fiercest counter-attack came at about three in the morning, when the whole ravine lit up in a blaze of fire. Absorbed in his work shoring up the captured position, Howard did not see the Russian soldier lurking 'behind a gabion, bent on his knee'. He did not notice the musket, as it was slowly raised and levelled. He did not know he was only moments from death. But Corporal Stanton did. Spotting the man, he seized a sword from the lifeless hand of a dead officer and brutally struck him down. 'Lieutenant Elphinstone and Stanton were working side by side at the time,' the official historian of the action later dryly recorded, 'but the former was unaware of his danger till the deadly act of the latter had removed the cause.'[1]

Towards dawn the Russian attacks finally faded, leaving the British troops to slump among the corpses to get what sleep they could. In his memoirs Captain Wolseley, by then a highly decorated field marshal, would describe that night's attack on the Quarries as the hardest fight he had ever experienced – and he had seen a few. One in three of the men involved in the action were killed or wounded. Elphinstone returned to the engineers' camp exhausted, but alive. His efforts that night had not gone unnoticed, however. In the morning Lord Raglan, the commander-in-chief of the British army in the Crimea, singled him out in the dispatches he sent London on the action, quoting the words of Colonel Tylden, who had told him that 'this officer deserves the highest praise for the creditable manner in which he executed this service'.[2]

The only obstacle that still prevented the British from entering Sevastopol itself was the enemy's Battery No. 3, the so-called 'Great Redan'. Designed by Colonel Franz Todleben, a fiendishly clever military engineer, the Redan crouched behind a huge hurdle of felled trees and a deep, stake-strewn ditch. Its ramparts bristled with guns and ill-disguised menace. To the British redcoats sheltering in their trenches it appeared impregnable.

Sunzel, Russian province of Livonia

SATURDAY 12 DECEMBER 1829

HOWARD ELPHINSTONE was born on 12 December 1829 at Kumenhof, his family's white-brick country retreat near the village of Sunzel, thirty miles outside Riga in Livonia (since 1918 Suntazi in Latvia). The villa, like similar properties belonging to other merchants from the city, stood in a vast, snow-covered landscape of lakes, forests and marshes. Nearby, a handful of miserable wooden dwellings housed the serfs who farmed the family's land. Like his brother and sisters before him, the new baby was christened in the large Lutheran cathedral which stood in a maze of crooked streets at the heart of the old city of Riga.

The child had an exotic lineage. From his mother Amelia he inherited the blood of the Germans who had settled the region centuries before the Russians arrived to claim it for their empire. His father Alexander Elphinstone, a recently retired officer of the Royal Navy, claimed an even more ancient and illustrious origin for his side of the family. 'I have', he declared on emerging from years of research in German archives, 'found that our family, *originally* Helfensteins, actually descended from the reigning dukes of Helfenstein, and have their whole history from the year *450*.'[1] Descent had certainly been proved as far back as the thirteenth century, and it was known that the Elphinstones had settled in the Orkney Islands by the sixteenth. The Royal Navy brought the family down to England in the eighteenth century, although Alexander remained loyal to his family's Scottish heritage, claiming kinship with the Lord Elphinstone whose title had been earned fighting the English on behalf of James IV of Scotland. Moreover, Alexander steadfastly maintained that he was the rightful heir to Arthur Elphinstone, the sixth Lord Balmerino and a descendant of the youngest son of the third Lord Elphinstone. Balmerino, a daring Jacobite military officer, had died childless following his execution for treason in 1746, leaving Alexander to contend later that his title should have then passed to the heirs of the second son of the third Lord Elphinstone, which he claimed as his own line.

Alexander's grandfather John Elphinstone, then a young naval lieutenant, had witnessed his cousin's beheading at the Tower of London (the last occasion this method was used under English law to dispatch traitors), receiving Balmerino's treasured claymore before the axe fell. In 1769, by now a highly respected captain and veteran of the Seven Years War against France, John was approached by Count Zakhar Chernyshev, the Russian ambassador in London, acting on behalf of Empress Catherine II. The Empress wanted to bolster the skills of her navy – then engaged in a bitter struggle against the Turks – with the help of an elite band of handpicked British officers. With the permission of the Admiralty, John travelled to St Petersburg with two of his sons, both lieutenants in the Royal Navy, and Howard Lord Effingham, an old friend who had volunteered to join him in his adventure. On 28 June 1769, the seventh anniversary of her accession to the Russian throne, the Empress received John 'in the most gracious and flattering manner' at her Winter Palace.[2] He was promoted to rear-admiral in the Russian navy, given a suite of luxurious apartments in the palace and allocated a place beside Catherine at dinner. 'I did not expect to find so much ease at the table of so great a Sovereign,' he recalled; 'she sat like the mistress of a private family, speaking to all with the greatest affability.' John marvelled at life inside the easy-going Russian court, though he could not fail to notice that the flattering attention he received 'caused jealousy amongst the courtiers'.[3] 'None of the Empress's attendants wear swords', he noted with amazement, 'nor has she any guards, and if she passes through any of the apartments, everyone knows they are to take no notice by bowing or any other mark of respect.'[4] When John declared that he would fit up a squadron of ships and lead them to victory against the Turks, the Empress 'clap'd her hands with joy'.[5] He was as good as his word. Within a year of his arrival, in May 1770, a squadron of Russian ships commanded by Elphinstone engaged the Turkish fleet at Nauplia in the Aegean, scoring a notable success. But the admiral's efforts were soon overshadowed by a greater Russian naval victory at the battle of Chesme.

Although Elphinstone seems personally to have played only a supporting role at Chesme, he claimed the lion's share of the victory, and duly returned to Petersburg to collect his spoils. But Count Alexei Orlov, a close intimate of the Empress and supreme commander of Russian forces in the Mediterranean, challenged the admiral's account of his role in the battle and began spreading rumours of negligence and misappropriation of funds. His name blackened by Orlov, John found himself dismissed by the Empress as belonging 'to the ranks of the mad who are carried away by their first impulse and pay no regard to logic'.[6] Furious at this humiliation, he stormed into the room of Count Zakhar Chernyshev, the Empress's confidant who had originally engaged his services, demanding satisfaction. 'I stepped to the door,' John later recalled,

bolted it, and came up to him with a countenance which terrified him, and my hand clenched close to his face, threatened him if he did not speedily do me justice, he himself must expect the consequences, as through low artifices I had been prevented from seeing the Empress, from whom alone I could look for redress. But now it was his duty, as he was the means of bringing me into the service. He begged me to be calm, embraced me, said he was my best friend, that every thing should be settled entirely to my satisfaction, so upon his repeated assurances I left him.[7]

The admiral was as wrong to trust the devious Russian courtier as he was naïve in attempting to negotiate the machinations of the Empress's court. He returned to England with a gold medal and 5,000 roubles – about £100,000 at today's prices – but without his promised pension or his bounty payment from the battle of Chesme, which he estimated at over 40,000 roubles. Worse still, when he reached London Elphinstone was arrested for the debts he had incurred refitting the Russian fleet at Portsmouth. Hearing of the admiral's fate, Lord Cathcart, the British ambassador in St Petersburg, observed that 'no foreigner was ever so much caressed; no one has been threatened worse, nor no man deserved it less'.[8] When his ceaseless demands for compensation went unanswered, John threatened to publish an exposé of his life in the Russian court. Eventually the State Council in St Petersburg relented, admitting 'that it was necessary for this restless man to be satisfied'.[9] The admiral was sent an *ex gratia* payment of 24,000 roubles to clear his debts. But there was still no pension, nor any sign of the prize money he felt he was owed. To his dying day in 1785, John nurtured a grievance against Russia – and Russians.

John and his wife Amelia – the daughter of the famously eccentric antiquarian John Warburton and 'the best looking woman of her age', according to one observer – had ten children. 'And such a set few can boast,' remarked one visitor to their house in Hampshire: 'all handsome, not one defect in the whole number, [though] they are and will be most of them short.'[10] Their second son Samuel remained in the Russian navy after his father's ignominious return to England and prospered despite the opprobrium attached to his distinctive name. On one occasion he travelled through the night to deliver some important dispatches to the Empress in person, arriving 'late at night in his fighting clothes, covered with dust and gunpowder, and severely fatigued with long and arduous duty'. The Empress called Sam Elphinstone 'my son' and made him a Knight of St George, her highest award for gallantry.[11] Inevitably, considering Catherine's rapacious reputation, there were rumours of a sexual affair. Nevertheless, the Empress welcomed Sam's marriage to her goddaughter Catherine Cruys, whose father Alexander Cruys, an eminent admiral in her navy, had fought beside the ill-fated John Elphinstone.

In addition to his great courage, Sam had a lively, inquisitive mind. In the lull before the outbreak of the Russo-Swedish war, working from his home in the naval port of Kronstadt, he embarked on an ambitious scheme to compile a compendium of every known fact necessary, in his opinion, to pursue a successful naval career, delving into fields from astronomy to natural history; horology to gunnery. Sadly, this remarkable work, the manuscript for which is now at the National Maritime Museum in London, was never completed; for in 1789 Sam died of the wounds he sustained trying to capture the Swedish king. Soon afterwards, his widow Catherine took their infant son Alexander back to England to be close to Sam's surviving family.

In 1798, after a patchy education in Parsons Green, then a small village to the south-west of London, Alexander followed the family tradition and entered the Royal Navy as a midshipman. At the end of the Napoleonic Wars he earned a footnote in history by being present at a dinner in Devon at which the fate of Napoleon was decided. The dinner was being hosted by his uncle Captain Thomas Elphinstone for their kinsman Admiral Lord Keith, Lieutenant Governor of Plymouth. A few miles out to sea the ex-Emperor of France lay incarcerated in *Bellerophon*, a British warship anchored in Plymouth Sound. During the dinner, urgent dispatches arrived from the Admiralty seeking Keith's opinion on where Napoleon should be sent. The table was cleared, maps were produced and the matter was discussed while Alexander stood guard at the door, 'to prevent the servants listening'.[12] The suggestion the officers sent back to London by return courier that night was that the former Emperor be confined on St Helena, a remote island in the South Atlantic. Their proposal was immediately adopted by the Admiralty, although it was kept a secret from the rest of the world until Napoleon had been safely dispatched.

After Sam's heroic death Catherine the Great had vowed to take care of the Elphinstones, but again the family's recompense was slow in coming: it was not until 1803, in the reign of the Empress's grandson Tsar Alexander I, that Catherine Elphinstone was finally granted a lease on an estate in Livonia. Her son Alexander was raised to the Livonian nobility and decorated *in absentia* with the Order of St Vladimir, an honour restricted to Russian noblemen defending the Empire against the French. Shortly thereafter Catherine Elphinstone died, and it was only with the peace of 1814 that Alexander was able to travel to Livonia to claim his inheritance – to find not only that the tenant on his estate had paid no rent since the French invasion of Russia in 1812, but that the law did not allow him to extend his mother's lease beyond its twelve-year term. Disillusioned and facing ruin, Alexander appealed to the governor general of Livonia for help, eventually securing a further term on the estate (although the post-war depression made it largely worthless). At this point, embittered by his own struggle against Russian bureaucracy, Alexander took up the fight begun by his grandfather Admiral John Elphinstone nearly fifty years before, for payment of the money owed to his family by the Russians after the battle of Chesme. 'I now remain', Alexander loftily informed Tsar Nicolai I in 1825,

> the representative of my grandfather and of a principal branch of
> the Elphinstone family who have been ennobled above 700 years
> and have served with honour in Palestine and every country they
> have been employed in. I therefore feel ambition of leaving my
> children some honourable proofs of the services of their ancestors
> in this country to which I am so much attached.[13]

In Livonia Alexander met and married Amelia Lobach, the daughter of a prominent Rigan merchant, Frederick Lobach, who owned a factory in the city. The Lobachs were Baltic Germans, members of the tight-knit Lutheran liberal elite who still dominated the city's affairs, despite Russia's century-old suzerainty over the region. They were cultured, hard-working people who wore the finest clothes, patronized the arts and, when they were not making money, enjoyed their large estates in the country. Their fortunes were built on linseed, hemp and flax, and on the valuable export trade in timber for shipbuilding. 'In Riga the rich live and let live and enjoy their wealth, without at all despising the wealth of others,' observed one English visitor. 'Different ranks and classes are not so sharply divided as with us, and no one asks after the rank, origin, or birth of a stranger. The man himself is alone looked to, and if he is endurable he will be endured.'[14] These qualities formed Alexander's and Amelia's eight children – four boys and four girls – all of whom survived childhood. The eldest boy, John, was named for his impetuous great-grandfather; the next, Nicolai, for his godfather the Tsar. Howard, the youngest boy, was given the name of his great-uncle Major-General Sir Howard Elphinstone. Sir Howard, Admiral John Elphinstone's youngest son and one of Sam Elphinstone's brothers, had ignored his family's ties with the navy to pursue a successful career in the army. A close confidant of the Duke of Wellington, he had earned his baronetcy directing many of the sieges in the Peninsular War as the commanding Royal Engineer.

In the early 1830s the lease on the Elphinstones' estate in Livonia finally expired, forcing them to leave. For some years they moved around the continent, a nomadic lifestyle which seems to have given all the children wanderlust in later life. They lodged first in Dresden, where the boys were patchily educated at military school, then in a modest apartment on the Champs de Mars in Brussels. Money was tight, despite Alexander's success in seeing his name added to a short list of British naval officers promoted in retirement to increase their pensions. But he still failed in his efforts to obtain satisfactory recompense from the Russian government for his grandfather's service: 'a duty which I owe to the memory of my distinguished predecessors, to myself, and to the children (all natives of the Imperial Empire) with whom my marriage to a Livonian Lady has been blessed'.[15]

The original Major-General Sir Howard Elphinstone, created first baronet after the Peninsular War on the recommendation of the Duke of Wellington. He encouraged his great-nephew and namesake to enter the Royal Engineers.

Alexander was not a well-educated man, but he was a very determined one. '*Remember* [that] I am a plain, downright sailor, and *say what I mean*,' he once declared.[16] So when no fewer than '6 harassing and expensive journeys to St. Petersburg' had met without success, the captain published his grandfather's Russian journals, hoping thereby to expose what he considered the venality at the heart of Catherine the Great's court.[17] Sprung at a delicate moment in Anglo-Russian relations, the publication of the journal seems to have finally exhausted the patience of the government in St Petersburg. Alexander was sent a substantial, and final, payment in settlement for his grandfather's service; although it was nothing like the £149,187 he had been hoping for.

Feeling vindicated and temporarily flush with money, in 1844 Alexander took his family back to England, to the appropriately named Livonia Cottage, a run-down house outside Sidmouth in Devon that he had purchased some thirty years before as a young naval officer. The house was renovated with the help of the Tsar's money, while the children decorated its windows with their coats of arms, both real and imagined, and the white elephant crests of the counts of Helfenstein. Meanwhile, their father turned his full attention to proving that he was entitled to the abeyant Balmerino peerage. He engaged an expensive genealogical agent to investigate the matter in Edinburgh, hiring a lawyer to prepare the case for court. The thirteenth Lord Elphinstone had initially been unperturbed by Alexander's dogged attempts to claim one of his family's ancient titles, believing them hopeless. His uncle Mountstuart Elphinstone, a famous Indian administrator, had even been encouraging, wishing Alexander 'all success'.[18] However, as time passed, Lord Elphinstone, to whom it was said the youthful Queen Victoria had once lost her heart, grew irritated by Alexander's demands. He ordered Scotland's foremost genealogist, Sir William Fraser, to resist the claim and to enquire after his own right to the attainted title, opening up a bitter breach between the different branches of the Elphinstone family.

LEVONIA COTTAGE.
(Capt.ⁿ Elphinstone R.N.)
Pub.ᵈ by J. Wallis R. Marine Library, Sidmouth Ap.ᵗ 1ˢᵗ 1826.

Levonia (Livonia) Cottage in Sidmouth, to which the Elphinstones retreated after losing their Russian estate.

While her husband plotted the return of his family to what he considered their rightful position in society, Amelia Elphinstone managed his chaotic finances and household with the utmost economy. How else, she exclaimed, 'could we keep up our position in the world?'[19] Brought up to a life of luxury in Livonia, Amelia had reconciled herself to her reduced circumstances through her strong religious faith and the conviction that 'to overcome difficulties stimulates the capacities of soul and will'.[20] Her portrait shows a young woman, growing slightly plump, with a steady gaze and simple but refined tastes. The rich ruby-red velvet gown she is wearing is unadorned but sumptuously expensive; her only jewellery is a long gold chain weighing heavily around her neck.

Amelia declared that she 'could endure anything except an ill bred child. It would soon bring me to the grave.'[21] She told her children never 'to be ashamed of your parents' and to remember that they were members of the Russian nobility and scions of the Scottish aristocracy. Scornful of provincial English society, the Elphinstones kept themselves to themselves in Devon. They preferred their own to the company of others, and spoke only German at home. It was an austere, God-fearing household. Well loved but ruled with a rod of iron, the children grew up resilient and self-reliant but also introspective and self-critical – and in some cases critical of their parents, too, as they grew older. Rosalie, the eldest daughter, complained that the family only ever ventured into 'circles where we are never eclipsed and even think it right to be thought the first and best'. Such a life, she observed sadly to her brother Howard, 'engenders great self-conceit'.[22] All the children painted well and played music to a high standard, but they made few friends and lived isolated lives, often dogged by a despondent sense of loneliness. As Rosalie confided to Howard, following a visit to London,

When every other person seemed enjoying themselves and looked happy being surrounded by hosts of their friends I felt *alone* and friendless. How often when driving with Lady Dymoke or Lady Mansell in their gay carriages have I observed many a poor creature looking at me with envy and thought 'Oh, if you only knew how far my heart was from feeling the happiness you imagine, you would pity not envy.'[23]

In Howard himself a tendency towards his sister's melancholy outlook engendered a fatalism which would later express itself in outrageous acts of bravery. Only the advent of a wife and children would eventually ease his burden – by which time it was almost too late.

3

The Royal Military Academy, Woolwich

1845

EACH IN TURN, the three elder Elphinstone boys entered the military service of the Honourable East India Company, the semi-private enterprise that controlled India under the nominal authority of the British Crown. Naturally, their father would have preferred them to join the navy; but with Britain enjoying a long period of peace, a career at sea offered few prospects of reward. The HEIC was a good alternative. It was cheaper to obtain a commission in the company's service than in the regular army, and promotion was more fairly geared towards talent than interest. (None the less, before entering his sons for the HEIC training school at Addiscombe in Surrey, Alexander Elphinstone was sensible enough to seek the assistance of his kinsman Mountstuart Elphinstone, once governor of Bombay and the company's most eminent former servant.)

Howard would have followed his brothers into the HEIC, had his father not heard in 1842, to his surprise, that 'the Engineer Corps had . . . taken a favourable turn [and] that a young man, *could now live on his pay*'.[1] Consequently, Alexander sought a place for 'little Howard' at the Royal Military Academy in Woolwich, where the Royal Engineers earned their commissions through examination, in contrast to the regular army where commissions were still traded. In theory, this made the corps open to all; but in practice entrance to the academy was still carefully vetted to ensure that the cadets were drawn mainly from the gentry. Howard's acceptance as a candidate for entry was a foregone conclusion, for his great-uncle and namesake Major-General Sir Howard Elphinstone RE, hero of the Peninsular War and an intimate of the Duke of Wellington, was still very much alive and living in retirement in Sussex. Accordingly, after passing the formality of an entrance examination in classics and mathematics, Howard entered the academy in June 1845 as one of sixty *neux*, or new boys.

The academy occupied an elegant eighteenth-century building on the south side of Woolwich Common, near the river Thames to the east of London. The one hundred and eighty or so 'gentlemen cadets' it housed were not seen as soldiers, nor were they subject to military law. Instead 'The Shop', as the academy became known to generations of cadets, more closely resembled one of the newer public schools. Fees of £80 a year were charged for a cadet's education, although these were reduced to £50 for the son of a retired naval officer such as Howard. In addition, a further 20 guineas was recovered for the cadet's uniform, books and equipment.

The similarity to life in an English public school left Howard at a disadvantage. Unlike most of the other cadets, he had received an uneven and largely private education abroad, mixing with few other English boys, and was unused to the culture of bullying, drinking and gambling which was rife inside the academy. This disorder had reached such an epidemic proportion by the 1840s that it sparked a series of riots in which the cadets clashed violently with boys from the local town. In fact, the unrest at Woolwich was merely a microcosm of the instability in the wider world; for this was a decade that saw revolutions sweeping the continent, sparking armed conflicts and unseating monarchs. In London the rise of the so-called Chartist movement for constitutional change caused such alarm to the political establishment that in April 1848 the Queen herself was evacuated from London ahead of a planned

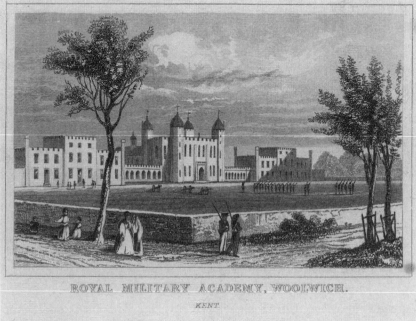

ROYAL MILITARY ACADEMY, WOOLWICH.

KENT.

Drawn & Engraved for DUGDALES ENGLAND & WALES Delineated

The Royal Military Academy in Woolwich, c. 1840. The training school for the Royal Engineers and Royal Horse Artillery, it was known to generations of gentlemen cadets simply as 'The Shop'.

mass demonstration. Howard's eldest sister Rosalie, who was in town at the time, witnessed the build-up to the rally, reporting excitedly that she had seen the police dispersing a large crowd in Trafalgar Square. 'The general belief is that if the military are allowed to use their arms it will soon be all quiet again,' she wrote.[2] Mercifully, such drastic measures were avoided. In heavy rain, the protest failed to materialize and soon afterwards the movement itself faltered and collapsed – a typically English reaction to radicalism in typically English conditions.

Despite so many distractions Howard worked hard at the academy, helped by some outstanding teachers. His mathematics tutor, for instance, was Professor Peter Barlow, a close associate of Charles Babbage, while Professor Michael Faraday, then at the height of his powers, taught him chemistry. Under their guidance Howard matured quickly, and the shy, self-absorbed boy who had left Devon soon became unrecognizable to his mother – so much so, that before his final examination Amelia Elphinstone admitted to her son that she had dreamt 'you had become so very conceited and that you were quite sure of passing a successful examination, relying entirely upon your own abilities and by no means on God's help'.[3] She need not have worried. Howard finished first in his class, receiving in addition a theodolite 'for his proficiency in the surveying class'.[4] On 18 December 1847 he was commissioned in the Royal Engineers, the elite professional corps of the British army.

Young Lieutenant Elphinstone left Woolwich looking for action, and for glory. Instead, after a period of training at Chatham and with the aid of some discreet string-pulling by his father, he was appointed to the staff of Colonel Harry Jones RE, the commanding engineer at Edinburgh Castle. Jones was a kindly, if somewhat irascible, veteran of the Peninsular War and an old comrade of Howard's great-uncle Major-General Sir Howard Elphinstone. Alexander was delighted with his son's posting, telling him that 'you must try to keep up these sorts of acquaintances of mine as it may be useful to you later on sometime'.[5] He also secretly hoped that the appointment would give his son the chance to delve into the family's history in Scotland to advance his own claim to the Balmerino title. But Howard was soon distracted by the many more pleasurable diversions that the old city had to offer, relishing his freedom both from the academy and from his overbearing father. He passed his evenings playing billiards at the regimental mess, dancing at the Assembly Rooms, going to the theatre or simply 'sauntering like a dandy about the town'.[6] There were girls to flirt with and parties to attend. One particularly 'disgraceful' dinner at the castle, he noted rather shamefully in his journal, left him with a 'dreadful headache' for days afterwards.[7]

Yet despite being frequently 'blown up' by Jones for being late to the office, Howard still worked hard and never lost the urge to improve himself.[8] In his spare time he attended lectures at the university; painted and sketched in the surrounding countryside; and, each evening, diligently practised his violin at the dingy lodgings in Darnaway Street that he shared with Anthony Durnford, a close friend from Woolwich. Like Howard, Durnford had been partially educated in Germany before entering the academy, but at six feet tall he towered over his friend. Nor can he have been an entirely restful companion. Although his Irish ancestry gave him great charm, Durnford's Celtic blood and bouts of heavy drinking could make him short-tempered and prone to melancholy; and his dangerous love of gambling was to lead directly to his violent and celebrated death years later in the Zulu War.

While Howard caroused in Edinburgh, his eldest sister Rosalie sent him long accounts of her secluded life in Devon with their parents. 'I see, more and more, we none of us are yet humble minded enough,' she sighed as she watched her father labouring over his genealogical charts.[9] In childhood, Rosalie had given her brother the warm affection he had lacked from his parents, so her early death in September 1851, after years of enduring debilitating but unspecified 'spasms', left Howard emotionally adrift. Many months later, the mere mention of his sister's name over dinner still, he admitted, 'stung me to the soul'.[10] In her last letter to Howard, Rosalie had cautioned him against becoming 'worldly-minded, proud and overbearing' – like their father, in fact.[11] Howard took her words to heart. He wrote 'read it often' on the letter, and carried it with him for the rest of his life.

In August 1850 Howard had glimpsed the royal family for the first time when they visited Edinburgh on their way north on holiday. The Queen and her husband Prince Albert were both enraptured by Scotland and since 1848 had enjoyed the lease on Balmoral, a modestly sized mansion on Deeside in the Highlands. This was only the third year that the royal couple had made the long journey north with their growing family – their seventh child Arthur having been born in May – and they were greeted with great enthusiasm. Howard ran down to see the special train arrive, watching in fascination as the long procession of royal carriages then wound its way up to Holyrood Palace through streets lined with troops and thousands of spectators. 'Nothing can describe the splendour of the scenes witnessed,' he wrote in his diary that evening, noting that 'the most remarkable feature seemed to me the orderly and well behaved spirit of the mob, no clouting or pushing or fighting, but everything went in the most decorous and well behaved manner'.[12] From her carriage, meanwhile, as recorded in her own journal, the Queen thought 'the sight a very fine one and the good Scotch people most enthusiastic'.[13]

The following morning, Howard noticed crowds gathering on the Mound to hear Prince Albert speak at the stone-laying ceremony for the new National Gallery of Scotland. Determined to see this grand event, he rushed back to his lodgings to 'encase myself in military uniform, well knowing that a red coat must pass anywhere, and I was not mistaken, for no opposition [was] ever offered me'.[14] Having thus secured a prime position in the packed grandstand – which, he happily observed, was 'crowded with all the beauty Edinburgh could boast of' – Howard listened as the prince delivered a short address in his heavily accented English. In the speech, which was later published, Albert praised the foundation of a 'temple' to the 'Fine Arts which have so important an influence upon the development of the mind and feeling of a people'.[15] According to the Queen, her husband had been very nervous before the event, as he always dreaded speaking in public. So when he returned to Holyrood, she was relieved to hear that 'everything had gone off beautifully'.[16] The next day the royal family continued on their stately way to Balmoral. Howard missed their departure, although he 'heard all at club while playing billiards'.[17] His curiosity was sated and, after all, he little expected to see them all again.

Opportunities for advancement in the Royal Engineers were scarce during peacetime. So Howard was delighted when, having failed in a hopeful application for a position in Hong Kong, he was posted to the Ordnance Survey, a branch of the engineers charged with mapping Britain. Then, in September 1853, after eighteen months spent tramping around the north of England with his surveying tools, Howard was unexpectedly summoned to London for a special assignment, probably on the recommendation of Colonel Jones, who knew of his drawing skills and fluency in German. He was to observe a series of military manoeuvres on the continent involving the armies of the self-styled 'Holy Alliance' of Prussia, Austria and Russia. His role was an official one, codified in diplomatic language; but, with relations between London and St Petersburg increasingly fraught over Russian ambitions in the eastern Mediterranean, it was also a spying mission in anticipation of war. For such a young officer – Howard was still only twenty-three – it was a remarkable appointment and testament to the high regard in which he was already held by his superiors.

For two months he travelled around Europe, attending not only the manoeuvres but the equally exhausting programme of social events which accompanied them as his hosts vied with each other to impress their many distinguished visitors. His first stop was Berlin, where he stayed at the embassy with Lord Bloomfield, the urbane British ambassador, and his wife Georgiana.[18] He considered the vast Schloss, the official residence of King Friedrich Wilhelm IV of Prussia, to be very 'shabby', noticing in particular how all the plaster on the walls seemed to be 'falling off'. Nor was he any more impressed by the King's wife Elizabeth, whom he adjudged 'a commonplace looking woman' – certainly for a queen – or by the Prussian army, which appeared overly theatrical and poorly equipped. Howard was particularly amused to see how the troops 'threw their feet forward in a most absurd manner' when they marched using the so-called goosestep.[19]

On 19 September a break in the proceedings gave Howard the chance to explore Sanssouci Park, a royal playground of palaces and gardens developed by Frederick the Great at Potsdam, a quiet town some twenty miles outside Berlin. Again he was slightly disdainful, deeming the palace of Sanssouci itself, considered a gem of baroque architecture, 'excessively small'. Charlottenhof, another palace built recently by the current king in an ornate Italian style, fared slightly better in his eyes, being equally small, 'but neat' and 'very pretty'. However, it was the 'grandeur' of the Neues Palais, its 'air of poverty notwithstanding', which made the greatest impression on the young English tourist. Completed by Frederick the Great in 1769 – 'to show', in Howard's words, 'that he was not yet impoverished' – this enormous palace loomed magnificently over the park: a vast two-hundred-room confection of rococo extravagance. Wandering through its deserted and dusty corridors, Howard came across the palace's greatest treasure, its famous *Muschelsaal*, or Shell Hall – and dismissed it as 'embellished in most hideous taste with precious minerals and jewels'. 'What a waste of money,' he concluded contemptuously before catching the train back to Berlin.[20] He could little have imagined how large a part the palace would later play in his life.

From Prussia, Howard travelled to Olmütz to observe the manoeuvres of the Austrian army. On the opening day he attended an open-air mass with the youthful Emperor Franz Joseph of Austria and the Tsar of Russia, Nicolai I (who was also his own elder brother's godfather). Then it was on to Warsaw for the Tsar's turn to show off his army – although in Howard's case at least, he signally failed. 'There appear to be two great drawbacks to the efficiency of the Russian Army,' he noted in his report.

> First the inferiority of the officers, the majority of whom seem to be of the same intellectual stamp as the men, without thought or energy; and secondly the absence of a proper commissariat . . .
> If these two points could be reformed I think the Russian troops would form a very superior force. They have one very good point, they don't run![21]

The manoeuvres concluded on Tuesday 4 October 1853 with a grand dinner at the Imperial Palace in Warsaw jointly hosted by all three monarchs. Afterwards, Howard and the other guests marvelled at an extraordinary display of fireworks which climaxed with the release of no fewer than fifteen thousand rockets over the darkened city. It was a portentous sight; but few of the spectators – except for the Tsar and his staff – knew that earlier that same day Turkey, an ally of Britain, had declared war on Russia. Within a year, this bold act would lead to war in the Crimea, where Howard would be faced by those self-same Russian troops he had coolly appraised; this time though, in bitter and bloody conflict.

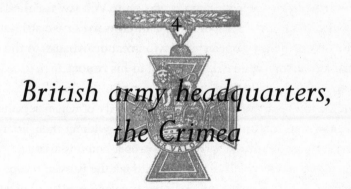

British army headquarters, the Crimea

17 June 1855, 10.30 p.m.

Ten days after the attack on the Quarries, Elphinstone pressed into a small, crowded hut at army headquarters. The oily air was draped with cigar smoke; moths whirled around the flickering candle, throwing shadows across the burnt, bewhiskered faces of the men gathered there. Harry Jones, Howard's old chief in Edinburgh, now a general, sat hunched over a map on the table; at his side, his adjutant Lieutenant John Cowell took notes. With London frustrated at the pace of the war and the newspapers increasingly critical of the conduct of the army, General Jones had supplanted the faltering Sir John Burgoyne as the commanding engineer for the campaign. From his youthful experience of the Peninsular War nearly fifty years before, Jones was confident that a huge combined allied attack on Sevastopol could lift the debilitating siege and end the war in triumph. As a stream of hastily written orders passed into the cool night air to begin their journey down to the trenches, few of the officers in the hut doubted that Jones was right. Even the date of the supposedly secret attack was deliberately propitious. The following day would be the fortieth anniversary of the Battle of Waterloo – the significance of which cannot have failed, however, to alert the Russians as they made their defensive preparations.

Of the men gathered in the hut, Howard had endured more

than most, having been present at the siege of Sevastopol since it began the previous October. In an environment where acts of heroism were commonplace his exploits, and his survival, were astonishing. Even before landing in the Crimea he had distinguished himself, saving the lives of four drunken soldiers as they struggled to cross the churning waters of the Bosporus in a frail boat.[1] He had consistently shown a 'singularly cool' attitude towards his own safety which to others had seemed at times almost suicidal. Gerald Graham, a fellow engineer who would win a Victoria Cross during the campaign and eventually rise to become a general, recalled

> walking in an advanced trench on the Right Attack with him when
> we had to pass a gap where there was no cover at all, thereby
> affording the enemy a sport like rabbit shooting, with us for rab-
> bits. When it came to Elphinstone's turn, he merely made a quiet
> remark after getting across: 'That was a good shot, considering I
> was running', the bullet having just grazed his coat.[2]

Another officer commented that Elphinstone 'was always ready for an adventure if it came in the way of duty'. Major Campbell, of the 46th Regiment, enjoyed recounting 'how he, Elphinstone, and another, had one night tried how far they could creep in front of the Redan before being stopped'.[3] In contrast to his swashbuckling reputation, however, away from the heat of battle Elphinstone was described by a senior officer as 'full of quiet humour, very observant and quick at detecting humbug or affectation'.[4]

Towards midnight, after a final glass of brandy and water, the small team of engineers who would spearhead the assault returned to camp for parade. Elphinstone, on orderly duty, stayed behind at headquarters, following Jones and Cowell to the small farmhouse which housed Lord Raglan, the commander-in-chief of the army. Outside, Raglan's staff officers clustered on the cool stone steps, smoking and talking, confident of success. Horses shuffled in the dark. There was a tension between the aristocratic Guards officers,

ROYAL ENGINEER PARK.

(RIGHT ATTACK)

The Royal Engineers' camp behind the British lines before Sevastopol in 1855. This drawing by Howard Elphinstone was published as the frontispiece to his heavily criticized account of the campaign.

who had bought their commissions, and the engineers, who were professional soldiers. The Guards blamed the engineers for embroiling the army in a lengthy and costly siege; the engineers considered the Guards to be arrogant popinjays.

The ride down to the front line was slow, with the horses frequently stumbling on the shot-strewn road. Ripples of applause greeted the silent procession as it passed the huddles of excited spectators. Beyond a line of cavalry drawn up to protect the trenches, the staff dismounted, unable to ride any further in safety. Elphinstone, who had spent many months painstakingly inching the attack forward, knew the layout of the complex trench system by heart. But most of the soldiers did not, and the trenches were packed with confused and frightened men, many drunk, who struggled with the ladders, axes and grappling irons needed for the assault. Scuffles broke out and it was only by drawing their swords that the staff officers could force their way up to the third parallel, close to the front line. Half a mile ahead, the Redan squatted menacingly against the flames lighting the city below. The staff crowded behind Raglan into a mortar battery. The confined space stank of stale wine, urine and excrement. It was three in the morning. With the agreement of his French counterpart, Raglan had scheduled the combined allied attack for dawn.

The movement ceased, a few hushed voices faded away and the trenches fell silent. The thousands of redcoats jammed into the slits in the stony ground were invisible in the dark as, terrified, they waited to fight. Elphinstone wanted to be with them; with the engineers who would direct the assault. They would end the siege, and with it the war, covered in glory while he was left behind alongside John Cowell – a man who, Graham had sneered, 'does not like danger for the sake of its excitement'.[5] Elphinstone clearly did. The waiting time was short, however; far too short. Before the first ribbons of dawn had unravelled across the sky, the sporadic rattle of musket fire drifted over the British troops from the French trenches to their right. It was followed by the sharp, hard thump of drums and the distant sound of Russian buglers raising the alarm. The Malakoff fort, the French target in the attack, burst into flame as its guns leapt into life. In the mortar battery, Raglan and the staff swivelled to peer through their glasses at their ally's fatally premature assault. Behind them, the British guns opened up a deadly barrage, the shots from the huge Lancaster guns tearing over their heads like a fleet of mad express trains as they hurtled towards the enemy. The Russians replied with a volley of shells which ripped open the night air before bursting in a deadly shower of red-hot, razor-sharp splinters. The air throbbed around them and the earth rocked beneath their feet.

Every eye strained to see the French attack. But again the Malakoff flared with gunfire, showing it was still in Russian hands. Below it the hillside crawled with blue-coated troops and sparkled with the flicker of musketry and the flash of sunlight on polished steel. Rockets were hastily fired to launch the British assault on the Redan. But the signal was lost in the fiery web spread over the battlefield; so Raglan ordered Harry Jones to hoist the flag of St George, England's traditional battle standard. Jones sent Lieutenant Cowell away to find a flagstaff, the young officer weaving through gales of grapeshot as he hauled one back above ground to the battery. After ramming the pole into a gabion, Cowell shouted across at Private Eadie to get the flag aloft quickly.[6] The signal at last made, the redcoats clambered awkwardly out of the trenches to advance. Some ran; others walked, stooping beneath their equipment like old men. Many fell at once, sinking into the bloodied ground. The attack soon dissolved into isolated pockets of men, each lurching blindly towards the Redan. In the reserve trenches, a young engineer called Charles Gordon watched in mounting horror as the Russians 'mowed down our men in dozens'.[7]

'There is no chance for them!' shouted Captain Wolseley, who was standing in the mortar battery beside Elphinstone and Captain Brown of the 88th Regiment. As Wolseley spoke, a shot bounded through an embrasure of the battery, tearing off the head of a gunner, ripping away Brown's arm and passing through the chest of Private Eadie, who was 'knocked . . . to pieces'.[8] The young soldier's guts sprayed around the battery, covering the officers with a warm film of torn flesh. Then General Jones, who had been peering above the parapet with Raglan, staggered back, falling into the bloody mess on the floor of the battery. A bullet had gouged a furrow out of the side of his head, leaving a claret-red stain to creep through his ruffled white hair. 'That was quite close enough!' exclaimed Raglan, clearly shocked by the carnage.[9]

The attack was a shambles; the day lost. By ten that morning it was over. Most of the engineers involved in the attack had been killed; one, Lieutenant Graves, a close friend of Elphinstone's from Woolwich, was missing. As swarms of flies descended to feed on the dead and dying, so the critics fell on Raglan. William Russell, *The Times*'s war correspondent, deplored the assault's 'defective and inadequate' planning, claiming that the British officers had been completely 'outwitted' by the enemy. 'So abortive and so weak was the attack', he fumed, 'that the Russians actually got outside the parapet of the Redan, jeered and laughed at our soldiers as they fired upon them at the abattis, and mockingly invited the "Inglisky" to come nearer.'[10] The Russians, in fact, were baffled by their enemy's plan. Years later Elphinstone revealed that Franz Todleben, the Russian engineering genius responsible for Sevastopol's defences, had told him when they met after the war that he thought 'it was odd the French and us did not divide the attack in proportion to our numbers instead of each taking half. Always thought the Malakoff the strongest point as there was room in rear not only to collect but to bring out reserves on each side.'[11]

Dazed and exhausted, Elphinstone rode back to camp. Then, after snatching a few hours' rest, he returned on duty to the front line. He was determined to do something about the carnage caused by the disastrous attack. He faced an appalling scene: the stinking trenches were heaped with the dead and wounded. But the horrors inside the trenches were as nothing compared to those outside in no-man's-land. 'It was agonising to see the wounded men who were lying there under a broiling sun,' William Russell reported, 'parched with excruciating thirst, racked with fever, and agonised with pain.'[12] The Russians had ignored the British request for an armistice that would have enabled the wounded to be retrieved, so the hillside below the Redan was still littered with bodies, weapons and discarded equipment. The gentle evening breeze carried on it the smell of death and the pathetic groans of the injured men who lay marooned on the battlefield. Seeing the white flag flying above the British lines, one or two of them weakly waved their caps for help. Others raised themselves up before falling back, each stilled by a single shot from the murderous Redan. Elphinstone scanned the battlefield for Graves. His job was to repair the battered front-line defences; but, tortured by the suffering and the thought of his friend lying alone and possibly alive in no-man's-land, he decided to act.

Some years before, Rosalie Elphinstone had been surprised by the findings of a light-hearted assessment of her brother's handwriting. 'We all think it so exactly like you,' she had mused, 'except the last two inclinations he gives you: that of sudden resolves and precipitant actions, which I think is very far indeed from your general calm and collected way.'[13] The graphologist had been correct, however. For now, without a second thought and with only a single sapper at his side, Howard clambered out of his trench and dashed onto the battlefield, stumbling over the bodies, many of them blackened and bloated by the searing heat. Seeing him, some of the forsaken men shouted out for help. But their cries were met by a deadly volley of Russian gunfire which swept down the hillside, killing the sapper instantly. There was little Elphinstone could do by himself except grab one of the abandoned scaling ladders and drag it awkwardly back to the British trenches. Yet he would not give up. As dusk fell and the horrific scene faded into the inky night, he called for volunteers to join him in a rescue party. None came forward. The drunk gawped while the sober turned away, their shame less than their fear. Angered, Elphinstone ordered six terrified redcoats at gunpoint to follow him. When it was dark, they stole back onto the battlefield, feeling for the living among the dead. Occasionally shots rang out from the Redan, halting the men in terror as they waited for the bullet to strike. But one by one twenty of the wounded were hauled back to safety among the debris of the British trench. Much of the engineers' discarded equipment was also recovered, denying the enemy valuable trophies. Towards midnight the sporadic fire escalated into a full-scale artillery barrage. The British guns barked back, some of their shells dropping so dangerously short that Elphinstone was forced to abandon his rescue mission for fear that they would kill him and his men. The body of Lieutenant Graves was later found near the Redan, a single bullet wound in his head.

After the terrible events of 18 June, the British camp fell into sullen despondency. Many of the infantry officers blamed the engineers for entangling the army in the debilitating siege, believing that a decisive battle at the outset might have secured Sevastopol at a stroke. 'We shall never take it', said one scornfully, 'till the last engineer is hanged.'[14] Broken by the disaster and stricken by cholera, Raglan died ten days later. The engineers resumed their relentless work, directing repairs to the trenches and leading the sappers as they inched the attack still closer to the enemy. The siege was now at a critical stage and the outcome of the war on a knife-edge. One day in early September, Elphinstone was given orders to establish a new rifle pit, directly opposite the Russian defences. Shortly after nine that evening, when darkness had fallen, he joined Lieutenant Ranken at 'the most favourable point of our line for starting an expedition across "the open"'.

'We advanced as cautiously as we could,' George Ranken later recalled,

> the shot and shell directed from our batteries at the enemy, and by theirs at ours, whizzing over our heads. We spoke in whispers and endeavoured to tread as lightly as possible; I groped about for a flower to bear off and send to my mother as a trophy, but my hand encountered nothing but thistles and grass. At length, after walking about thirty or forty yards, Elphinstone stopped, and told us

he thought we had reached the right place. He had no sooner said this, and our small working party halted to wait for our work-men, when a low whistle was heard from the Russian sentries, lying concealed around, and we perceived we were discovered. Our men in the trenches had been told we were out, and directed on no account to fire. Our discovery was immediately followed by a volley of musketry, directed at us from all around, and our men, in spite of the warnings given them, seeing the blaze of the Russian muskets opened an indiscriminate cross fire on every one (ourselves included). We took to our heels and made for our own trenches as fast as our legs would carry us, and happily reached them in safety. Three of our working party, however, had been wounded, and they were forced to abandon their tools and gabions.[15]

Then, on 8 September 1855, the allied guns launched a fero-cious new barrage, spitting tons of hot metal into the Russian fortifications. Towards noon Elphinstone left the dugout in the front line where he was stationed to see the French tricolour flying above the Malakoff fort. Around him, redcoats rose from the British trenches, as they had done before in June, but this time surging forward with a roar. For a time it seemed that the Redan itself might fall. Through the churning smoke, Colonel Windham of the Coldstream Guards could be seen on its ramparts, waving his sword in triumph. But seconds later, the Redan erupted into flame, Windham was lost in the smoke and the invaders were spat out by a ferocious counter-attack. 'Bleeding, panting, and exhausted, our men lay in heaps in the ditch beneath the parapet,' William Russell wrote, 'sheltering themselves behind stones and in bomb craters.' Many stumbled back down the hill, throwing away their weapons, running 'the gauntlet of tremendous fire' before dropping back into the trenches, sobbing with fear and pain.[16] 'We should have carried everything before us if the men had advanced,' stormed Charles Gordon, shocked at this turn of events and disgusted by the soldiers' cowardice, 'but they did not behave as they ought, as the number of officers killed shows.'[17] Appalled and outraged by the unfolding disaster, Elphinstone lifted himself higher above the parapet to get a better look. In an instant, he was hurled backwards into the trench, as if struck in the face by a sledgehammer. The rest was darkness and pain.

George Ranken tumbled back into the British trenches soon afterwards. 'All was shame, rage and fear,' he wrote later; 'the men were crowded together and disorganized.'[18] He pushed through to the engineers' hut where Elphinstone should have been, but it 'presented a most lamentable spectacle'. Inside the remains of the hut he found only 'a poor gunner with his leg badly shattered by the splinter of a shell. In front, in the centre of the roadway, lay a rifleman dying, covered with blood about the head and face, and foaming at the mouth.'[19] There was no sign of Howard, so when a naval officer came up and urgently asked for his orders, Ranken took charge of the situation himself. 'Though my duty, strictly speaking, was over,' he wrote, 'yet I felt I was called upon to supply Elphinstone's place at a time like this.'[20]

When the smoke of battle had cleared, Elphinstone's servant came down from the engineers' camp to search for him anxiously. No-one knew where he was. The dugout was deserted and the wounded had been taken away. Then, while fearfully scouring the carts loaded with piles of the dead, the servant recognized the boots he had polished that morning. Howard was lying insensible among the decomposing corpses, his uniform in tatters and his face smeared with blood. The servant pulled the inert body from beneath the heap of rotting dead and, calling for help, carried him up to the doctor's hut behind the lines, barely noticing the huge explosions rocking the city below.

5

Balmoral, Scotland

MONDAY 10 SEPTEMBER 1855, 10.30 A.M.

' FROM GENERAL SIMPSON, ma'am!' Lord Granville exclaimed, waving the telegram above his head: 'Sevastopol is in the hands of the Allies!'[1] The Queen clapped her hands, her eyes sparkling with excitement. Prince Albert said they must light the beacon. With a rush of crinoline and the clatter of abandoned coffee cups, the household bustled out of the drawing room to find overcoats and galoshes. The castle was thrown into a happy confusion as the procession was joined by the servants, keepers and workmen from the village. Led by John Brown and with Ross on his pipes, the prince steered the noisy crowd up Craig Gowan, where a bonfire was lit and the victory toasted in whisky. Victoria watched the celebrations from the castle, laughing at the distant figures pirouetting in the firelight.

6

Livonia Cottage,
Sidmouth, Devon

THURSDAY 27 SEPTEMBER 1855

'MY DEAR SON HOWARD has written himself,' Captain Elphinstone scrawled hurriedly to his lawyer;

> he gives a short account of the battle and that he was wounded in the head which is still bound up, as well as one eye and the other rather weak, but he says he feels much better now and is taken great care of. The date of his letter is the 16th September. Today I have to write many letters in answer to enquiries about my son, so you must excuse my adding more but the moment I know anything more about him I shall let you know.[1]

The captain was forced to wait until 20 November before he could welcome his son home from the Crimea in person. He was 'very weak', his father reported, 'but in *bodily* good health, except his right eye, which he fears he will lose'.[2] (In fact, both eyes were saved but sight in the left was lost.)

Howard recuperated at Livonia Cottage for five months before reporting back for duty. The wound he had suffered was a familiar one. Debris thrown up by enemy shot was a constant danger in the trenches. Garnet Wolseley had suffered an almost identical injury shortly before Howard and, like him, had similarly lost the sight in one eye. But many men came back from the

Crimea physically scarred and, although serious, Howard's wound would not prevent him resuming his military career. The emotional damage was less well understood, hardly even taken into account. The term 'shell shock' was quite unknown, let alone recognized as a medical condition. Yet in the year before he received his wound, Howard had endured eighty-one days and ninety-one nights on duty in the trenches, almost certainly a higher total than any other officer or soldier in the whole army, incurring untold damage to his psychological well-being. The best evidence for the impact of such relentless mental and emotional stress is Howard's journal which, when resumed, revealed a graver-minded man than the one who had sailed in such high hopes to the Crimea. He was also far warier of other people, finding it difficult to form close relationships. His experience of war and his disability stripped away his confidence, leaving him insecure, withdrawn and highly sensitive to the opinion of others. But he was no less industrious. Conscious of his own failings, he set about studying the behaviour of others, as if by imitation he could improve and mend himself. This approach was revealed a year later, when he dined with an old friend from Woolwich. 'Study Egan's manner of conversing more,' he told himself; 'learn the method in which he dresses his speeches; for he is interesting beyond doubt, and always pleasing, and agreeable. He is so thoroughly master of all the subjects he broaches, and draws others' conversation so very pleasingly into his own channels, i.e. those with which he is acquainted. It is an act to acquire.'[3]

On his return to the Royal Engineers, Howard was promoted captain and sent once again to observe the annual military manoeuvres in Prussia. So impressed was the Duke of Cambridge, the Queen's cousin and head of the army, with the reports and drawings which Howard conscientiously filed from Coblenz that he forwarded them to the palace for the personal 'perusal' of Prince Albert, a keen student of warfare.[4] The prince read the reports with the 'greatest interest', praising Elphinstone's diligence and his considerable talents as a draughtsman.[5] When

Howard came back from the continent, he was sent to the newly instituted Topographical Department in Charing Cross, where his drawing skills, apparently unaffected by his injury, could be best used in mapmaking. He was also given the demanding task of preparing the first volume of an official account of the war, which he illustrated with his own drawings and those of other engineers such as Charles Gordon. As Howard had been evacuated from the Crimea before the end of the conflict – which following the fall of Sevastopol drifted on until March 1856 – the work would be completed by General Sir Harry Jones, now head of the new army staff college at Sandhurst. 'The war has certainly proved a good mistress to him,' Elphinstone quipped ruefully after visiting his former chief's comfortable residence in Surrey.[6]

In October 1856 Howard was present at a regimental dinner in London attended by other veterans of the war, including General Jones's former adjutant John Cowell.[7] Cowell had returned from the Crimea something of a celebrity, having entered Sevastopol after the city fell and theatrically seized a Russian flag. Hearing of his exploit, the Queen had invited Cowell to the palace to tell his story. But there was also another, more surreptitious, reason for his regal summons. Prince Albert had asked General Jones to enquire discreetly after an officer prepared to act as a 'military governor' to eleven-year-old Prince Alfred, the royal couple's second son. Affie, as he was called by the family, was struggling in the schoolroom beside his unruly elder brother Albert Edward (universally known as Bertie), the Prince of Wales and future King. Despite the best efforts of the princes' tutor Frederick Gibbs, the two boys constantly squabbled and fought, preventing each other from working. Their father had therefore decided to separate the children, placing each in his own household under the supervision of a governor with wide-ranging powers. In doing this, Albert, to whom the Queen had given *carte blanche* in the education of their children, was only continuing a tradition established during his own childhood in Coburg, where his upbringing had been assigned to a young German called

John Cowell, Howard's contemporary in the Royal Engineers, who negotiated his entry into court.

Christoph Florschütz. Florschütz had been engaged by Baron Christian Stockmar, a Machiavellian figure employed by the prince's hedonistic father, the Duke of Saxe-Coburg-Gotha, as his principal adviser. Prince Albert was especially keen to select his own sons' governors from within the army, as he wanted to give their education a distinctly martial tone. Moreover, using governors would allow him to discipline his sons by proxy without damaging his own relationship with them. 'It is not possible to be on happy friendly terms with people you have just been scolding,' Albert told his wife.[8] When Cowell visited the palace for his interview, Bertie had already been packed off to a house in Richmond Park with Robert Bruce, a colonel in the Guards.

The Queen thought Cowell a 'remarkably nice, steady and amiable young engineer officer'.[9] Like Charley Gordon, his closest friend in the Royal Engineers, he was also a man of deep religious conviction. With these qualities and on the personal recommendation of Harry Jones, Cowell was duly appointed Affie's governor; his lack of aristocratic credentials proving no obstacle to this prestigious appointment. Within weeks he found himself living in the Royal Lodge in Windsor Park with the young prince and the prince's tutor, a stolid young clergyman called William Jolley.

A year later Prince Albert, now officially styled Prince Consort, began casting about for a governor for his third son, Arthur. The need was not immediate. Bertie and Affie had been fifteen and eleven respectively when they left home, whereas Arthur was still only seven and under the care of the maids in the royal nursery. But the cause was very great indeed, for Arthur was the Queen's most adored child: '*dearer* than any of the others put together', she told her husband; 'thus *after you* he is the *dearest* and *most precious* object to *me* on *Earth*'.[10] Born on 1 May 1850, Arthur had been named for his godfather, the legendary Duke of Wellington, whose birthday he providentially shared. A life in the army had been intended for the prince from his birth; for, being Victoria's third son, he was unlikely ever to inherit the throne. His mother's close interest therefore demanded special care in the choice of a governor for Arthur – a fact impressed upon General Jones when he was again asked for his assistance in filling the post.

Jones's first candidate was Edward Stanton, a colonel in the engineers who had recently returned from surveying the Danube with Charles Gordon. However, Stanton awkwardly declined the honour, preferring his current post as commanding officer of the Royal Engineers at Chatham to minding the mundane affairs of a seven-year-old boy. In a tense meeting with Jones, Stanton tactfully pleaded the insurmountable age difference between the prince and himself, which, he declared, 'would make companionship out of the question'.[11] Writing privately to Cowell, who was acting as the Prince Consort's intermediary in the matter, Jones hinted at the 'other reasons' behind the colonel's decision. Besides reluctance to abandon a comfortable position at Chatham, these included professional embarrassment at accepting such a demeaning role and the very real fear that leaving the engineers for any length of time could cost him dearly in terms of future promotion.[12] Regardless of the importance the Queen attached to the position, Jones recognized that only a younger, less senior officer would ever consider it, as he would have less to lose. Happily, the ideal candidate was close at hand. 'I know not of any officer so well qualified in every way as Captain Elphinstone,' Jones reported to the palace. 'He is a good linguist, draws well, good tempered, and is a good officer of Engineers, and would, I am of opinion, make an excellent companion for the young Prince.'[13] The general was certain he could persuade Elphinstone to accept the position.

The Prince Consort was impressed by Elphinstone's qualifications, recognizing his name from the Prussian military reports. On 8 September 1857 he asked Cowell to sound out his fellow engineer and to discuss with him the '*modus operandi*' of the post, 'explaining, from your own experience, the duties to be performed and the privations attached to their conscientious performance'.[14] As there seems to have been some unnecessary urgency attached to the prince's request, Cowell arranged to meet

Elphinstone a few days later on the quayside at Southampton and talk the matter over with him as they crossed the Solent together in the royal steam yacht *Fairy*. The Queen was expecting Cowell and Prince Alfred at Osborne House, the royal family's retreat on the Isle of Wight, so there was no time for a longer discussion. Only hours before his meeting with Elphinstone did it occur to Cowell to inform the Prince Consort about his friend's war wound, presumably to allay concerns that it might frighten Arthur. 'It has not affected his appearance in the least nor his vision in the right eye,' Cowell assured the prince. 'It is hardly visible in the pupil to a careful observer, as the loss of sight was caused by being hit about half way between the eye and ear.'[15] The substantial whiskers which Howard sported, like other veterans of the Crimean winters, possibly masked some of the scarring on his left temple. But he remained highly conscious of it, always preferring to pose for photographs showing his right profile.

As *Fairy* hauled itself through the grey-green waters of the Solent, Cowell talked candidly to Howard about his life as a governor in the royal household. At the private pier for Osborne, the two officers parted: Cowell to continue up to the house with Prince Alfred, while Elphinstone returned to the mainland by packet boat, having promised his answer within the week. He had obviously expressed serious reservations about accepting the post: Cowell told the Prince Consort that he thought nothing would induce Elphinstone to resign from the Topographical Department 'short of the prospect of active service in a European war. He sees that if he left his Corps for an indefinite period, he would on his return to it find himself in all probability in a much lower position than he now occupies.'[16] This, of course, had been Colonel Stanton's principal objection too. Indeed, the question as to whether officers seconded to court should enjoy the same promotion rights as those on active service was such a sensitive issue that when Prince Albert's private secretary Charles Grey became due for an army promotion in 1860 the matter was debated on the floor of the House of Commons. Pointing out that the Queen had surrounded herself with 'officers of distinction', Sidney Herbert, the Secretary of State for War, remarked that to

> make it the rule that the moment a man accepts a Court place, a black mark shall be set against his name, that his past service shall not count, that he shall be debarred from receiving the legitimate honours of his profession; and you exclude from the places which it is in the best interests of the country to have filled by the best men, the very officers whom you would yourselves select, as the best persons to discharge the duties.

Benjamin Disraeli, speaking for the opposition, agreed. If the acceptance of a place at court by an officer was seen as a bar to promotion, he argued, the royal household would be staffed by 'a very inferior class of military men'. 'It is not for the interest of the country', he pronounced, 'that our Sovereigns and the Princes of their families should be surrounded by military parasites; but rather that they should be surrounded by men of independent feeling, of high qualities, and with a sense of responsibility.'[17] Grey received his promotion to lieutenant-general; but the debate had failed to resolve the wider issue, as Elphinstone would later discover.

Back in London, Howard sought the advice of Harry Jones before giving his answer to the palace – unaware, perhaps, of the general's close personal interest in the affair. His concern had now shifted to his suitability for such a task, believing his personality to be unsympathetic to the needs of a young child. Jones, unwilling to fail the Prince Consort again, brushed aside Howard's concerns. 'The great point will be', the general observed sagely, 'whether you will be able to make the boy your friend.'[18] Jones revealed that in similar circumstances he had personally insisted to the Prince Consort that John Cowell should be treated 'as a companion and friend' by Alfred, and not seen by his young charge as simply another tutor.[19] Nevertheless, Elphinstone returned to his lodgings in Bury Street still reluctant to accept the post. We do not know whether he asked his father for an opinion; if he did, it seems

General Sir Harry Jones, Howard's mentor and commanding officer in the Crimea, who selected him for the post of governor to Prince Arthur.

unlikely that Alexander, who was somewhat of a snob, would not have urged him to accept it – having also, of course, an ulterior motive for encouraging his son to enter court, one quickly seized upon by his rivals for the Balmerino title. Sir William Fraser, Lord Elphinstone's genealogical agent, later suspected that Howard would 'take advantage' of his position at court 'to forward' his family's claim to the Balmerino titles. 'Such a connection might facilitate their getting an act of restoration from the attainder of the last lord [Balmerino],' Fraser warned Lord Elphinstone, 'but before they can apply to the Queen or the House of Lords, they must show that they are the nearest heirs male of the Balmerino branch. This they have hitherto failed to do.'[20]

Such an outcome mattered little to Howard as he sat in his room agonizing over his decision. He was more concerned about how a young boy would respond to a man scarred by war and with a tendency to brooding introspection. Uncertain what to do, he fired off a letter to Cowell seeking final reassurance. 'Now honestly and candidly,' he wrote, 'give me your opinion as to whether my intended young charge and me would get on well. Is mine a character that he would take to? For I am *well* aware that it is not one that *all* boys would like.'[21] The reply from Osborne House was swift and encouraging. 'I can say no more than that I firmly believe Prince Arthur's character and disposition to be all that I could desire in undertaking such a charge,' Cowell wrote. 'He is a boy of much feeling, upon whom justice and kindness would make a strong impression. This being my opinion of him, and knowing what I do of you, I have every reason to suppose that yours is a character he would take to, and more so, after you had acquired an influence over him by commanding his obedience.'[22]

His misgivings eased, if not entirely erased, by Cowell's soothing words, Elphinstone formally accepted the position the next day. The Prince Consort was delighted, telling his mentor Baron Stockmar that Arthur's new governor 'promises well'.[23] None the less, the prince asked Harry Jones, rather ominously, whether Elphinstone 'had well considered the offer before accepting it'.[24] Certainly, the speed of the appointment, no more than a month from beginning to end, appears to have taken everyone aback. The terms of Elphinstone's employment at the palace were agreed with Charles Phipps, the Keeper of the Privy Purse. He would receive £300 a year, the same amount as Cowell but considerably less than the £1,000 a year paid to Colonel Bruce for minding the heir to the throne. He would also be given his own servant, a travel allowance, and board and lodging in the royal residences. Moreover, as a mark of the prestige the Queen and Prince Consort attached to his position, Howard would be admitted to the royal household, the closely guarded inner circle of courtiers surrounding the monarch and a sanctum strictly barred to mere tutors and governesses. He would be employed initially for one year starting in 1859. As large numbers of troops were currently being sent to India to suppress the mutiny there, the palace sought, and received, an assurance from the War Office that Elphinstone would not be posted overseas in the meantime.[25]

The terms of his appointment settled, on 6 November 1857 Elphinstone was summoned to Windsor for his first meeting with the Queen. The appointed day was cold and foggy, but when Howard arrived the Queen was taking her afternoon drive in the park as usual, forcing him to wait for his audience in the Grand Corridor. This thoroughfare, the principal artery of the castle linking the private apartments, was thickly carpeted, richly furnished and hung with magnificent portraits of kings and statesmen. One frequent visitor to the castle recalled the scent of flowers, regardless of the season, which hung in the air, and the smell of 'old furniture kept very clean'.[26] A particularly striking painting on one wall, which Elphinstone can hardly have failed to notice, was *The First of May* by Franz Winterhalter: a depiction of the elderly Duke of Wellington offering his infant godson Arthur a bejewelled casket, watched indulgently by the Queen and Prince Albert.

The audience chamber itself was a small room, intimate even, though lavishly decorated. Howard was probably received by a maid of honour, as convention dictated, before the Queen

The Lower Ward of Windsor Castle, photographed by Roger Fenton in 1860, months after Howard's arrival at court. On the left is St George's Chapel, the scene of so many royal family occasions, both happy and sad.

herself entered with a lady in waiting and possibly Charles Phipps. Still only in her thirties, Victoria was a short, plump woman, about five feet tall, with mousy-coloured hair drawn tightly back above a slightly flushed, moon-shaped face. She had the slightly protuberant eyes and hooked nose common to most of the Hanoverians, as well as their receding chin. Her mouth was small and often pursed, as she was conscious of her poor teeth and over-prominent gums. She was most certainly not an attractive woman, but she was a captivating one; and, holding Howard in the gaze of her china-blue eyes as she approached ('as if moving on skates', according to one awed palace guest), she was a most impressive figure.[27]

Elphinstone bowed, walked forward and, dropping to one knee, brushed the Queen's outstretched gloved hand with his lips. Victoria spoke in a highly distinctive, lilting voice, possibly – as Howard may have himself – with a slight German accent. They talked of the war and of Arthur. Although the Queen was preoccupied by the forthcoming marriage of her eldest daughter Victoria (Vicky) to Prince Friedrich Wilhelm of Prussia, scheduled for January 1858, the new governor clearly left a good impression. Writing in her journal that evening, Victoria described him as

> gentlemanlike, quiet and pleasing and . . . a very distinguished officer, having been long in the Crimea, where he led the attacking party who carried the quarries on the 7th of June 55, and the assault on the 8th of Sept: 55. He is said to be an excellent linguist, draws and paints well, and is fond of music, all of which we are very glad of.[28]

Elphinstone was also not unattractive to the Queen, a woman who took a keen interest in the physical appearance of the men around her. Later she would pronounce him as 'good looking, but short'.[29] Moreover, Cowell had been right: the wound 'does not show'.[30]

On 22 March 1858 the board of officers in Whitehall charged with administering the Victoria Cross met to consider the latest candidates. The award had been founded in January 1856 to recognize outstanding acts of bravery in the face of the enemy by British soldiers, regardless of rank. The Queen viewed the cross as within her personal gift – Albert himself was credited with its design – so she viewed its winners proprietarily and as the elite of her army. Two of the cross's earliest recipients, Major Lindsay (later Lord Wantage) and Major Teesdale, were already working at the palace as equerries and more would follow. At Bertie's urging, both officers sat to Louis Desanges, an artist who was compiling a gallery of heroic images of the actions for which the cross had been won.

Elphinstone had not appeared among the first crop of recipients, but his name was submitted now. The board was asked to consider his 'fearless conduct' in leading the rescue of twenty wounded men after the disastrous attack on the Redan of 18 June 1855. Howard's exploits in the Crimea had already been widely noted. He would himself recall, with uncharacteristic immodesty, how his name had been mentioned in dispatches during the war 'no less than 9 times – a number of times I believe quite unparalleled in the case of a subaltern, either in the Crimea or in India'.[31] In addition to this remarkable distinction, the Sultan of Turkey had given him the Order of the Medjidie, and earlier that same year he had been to Paris to collect the *Légion d'honneur*, France's highest award for gallantry, from the hand of Emperor Napoleon III himself.

The board rubber-stamped the submission, passing it to the Duke of Cambridge for his endorsement. The duke nodded it through to Frederick Peel, the Secretary of State for War, for final approval and submission to the Queen. But here it hit a snag. Edward Pennington, a pernickety civil servant at the War Office, complained that the application, for an award arising from the Crimean War, was too late and could not be considered. Official attention had shifted to India, where a number of native regiments had violently mutinied, sparked by high-handed British attitudes towards their culture and Hindu religion. No-one at the War Office, however, least of all the secretary of state, was prepared to contradict the Duke of Cambridge. Instead Peel, in a letter confirming Elphinstone's award, politely asked the duke to complete any remaining Crimean War claims 'at an early period'.[32] The duke replied haughtily that he found all such appeals 'impossible' to resist, and would continue to do as he pleased – which he did.[33]

The Queen signed Howard's award on 1 June 1858 and it was announced in the *London Gazette* the next day. The citation declared that Elphinstone had,

> on the night after the unsuccessful attack on the Redan, volunteered to command a party of volunteers, who proceeded to search for and bring back the scaling ladders left behind after the repulse; and while successfully performing this task, of rescuing trophies from the Russians . . . conducted a persevering search, close to the enemy, for wounded men, twenty of whom he rescued and brought back to the trenches.[34]

Howard's own recollection of that night's dramatic events differed from the official version in one crucial respect. '*Being unable to find volunteers,*' he revealed in his unpublished report, 'I ordered a party of 6 men of the line to accompany me.'[35] His own bravery was beyond question, but that of his men had been spun for public consumption. Moreover, the timing of Howard's award, coming as it did so soon after his still confidential appointment to the royal household, inevitably suggests some high-level string-pulling, a feature of the Victoria Cross which lingers to this day. He fully deserved the decoration; but, through no fault of his own, the manner of its grant was controversial.

The day of the presentation, 2 August 1858, dawned bright and clear. 'Queen's Weather', it was called. By ten, Southsea Common near Portsmouth was bathed in brilliant sunshine as the first people arrived, 'clad', sniffed *The Times*'s metropolitan

correspondent, 'in all the eccentricities of English seaside costume'. They came by train and carriage, or simply walked from the
neighbouring villages. By three, the common had been 'converted
into one of the most densely populated places of its size in
Victoria's dominions'. The esplanade was packed, everyone pressing forward to peer across the sparkling silver-blue sea towards
the Isle of Wight, which lay basking on the horizon. By half-past
three the best seats − naturally, those nearest to the royal dais −
were creaking beneath the bottoms of the most fashionable people
of Ryde, who sat sweltering under cotton parasols and black stove-
pipe hats. Hundreds of troops then began filing onto the scorched
grass, led by the artillery whose guns leapt wildly over the uneven
ground.

When the lines of troops had settled uncomfortably in the
trembling heat, twelve men quietly emerged from one corner of
the common to be greeted by a growing roar of approval from the
vast crowd. The men marched smartly to the dais, gathering there
in order of rank. Howard stood between Captain Dighton Probyn
(later equerry to Prince Alfred and Keeper of the Privy Purse to
Edward VII) and Captain Alfred Jones, both of whom had earned
their crosses in the Indian Mutiny. Howard was wearing the dress
uniform of the Royal Engineers: a double-breasted scarlet coat
with garter blue collar and cuffs studded with gold buttons and
draped in gold lace. On his head, worn in the 'Nelson' or English
fashion, was a black beaverskin bicorn hat topped by a creamy-
white swan feather plume.

Shortly before four, sailors could be seen in the distance
climbing the rigging of the warships perched out on the Solent. A
salute ran across the line of ships, 'darting from the tall massive
sides of the men-at-war in broad red sheets of flame and clouds of
smoke till the very air seemed to move'. Then Fairy emerged
through the black powder smoke, weaving between the towering
warships as she scudded towards Portsmouth bearing the royal
party. By half-past four, reported one journalist, 'the people were
anxious and Victoria's reputation for punctuality seemed in

danger'.[36] Then the crowd shifted and, amid a flurry of waved handkerchiefs and raised hats, the royal family and their entourage appeared at the edge of the common. The Queen was in a landau sitting beside two of her daughters, Princesses Helena and Alice. Riding alongside were the Prince Consort and the Duke of Cambridge, both in full dress uniform. With a crunch of arms, the troops on the common came smartly to attention, lowering their flags in tribute. Reaching the dais, the landau paused and Victoria stepped out, waiting for her husband and the duke to join her. Beside her, on a low circular table draped in scarlet cloth, were twelve small, gun-metal black crosses: each one worthless in monetary terms but of inestimable value to its recipient. There were no speeches or elaborate ceremony. Instead, each man simply stepped forward as his name was called, bowed, saluted and paused while the Queen fixed the cross to his coat, her short fingers fumbling awkwardly with the pin. Giving her cross to Elphinstone, she noted that evening in her journal, gave her 'particular pleasure'.[37]

The Coburg Bow

WINDSOR CASTLE, 1858

WHEN PRINCE ALFRED entered the navy as a midshipman in September 1858 his redundant tutor, the Reverend William Jolley, was re-engaged to teach Prince Arthur. Jolley's appointment was a stark reminder to the Queen that her favourite child was about to enter a 'new epoch in his life'. Responsibility for Arthur's care would soon transfer from Lady Caroline Barrington, the formidable lady superintendent of the royal nursery, to his new governor Howard Elphinstone. She wept at the thought of Arthur leaving the nursery for his own household, of his passing from 'female to male hands'. Victoria had willingly given her husband responsibility for educating their sons, but now she urged him to remember that, at eight years old, Arthur was three years younger than Alfred had been when he moved to the Royal Lodge with John Cowell. Trying to be 'sensible and reasonable', she pressed Albert to keep Arthur at home until he was at least twelve, pointing out that he could not join the army in any case for several more years.[1] The Queen confided to her eldest daughter Vicky, now in Berlin following her marriage to Prince Friedrich Wilhelm of Prussia, that she would 'take good care, that he is not treated as Affie was, but remaining with us as long as he possibly can'.[2]

Despite the secrecy surrounding Howard's appointment,

rumours that a governor had been employed for Arthur quickly circulated within the close-knit, gossipy world of the royal household, unsettling the women already charged with the prince's care. In September 1858 Louise Rollande de la Sange, Arthur's French governess, plucked up enough courage to raise the matter with Lady Caroline. After being reassured that the Queen was pleased with her own work, Louise pressed the lady superintendent to confirm the rumour that a governor had been engaged for Arthur. Lady Caroline admitted to the Queen later that she had considered Louise's anxious enquiry to be 'a good opening for breaking to her Your Majesty's intention'. Turning to the governess, she revealed 'what she doubtless already knew', that a governor had indeed been appointed to Arthur and, in consequence, that her own services would no longer be required.[3] In reality, both women knew that Louise was being sacked, as a governess would still be needed to teach French to the other children. Louise was stunned – not so much at the confirmation of Elphinstone's appointment, which she had long anticipated, but at her own fate. She later complained to Prince Albert that 'she never expected to hear that *she* was to leave us, but merely that Arthur was to leave her'.[4]

At first Louise 'made no fuss'. But by that evening, having absorbed the devastating news of her dismissal, she had become, in Lady Caroline's words, 'more difficult to manage'. Her eyes moist with defiant tears and her hands clasped tightly in front of her, she challenged the lady superintendent to reveal the true reason for her dismissal. She was heavily in debt, she sobbed, and as her husband earned only a 'very small salary' as a civil servant in France, losing her place at court would make them both 'very poor'.[5] Shaken by the governess's outburst, the lady superintendent revealed what Louise most feared: she was considered too old, and her health too uncertain, to continue any longer in the royal schoolroom.

The Queen thought Louise 'imprudent and foolish' to have got herself so deeply into debt, a failing which set such a bad example to the children. But she was not unsympathetic to the governess's plight, conferring on her a pension of £100 a year – a generous award when Louise might reasonably have expected, like so many other governesses in her position, to leave with nothing.[6] In fact, the real reason for Louise's dismissal was the Queen's desire to find someone else to take care of Arthur's younger brother, four-year-old Prince Leopold, whose delicate health was causing concern. Indeed, a new governess specifically charged with looking after Leo had already been engaged. Colonel Bruce's sister Augusta, a favoured lady in waiting at court, had found the ideal replacement for Louise in Marie Hocédé, 'a *very young* widow' of twenty-four, 'with pretty eyes and hair'.[7] Marie would start work at the same time as Howard.

Shortly before Prince Alfred went to sea for the first time in October 1858, Elphinstone was invited for a 'dine and sleep' at Windsor Castle. This would give him an insight into the so-called 'Windsor System' that governed court life before John Cowell departed overseas with the prince. Sir John Burgoyne, who stayed at the castle in 1855 after his recall from the Crimea, has left a vivid account of the sort of accommodation the castle offered to its 'dine and sleep' guests. In a letter to his wife, Burgoyne described being shown to 'a bedroom with dressing-room adjoining, and on the other side of the bed-room a sitting-room, all most comfortable, and with excellent fires; writing apparatus very complete, and everything one can possibly want, except books'.[8]

Elphinstone's visit began with a tour of the castle and lunch with the equerries, men his own age, many of whom he might have known already from the army. The equerries' dining room, which was located beside the hall inside the visitors' entrance to the castle, had the reassuring feel of a regimental mess, with military prints on the walls, comfortable armchairs and scattered copies of the *United Service Journal*. After lunch Howard was presented to the Prince Consort, who 'bowed graciously twice; then gave his hand'.[9] (Albert's German habit of nodding sharply from the neck in greeting was labelled the 'The Coburg Bow'.[10]) The

The Prince Consort photographed shortly before his death, clearly showing the strain of his punishing self-imposed work regime.

prince was only thirty-nine, but a heavy workload and indifferent health had aged him greatly. He was also notoriously awkward in conversation, forcing Howard to break the 'momentary dead silence' which followed their introduction by rashly launching into a discussion about his starting date at the palace. February 1859 had already been agreed upon, but under the silent scrutiny of the prince, Howard blurted out that he could begin work two weeks earlier on 14 January, denying himself a holiday after finishing at the Topographical Department. 'I wish I had insisted more firmly on the 1st,' he wrote ruefully in his journal that evening.[11]

The tension broken, the prince firmly presented to Howard his views on education, a subject on which he had very decided opinions. A knowledge of history, languages and the classics was obviously important, he declared, but so too was an appreciation of painting and of music. A rural upbringing was essential, the prince believed, with plenty of riding and walking. 'How much might be learnt out of doors,' he told Elphinstone, 'by teaching a boy birds, the different plants, botany, geology, even the formation and variety of pebbles. It fixes the mind early.'[12] He wanted his son to try everything, better to understand the skill of others. Three hours of lessons a day would be ample to begin with. Arthur was cleverer than his two elder brothers and the Queen, he reported, was concerned that such a 'wide awake' child would be harmed by overwork. She was also 'perfectly certain' that his governor would have no trouble with her son's behaviour.[13] The only difficulty with a private education away from other children, mused the prince, was the 'want of emulation, which stirs up the boy's energies'. If the boy should consequently show any lack of application, Elphinstone was to reason with Arthur. 'I certainly felt inclined to say', thought the astonished governor, who was better used to military discipline, 'that I should insist on my dictum being obeyed.'[14]

The Prince Consort's outlook had been formed by his upbringing in Germany under the close scrutiny of Baron Christian Stockmar. Stockmar was now living in quiet retirement in Coburg, but he remained an *éminence grise* to the English court.

Originally physician to the Queen's uncle Prince Leopold (brother of her mother, the Duchess of Kent; husband of George IV's ill-fated daughter Charlotte; and, since 1831, King of the Belgians), Stockmar had steered Victoria through the difficult early years of her reign, while simultaneously grooming Prince Albert – the son of his patron Ernest, Duke of Saxe-Coburg-Gotha – for the role of Victoria's husband. But the eventual marriage of Victoria and Albert was only the first step in realizing Stockmar's wider dream of creating a modern constitutional monarchy at Windsor and seeing England allied with a unified Germany led by Prussia. The birth of the Prince of Wales in 1841 had spurred the relentless baron into drafting a typically methodical memorandum outlining his precise ideas on the education of royal princes. In this lengthy document, Stockmar blamed the 'glaring' errors of the sons of King George III on their deplorable tutors. These were men, he claimed, who were 'either incapable of engrafting on their minds during their youth the principles of truth and morality, or . . . most culpably neglected their duties, or were not supported in them by the Royal parents'. Moreover, several of the Hanoverian princes, including the Queen's own father, the Duke of Kent, had been taught overseas. In Stockmar's opinion, this had earned them the hatred of their own people as the British were deeply preju-diced against foreigners.

'The education of the Royal Children', Stockmar con-cluded, 'ought to be from its earliest beginning a *truly moral and a truly English one.*' As a child's education 'begins the first day of his life', he insisted, the royal princes should from an early age be 'entrusted to persons only who are themselves morally good, intelligent, well-informed and experienced'.[15] Recognizing the benefits, as well as the risks, of imitation by very young children, the baron also stipulated that the royal children should be sur-rounded only by 'those who are good and pure, who will teach not only by precept but by example', such as artists, musicians and military heroes.[16] Stockmar's prescription held great sway with Victoria and Albert, and certainly had some influence on

Howard's appointment. But it was far too rigorous for all except the very brightest of their children, such as Vicky and Alice, proving disastrously counter-productive for the less able, like Bertie and Affie. Time alone would tell of its effect on Arthur.

After being lectured by the Prince Consort, Howard returned to his room to dress for dinner. Towards eight, the groom of the chambers – 'a gentlemanlike foreigner (but speaking perfect English)'[17] – knocked gently on his door before leading him through the labyrinth of passages to the Queen's dining room. Other guests at the select royal dinner that evening included the Prince Consort's private secretary, Charles Grey, and Count Lauradio, the Portuguese minister in London. Behind each of their chairs stood a footman dressed in red livery. Victoria relished her food and was a notoriously quick eater. Apart from a perilously sweet tooth, she generally preferred simple fare such as boiled chicken, a grilled sirloin steak or 'perhaps a slice of game' to the more exotic concoctions of the royal kitchens.[18] The vegetables at the royal table were always those of the season, with Victoria enjoying in particular 'a great weakness of potatoes, which are cooked for her in every conceivable way'.[19] Pudding was usually fruit, much of it grown in the glasshouses at Frogmore House, the residence of her mother the Duchess of Kent in Windsor Park. Naturally the best wines were consumed in the royal palaces, although the Queen herself generally favoured a tipple of whisky, a habit recently acquired from her visits to Scotland. Throughout dinner, music was supplied by a regimental band playing in the next-door room. It is likely that Howard, who was generally reserved in company, said little over dinner, the first of hundreds he would attend with the Queen. Victoria's journal, however, reveals that the conversation centred on the recent capture by the Portuguese of a French vessel engaged in the slave trade, a subject which roused the excitable Portuguese minister to indignant fury.

The meal ended when the Queen had finished, regardless of the progress made by her guests. She then led the way to the White

Drawing Room, said to be her favourite in the castle and described by one visitor as 'a vision in white and gold'.[20] It was smaller, more intimate, than the grander Green Drawing Room next door, and was dominated by the enormous porcelain vase which stood in the window, a gift to Victoria from Tsar Nicolai I. The fire in the grate burned beech logs – never coal, which the Queen disliked – while hundreds of candles lit the many candelabra. With such a small party it is unlikely that games of cards or chess were begun that evening (if they had been, the Queen would have expected her guests to gamble only with new and unused coins of her realm[21]). Instead, there may have been a short musical entertainment, or Victoria may simply have sat on a sofa and spoken to her guests in turn (etiquette preventing them from initiating a conversation themselves). Unless invited forward, everyone was obliged to remain standing and facing the Queen while in her presence. The gentlemen generally pressed themselves against the walls, holding muttered conversations beneath their breath. The party quickly broke up when Victoria retired to attend as usual to some official papers before bed. At this point the ladies returned to their rooms while the men headed gratefully towards the distant billiard room for a cigar – smoking being strictly forbidden elsewhere in the castle. 'Dine and sleep' guests usually left the castle early the next day – 'after a visit', Burgoyne had concluded, 'which even to the most *blasé* must be a memorable and delightful experience'.[22] To Howard, however, it would soon become a very familiar daily routine.

PART TWO
Windsor

The new governor

WINDSOR CASTLE, 15 JANUARY 1859

'**M**AJOR ELPHINSTONE, Arthur's new tutor, comes to the House today,' the Queen wrote to Vicky on 15 January 1859.

> Arthur will I think go to him on Monday or Tuesday. Collins (Affie's servant) will be his servant. On Thursday, the new Governess Mademoiselle Hocédé comes, on Thursday poor Rollet goes! All this with the state of Expectation about you [the princess was expecting her first child] and the excitement about Italy and France, and besides Bertie's journey and Affie's voyages does really keep one in a great agitation and fuss.[1]

Lady Caroline Barrington met Howard (gazetted major four days earlier) on his arrival at Windsor, taking him straight up to the children's apartments overlooking the South Terrace of the castle. Lady Caroline had tried to put the 'most painful business' of Louise Rollande's dismissal behind her, but the mood in the schoolroom was still subdued. Louise was tearfully packing her bags, while the remaining governesses, Karolin Bauer and Sarah Hildyard, viewed the newcomer warily. More used to army mess life, Elphinstone would discover that he had unwittingly entered an enclosed feminine world, one fraught with insecurity and bruised by the loss of a much-loved colleague. Emotions were equally highly charged in the nursery, where the maids in their stiffly starched pinafores were 'inconsolable' at the prospect of losing Arthur to his new governor.[2] They listened glumly as Mary Thurston, the head nurse, lectured Elphinstone sternly on the prince's daily routine.

In the few days left before he officially took charge of Arthur, Howard composed a timetable of lessons for the prince's tutor William Jolley to follow. The Queen had specified that her son's lessons last no longer than half an hour, or three-quarters of an hour at the utmost. 'It should be *clearly* understood', she told Albert, 'that a *little* boy of *8* and *½ cannot* study.'[3] This was the firm opinion of the Queen's doctor Sir James Clark, whose advice she never questioned. Howard therefore proposed seven half-hour lessons a day, six days a week, for the prince, starting at eight in the morning and finishing at seven in the evening. Sundays, family birthdays (and there were already many), his parents' wedding anniversary and Christmas were counted as holidays. Otherwise Arthur would be taught every day of the year, with William Jolley accompanying the prince and his governor as they moved between royal residences.

Every day would begin with a session of music followed by a period of unsupervised study, or 'prep'. After breakfast, generally taken with his parents at nine, Arthur would have two hours' playtime. At eleven-thirty lessons resumed, with instruction in French or German with the governesses followed by writing and arithmetic with Jolley. After lunch at two, Arthur could play with his brother and sisters watched over carefully by Elphinstone. Tea was at four in the nursery, although on fine days the children would often be invited to join their mother for this important ritual at her summer house in the garden. Victoria had a particular weakness for afternoon tea, enjoying the many treats served up by her confectionery cooks. A typical offering included 'chocolate sponges, plain sponges, wafers of two or three different shapes, biscuits, drop cakes of all kinds, *petits fours*, Princess and rice cakes, pralines, almond sweets, and a large quantity of mixed sweets'.[4] (Such indulgence inevitably took a heavy toll on Victoria's diminutive five-foot figure, which had swelled to twelve stone by the 1880s.) After tea, there would be more lessons in history or geography before a final session of French with Marie Hocédé.

Tuesday, the day of 'great domestic changes', finally dawned.[5] After breakfast that morning, the Queen and Prince Consort toured the suite of rooms, below their own, allocated to Arthur and his governor. The rooms had recently been vacated by Prince Alfred and were still cluttered with his wooden ship models. Albert, who was obsessed with his children's security, carefully checked the locks on the doors and windows while Victoria discussed final arrangements with Elphinstone. Having dreaded this moment so long, she now felt reassured by the governor's calm authority, describing him as 'so quiet and nice, and so anxious to do what is right'.[6] When the Prince Consort was satisfied with his son's protection, Arthur was fetched from the nursery, running in 'full of expectation' at the exciting change to his life.[7] He was a small child for his age, with the pale, delicate looks and large blue eyes of all his brothers, and fair hair which still retained a few babyish curls. The young prince shyly received his introduction to Elphinstone, who bowed smartly and, smiling, shook his small hand. Albert took one more careful look around the room, told his son to be 'good, obedient and studious', and departed with the Queen, leaving Howard alone with the prince.[8]

The major was keen to establish a routine and to impose his authority on the young prince as quickly as possible. He had no experience or training for his task beyond his own rigid upbringing. But from his later actions it seems that before taking up his duties he had studied the work of Dr Daniel Schreber, a bestselling German educationalist – probably at the urging of the Prince Consort. Schreber, who was strongly influenced by Martin Luther's principle that 'there are no better works than to obey and serve all those who are set over us',[9] advocated taking a firm approach when dealing with children. 'The little ones' displays of temper, as indicated by screaming or crying without cause, should be regarded as the first test of your spiritual and pedagogical principles,' he wrote in 1858, just months before Howard started at the palace.

> Once you have established that nothing is really wrong, that the child is not ill, distressed or in pain, then you can rest assured that the screaming is nothing more than an outburst of temper, a whim, the first appearance of wilfulness [to be met with] mild corporal punishment repeated persistently at brief intervals until the child quiets down or falls asleep . . . This procedure will be necessary only once, or at the most twice, and then you will be *master* of the child *forever*. From now on, a glance, a word, a single threatening gesture will be sufficient to control the child.[10]

The doctor summed up his view of the relationship between a governor, or tutor, with his pupil as an 'indispensable process of learning to subordinate and control his will, [until the boy is able] to distinguish for himself the difference between what is permissible and what is not'.[11]

Howard ordered work to begin at once, although William Jolley soon found his new pupil as difficult to teach as his elder brothers had been. Between lessons, while Jolley recovered his composure, the prince took his hoop out to the castle terraces or set out the tin soldiers his sister Vicky regularly sent him from Berlin. From afar, the Queen noticed almost immediately how 'nicely' Howard played with her son.[12] Most afternoons the prince was taken for a drive, often to visit his grandmother the Duchess of Kent at Frogmore House. When news came from Berlin of the birth of the Queen's first grandchild, Prince Wilhelm of Prussia, the duchess hosted a children's ball to celebrate the event, decorating Frogmore with flowers and Prussian flags. 'All the children, big and small danced so merrily,' her delighted daughter wrote in her journal.[13] Howard thought the Queen looked 'as happy as any one of the children' on such occasions.[14] It was all too much for one four-year-old girl, who fell asleep curled up on her mother's train during the ball. Seventy years later, by now an elderly woman, she recalled how she had 'thought it cruel when I was roused to dance with the Prince Consort, and I remember my difficulty in reaching his hand to try and make an arch high enough for the country dance couples to pass through'.[15]

Each evening, Elphinstone entrusted Arthur to the prince's valet Collins, 'a good, careful, gentle well-behaved servant', according to the Queen.[16] Unless summoned to the royal table, Howard then joined the rest of the household for dinner, exchanging his daytime attire of black morning coat, trousers and waistcoat for the 'Windsor Uniform' of dark blue tailcoat with scarlet collar and cuffs. He then made his way to the octagonal oak-panelled dining room overlooking the North Terrace of the castle where the household gathered to eat. Those royal employees excluded from the elite of the household, such as the doctors, governesses, tutors and librarians, ate alone in their rooms.

The Prince Consort, under Baron Stockmar's guidance, had wanted a court populated by men who had distinguished themselves in the arts, sciences or military, and clever women from the best and wealthiest families in the land. The overtly political element, tinged with sexual intrigue, that had so bedevilled the early years of the Queen's reign had been ruthlessly purged, leaving a court of intensely loyal but often insecure people. The sotto voce conversation over household dinner was therefore no longer dominated by racy gossip but, in the words of an awed young maid of honour, 'on very courtly and regal subjects'.[17] 'Discretion was extreme,' recalled another with a slight shudder.[18] Nevertheless, rivalries and jealousies simmered beneath the stately surface as they had always done in the palace, with the courtiers jockeying for position and favour.

At the head of the household, and its dining table, were its officers: those men handpicked by the Lord Chamberlain – a political appointee who was rarely present at court – to ensure the smooth running of the palace 'above stairs'. They included the

Keeper of the Privy Purse, Sir Charles Phipps, and the Master of the Household, Thomas Biddulph. The post of private secretary to the Queen had yet to be formally recognized, but the patrician Charles Grey fulfilled an equivalent role for the Prince Consort, wielding great influence over court in consequence. Of greater personal importance to Victoria were her ladies of the bedchamber, the twittering Lady Ely and the long-suffering Lady Churchill. Both women were the soul of discretion and in them the Queen placed the very highest confidence.

This knot of permanent courtiers was surrounded by a revolving cast of aristocratic equerries, ladies in waiting and maids of honour; each of whom served on a rotating basis, generally for a month at a time, three times a year. Being 'in waiting' was a dull life as days, even weeks, could pass without a summons to attend the Queen. But it was also a useful means of securing a place in society, and an excellent opportunity for the unmarried to find partners. Henry Ponsonby, for instance, possibly Queen Victoria's most famous courtier, ended up marrying Charles Grey's granddaughter Mary Bulteel, who had been a maid of honour when he joined the court as an equerry in 1857.

Howard told John Cowell that he had experienced the 'greatest kindness from everyone' on entering court.[19] But in truth he fitted only uneasily into its narrow, nepotistic, flirtatious world. It may have been the trace of a foreign accent in his voice or his close cultural and intellectual rapport with the Prince Consort that made it so difficult for him to make friends, for Albert was widely disliked. One maid of honour reported how Carl Haag, the Prince Consort's favourite German painter and, like Howard, his soulmate, was put through 'a process of *snubbing*' when he stayed at the palace, 'which I must own he richly deserves'.[20] Certainly Prince Albert's aloofness was deeply resented by the rest of the court. Mary Bulteel defined it as the 'cold egotism which seems to chill you in all Royalties; and prevents you from forgetting the difference of position between them and their *entourage*'. Mary doubted the prince had a single friend among the English members of the household, as 'his way of giving orders and reproofs was rather too like a master of a house scolding servants to be pleasant'.[21] In contrast to her husband, the Queen, or 'Eliza' as she was nicknamed, was warmly respected by her household – despite a stubborn and tempestuous nature and her disconcertingly middle-class moralizing attitude.

Inevitably, given the English courtiers' dislike of the Prince Consort and indeed of foreigners generally, Howard gravitated towards the German faction at court: men like the prince's German secretary Dr Ernst Becker, and his scholarly young librarian, the 24-year-old Carl Ruland, both protégés of the Svengali-like Baron Stockmar. Used to the *esprit de corps* of the army, these men were more congenial company to Howard, who found it difficult adjusting to the secluded, often spiteful world of the household, where jealousies were magnified and feelings suppressed. Charles Grey and Thomas Biddulph were remote figures, and while he viewed Charles Phipps as a 'kind father', he also considered him an incompetent ditherer.[22] The major's good looks, heroic disability and romantic family background nevertheless attracted plenty of female admirers. One maid of honour considered him 'the pick of the court for pleasantness and kindness'.[23] Another found him 'very agreeable' after 'the others [who] struck me as cold and stiff'.[24] Such flattering attention was quickly seized upon by the other men at court.

'Elphinstone,' Arthur Hardinge said loudly over dinner one evening, when Howard had been at the castle for a few weeks: 'I produce this for your especial benefit.'

The table fell silent as all eyes turned expectantly towards the Coldstream Guardsman. 'When you intend to propose you should not delay, because you fancy your love is safe, and that there be no hurry.' Hardinge paused dramatically, relishing his moment: 'It is a dangerous proceeding!'

There was loud laughter. Elphinstone wrote later in his journal that he felt 'uncomfortably warm' with anger and embarrassment at the banter. He saw John Cowell glance at

Horatia Stopford, the pretty daughter of a colonel who was also new to court. Horatia looked mortified, her face 'red as fire'. Lady Ely's flustered efforts to change the subject only made matters worse.

In a similar situation, others might have brushed the incident aside, enjoying the joke. But Howard dwelt on it, analysing his own conduct and feeling pity both for himself and for Horatia. 'The odd thing is', he thought, 'that nothing has passed, or to my mind anything gone so far as to show even a strong *partiality*. This has made the matter *very* awkward, and I really do not see how I am to get honourably out of it. I must be *much* on my guard tomorrow, and not show any change.'[25]

Such anxiety and discomfort increased his brooding introspection. Back in his room, he compiled a list of principles to read morning and night, as if imposing order and routine would ease his predicament:

1 Practice self esteem, but avoid arrogance, do or say nothing mean underhand.
2 Adhere strictly to truth.
3 Be always cool and calm; never flurried. It is the only way to acquire moral weight.
4 Never say even a harsh word of others; but on every occasion be careful.
5 Think well of the consequences of what you say. Be cautious, very cautious.
6 Has the mind been FULLY occupied. No busy idleness ever doing useless easy work.
7 Be agreeable in conversation; be less authoritative, especially upon unknown matters.
8 Recollect you are not an nonentity, but meant to influence others; think therefore.
9 Vigour, efficiency and thoughtfulness to characterise everything you do.
10 Draw out a nightly plan of work.[26]

The Queen kept a wary eye on the major, sending him messages, sometimes several times a day, closely enquiring after her son's welfare. Often these were no more than polite requests for Arthur to join her for a drive, or for a trip to the theatre. But she also fussed endlessly about the temperature in the prince's bedroom – which she always considered too high – or about the dangers of playing on wet grass. Sometimes the notes betrayed irritation; when Arthur failed to appear for church, for instance, or at a child's tea party. Nevertheless, progress was good at first. After a month, the Queen told her uncle Leopold, the King of the Belgians, that Arthur was getting on 'delightfully with his *very* amiable and sensible tutor'.[27] Her son could now dress himself, did everything he was told and, his governor reported, 'works so well by himself'.[28] In fact, Arthur's behaviour was already causing Howard some difficulty. Like his elder brothers, the prince was easily distracted in the schoolroom and, when admonished, would turn sulky and petulant. To punish him, Elphinstone began revoking the prince's holidays and denying him playtime with the other children. Lessons were lengthened and examinations introduced to test the prince's academic progress, a radical experiment in an environment where competition was considered uncivilized. This stricter regime was tacitly encouraged by the Prince Consort, a strict disciplinarian and, unlike his wife, a firm advocate of the corporal punishment of his children. But it caused the Queen great unease.

In the spring the court moved to London for the social season, with Arthur and the major settling into Bertie's old rooms at Buckingham Palace. As the children were under far greater public scrutiny in town than at Windsor, Howard was instructed to ensure that Arthur always wore his kilt, an affectation imposed by the Queen on all her sons to demonstrate her liking for Scotland. In April a children's fancy-dress ball was held at the palace to celebrate Prince Leopold's sixth birthday. Arthur and Leopold appeared as the sons of Henry IV of France, wearing white satin tunics beneath pale blue velvet capes trimmed in gold and decorated with fleurs-de-lis. Their sisters Helena and Louise dressed up as Swiss peasants, wearing straw bonnets and with their hair tied in plaits. All the children were paraded in the picture gallery before supper, afterwards pressing noisily into the ball-room where they danced, in the words of the delighted Queen, 'without ceasing' until midnight.[29] The major was charged with steering Arthur around the room to ensure he partnered all of those children who mattered, such as his fat and clumsy cousins from Saxe-Coburg. 'The children all enjoyed it so much,' Victoria wrote in her journal before going to bed, 'no one more than little Leopold.' There was no dance to celebrate the ninth birthday of 'our precious little Mayflower' a few days later on 1 May, however, as the occasion was eclipsed by a service of thanksgiving for the end to the Indian Mutiny. But Arthur's present table was still piled as high as his brother's had been, with (among much else) a gold watch from his parents, an inkstand from Bertie and 'numberless military toys' from the rest of his family.[30]

Feeling as isolated within the household as the German Prince Consort often felt in his adopted country, Howard steadily forged a genuine friendship with Albert, a bond based on a shared outlook, a common language and a mutual interest in military affairs, the fine arts and science. Occasionally Howard would join the Prince Consort in the library at Windsor to help Ruland and Becker catalogue the royal collection's holding of works by Raphael, filling his own sketchbooks with scattered vignettes from the Italian master at the same time. Albert was a hard taskmaster: Howard noted in his journal that he was often chided for failing to keep up. But he was also an encouraging one, entrusting the major with overseeing the establishment of a military library under royal patronage at Aldershot, the sprawling new army camp in Hampshire. The library, like the Great Exhibition of 1851 that had been his vision, was a further demonstration of Albert's ceaseless urge to educate and inform, and of his desire to win the approval of his wife's still sceptical subjects.

Seeing him so often close at hand, Howard was struck by the

disparity between Albert's coldness in public and the warm affection he showed towards his family. Unlike Victoria, he played openly, even riotously, with his children, revelling in their games and practical jokes; and he was equally happy quietly cuddling two-year-old Princess Beatrice on his knee while a governess read aloud to her. As the two men passed hours together in the library, the normally reserved prince gradually opened up to Howard, offering his views on art and music. Sometimes he even made unguarded remarks about the people he had encountered, once confiding to the major that he had never liked Lord Raglan, the still widely revered commander-in-chief of the army in the Crimea, 'because he was not sincere'. 'He had always a smiling face,' the prince continued, 'and pretended to agree with you, or at all events never ventured to differ, and you saw that the arguments he used were insincere, that they were based more upon your own views. I never could feel comfortable with such a man.'[31] In the cloistered world of the court, Howard was unsure whether this was a thinly veiled attack on his own reticence or a compliment to his integrity. The prince had little time left to make himself better understood.

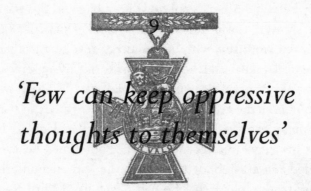

9

'Few can keep oppressive thoughts to themselves'

OSBORNE HOUSE, JULY 1859

THIS TIME WHEN ELPHINSTONE stepped onto the landing stage for Osborne House he would not be returning forthwith to the mainland, as he had two years before after his conversation with John Cowell about his proposed appointment at court. Instead, a liveried footman took his bags while he, climbing into the waiting brougham, continued up to the house.

Completed ten years earlier, Osborne House sprawled over the crest of a hill above the sleepy village of Cowes on the Isle of Wight. As Albert had intended, its profusion of terraces, porticos, towers and balustrades gave the house an exotic Neapolitan feel, in marked contrast to the sober Georgian manor house it had replaced. Inside, servants scurried from room to room and the tiled floors rang with the shouts of the children as the royal family gathered for its annual summer holiday. Bertie had already arrived with Robert (now General) Bruce; the Duchess of Kent was on her way; and Affie and Cowell were expected any day.

Despite the generally relaxed air, William Jolley, who was lodged in an outlying cottage on the large estate, continued to teach Arthur. But there was still plenty of time for the children to enjoy swimming, sailing and noisy paper chases during the long afternoons. Howard and the young prince would comb the cliffs for fossils or the beach for shells, proudly displaying their trophies

Osborne House on the Isle of Wight, the royal family's summer retreat and the Queen's preferred venue for Christmas after Albert's death.

in the museum of curios at the Swiss Cottage, an extravagant wooden folly built for the children in the grounds to the house. Near the Swiss Cottage was the Victoria Fort, a series of miniature military earthworks constructed by Affie under Cowell's supervision a couple of summers before. Not to be outdone, the following year Howard and Arthur would build the Albert Barracks of the Victoria Fort, a scaled-down version of the latest military design using bricks made on the estate. The foundation stone was laid with due ceremony by fourteen-year-old Princess Helena, who buried beneath it a few gold coins, a scroll containing the name of the building and a list of the people present. 'I think it will form a pleasing memento to Prince Arthur in after-life,' Howard proudly told the Queen, 'and remind him of the first building he constructed.'[1]

Yet all was not well. Over the summer Howard felt increasingly lonely and insecure, convinced that he was falling out of royal favour. 'Few can keep oppressive thoughts to themselves,' he reflected; 'they must have someone, to whom they can occasionally unburden themselves.' Yet he had no-one. He shared with William Jolley responsibility for Prince Arthur; yet there was an unbridgeable divide between himself, a member of the Queen's elite household, and Jolley, who was not. Propriety, meanwhile, prevented his becoming socially intimate with the governesses. Except for his violin, his companion since childhood, he had no close friend, no outlet for his anxiety. Then a solution to his loneliness struck him. 'Why not adopt a book,' he declared, 'to which you can tell all, and always? Will it teach as much as a person, if locked up? I'll try. Time, will alone show the result.' So, 'to relieve the mind', he took up his journal again, using it as others might use a confidant or friend.[2] And whereas his earlier entries were largely a record of events, those he made now expanded into searching, and often self-critical, examinations of his own behaviour.

His principal, paradoxical, concern was that 'I am always inclined to fancy that my position is beneath me, or else I am

*Lieutenant Elphinstone (pictured right) directing
the rescue of the wounded and the recovery of discarded
equipment following the disastrous British assault on
the Redan on 18 June 1855. Painted by Louis Desanges
for his Victoria Cross Gallery, c.1860.*

INSET: *The Victoria Cross*

Captain Alexander Elphinstone RN, Howard's pugnacious father, who fought to restore his family's fortune and laid claim to an extinct Scottish peerage.

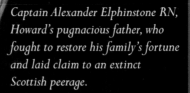

Amelia Elphinstone, the god-fearing daughter of a wealthy Livonian merchant who declared that she 'could endure anything except an ill bred child'.

July 1850

ABOVE: *'Our lodgings [in] Edinburgh 10 o'clock at night' painted by Howard in July 1850 while stationed in the city as a young subaltern.*

LEFT: *Captain Elphinstone RE, VC, photographed after the Crimean War and before entering court.*

Queen Victoria and Prince Albert: hand-tinted photograph by John Mayall, 1861.

Prince Arthur.

Prince Alfred.

The Prince of Wales.

Dr. Becker — 1859.

RIGHT: *Dr Ernst Becker, the Prince Consort's scholarly German Secretary, who befriended Howard in his early days at court.*

BELOW: *The Reverend William Jolley, Prince Arthur's stolid tutor.*

OPPOSITE PAGE:

TOP LEFT: *Carl Ruland, the Prince Consort's librarian, who left the palace under a cloud.*

TOP RIGHT: *Sir Charles Phipps, Keeper of the Privy Purse, who set the terms of Howard's employment.*

BOTTOM: *Household group on the terrace at Osborne House in about 1859. Howard (distinguished by his lack of height) is standing right. Henry Ponsonby, future private secretary to the Queen, towers in the centre. Thomas Biddulph, Master of the Household for fifteen years until 1866, is on the left.*

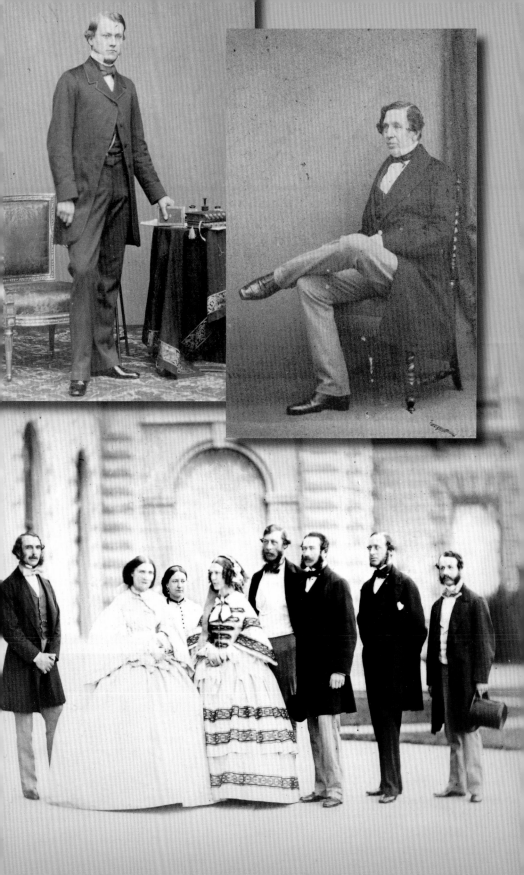

Howard Elphinstone in court uniform:
pencil drawing highlighted in watercolour
by unknown artist, c.1860.

THE ALBERT BARRACKS, 1860, MODEL FORT, AND REDOUBTS.
BRICKS MADE BY THE ROYAL CHILDREN.

The Albert Barracks in the Victoria Fort beside the Swiss Cottage at Osborne House, built by Prince Arthur under Howard's supervision in 1860.

unable to uphold it sufficiently.'[3] Plummeting self-confidence had clashed against the rigid self-belief instilled in him as a child by his father. Hard as he tried, he knew he could never adopt the apparent nonchalance of the other governors. Noting that Colonel Bruce, for instance, was 'much thought of' by the royals, Howard vowed 'to watch him closely and see how far you could imitate'. The colonel's type was a familiar one to him from the trenches of the Crimea: a titled Guards officer 'with very great tact, and fine manners; suavity itself, and pride insuperable'. But Bruce's bluff exterior hid a formidable intellect which 'braced and bent to enter into your views'.[4] Howard noted how the colonel always spoke cautiously and deliberately, quietly slipping away from any indiscreet conversations. He also jealously protected his position beside the Prince of Wales, quizzing Howard closely when he heard that Bertie had been seeking his advice. 'Does the Prince often come down to your room?' Bruce asked sharply, before adding slyly: 'I thought perhaps that he might bore you a good deal from what the Prince Consort told me.'[5]

Howard should have felt at greater ease with his contemporary John Cowell. But the Queen herself had noticed that the two men were 'very different', telling Vicky that Elphinstone was the 'more accomplished' of the two, speaking 'German beautifully and French well [and being] . . . very fond of music'.[6] Like Charles Gordon, his closest friend in the engineers, Cowell was a spiritually intense man who enjoyed tackling the less devout Elphinstone in tedious doctrinal debate. While admitting that Cowell was 'too agreeable in his manner to dislike', Howard decided 'that there is to my mind an arrogance in his manner which will always prevent my making a *friend* of him'.[7]

Elphinstone did recognize, however, that his fellow governor was very popular at court, while he patently was not. So he resolved to watch Cowell closely, quickly observing that his success, unlike Bruce's, relied not on aristocratic guile but on 'self-confidence and politeness'.[8] Howard observed how Cowell always spoke slowly and deliberately: 'He is never hasty, nor is it possible to heat him in argument. He remains quite cool and whether speaking to the Prince or others affects openness and candour.'[9] This approach gave Cowell 'immense weight' with the royals. Cowell also, Howard noted wryly, made certain to see 'the Prince Consort often, so as not to be forgotten'.[10] Such caution and calculation stood in stark contrast to the impulsiveness of the Elphinstones. But Howard recognized that unless he adjusted his behaviour, his career at Windsor might be as short-lived as his great-grandfather's had been at the court of Catherine the Great. Bruce and Cowell appeared poised and self-assured. 'Can you not do the same?' he asked himself. 'It requires an *effort*, but I ought to have seen enough of the world to know *that without great effort one cannot attain too much.*'[11]

In the late summer of 1859 the major joined the royal family on their annual pilgrimage to Scotland. The Queen had been quite explicit in her instructions. 'When the Court moves', she decreed, 'the children (unless as a special exception) always go with us.'[12] On 29 August, therefore, following a light supper at Buckingham Palace, the royal party left Euston Station on an overnight train for Scotland. There was little chance of sleep, or sustenance, as they clattered, jolted and shuddered their way north. Short stops at remote rural stations were greeted by a flurry of flying shawls, coats and hats as the household tumbled onto the platform to seek refreshment, or relief in private. When they reached a blustery Edinburgh at eight the following morning, everyone was cold, tired and hungry, so the salute fired from the castle ramparts was barely noticed. Just nine years before, Howard had watched a similar scene as a young subaltern stationed in the city. Now he gazed back at the crowds from his seat in a royal carriage, marvelling perhaps at the change to his life.

After a few hours' rest at Holyrood, the royal party continued their journey – forcing Howard to apologize to his father's lawyers, who called at the palace after he had gone hoping to discuss the Balmerino case. At Banchory the travellers left the royal train to complete the last leg of the journey by road. The rain pounded down on the shiny black canvases of the carriages as they lurched along the uneven country lanes. Inside, the household sat shivering and dripping. The more seasoned members always dreaded the annual visit to Balmoral, not sharing the royal couple's infatuation with remote, rural Scotland. Eventually the procession emerged from a gloomy forest of conifers and turned towards the silver-grey castle looming through the mist. A stream of footmen appeared carrying umbrellas, their red coats the only spots of colour in the bleak scene. The household entered the castle through a small doorway at the foot of a great tower, hurrying to escape from the rain. Newcomers were invariably struck by the vivid decoration inside: a lurid mixture of multi-coloured tartans punctuated by glassy-eyed sporting trophies. Nevertheless, Balmoral had a modern, luxurious feel after the medieval austerity of Windsor, with running baths and flushing water closets.[13] Howard was given a room beside Arthur's in the royal apartments; beneath his window the river Dee gurgled and gushed its way through the castle grounds.

The Queen was at her happiest in Scotland, surrounded by her family and Scottish servants. Every day after breakfast, there was a whirl of happy activity as children were scooped up, picnic baskets packed and expeditions launched to walk or ride in the heather-clad hills that embraced the castle. Most days Albert organized a shooting party, but Elphinstone rarely joined in, preferring to walk the hills discussing literature with Ernst Becker than to stalk them with a gun. Moreover, he was experiencing great difficulties with Arthur, whose behaviour was now so bad that his governor had felt it necessary to confine the prince to his room for hours at a time. When his detention made little difference, the prince was beaten. But the boy's screams soon caused Howard to be called to the Queen's cluttered sitting room, where Victoria sat working on her papers. 'Before her', the governor noticed, his eye absent-mindedly drawn, as usual, to anything artistic, 'is the miniature of the Prince Consort, a very fine one and very like. I have an engraving done after it.'

Balmoral Castle, photographed by Roger Fenton soon after its completion in 1856.

'Is Prince Arthur improving,' Victoria asked, looking up from her work, 'and what is the cause of his naughtiness?'

The major was unrepentant, explaining that he had been forced to punish the prince for his incessant lying. The Queen was anxious to avoid a confrontation with Howard, knowing that he operated under her husband's, and not her, authority. Admitting that her son was 'inclined to deceive', she suggested that he start learning Latin to occupy him – an idea, she added hastily, which had originally been the Prince Consort's. But Howard strongly objected to her proposal, claiming that 'the difficulty of confining his attention would be too great'. 'Strong measures might have to be resorted to,' he continued forcefully, 'as it would not do to commence and show the boy that you are obliged to abandon it. He obtains the mastery [while] to persist on the contrary might sour his temper. It is fine now, but will it stand proof against continual scolding?' As if to lighten the tense mood, the Queen then revealed, 'with a laugh', that 'she herself hated lessons', though 'the Prince Consort on the contrary liked them above all else'.[14]

Ten days later, having achieved little improvement in the prince's behaviour, Elphinstone was again summoned. This time Victoria tried a different approach. 'The Prince Consort told me', she began with an air of defiance, 'that he was afraid that you had seen nothing of the country from your being so constantly kept at home with Prince Arthur. You ought to let him go with his sisters, if you wish to go out.'

'I replied that I did not by any means object to this confinement, so long as I found that I was doing good,' Elphinstone recalled vehemently.

But the Queen's message was unmistakable. Her son's continued confinement was causing comment around the castle, while the governor's self-imposed isolation was harming his own position. Howard knew that he was at fault, admitting that he 'ought to have gone out shooting' with the Prince Consort rather than stay behind at the castle.[15] He had perhaps been following Dr Schreber's formula for good child management a little too closely.

So he relented, and that afternoon took Arthur out on a picnic ride with the Queen, Lady Churchill, Bertie and Princess Alice.[16] As usual, Victoria's pony was led by John Brown, a large, taciturn Highlander with watchful eyes and a face apparently hewn from granite. Behind the party trailed a young ghillie, carting a bulging wicker hamper on his back. Soon, however, even the sure-footed ponies found the steep, stone-strewn tracks difficult to negotiate. So the party dismounted and continued on foot, laden down with parasols, telescopes and sketching equipment. 'One had heather up to one's knees,' Victoria happily recalled, 'holes, slipping ground, and stones 2 or 3 ft high to get over. I tried my best, but could never have got on, without Brown's help.' It was 'the most difficult ascent, I have ever made', she claimed, noting it had taken an hour to reach the summit.[17] After a windswept picnic, Arthur played with Bertie, while Elphinstone sat sketching beside the Queen. 'But what a difficult thing to get the colouring of the hills,' he complained; 'one is always at fault, and cannot give the delicacy and smoothness the scenery ought to have.'[18]

'The going down was a wonderful but very amusing affair,' Victoria wrote later. The children tumbled down the hillside, whooping with joy, while John Brown, 'in trying to keep me up, came down his whole length'.[19] When Lady Churchill then slipped over in the heather, landing in a confusion of skirts, John Brown hurried down to assist.

'Your Ladyship is not so heavy as Her Majesty,' he mumbled as he helped the blushing lady of the bedchamber to her feet.

'Am I grown heavier, do you think?' teased the Queen, over-hearing the remark.

'Well, I think you are,' Brown replied, unabashed.[20]

Sixty years later, Arthur would recall the last few days of this holiday, which had begun so badly for him, as among the happiest of his whole childhood. 'I remember accompanying my father to spear salmon in the Dee,' he told his biographer in 1926, 'when all the keepers, gillies and people on the estate took part. I enjoyed wading in the river. After a successful day of deer-stalking, the deer were shown in front of the castle by torchlight when the pipes were played and reels were danced by the people of Balmoral.'[21] Elphinstone perhaps relaxed a little too much. His casual suggestion one morning that he take Arthur for a ride with John Brown was greeted with incredulity by the Queen. 'Impossible,' she exclaimed. 'Why, what should I do without him! He is my particular ghilley!'[22]

Victoria dreaded the return to England. 'You cannot conceive', she confided miserably in Howard, their recent disagreement entirely forgotten, 'what a *complete* change it is. Not only the weather, but the entire change of living. I can no longer go without being followed by a crowd. It makes one feel inclined to become quite like a naughty child.'[23] The major, however, was still preoccupied by his own worries as he left Balmoral for the long journey south. Shaken by the rebuke over Brown, he was trying to 'efface the bad impression which many things have led me to believe that I have made there'.[24] Back at Windsor, he anxiously studied the royals for signs of approval. At least, he noted wryly, the Duchess of Kent seemed pleased to see him.

10

'Vraiment un peu trop extravagant'

CHRISTMAS 1859

IN NOVEMBER 1859 Vicky visited Windsor with her new husband Prince Friedrich Wilhelm of Prussia, or Fritz as the family called him. The prince cut an impressive figure, over six feet tall with a ramrod back and sandy-coloured whiskers. The day after they arrived a banquet was held in the Waterloo Chamber to celebrate the princess's eighteenth birthday, followed by a presentation in St George's Hall of *The Evil Genius*, a comedy in three acts. All the royal family loved the stage and the art of dressing-up, especially the Queen – although she was highly suspicious of actors. She later told Howard to ensure that Arthur '*never* goes *behind* the scenes' when attending the theatre.[1] Performances of short plays, or elaborate *tableaux vivants* presented by the children, marked every family occasion. Arthur was always the most enthusiastic member of the cast, his love of acting developing into a passion for charades. Fortunately, Howard shared this royal enthusiasm, otherwise the palace entertainments might have grown wearisome. As a young subaltern in Edinburgh he had attended a reading by the renowned actress Fanny Kemble, while throughout his court career he always happily submitted to the indignity of fancy dress when called upon.

A few nights after the birthday banquet, Fritz visited Elphinstone in his room to discuss military matters. The two men

93

were close in age and in outlook. Despite a rigid upbringing, Fritz had wide cultural interests and very liberal views compared to the crushing conservatism prevalent elsewhere at the Prussian court. Vicky encouraged her husband's enlightened opinions, but they clashed dangerously with those of his father Wilhelm, the Crown Prince and next in line to the Prussian throne. Above all else, the prince was fascinated by the art of war, and when he met Howard their conversation was 'chiefly on military matters'. A discussion on the British army's new camp at Aldershot – a further initiative of the tireless Prince Consort – prompted Fritz to remark that most British soldiers were mere 'boys' compared to their Prussian counterparts. He then disclosed details of Prussia's latest secret weapon: a breech-loading rifle called the 'needle gun'. In trials the rifle had performed six times faster than a musket, impressing the watching officers. 'They don't misfire,' the prince revealed, 'and from experience they find that their men do not fire away their ammunition too rapidly.'[2] Such a weapon would obviously give the Prussians a clear advantage in any future conflict. Howard was enthralled, and 'particularly pleased' with the prince's open and relaxed manner towards him. 'There was none of the hauteur which I had previously ascribed to him,' he noted, clearly delighted to be treated as an equal by the earnest young Prussian.[3]

In December the royals returned to the Isle of Wight for a short stay at Osborne before the Christmas holiday. But the house was most decidedly '*not* a winter residence', Howard complained, '[as] the Italian architecture of the whole place is so unsuited at this time of year'. All the colour and warmth of the summer had drained away; leaving a cold, desolate air. Vases which in summer had burst with 'geraniums and bright coloured garden gems' now stood in 'damp nakedness almost an eyesore' on the bleak, leaf-strewn terraces. The Prince Consort, however, was in unusually high spirits: singing comic songs to the children, organizing indoor games and telling 'very amusing' stories after dinner.[4] 'What a wonderful memory the Prince has!' marvelled Elphinstone. 'I have never met any to equal him in that respect.'[5]

On 12 December, having let it slip that it was his thirtieth birthday, Elphinstone received a variety of presents from the children. Arthur gave his governor an antique gold seal, while 'sweet little' Princess Louise shyly handed him a wooden watch stand. 'When I tried to thank her,' Howard wrote, 'she modestly ran away, to avoid receiving them.'[6] These presents were the first modest contributions towards an eventual treasure trove of royal gifts which Howard would accumulate over his years at court, culminating in a priceless Stradivarius violin (now known as the 'Elphinstone Strad').

Howard's birthday came towards the end of his one-year probation period as Arthur's governor. The Prince Consort marked this milestone by asking him to stay in his post for a further three years, until the end of 1862. Howard was 'truly gratified' by the prince's offer, but was also surprised. Writing to accept, he confessed that he was aware his 'humble efforts although well meant, have not infrequently led me into errors of judgement and even in action for which, I fear, my inexperience alone must plead'.[7] In his letter to Howard confirming his offer, the Prince Consort broached the subject of Prince Leopold's future education for the first time. During the summer, the Queen's irritation with her youngest son's fragile health, which so often caused him to miss out on normal family life, had spiked into anxiety. The young prince's medical condition could no longer be ignored, and it was becoming obvious that his new governess Marie Hocédé could not cope alone. Leo took days, weeks sometimes, to recover from bumps and bruises which other children of his age shrugged off in an instant. Howard suspected something was seriously wrong with the prince. One day he noticed how 'the poor little fellow's head' had swelled 'dreadfully' after barely '*touching*' a table.[8] The doctors talked vaguely about 'the peculiar constitution of his blood vessels which have no adhesiveness'. But they were at a loss as to what to do, beyond hoping that Leopold would one day grow out of his baffling complaint. The prince's troubling symptoms were in fact the consequence of haemophilia, a condition in which the blood fails to clot; but this disorder had yet to be properly recognized, and an effective treatment was years away. In the absence of any better suggestions, the Queen recommended giving her son hot baths, and doses of iron to bolster his blood. No less ignorant, Elphinstone proposed rigorous outdoor exercise for the prince, combined with standing him a 'dozen times a day' against a board to improve his stooping posture (ill-informed advice lifted directly from Dr Schreber, who was a firm believer in 'good posture' as a means of education).[9] Yet he held out little hope of success, remarking gloomily that the Queen 'did not speak' about her youngest son 'with that *sadness*, which I am afraid it may be necessary to do hereafter'.[10] When asked by the Prince Consort, Howard 'gladly' agreed to take charge of Leopold as well as Arthur, but he was understandably nervous about accepting such a hazardous task, one for which he was woefully ill-qualified.[11] 'Should he be placed under my care,' he thought unhappily, 'I trust sincerely for a change in his health, as some accident might cause his death while with me.'[12] When he confided this concern to John Cowell, he was told simply to 'speak to the parents about it' – something he could never do.[13]

By 19 December, Osborne was blanketed in deep snow. 'I never saw anything more lovely than the trees loaded with snow,' wrote Eleanor Stanley to her mother, as she gazed out of her bedroom window over the white-blanketed garden and down to the sea. The maid of honour counted no fewer than sixty loads of ice being carted to the cavernous ice house, in preparation for the summer. To Arthur's delight, William Jolley was caught in a snow-drift on his way up to the house, forcing the cancellation of his lessons for the day. Bertie wanted to go skating, 'but the Queen and Prince were nervous about it, as the pond is tolerably deep, and there is no "humane" apparatus here, as on the Serpentine, to serve impudent youths'.[14] Instead, feeling 'infected with good humour', Howard took Arthur and Bertie outside to build a snow-man on the croquet lawn. Spotting them from his first-floor study window, the Prince Consort hurried outside to join them, producing a carrot for the snowman's nose and one of Affie's 'hideous' old hats for its head.[15] Albert then 'most energetically' pulled all the children on a sledge, stamping down the snow to make a better slide.

By Christmas Eve the snow had gone and Osborne was once again deserted. The royals were back at Windsor Castle, decorating the 'Christmas room', a small chamber beside the King's Room in the heart of the private apartments. During the evening, presents were distributed among the household. Howard received photographs from the royal children, a gold and malachite inkstand from Victoria and Albert, and an ivory paper knife and notebook from the Duchess of Kent. In return, he gave Arthur a photograph of himself, mounted in a silver frame. As a mark of their special favour, Elphinstone and Ernst Becker were invited ahead of the rest of the household to view the lavish display of the family's own gifts in the Christmas room. The children were in 'ecstasies' at the mountain of toys, although Elphinstone rather primly thought such a 'tremendous' number far more than they could possibly ever appreciate. Only eleven-year-old Princess Louise seemed embarrassed by such largesse, sidling up to Howard to confide sweetly that it was all *Vraiment un peu trop extravagant*.'[16]

After Christmas, Victoria sent for Elphinstone to discuss Arthur's progress. 'She was engaged in some needlework,' he recalled: 'unusual, for generally she is at her journal or else letters.' Unaware that Jolley had just given the prince a bad report, Howard assured the Queen that her son's work was improving. Yet it was soon apparent that a progress report on the prince was not the real reason behind their meeting, so his blunder was ignored. Victoria was more concerned about the governor's relationship with her son, in particular his use of corporal punishment on the prince. She had evidently dwelt on their awkward conversation at Balmoral the previous summer.

'I don't think that your severity has in any way diminished the affection he bears for you,' she said uneasily, as if to reassure him.

'I always endeavoured to make him *feel* the justice of the punishment and *acknowledge* it, when I punished him,' Elphinstone replied, with more force than was strictly necessary. Only later did he appreciate the generosity of the Queen's remark, and the clumsiness of his reply. 'I ought to have expressed myself more fully and feelingly,' he reflected ruefully, 'for it was particularly gracious of the Queen to do this.'[17]

But 1859 did not end 'very happily for poor Prince Arthur'. His work deteriorated and his lying became more frequent, culminating in a violent clash with his governor. 'Many raps . . . did the poor little boy get,' wrote Elphinstone hopelessly, 'and his crying was unquestionably very loud. I wish I could find some other mode of punishing!!' In despair, the Queen now began throwing out 'strong hints' that she disapproved strongly of Elphinstone's methods of discipline, even though they were condoned by the Prince Consort. On New Year's Eve she sent for him again, her patience finally exhausted. She could not accept, she told Howard, that Arthur was as badly behaved as his elder brothers, or that he needed punishing so severely or so often. He might occasionally 'scheme', she admitted, but he would never tell a 'direct falsehood' – unlike Affie, whose 'love of truth is not very great'.[18]

'I have been thinking over it,' she continued, in a more conciliatory manner, 'and must admit that Prince Arthur has far less pleasure than any of his brothers and sisters. Might not this create a feeling of apparent injustice and consequent irritation? Not that there are any grounds for it, because he has not been good. Still having lost two holidays, from Christmas Day and New Year falling on the Sunday, might it not be as well to give him one holiday?'

'It was impossible to say anything against it,' fumed Elphinstone, feeling his authority undermined. Reluctantly, he agreed to give Arthur an extra holiday on Twelfth Night, on condition that the prince did not play with his friends that day. But he defended the beatings, insisting that 'remaining quiet without speaking, or being locked up had little effect' on the prince. The

Queen 'persisted no further, but it is evident she does not wish it', he confided unhappily to his journal. Her meaning was unmistakable: he was to change his ways or face the consequences, regardless of his friendship with Albert. Hours later, Howard joined the Queen in the ballroom to hear 1860 heralded by 'a great crash of drum, cymbals and all the trumpets'. 'Everyone was wishing each other a happy New Year and shaking hands,' he noted back in his room, but he could not hide his unhappiness.[19] His first year at court was over; but he was doubtful he could, or would, survive another one.

'One cannot exercise too much tact up here'

WINDSOR CASTLE, 1860

> The New Year has commenced, and the old one has gone. Upon the whole it has not appeared long to me, although the many things I have seen here might have conduced towards it. Would that I could review carefully and judiciously my last year's conduct, and see in what way, both morally and physically I have altered or improved. The change is very slight, and by my present humour, I should say not for the better, perhaps.[1]

ELPHINSTONE SAT BACK from his desk in a sombre, reflective mood. A year after entering court, he could count on the support of the Prince Consort. But the Queen's trust was far less certain, and he had yet to earn Prince Arthur's respect, let alone his affection. He had also struggled to make friends in the close-knit world of the court, preferring the company of Prince Albert's serious-minded German staff to the English aristocrats who dominated the royal household. This approach left him feeling isolated and alone, but appearing arrogant and aloof. 'One cannot exercise *too* much tact up here,' he told himself; 'make yourself *felt*, but that with *modesty* and consideration for others.' He was tired, exhausted by the responsibility of his position and the scrutiny of others, and frustrated by the Queen's interference in his work. He admitted that 'the great anxiety that I used to evince to exert myself to please the Queen and Prince Consort is *very* much diminished'.[2] The invitations to the royal dinner parties had dwindled, and when his friend Ernst Becker abruptly left the castle after Christmas, feeling 'very unhappy', Howard's sense of vulnerability increased yet further. 'I feel myself much in the position of a man who having played for a high game, finds the ground beneath him slippery,' he wrote miserably, 'and every step he takes tends more and more to hurl him down.'[3]

On Twelfth Night, Elphinstone organized a gymkhana for the children in the riding school. Back in his room, he found a message from Victoria telling him that, as it was a holiday, the Prince Consort thought Arthur should be allowed out to play with Albert Grey, the son of Charles Grey and the young prince's best friend outside his family. It was the final straw. Feeling his position challenged, Howard angrily rejected the suggestion. In a hastily scrawled note, he ill-advisedly reminded the Queen that he had expressly forbidden the prince from playing with any of his friends that day as he was still being punished for his behaviour at Christmas. Within minutes, he was summoned to the Queen's sitting room. Victoria's tone, 'although kindly', was distinctly frosty. 'It would be better not to lay down prospective conditions with Prince Arthur,' she told him, carefully, 'as that binds one down to fulfil those threats although it becomes awkward. Don't you think that *immediate* punishments are better?'[4]

That evening Howard received an unexpected visit in his room from an 'earnest'-looking Albert. The Prince Consort apologized awkwardly for not answering the governor's ill-tempered note to the Queen himself: 'which I intended to have done, as I have been very busy'. Howard's outburst had clearly compromised the Prince Consort, causing a row between the royal couple. 'I must be more cautious in future,' the governor vowed, sensing Albert's hurt and realizing his mistake.[5]

An uneasy peace settled briefly over the castle. Then, within days, Arthur turned 'sulky' again after being ordered to prepare a double dose of poetry. The prince kicked off his shoes, sat on the ground, yelled and noisily stamped his feet. After weeks of provocation, Howard finally snapped. He grabbed the prince by his collar and gave him 'a good box on his ears'. 'I would not have done this,' he wrote later, justifying his action, 'but that he had several times that day tried to disobey me, and I therefore thought it inadvisable to let it pass this time without severe punishment.' The boy's screams were so loud and so long, however, that within minutes the Queen herself rushed into the room. After calming the hysterical Arthur, she turned white-faced to the governor and quietly 'asked me to go upstairs to her'.[6]

Howard probably expected to be dismissed. Perhaps he deserved to be, even desired to be. But instead Victoria was again conciliatory, telling him calmly that 'she hoped this would not occur often as it was annoying to hear those screams so frequently'. They discussed the problems Howard was having with her son. He explained at length how he found it impossible to make the prince concentrate on his lessons and to obey him. Victoria listened in silence, obviously keen to help. She now agreed that letting her son mix with children outside his own family, something Howard had been promoting for months, might be of 'great advantage' to Arthur.[7] Albert Grey would be allowed to join the prince in the schoolroom. Suppressing her fear of infection, Victoria even gave permission for Arthur to be taken down to Eton several times a week to play with the boys at the college. Howard told her later that the visits helped to '"rub off" [the] little eccentricities and softness of character which a home education must unavoidably produce'.[8]

For the time being, at least, Howard's place seemed secure. The Prince Consort may have reasoned with the Queen behind the closed doors of the royal apartments. She had certainly shown no hesitation in the past in ridding herself of servants or staff in whom she had lost confidence, like Madame Rollande. But the education of her sons was her husband's responsibility: the method his design, and Howard his choice of governor. So while the major still enjoyed the confidence of the Prince Consort, his position was safe.

A week later, on the anniversary of his first day in charge of Prince Arthur, Howard received a letter from Victoria praising his 'zeal and devotion'. 'She trusts', she wrote, a little disingenuously,

> that he will admit that the Queen never has interfered with the salutary and necessary strictness which Major Elphinstone has wisely shown in enforcing obedience and attention on the part of Arthur. The Queen loves her children *far* too dearly *ever* to wish to see them indulged or spoilt, even when they are so worshipped, as she may *here own* to the Major, she has our little Arthur, from the day of his birth. He has never given us a day's sorrow or trouble, she may truly say, but ever been like a little ray of sunshine in the House![9]

Out of the envelope tumbled some photographs of Arthur.

The governor was 'deeply touched' by this unexpected gesture, declaring that Victoria's letter was 'worth handing down to one's relations and it is written with so much feeling that it ought to be carefully kept from vulgar gaze'. The Queen's well-timed action was an astute piece of management which raised the governor's flagging spirits and renewed his enthusiasm for his task. 'This may seem vain but is natural', Howard wrote in his journal, 'when you see that your labour for others is duly appreciated, it is *then* only that you get encouraged to proceed vigorously.'[10] In his reply to Victoria he tried to express his thanks properly, but only 'a bundle of words' came out and he later bitterly regretted that he had not thanked her in person.[11]

Any thought of abandoning his post was pushed aside. With fresh energy and having 'determined to keep my position with the young Prince', Howard drafted another set of objectives to help him improve his relationship with his young charge:

1   Never order him to do anything unless it is *necessary*.
2   Keep your temper cool in every possible emergency, and *never* speak harshly.
3   In joining in his games take great care that you do so only by

keeping your position well and thoroughly; enter more in them as if to please him.

4   Take great care that he does not read your thoughts.[12]

Meeting Elphinstone on the castle terrace a couple of days later, Victoria made no mention of her letter. She expressed her fears for Leopold, asking the major to speak with Madame Hocédé about his ideas for handling the prince, 'as she admitted that they seemed good'. Turning to the problems he was having with Arthur, the Queen revealed, in a 'motherly' way, how difficult it had been for the Prince of Wales to make friends at the same age. 'He used to ill-treat and beat the boys [so] that the parents . . . *refused* to send their children,' she recalled sadly.[13] The Queen habitually compared Bertie unfavourably to her other children, having placed such high expectations on him. 'One cannot fix his attention, even at a novel,' she would admit to Howard; 'in fact he would wish to be doing absolutely nothing whatever; throw himself down upon a chair, or else on the good nature of others.'[14] At such moments of intimacy, Howard felt 'devoted heart and soul' to Victoria, sensing the vulnerability beneath the weight of her position. When that evening at dinner, she had then leaned across John Cowell to deliberately speak with him, his heart had burst with pride.

It took longer for the Prince Consort to forgive the major's impertinence towards his wife. For weeks he seemed to brood over the affair, ignoring the man of whom he had made a friend. 'He used to come down and speak frequently with me,' Howard lamented; 'that he never does now, and generally I think, when an interview occurs, shortens it as much as possible. It may be fancy on my part, yet I doubt it.'[15] In fact Albert had many other things on his mind. He was struggling with an impossible workload while suffering from headaches and bouts of severe stomach pain. Ignoring the pleas of his family to slow down, he recklessly kept working as if fatally driven by some hidden demon.

Howard's discomfort in January 1860 was exacerbated by

the long-awaited publication of his first volume of the official account of the Crimean War, entitled *The Journal of the Operations conducted by the Corps of the Royal Engineers*. The reviewer for *The Times* (possibly William Russell, who had memorably covered the war for the paper) lambasted the major's stilted writing style, his vagueness and his attempt to gloss over the worst aspects of the conflict to show the Royal Engineers in the best possible light.[16] The *United Service Magazine* went further still, regretting that so important a task had been given to 'such an incompetent hand'. The editor queried why the choice of author had been left to Sir John Burgoyne, the head of the Royal Engineers, who so obviously wanted to show his own actions in the 'best colour', having been recalled from the Crimea for ineptitude and replaced by Harry Jones. There was even a suggestion, vehemently denied, that some of the documents Elphinstone had published as an appendix had been doctored or 'written after the event'.[17] Another critic raged that the book was 'as unjust to our noble Crimean Army and its illustrious commander as it is discreditable to its authors'.[18]

Burgoyne publicly defended Elphinstone, accusing his critics of trying to scapegoat the engineers for the wider failures of the campaign. For Howard, however, the most personally damaging aspect of the hostility which greeted his book was the accusation that, by promoting Burgoyne, he had disparaged the memory of Lord Raglan. 'Of all the attacks on Lord Raglan,' sniffed the *United Service Magazine*, 'this, which strikes with a muffled dagger, is the unkindest. As we read, we cannot forbear to exclaim – *Et tu, O Brute!*'[19] Such notoriety was unwelcome to Elphinstone inside the royal household, where many officers still worshipped Raglan. Fortunately, as Howard knew, the Prince Consort was not among Raglan's admirers; had this not been the case, his position at court might well have been compromised by the controversy, coming as it did at a time when a coolness had grown up between Albert and his son's governor. None the less, his critical mauling stung him badly. Writing to Albert some months later on library matters, Howard referred sharply to the *United Service Magazine* as 'not a good periodical [but] the only military one we have that is worth mentioning'.[20] In contrast to its first volume, the second volume of *The Journal of the Operations conducted by the Corps of the Royal Engineers*, written by the vastly more experienced and politically astute General Sir Harry Jones, was much better received. The *United Service Magazine* praised it as 'honourable to his character, and unleavened by apocryphal documents'.

When Albert did eventually talk to Howard again after the *froideur* of the New Year, their conversations were on political and military affairs, not on Arthur's education. The Prince Consort was fixated by the threat of war with France, whose meddling in Italy's current struggle for independence from Austrian control risked triggering a conflict. During a long discussion on England's security, the prince expressed his exasperation at the objections of the new Chancellor of the Exchequer, William Gladstone, to improving the country's coastal defences, on grounds of cost. 'If they allow me to buy the land,' Albert exclaimed, 'I would make it more than productive, by purchasing far more than required, and when the existence of forts and barracks commenced, to bring settlers to the place, and parcel it out in lots.'[21] Troops were as important as forts to the country's protection, and in June 1860 Howard took Prince Arthur to Hyde Park to see the Queen review the Volunteer Defence Force, another innovation of the Prince Consort's to bolster the country's defences. A week later came the much-publicized launch of an annual rifle-shooting competition on Wimbledon Common, designed to improve the nation's aim. Watched by Howard and thousands of spectators, the Queen opened the event by hitting the bull's-eye of a target at four hundred yards using a carefully fixed pre-sighted rifle.

Elphinstone was back in favour with Victoria and Albert, but he still had to settle comfortably within the aristocratic world of the court. He was also distracted by his father's attempt to resurrect the Balmerino title. Back in March, James Law, Captain Elphinstone's solicitor in Edinburgh, had travelled four hundred miles to discuss the case with Howard on the private pier for

Osborne House. He then reported that Howard's elder brother Nicolai had returned from India determined 'not [to] leave a stone unturned to gain his object, provided that it can be done by reasonable means'.[22] Nicolai had had a 'fight' with Lord Elphinstone's lawyer, provoking fury in Scotland. Only months later, the sudden deaths in quick succession of the thirteenth and then the fourteenth Lord Elphinstone brought matters to a head. Unwisely, Howard took advantage of the double tragedy to write to the editor of *Lodge's Peerage* – a genealogical survey of low repute – claiming his family's collateral descent with the new Lord Elphinstone, a key feature of his own family's claim to the Balmerino title. It was an ill-judged move which was bitterly resented by the Scottish Elphinstones and undermined his father's case. Howard would need to rein himself and his hot-headed brother in before their family's spiralling legal conflict further damaged his fragile position at court.

12

'Be careful, careful, *in* explanations *with the Queen; you have offended* twice'

WINDSOR CASTLE, 1860

'SINCE MY LAST ENTRY I have been to London and back again to Windsor,' Elphinstone wrote in his journal on 7 April 1860; 'about a month has elapsed. But whether fancied or real, I know not, but I appear to feel myself in a different position . . . Take care, take care however of arrogance, that insupportable presumption. Nothing can atone for it.'[1]

Life had returned to normal since the crisis at Christmas, when it had seemed that Howard's impertinence might end his career at court. It was Prince Leopold's seventh birthday and an expedition was planned to Virginia Water, the picturesque lake at the far end of Windsor Park, with its grottoes and follies. As the Queen and Prince Consort had wished, Howard was now in charge of Leo as well as Arthur – notwithstanding the major's reluctance to take on such a perilous charge. Leo's bleeding episodes were becoming progressively more severe, heightening Howard's fear that the prince might die under his care. He also saw difficulties looking after the two princes 'judiciously' and on an equal basis. Arthur was now a boisterous nine-year-old while his younger brother was not only physically weak but, having been mollycoddled since birth, also 'very touchy' and 'thinks too much of his dignity'.[2]

In a long memorandum entitled 'On Prince Arthur and Prince Leopold living together', Howard had laid down a series of conditions for his management of the children. 'The great difference in strength, age and character of the two Princes', he told the Queen, 'will necessitate that for the present they should, as a rule, be kept apart, and that their joint participation wither [whether] in lessons or amusement, be the exception.'[3] Howard also prescribed more exercise for Leo, as 'he is so intelligent that a little less work could do him no harm mentally, whereas it certainly would benefit him physically'. The futility of this advice became evident almost immediately when the prince badly sprained his ankle out walking. Nevertheless, his frailty did not prevent Leo from joining Arthur in his pranks. On one occasion the boys provoked outrage from the Prince of Wales by throwing water at him. 'I don't like making complaints,' Bertie thundered at Elphinstone, 'but really I am obliged to do so now, as I think that some one should look after them when they are alone.'[4]

Anxious to avoid a repeat of the disciplinary problems he had encountered with Arthur, Howard reviewed his own conduct now that he was in charge of two princes. He composed another set of principles, entitling this one: 'Be the perfect gentleman with the young Princes':

1 Be careful to maintain your superiority by gentleness, firmness, coolness.
2 Be careful not to abuse, or laugh at them.
3 Give as few orders as possible, and those always distinctly.
4 Always speak kindly, but firmly.
5 Never accept a provocation. Quiet resolution is the only power.
6 Never write *anything* which opens another subject or may lead to consequences.
7 Be *careful, careful*, in explanations with the Queen; you have offended *twice*.[5]

In September 1860 Victoria and Albert went on a visit to Germany, leaving Howard alone with the princes at Osborne House. As Leopold was too frail to join his brother and governor on a walking tour of the Isle of Wight, he remained behind under the supervision of Sir Edward Bowater, an elderly courtier and not, according to Howard, 'a lively man in a solitary abode'.[6] During their expedition around the island, Arthur and Elphinstone tried to stay incognito in local hotels, passing their time exploring churches and ruined forts. Collecting fossils was still a favourite pastime. Charles Darwin's *On the Origin of Species* had recently been published and Howard was convinced, as he told the Prince Consort, that the study of geology would give Arthur 'more enlarged and general ideas'. The young prince would discover that 'what he had hitherto considered as layers of dirty mud and clay, contained after all the remains of some very beautiful shells and the remains of animals that must have lived many many years ago'.[7] Away from the oppressive routine of court life and the rigid discipline of the schoolroom, the governor's difficult relationship with his charge gradually improved, each seeing the other in a new light. For the first time, Howard noticed with pleasure that the prince was 'anxious to do his best to please *me*', rather than simply to avoid punishment.[8]

During the tour, news reached Elphinstone from Germany that the Prince Consort's stepmother the Dowager Duchess of Coburg had died, plunging the court into mourning. Then Albert himself was nearly killed in a driving accident. Howard sent a 'badly worded and stupid letter' of sympathy, admitting that 'I really did not know what to say'.[9] In his reply from Coburg – which he signed 'ever yours truly Albert' – the prince stoically assured Elphinstone that he was 'recovering well and rapidly' from the accident, having suffered no more than minor cuts and bad bruising.[10] In fact, the incident had shaken him badly. Albert confessed to his eldest daughter Vicky that as his carriage careered out of control he had been convinced that he was going to die. Visiting the Rosenau, his childhood home near Coburg, a few days later,

Albert stood and cried, so sure was he that he would never see it again.

This dismal mood lifted in December when once again the family assembled at Windsor Castle for Christmas. It was an unusually large gathering this year. Except for Vicky, who remained in Berlin, all the children were there: Bertie was back from a highly successful tour of North America and Affie was briefly home from sea. They were all curious to meet Prince Ludwig of Hesse and by Rhine, the heir to a small duchy in Germany, whose engagement to Princess Alice had recently been announced. Louis, as he was known in England, was a shy, easy-going man; the perfect foil to the intense and serious-minded princess. 'It was royalty putting aside its state,' reported one guest at the festivities, 'and becoming in words, acts, and deeds one of ourselves, no forms and not a vestige of ceremony.' Even Albert 'lost his stiffness', happily dodging Arthur while his son took pot shots at him with a wooden rifle.[11] Christmas Day was celebrated with a banquet consisting of dozens of roast turkeys and geese, barons of beef and a specially prepared pie stuffed with a hundred woodcock. After some party games, the gentlemen retired to the billiard room where Captain Du Plat, one of the Prince Consort's equerries, 'cleared the remainder out of every silver coin they possessed'.[12] After all the arguments a year before, it was a happy and relaxed family occasion. No-one could know that it would be the last for many years.

Eighteen sixty-one even began inauspiciously. Just days into the New Year one of the Queen's physicians, William Baly, was killed in a freak accident when the floor of the railway carriage he was travelling in collapsed, hurling him beneath the wheels of the train. 'He was so mangled', an appalled and increasingly fatalistic Prince Consort reported to Baron Stockmar, 'that his servants were unable to swear to the identity of his body, when it was shown to them, until their attention was called to his clothes.'[13] Baly's successor was William Jenner, a gruff, self-confident man who later 'horrified' one maid of honour 'with his ugliness, which is something suggestive to me of Voltaire'.[14] The new doctor faced a heavy workload. The Prince Consort was still suffering from intermittent stomach pain, while the health of the Duchess of Kent, Victoria's 74-year-old mother, was causing mounting concern. Jenner's most pressing task, however, was tackling Prince Leopold's bleeding attacks, which had worsened since his move into Arthur's rooms the previous year. Now no more than a sneeze could provoke a nosebleed lasting hours, upsetting the prince and terrifying his mother. On her suggestion, a bell was placed beside the prince's bed so that in an emergency Leo could rouse Howard, who slept in the adjoining room with the door ajar. There was still no attempt to arrange proper medical supervision. Leo's debilitating condition was known only to a few trusted people inside the palace, and to none without, and the Queen wanted to keep it that way. Instead, Carl Ruland was recruited to cover for Howard when he was occupied with Arthur, although the librarian was equally unsuited for the role. Meanwhile, everyone waited for the inevitable crisis to overwhelm the young prince.

As it was obvious that Leo would never lead a normal life, Howard developed a special routine to deal with his needs. He did so mindful of Leo's natural desire to leave the childish environment of the nursery for the world enjoyed by his elder brothers and sisters. The prince would be protected, but not smothered. Unlike the other children, Leo would be allowed snacks between meals to build up his strength, while his lessons would be restricted to just two and a half hours each day.[15] (As Leo spent so much of his ample spare time reading alone in his room, this hardly hindered his academic progress.) To avoid more accidents, Howard stopped the boys from playing together too roughly, while a footman was detailed to linger behind Leo wherever he went in case he needed carrying. Leo would eat with the rest of the family, unless he was unwell, when he would take his meals in his room with Howard. 'In case of *serious* illness,' Howard decreed, 'which has not yet occurred, it might be preferable to remove the Prince entirely from Prince Arthur's rooms and put him under the charge of one of the Governesses, with one of the maids from the nursery to attend upon him, and then keep him separate from the nursery, to which he could not well return.'[16] The young prince resigned himself to the well-intentioned strictures placed on his life, objecting only when they forced him to miss a party or a family celebration.

In March 1861 concern for Leopold was overshadowed by the death of the Duchess of Kent from cancer. The Queen, who had watched her mother die, threw herself into an extravagant paroxysm of grief, pushing her children away and hiding in her room for almost a month. For a woman of forty-one living in the 1860s, Victoria had surprisingly little direct experience of death, or of the elaborate rituals which had recently come to surround it. Remarkably, all her nine children had survived infancy, while she had been too young at the time to remember her father's death. Such ignorance left her woefully unprepared for the shock of her mother's death, or for the worse trial to come.

On Sunday 24 March, eight days after the duchess had died, Howard took the princes down to Frogmore for a private service of remembrance. The drawing room, the scene of so many happy children's parties, was now shrouded and dominated by the duchess's lead-lined coffin. Before they left the castle, the Queen had given each of her sons a photograph of their grandmother which she asked Howard to frame.[17] The next day, in the darkness before dawn, the coffin was silently carried up to St George's Chapel within the castle precincts, where it was placed beside the magnificent marble tomb of Princess Charlotte (George IV's daughter who had died in childbirth, paving the way to Victoria's accession). Later that morning Elphinstone escorted Arthur to the Chapter House, where they joined the other mourners who would follow the coffin up the aisle for the funeral service. Leopold, who was too young to participate in the rituals, was taken to join his mother in a stall above the altar. The solemn procession halted in the choir, where a grave had been opened into the royal vault. Here the body would rest until a mausoleum, begun in the duchess's lifetime, was finished in the grounds at Frogmore House. The coffin, in its covering of royal crimson felt, seemed like a drop of blood in the inky black of the shrouded chapel. Deeply moved, the Prince Consort shook with silent sobs as the Dean of Windsor uttered the committal prayer. Outside the chapel's ancient walls, guns were fired as the coffin slowly descended. Finally, a mourner stepped forward to drop a handful of earth into the grave with a 'sharp tacking sound'.[18]

Frogmore now became a shrine to the duchess. Most days the Queen went there alone 'to weep and pray'.[19] She insisted that the sitting room, with its caged canary bird and unfinished needle-work by the chair, should remain exactly as her mother had left it. That October, seven months after the duchess had died, Victoria was still writing to thank Elphinstone for 'the kind and *tender* feel-ing which prompted him to take our darling Arthur to that *hallowed* spot at Frogmore', the mere thought of which touched her '*very deeply*'.[20] For weeks she ate alone, finding any company too upsetting. Birthday parties were cancelled, outings to the the-atre banned and requests for audiences ignored. Eventually she retreated to the White Lodge in Richmond, leaving the children behind with their governors and governesses and abandoning her ailing husband to an even heavier workload.

Wisely, the Prince of Wales had hurried back to Cambridge University after his grandmother's funeral, anxious to be away from such a gloomy scene. In May he invited Arthur and Elphinstone down for the weekend, enjoying escorting them around the colleges. But the prince could not entirely avoid the attention of his parents. Two days after Elphinstone and Arthur returned to Windsor, Bertie was visited by his father who, stern-faced, lectured him on his behaviour. Albert had been alerted to rumours that Bertie was mixing with the wrong sort of students at the university and, worse, consorting with women from the town. On 14 May, during a long walk with his father at Madingley, the Tudor mansion in the Cambridgeshire countryside where he lodged with General Bruce, Bertie was warned about his conduct and of the need for sexual restraint. Back in Windsor, his mother seemed more concerned about her heir's table manners. She briefly emerged from her mourning to chastise Bertie for 'lolling' at the table 'and leaning back as if you were eating in your *own* room after a great fatigue. This, dear child, will NOT do for *any* person in your position, or any gentleman.' The only person she knew with worse habits, she declared, was the Duke of Cambridge, although he could be excused on account of his age. 'Young people cannot know these things unless they are told,' the Queen continued, 'and in these days of *bad undignified* manners, it is DOUBLY necessary that *you* should set the *very best* example.'[21] Bertie meekly replied that 'when one is not thinking, habits grow upon one unintentionally'.[22] Knowing of the warm regard that her son felt for him, the Queen sent Elphinstone, rather than General Bruce, a copy of her rebuke, together with Bertie's chastened reply.

Leopold had remained quietly behind at Buckingham Palace during Arthur's and Howard's flying visit to Cambridge; but he rejoined them for the royals' customary trip to Osborne House to mark the Queen's birthday on 24 May. Coming so soon after the death of the Duchess of Kent, the celebrations this year were naturally subdued. Victoria had insisted that there should be 'No music (that would kill me), no change of mourning and dine merely *en famille*'.[23] The next day, without warning, Leopold began passing blood in his urine. Doctor Jenner advised rest, prescribing laxatives to prevent the prince 'straining'. Elphinstone, who had dreaded just such an eventuality, passed Leo back into the hands of Lady Caroline Barrington, the lady superintendent of the nursery, who had been urgently summoned from the mainland. To make matters worse, both Arthur and Leopold then caught measles from Louis of Hesse-Darmstadt, who was still hovering around court waiting to marry Alice. Amid the panic, the Prince Consort insisted that the royal family return early to Buckingham Palace to attend the opening of the Royal Horticultural Show at South Kensington, one of his pet projects. His wife was furious, loudly complaining at having to return to London 'for no earthly reason but that tiresome horticultural garden'.[24] Arthur was well enough to travel (accompanied by Howard), but Jenner rightly insisted that Leo stay in bed at Osborne. 'They say there is no danger whatever at present,' the Queen told Vicky, 'but I own I think it both cruel and wrong to leave a sick child behind.'[25] The doctor's caution was justified, however. Hours after his parents departed, Leo developed a dangerous nosebleed. For several days his life hung in the balance. Eventually, as the Queen steeled herself for bad news and a 'dreadful journey' back to Osborne, Jenner managed to staunch the bleeding by cauterizing the prince's nose. 'Surely he must be meant for some great things,' marvelled Victoria when she heard of Leo's reprieve, 'to have been spared in the midst of such frequent illness!'[26]

Within days, Leo was playing happily again at the Swiss Cottage. But the emergency shook the Queen out of her complacency. She now recognized that the arrangements put in place for her youngest son's care were clearly inadequate, even misguided. Leopold could never be treated like a normal boy, nor could the gravity of his condition be ignored. All talk of exercise regimes and special diets was quietly dropped. Instead it was settled that Leo would spend the winter recuperating in the South of France under the supervision of Theodore Günther, a young German doctor practising in England who had caught the eye of Victoria and Albert – and whom they hired in preference to seeking help within the gossipy world of the English medical fraternity. In his letter of engagement, it was explained to the doctor that Leopold suffered 'a certain general weakness of the constitution which manifests itself particularly through a tendency towards haemorrhages, (from the nose, the gums etc.)'.[27] Elphinstone nominally remained Leo's governor but, as he was occupied with Arthur, Sir Edward Bowater would accompany the prince and Günther to France. Leopold was delighted at the prospect of his holiday, telling Howard that he was 'very glad to hear that I am going to France'.[28]

Before breakfast on 2 November 1861, in conditions of the utmost secrecy, a small crowd gathered on the steps of Windsor Castle to see Leopold off. The prince was neatly dressed in a grey jacket, waistcoat and knickerbockers, 'which is what little boys wear nowadays', reported his tearful mother.[29] As the trunks were loaded into the waiting carriages, the Prince Consort drew Sir Edward Bowater to one side.

'You'll take care of the boy, won't you?' the prince asked anxiously.

'I will, sir,' replied the old soldier, 'as if he were my own.'[30]

After a final kiss from his mother, and a few more tears, Leopold was gone: his carriage clattering out of the castle courtyard and into the autumnal mist. Arthur and Howard accompanied him as far as Folkestone, where they waved him off to France from the quayside. Only when the court went back into mourning a week later for the death of Prince Ferdinand of Portugal did the major suddenly realize that he had forgotten to pack any black-bordered writing paper in Leo's luggage, in case of an unexpected death in the family.

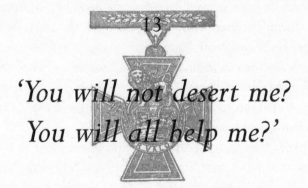

'You will not desert me? You will all help me?'

WINDSOR CASTLE, 1861

PRINCE ARTHUR WAS NOW approaching the age his elder brothers had been when they were sent away to their own households, a landmark long dreaded by his adoring mother. In July 1861 Victoria 'put down my feelings, wishes and objections' regarding her son's future in a long letter to Albert. While she accepted Howard Elphinstone's advice that Arthur needed to be kept '*quiet* to prevent his attention from being distracted', she begged her husband not to allow the prince to become 'completely exiled' from court. She suggested that Arthur spend each week with his governor at a royal residence near London, while returning to her at weekends. Several houses were considered before the Queen settled on the White Lodge in Richmond Park, where Bertie had previously lodged with General Bruce. It was agreed with Albert that the move would take place early in 1862.[1]

Shortly after Leopold sailed for France to recover his health, rumours began circulating in London that Bertie had enjoyed a sexual liaison with a young actress called Nellie Clifden. The Prince Consort was devastated by the gossip, fearing simultaneously scandal, blackmail and disease. He feverishly imagined the whole monarchy collapsing beneath the shame of his son's misdemeanour. On 25 November Albert again set out to confront his son at Cambridge, determined to discover the truth behind the talk. Already in poor health, he returned seriously ill, having taken a long walk in the rain with his remorseful son. He was flushed with a low fever and complained of pain in his back and legs. Even Victoria, who was used to the complaints of her hypochondriac husband, admitted that she had never seen him 'so low'.[2] As usual, however, the doctors were sanguine, assuring the Queen that Albert would recover quickly.

More alarming were the reports from the secluded Château Leader near Cannes that Sir Edward Bowater, Leo's guardian in France, had fallen dangerously ill. Concerned primarily about Leo's welfare, Elphinstone wondered 'how it was that Sir Edward's physician permitted him to travel with such an illness; or was the nature of his disease really not known before he left England?'[3] The major had given Theodore Günther strict instructions to move Leo to a hotel in just such a crisis. But these were ignored by the doctor, who thought it better to keep the prince away from the public gaze. Irritated by Günther's insubordination, Howard asked to see the Prince Consort to discuss the problem. But he found Albert so worn out by illness and overwork that he could barely concentrate on the issue. A crisis over the detention of a British steamer by a Union warship off New York threatened to plunge the country into America's civil war. A masterful memorandum by the prince averted this calamity, but it used up the last drops of his once formidable energy. In his increasingly paranoid state, Albert confessed that he had even stopped opening his letters 'because they may contain bad news about Leopold'.[4]

While Sir Edward languished in France and the Prince Consort declined at Windsor, preparations began as usual for Christmas, always a highlight of the royal year. On 7 December Howard sent orders for Günther to spend £10 on gifts for Leo, suggesting as ideas books and toy soldiers. He closed his letter by informing the doctor that

the Prince Consort has been suffering lately from severe colds and inflammation and has been confined to his room for more than a week. Perhaps it may be as well that Prince Leopold should know this, for although the Prince Consort's illness is far from being serious still it prevents him from reading and writing, and obliges his Royal Highness to keep very quiet.[5]

Elphinstone's words betrayed no real alarm about the prince, but elsewhere in the castle that same day the Queen admitted in a letter to Vicky that her husband's illness 'was displaying some ominous signs'.[6] Dr Jenner had found a rash of rose-pink spots on the prince's stomach, a classic symptom of 'gastric fever' or typhoid. Nevertheless the doctor, who considered himself an expert in this field, was convinced that the prince would make a full and speedy recovery. Moreover, no attempt was made to prevent either the Queen or Princess Alice from approaching the patient, a normal precaution in such cases. At first Jenner's confidence seemed justified. On 8 December the prince's diarrhoea eased and his racing pulse steadied. During the afternoon, he asked to be moved from his own bedroom into the King's Room nearby. The morbid symbolism of this curious request should have alerted Albert's family to the seriousness of his condition, as this was the very room where both William IV and George IV had died. Noiselessly attended by his German valet Rudolf Löhlein, the prince then lay down on a sofa by the window to gaze up at the clouds as they scudded across the wintry sky. Meanwhile the doctors did little beyond occasionally dosing the prince with brandy and holding huddled conferences in the corner of the room. In the evening, Victoria sat by her husband's bedside to read to him. '*Liebes Frauchen*,' he whispered, over and over again, as he held her small, soft hand and tenderly stroked her tear-stained face.[7]

For several days the prince sank beneath his fever, seldom rallying and apparently resigned to his fate. A press blackout was imposed, the anodyne court circulars which were issued each morning giving little hint of the drama unfolding at the heart of the castle. Even those living close to the prince were unaware just how grave the situation was. On 9 December Howard could still assure Günther in France that the Prince Consort was showing 'no unfavourable symptoms'. He did ask, however, for the doctor to send his daily bulletins on Leo's health to the Queen and not to the Prince Consort, 'as His Royal Highness will not be able to attend to any business for some time'.[8]

Jenner remained steadfastly optimistic that his patient would recover even when Albert's mind began to wander, a dangerous sign. 'In that feeble state', Howard recalled later, presumably having spoken with Löhlein, 'recurred to him the scenes of his early childhood which he wished to see again, to hear the birds twittering about the woods at Coburg and be again in his warm hearted home, away from the cold frigidity of England'.[9] On Thursday 12 December the fever markedly increased, shaking the prince into a delirium. He fretted wildly about Leopold's health, and Vicky's safety in Germany. His breathing grew more rapid and towards midday he began to vomit gobbets of foul-smelling, bloodied mucus into the bowl held by Alice. In a moment of clarity, he asked his daughter whether Vicky knew of his illness.

'Yes,' she said, with tears in her eyes, 'I told her you were very ill.'

'You did wrong,' he murmured, 'you should have told her I was dying.'[10]

Friday 13 December was worse. Unable to speak, the prince simply sat looking blankly out of the window. Jenner still assured the Queen that he had seen worse cases survive; but with less authority now, his face showing confusion and concern. Her mother paralysed by dread, Alice summoned Bertie to the castle while Charles Phipps warned the Prime Minister, Lord Palmerston, to expect the worst. At five the palace issued a terse statement which referred to the 'unfavourable character' of the prince's illness. For most people these were the first real indications of the impending tragedy. Astonishingly, it was only when Albert's equerry Charles Du Plat called on him in his room that evening that Howard himself 'felt any alarm about the Prince Consort'. When, grave-faced, Carl Ruland then grimly confirmed

Du Plat's report, Howard rushed upstairs to the private apartments where he received an 'unsatisfactory' bulletin on the Prince's condition.[11]

Albert grew calmer as the evening wore on. When Charles Grey raised a glass of brandy to his blue-tinged lips, he even wanly smiled, weakly toasting his secretary. But he knew that he was dying. 'Look at my tongue,' he whispered hoarsely to Phipps as he revealed it to be blackened and swollen with the infection.[12] Then the prince shakily arranged his thinning hair and folded his arms across his chest as if preparing for the end. Around midnight, exhausted by worry, the Queen lay down in the next room to rest. 'The country, oh, the country,' she wailed, time and again; 'I could perhaps bear my own misery, but the poor country.'[13]

Before dawn, Bertie rushed in from Cambridge, looking tired and fearful. At six, Victoria was roused with the news that her husband had rallied slightly. In her dressing gown and with her hair still loosely tied, she hurried to Albert's bedside, finding him lying there 'bathed in perspiration', his eyes staring vacantly up at the gilded ceiling.[14] Strangely, during the night Biddulph, Bruce and Grey had moved the prince's bed to the centre of the room, as if they were preparing a stage for the final act. 'Never can I forget how beautiful my darling looked lying there with his face lit up by the rising sun,' Victoria would write.[15] The only 'alarming thing' seemed to be Albert's breathing, although she knew that the 'dusky' pallor of his skin 'was not good'.[16] At nine, the palace blandly reported 'no change' in the prince's perilous condition.

Howard felt 'some presentiment' all day. 'I was afraid all hope was gone,' he wrote afterwards, 'yet I could not believe it possible that so great a calamity would visit the Queen.'[17] He kept Arthur quietly occupied in the schoolroom, away from the hushed voices outside the sick man's chamber. After lunch they went for a walk in the castle grounds to escape the oppressive atmosphere inside. They returned at five to hear that the prince had reached a 'most critical state' and that Arthur had been urgently summoned to the King's Room. Bertie, Alice and Louise were there already, all tearfully clustered around the bed. Each in turn stepped forward to grasp their father's lifeless hand, although only Arthur kissed it.[18] The young prince was deeply shocked by his father's condition, having received no warning of its seriousness. As he was led away, he sobbed that 'the face had so changed since he saw him last'. Howard took Arthur back to his room, still struggling to absorb the unfolding tragedy himself. He then dined quietly with Ruland, each trying to convince the other that all might yet be well. Finally, unable to bear the suspense any longer, 'an unaccountable feeling . . . induced us to go into the corridor upstairs'. It was now eight o'clock on the evening of 14 December 1861.

'I shall never forget the few hours I spent there,' Howard recalled.

> The old corridor with its historical pictures, busts of great men
> and bijouterie, usually the scene of many a gay chat of Household
> members before going, or after having been to dinner, presented
> now a very dim aspect. A few gloomy faces, fearing the worse
> were patiently sitting and anxiously watching each doctor's face as
> they came from the prince's room. But each report was different;
> hope and despair were alternately dealt out, that no one could
> form an idea of the truth.

At about half past ten, an ashen-looking Dean of Windsor, his robes trailing behind him, swept down the corridor and into the darkened room where Albert lay dying. Then the doctors were urgently called for, and the quiet was broken by the sudden opening of doors and the noise of crying and running feet. 'We knew now it was past hope,' the major wrote, 'and heard shortly after that it was all over.'

One by one the household were called in: 'first Phipps, then Bruce, then Lord Alfred [Paget, a favourite gentleman in waiting to the Queen]; Ruland; Seymour; the Dean; Grey; Du Plat; Biddulph; lastly I'.[19] Howard was taken aback by the sight which confronted him, suggesting confusion in his mind until the very end. He had expected to see the prince's body; instead he found himself in the small ante-room where the family's presents were displayed at Christmas. The Queen was lying prostrate on a sofa, Alice beside her on the floor tenderly cradling her mother's head. Behind them stood the Prince of Wales, looking 'deeply affected but quiet', and fifteen-year-old Princess Helena, who was sobbing 'violently'. Shocked at the intimacy of this scene, Howard hesitated and 'almost retreated' before 'the voice of the Queen and her outstretched hand called me to my senses'. 'Unable to speak', he stepped forward, kneeling before Victoria. She clutched at his hand and 'with a violent effort' cried: 'You will not desert me? You will all help me?'

Howard answered 'from the very depths of my heart'. He promised Victoria his devotion and loyalty, expressing his grief at the tragedy which had struck her family. When he stood up, Bertie grasped his hand and looked him steadily in the eye; Howard not 'forgetting to return the gentle but meaning pressure' in the gesture. He then stepped into the next room, where Albert's body lay covered by a sheet. Howard had seen death many times in the Crimea, but rarely in so tranquil a form. The prince's face looked 'calm, peaceful . . . Beautiful noble head it appeared'. In the shadows Löhlein was quietly preparing to lay out his master's body and, although the Queen had expressly forbade it, an artist had already been summoned to make a death mask. 'He had gone without a struggle,' Howard remarked, 'but likewise without saying a word.' England's German prince had slipped from the world as silently as he had often occupied it, aged just forty-two. Looking back, Howard was struck by the prince's dark fatalism, that peculiarly German trait born of the forests of northern Europe – and a trait not entirely absent from himself. 'The Prince always had a fixed idea that he would die of the first fever he got,' he mused. 'It proved true; although I dare say that this presentiment might have accelerated it, as he never even tried to rally from the moment the illness commenced.'[20]

As the various members of the household filed silently back

to their rooms, Victoria was given opiates and helped to bed. 'Her sobs and cries as she went along the passage were terrible,' Charles Grey wrote at the end of that dreadful long night.[21] In a letter to his parents Carl Ruland described the Prince Consort's death as 'a disaster for the entire family, for England, for the whole of Europe. What he was as a person no-one can judge better than myself. Did he not treat me as his own son?'[22] The librarian could not hide his concern that, with the loss of his employer, he faced a very uncertain future.

When Howard finally reached his room, he found two messages waiting for him. One was a telegram from France, bluntly informing him that Sir Edward Bowater had died earlier in the day, just hours before the Prince Consort. The other was a short, laboriously written note from the children's apartments. 'Dear Major,' he read, 'please come and say goodnight to me. Arthur.'[23]

14

'Her grief and anguish are indeed INDESCRIBABLE'

WINDSOR, 1862

THE OTHER CHILDREN heard in the morning. 'Oh, why did not God take me?' sobbed thirteen-year-old Louise, 'I am so stupid and useless.'[1] 'Why has earth not swallowed me up?' cried Vicky in Berlin, when she read the telegram.[2] Writing from the Château Leader, Leopold told Howard that he was 'very, very grieved to hear of the death of poor dear papa, who I loved so very much'.[3] 'Poor child,' Elphinstone confided to Theodore Günther, who had broken the news of his father's death to the bewildered prince,

> little can he conceive the awful loss he has sustained in the sudden
> death of his natural protector, who, we all hoped would have
> guided his youthful aspirations, and instilled into him that high
> tone of morality, activity and unselfishness which were the pecu-
> liar characteristics of the Prince himself. His death has taken every
> one aback, so little was it expected a week ago, and we can hardly
> realise it to ourselves.[4]

The major sent Leo books and toys and ordered Günther to send him the prince's medical reports to spare the Queen more anxiety.

Two days after Albert died, Elphinstone reported to Lady

126

Bowater, who was herself grieving the loss of a husband, that 'the Queen is bearing her awful calamity most beautifully, most nobly, devoting herself to her children and her duty, with a high minded-ness to call forth our deepest admiration. May she have strength to keep it up.'[5] In truth, Victoria was paralysed by shock. She retreated behind the locked doors of her room, leaving her dazed court in a state of utter disarray. Years later, Howard could still vividly remember how the Prince Consort's untimely death 'threw us all into consternation'.[6] A 'dark, overwhelming cloud' settled over the castle, suffocating the people trapped inside.[7] The business of state ground to a halt; letters went unanswered, docu-ments unsigned, speeches unread. Only now that the prince had gone was it apparent how hard he had worked and how much he had achieved in his wife's name. As the days passed, many in the household even began to worry about the Queen's sanity, so crushing seemed her grief. Others, such as Albert's former equer-ries and his devoted German staff, feared for their jobs. General Grey wondered whether the court would ever fully recover from the blow. 'Who is there now,' he asked Charles Phipps, 'when dif-ficulties and jealousies arise, as it is too much to hope they will not. Whose moderating influence will be sufficient to restore har-mony, as in the most difficult circumstances, *he* never failed to do.'[8] Phipps agreed. 'There is no head to judge,' he observed sagely, 'no authority to decide.'[9]

On 18 December, the Queen emerged to select a site at Frogmore, close to her mother's recently completed tomb, 'for a Mausoleum for us' – that is, for her husband and herself.[10] She then summoned her children and departed for Osborne House, trailing the disconsolate household behind her. Five days later, Howard and Arthur briefly returned to Windsor to attend the Prince Consort's funeral. They carried with them from Osborne wreaths tied by Alice, Helena and Louise, and a bouquet of violets selected by Victoria. Through the tightly drawn blinds of the railway car-riage which conveyed them from Southampton to Windsor they glimpsed the crowds lining the station platforms in silent tribute to the dead prince. Only in death, it seemed, had Albert finally earned the affection he had always craved from his wife's subjects.

By eleven on the morning of the funeral, Arthur and his governor had joined the other family mourners, all of them male, in the Oak Room at the castle. They then followed the hearse down to St George's Chapel and, for the second time that year, took their places behind a coffin as it was borne up the aisle. The court correspondent of *The Times* reported that Arthur's face appeared 'red and swollen' from days of crying. Bertie tried to console his younger brother, but when the choir began a dirge Arthur broke down completely, 'as if his very heart was breaking'.[11] A lady in the congregation saw Arthur bravely try to stifle 'his sobs by biting his pocket handkerchief'.[12] But his grief overwhelmed him. Eventually Howard took the prince out of the chapel altogether, heading back to the Isle of Wight before the other mourners had even noticed they were gone.

Christmas was miserable. Instead of the usual extravagant presents, the household received black-bordered photographs of the Prince Consort, while the royal children were given locks of their dead father's hair. Lady Augusta Stanley memorably compared the feeling at court during these first weeks of loss to that of Pompeii after the eruption, with 'the life suddenly extinguished'. 'You are all so thin,' remarked one shocked visitor at a household lunch in January 1862, 'there are such lines of care on every face.'[13] When Vicky, devastated by her father's death, arrived from Germany she described seeing her family wandering around 'like sheep without a shepherd'.[14] Victoria was slowly pulling her family, her household and, if she could, her whole country into her pit of despair. In March she told Elphinstone that 'her *grief* and *anguish* are *indeed* INDESCRIBABLE and can only *end* with THIS *life*'.[15]

The Queen was unobserved in her grief, but she was not unobservant. Her fragile emotional state made her fearful of further calamity or disturbance. On one occasion she castigated Howard for allowing Arthur to go outside with Prince Ludwig of

Hesse and by Rhine without a chaperone. 'Does Major Elphinstone think that Prince Louis will prevent any teazing [sic]?' she snapped.[16] She then vetoed his idea of giving Arthur a bow and arrows to cheer him up, citing Albert's objection to them on safety grounds. Instead, the prince would receive yet another photograph of his dead father for his crowded mantelpiece.

With Victoria clinging morbidly to her husband's image, everything was seen through the prism of his memory. Objects which Albert had once owned or touched, even the people he had employed, became sacred relics. A decree was issued that the King's Room at Windsor should remain exactly as it had been at the time of his death – not in the German tradition, as an ossified *Sterbezimmer* or death room, to gather dust behind a locked door, but as a living memorial to the dead prince. For the next forty years, the bedsheets would be changed daily while maids would bring in hot water for shaving and lay out clothes which would never be worn. Many members of the household were astonished at such obsessive rituals. Visiting the room one day with the Queen, Charles Grey watched in bemusement as she 'stooped down and kissed the pillow!' 'Don't talk of this,' Grey ordered his wife, '[but] his hats and gloves [are] out as usual, and the pocket handkerchief he last used lying as he left it on the sofa!'[17]

The bereaved Queen saw her children differently now: no longer as individuals, but as '*his* flesh and blood'; literally the living embodiment of their father. Victoria told Howard that she wanted 'her boys, especially the younger ones, to become very intimate with her'.[18] When the Queen eventually returned to Windsor, leaving Arthur and Elphinstone behind at Osborne, she complained that 'the *silence below* added to the *awful silence* nearby, is very painful'.[19] Given his mother's vulnerability, sending Arthur away to his own household after Christmas as planned was out of the question, so the move to White Lodge was delayed for several months.

If Albert's death marked a profound shift in the way the royal children were treated by their mother, it also radically redefined the roles of those people charged with their care. In particular, the Queen now saw Howard Elphinstone – the man in her inner circle whose manners, background, education and interests most closely resembled those of her dead husband – as a surrogate father to her children and confidant to her. The entrance of this personal dependence into his responsibilities made it highly unlikely that Howard would be returning soon to his stalled career in the army. In fact, he had little option but to stay at court. In an open letter to Arthur, Victoria asked her son to inform his governor 'how much I felt ALL he said about . . . adored Papa, and HOW much I FELT all his kind sympathy in my *terrible* grief! With so kind a friend as dear Major who watches over you so tenderly and who will constantly remind you of *your* terrible loss, I feel you are *as safe* as *our* fond hearts could wish.'[20] For Howard, the death of the Prince Consort had meant losing a mentor, ally and friend. But the catastrophe also changed the direction of his life. In the aftermath of Albert's death he showed Victoria that depth of sympathy which she felt she lacked from others in her household. In tribute, she later accorded him her highest compliment, writing that '*Few men feel* as Major Elphinstone and not many women even.'[21]

After the trauma of the Prince Consort's funeral, the major was understandably anxious to keep Arthur away from Windsor for as long as possible. Helena, who had accompanied her mother back to the castle, told her brother miserably that on seeing their father's room again she had felt 'as if my *heart* must break'.[22] But the dreaded return could not be delayed for ever. On 14 March, the first anniversary of the death of the Duchess of Kent, Arthur and Elphinstone were summoned from Osborne House to attend the stone-laying ceremony for a second mausoleum at Frogmore. Designed in romanesque style with an interior inspired by Raphael, this new tomb would house the body of the Prince Consort and eventually also that of the Queen herself. Such an exotic creation fared badly at the conservative-minded court. Seeing the completed building, one young maid of honour, Lucy Lyttelton, would sum up the feelings of many when she exclaimed that it 'does so jar upon one's English feelings'.[23] But Howard understood its significance to the Queen. He assured her that 'no excuse would be of sufficient importance' to justify Arthur's absence from the stone-laying ceremony.[24] In due course, the mausoleum became the focal point for the Queen's mourning, with a service held there on 14 December each year to commemorate the dead prince. The royal calendar, which was already shaped around numerous family anniversaries and birthdays, was becoming studded with dates framed in black.

On 3 April Howard and Arthur travelled to Dover for Leo's mournful homecoming. Before they left, the Queen instructed the major 'to take care and make poor little Leopold understand that his return will be a very sad one, that he comes back to a house of mourning and that his poor broken hearted mother cannot bear noise and excitement'.[25] Leopold had been seriously ill when he sailed for France, so the little boy who met Howard and Arthur on the quayside at Dover was almost unrecognizable. 'He has grown,' Howard reported, 'not only in height but much stouter. His shoulders and chest are much broader. His face, neck and hands are quite bronzed, and he has altogether a much more healthy and a far stronger appearance than formerly. In comparing him to Prince Arthur, one would at first sight say that he was the stronger of the two.'[26] During the crossing to the Isle of Wight, where he would be reunited with his mother, Leo listened quietly as Elphinstone told him about his father's death, and how life had irrevocably changed at home. The dramatic contrast at court was particularly marked to the grown-ups who had accompanied the prince to France the year before. Attending church with the household at Osborne House, Louisa Bowater was struck by 'the deep mourning, the seats draped with black, the vacant chair and name omitted in the prayers'.[27]

Despite appearances, Leopold's health was still extremely fragile. Hopes that his sojourn in France might have eased, even cured, his distressing condition were quickly dashed when a minor bump with Arthur during a game of croquet put the prince's arm

in a sling for weeks. Resuming responsibility for both the boys –
one of them boisterous, the other an invalid – placed a great strain
on Howard. He complained that Arthur's behaviour, which had
improved over the winter, worsened when he was with his
younger brother. He believed Leo's painful disability 'woefully
fed' Arthur's 'own importance and his vanity . . . He cannot help
feeling how dependent his brother is, and how much more he can
do himself both bodily and mentally, he consequently takes every
opportunity of putting him down.'[28] Moreover, Leo was now old
enough to suffer in comparison with his brothers and sisters.
Already a highly sensitive child, he was becoming withdrawn and
moody. Howard warned the Queen that if the princes lived
together – the Prince Consort's original intention – Arthur 'will
get very overbearing as he takes every opportunity to give *com-
mands* to his brother, and if not carried out, he either has recourse
to anger or else, worse still, to scheming'.[29]

But the major was equally reluctant to accept any more help
from Theodore Günther, Leo's medical attendant in France, whose
official position back in England was unclear. Citing unspecified
rumours of Günther's conduct in France, Howard tried to have
the German dismissed, telling the Queen that he did not think
'Doctor Günther will do to remain permanently with Leopold'.[30]
Victoria, who was sceptical of such reports, believing them 'at
best . . . an exaggeration',[31] referred the major to Lady Bowater,
who had observed the doctor and her son in France. Wary of the
damage such gossip might cause in the close-knit world of the
court, she also ordered Howard 'not to speak to any of the gentlemen about what he mentioned to her, except to Mr Ruland'.[32]

The surprising mention of the librarian's name revealed the
extent to which Victoria had turned to her husband's German staff
in the aftermath of his death. Albert's four English equerries had
simply been absorbed into the Queen's household, while his secretary Charles Grey had been confirmed in post, responsible now
to Victoria – her first official private secretary. But Carl Ruland
had been re-engaged as Victoria's German secretary, an additional

position which seemed to challenge that of General Grey. Ruland was delighted with his promotion, telling his parents that his new post was an 'extremely confidential role'. 'I hope you are not disappointed that I have fulfilled the Queen's wish,' he continued, 'and will not leave her. Had I gone, what would I have done? Teach? That no longer takes my fancy after the responsibilities I have had here. Here, on the other hand, my life and work have a meaning if, as they all say here, I can be of help to the entire family.'[33]

Rudolf Löhlein, the Prince Consort's faithful German valet, was made principal personal servant, another new and controversial post. Like Ruland, Löhlein now had close access to the Queen, an intimacy which unsettled the household. 'I have all your feelings about Löhlein and Ruland,' Charles Grey confided to Charles Phipps barely five months after Albert had died,

> and see as little as you do what is to be done. These are in fact the men who have the Queen's confidence on all subjects, and who see her at all times, and who carry her orders. I confess I was somewhat shocked at receiving through Löhlein, a verbal message as to the purport of a letter I was to write to the Prime Minister, on the subject of a difference with another of her ministers.

Procedural niceties aside, Grey was clearly affronted that the Queen felt more at ease discussing sensitive matters of state with a servant like Löhlein ('and Ruland I suppose she looks on as little better') than with him. 'The time will come', Grey gravely warned, 'when we must make a stand against receiving orders through these improper channels.'[34] Irritation among the courtiers at Victoria's familiarity with her servants, compared to the stiffness she often displayed towards them, would surface time and again in the latter stages of her reign. A typical reaction was that of the aristocratic Mary Bulteel, who complained that the Queen 'vulgarised' her 'standards of taste' by keeping such low company.[35]

Unlike Grey, Howard spoke the language used by the Queen and her German servants, giving his opinions added authority. Yet he too quickly discovered the hazards of navigating the hidden channels of Victoria's complex relationships with those servants. After seeking Ruland's confidential opinion on Theodore Günther, as he had been ordered, the major was furious to discover that the librarian had gone behind his back to the Queen and offered to replace him as Leo's governor. When Howard complained to Victoria about Ruland's action, he was told that he should '*not* take the slightest notice of what has passed. Mr Ruland's only anxiety is to be of use, as he ever has been and is, and he never dreams of interfering with Major Elphinstone's authority'. As to the problems he was still experiencing with Günther, Victoria declared that the German doctor was to '*act* WITH Major Elphinstone in educating Prince Leopold'. Günther had been employed by the Prince Consort and 'whatever he ordered and wished is the Queen's *law*'.[36] This was a refrain which would become all too familiar over the coming years.

In the spring Leopold followed his mother to Scotland, leaving Arthur and the major to explore the south coast of England in the royal steam yacht *Vivid*. On 8 May they moored off Sidmouth, but the large crowds that gathered on the beach denied Howard the chance of landing and visiting his parents at Livonia Cottage. The Queen was struck by the symbolism of the visit, however, reminding Arthur that 'my father died at Sidmouth when I was only 8 months old!'[37] The letters which Victoria now wrote to Howard from her Highland retreat were quite different in tone from those that had gone before. It was as if the tranquil surroundings of her Scottish home, the scene of so many happy and shared memories, made Victoria value his friendship more highly. 'The heart is *completely* broken,' she wrote to Howard on 18 May 1862, 'and the sense of desolation and longing *increases* as time goes on. It is *impossible* to bear such a complete shipwreck of *all* that was dearest and nearest and the destruction of *what was* necessary to the well being and very existence of the Queen's difficult and lonely position!'[38]

Although the Queen steadfastly refused to acknowledge it, one pressing family event was looming up fast through the fog of sorrow: the marriage of Princess Alice to Prince Ludwig of Hesse and by Rhine. In a break from tradition, the Queen insisted that the wedding take place quietly in the dining room at Osborne House rather than in the splendour of St George's Chapel as had been planned. Her only concession to the happiness of the occasion was to allow her ladies, though not herself, a few hours' respite from their mourning dresses. Nevertheless, the bride still wore a black undergarment beneath her white wedding gown, while her mother passed the entire ceremony gazing mournfully at a large, strategically placed portrait of Albert. Afterwards, with an unmistakable hint of satisfaction, the Queen described the proceedings to Vicky as 'more like a funeral than a wedding'.[39] The recent death of Bertie's governor General Bruce, from a fever he had caught touring Palestine with the prince, merely added to the overwhelming gloom of the occasion. Their ordeal over, Alice and Louis gratefully escaped to his modest palace in Darmstadt.

One consequence of Alice's marriage and Bruce's death was the momentum it gave Victoria in her search for a bride for Bertie, now dangerously adrift after the loss of his father and governor in quick succession. Before he died, Albert had picked out Princess Alexandra, the daughter of the Crown Prince of Denmark, as a suitable wife for his son and thus consort to the next King of England. Vicky, who was well placed on the continent to assess the princess, had enthusiastically reported that Alix was 'one of the most ladylike and aristocratic people I ever saw [with] very fine white regular teeth and very fine large eyes'.[40] Whatever Bertie, who had met Alix briefly in 1861, thought of the plan to get him married off, he wisely kept it to himself. His stock was currently so low with his mother – who irrationally blamed the Nellie Clifden incident for fatally distressing her husband – that he was powerless to resist her will. He may have confided his feelings on the matter to Howard when they met for a surreptitious smoke in the gun room at Balmoral in August. Their meeting, and others that summer in Scotland, suggests that Bertie turned to Howard for advice in the months after his father died, preferring the major's company to that of the elderly courtiers charged by his mother to look after him after the death of General Bruce.

Although Victoria never questioned her late husband's choice of a wife for Bertie, she was understandably anxious to see the Danish princess for herself before giving her formal approval to the match. In September 1862 a meeting was engineered between the two women in the garden at Laeken, the country retreat of the Queen's maternal uncle King Leopold of the Belgians. The introduction fitted conveniently into an emotionally charged pilgrimage which Victoria had arranged to the Rosenau, the Prince Consort's birthplace outside Coburg. The eighteen-year-old Danish Princess passed her daunting test with flying colours, the Queen extolling her 'beautiful refined profile and quiet lady-like manner'.[41] Afterwards Prince Arthur and Howard appeared in the garden on a pre-arranged errand to present the princess with a bouquet of flowers, which they had purchased earlier that morning in Brussels. While the royal party continued on to Germany, a nervous Bertie was left to complete the task begun by his father.

News of the engagement reached the Queen and her entourage at Reinhardtsbrunn, a ducal hunting lodge near Gotha, where they had paused on their way to the Rosenau. Howard was among the first to congratulate her – not only on 'the choice of the future Princess of Wales, but likewise on the very satisfactory manner in which the Prince himself has passed through the ordeal, and how pleased he seems with *his* choice. May she have that influence on his future character which Your Majesty so anxiously wishes for!'[42] Writing from Brussels, an overjoyed and clearly relieved Bertie admitted to Elphinstone that 'I don't think I have ever had real happiness till now.'[43] His engagement, which would be followed by his coming of age on 9 November, had awoken the much-maligned prince to the gravity of his destiny as the future King of England. 'As you so rightly say,' he confided to Howard,

'one now becomes "the man"; and I know now that all the responsibility of my actions, come upon me. But I am glad that it is so, as
I am sure that you will agree that it [is] far pleasanter to bear the
responsibility oneself, instead of having other people to bear it for
you.'[44]

The family's excitement at Bertie's news was soon eclipsed
by renewed concern for Prince Leopold, who had accidentally
pierced the top of his mouth with a pen while at the
Reinhardtsbrunn. The wound was insignificant – Howard
described it as no more than a 'slight scratch' – but the prince hid
it for a time and soon the bleeding could not be stopped.[45] For several days the prince again lingered painfully between life and
death. Rudolf Löhlein kept vigil by Leo's bedside, as he had for the
boy's father in December, while the best surgeons were urgently
summoned from Berlin. Sensibly, the major took Arthur away
from this distressing scene, embarking with him on a hiking tour
of the surrounding mountains. This was an activity Howard always
enjoyed, in an environment he loved as it evoked memories of his
own childhood on the continent. He filled his journal with
remarks on the many places of antiquarian interest they passed,
while his sketchbooks soon overflowed with images of the dramatic landscape.

To those used to the comforts of a royal lifestyle, the accommodation the major and the young prince encountered during
their expedition was distinctly rudimentary: often no more than a
damp palliasse in a remote inn after an unappetizing meal. Such
matters scarcely bothered a man who had survived the trenches of
the Crimea, yet the major was impressed by Arthur's resilience.
Writing to the Queen, he declared that the trip had helped her son
to conquer 'that daintiness in food which Your Majesty is aware he
has got to an extraordinary degree and which unless conquered
soon will cause him much misery in after life during his soldier's
career'.[46]

On 8 October the Queen arranged for Howard to meet
Baron Christian Stockmar, the Prince Consort's former mentor, in

Coburg. Despite his advanced age and failing health, the baron still commanded considerable respect among the English court, being widely credited with having steered the monarchy through the turbulent constitutional waters which had rocked its counterparts on the continent. Mary Bulteel described him, with perhaps equal amounts of acerbity and admiration, as the 'clever wire-puller behind the scenes'.[47] As Stockmar was also the principal architect of the royal children's education, the Queen was anxious that the major 'should have some opportunity of talking to him (without the Princes) of Prince Arthur, his education and his future, and hearing his opinion, which is always most wise'.[48] Howard was impressed by the wizened old man. 'What a mixture of perfect goodness, wisdom, and consummate knowledge of the world!!' he exclaimed in his journal; 'should like to see much of him.'[49]

Homage having been paid to Stockmar, the royal journey reached its climax with a highly charged visit to the Rosenau, the mock-medieval retreat of the dukes of Saxe-Coburg-Gotha and the hallowed birthplace of the Prince Consort. This was a place, Victoria gushed to Howard, 'where the very air seems to breathe of her precious one'.[50] Buildings, like people, now stood in tribute to her lost Prince.

15

'The only Prince in our poor house!'

GREENWICH, 1862

'IN 1862 I LEFT HOME and took up my residence at Ranger's House, Greenwich Park,' Prince Arthur recalled in 1926 when he was seventy-six. 'The only person living with me was Major Elphinstone. My tutor lived out, and came daily to give me lessons. My life was then a very lonely one and I had to work very hard.'[1]

Wrenching Arthur from his mother's side was very painful. But the matter had been discussed, and settled, with the Prince Consort before he died, so the Queen was resolute. Bertie told Howard that he thought it would do his brother 'a deal of good being away from home', joking that otherwise he might become 'very lazy . . . like his eldest brother'.[2] Arthur's mother saw things differently. She feared that her favourite son would 'become a *stranger* to that sad, fatherless home', and as distant towards her as Bertie and Affie had become. 'She is so anxious', she told Elphinstone, 'that Prince Arthur should be very confidential and open with her, and never fear to say or ask anything. She says all this openly to Major Elphinstone as she is *so* anxious that our child's *confidence* should be *made* to *her* and to *himself*.'[3] Howard suspected that the breach between Victoria and the older boys had been caused not by any lack of intimacy, but by their associating home with work and travel with enjoyment. He proposed therefore to keep Arthur's new residence '*solely* for work' to engender in the prince a longing for his mother and home: another theory lifted directly from Dr Schreber's handbook on child education.[4] The prince's unhappy recollection of this period in his life suggests that Elphinstone's strategy was successful, although at great cost to his own relationship with the boy.

Another reason for introducing a stricter regime was the major's impatience with Arthur's behaviour. This had deteriorated to such an extent that Howard had again resorted to punitive measures. There was never a suggestion that the bereaved young prince might have needed sympathy rather than scolding, or love rather than a beating. But Howard had never sought Arthur's affection, believing it was not his to seek. On the contrary, the major considered it his duty to emphasize through his own severity the compassion of the Queen. He promised Victoria that 'whatever punishment the Prince received, . . . he was the one who ordered it; whereas every reward, however trifling, has invariably been represented as coming direct from Your Majesty'.[5] The Queen accepted this approach, which had been formulated years before by Baron Stockmar and the Prince Consort; yet she still recoiled from seeing her son punished so harshly. During her husband's lifetime she had felt powerless to intervene, merely hinting at her opposition to it in her conversations with Howard. Now, however, she was in sole charge. So, after watching the major humiliate the prince once too often by ordering for his food to be cut up like an infant's, she demanded that in future, 'when Major Elphinstone has reason to punish Prince Arthur he would let her know'.[6] But she was careful not to antagonize the governor, assuring him that her son 'seems *as fond of* and *attached* to *Major Elphinstone as ever*', despite their frequent clashes.[7]

During the Prince Consort's lifetime it had been decided to send Arthur to the White Lodge in Richmond Park. In the summer of 1862, however, another, more suitable, grace-and-favour house unexpectedly fell vacant, following the death of its intended occupant Earl Canning, a former Viceroy of India. The Ranger's House was a handsome red-brick villa standing in a prominent position on the edge of Blackheath, above Greenwich Park and the City of London. Built in the late seventeenth century, the house had enjoyed a series of colourful owners, notably the dilettante fourth Earl of Chesterfield. Over the years the property had been enlarged and improved with the addition of bow-fronted wings and a large gallery to display Chesterfield's art collection. In 1807 the house had become Crown property and home to the Ranger of Greenwich Park, a royal sinecure recently held by the former Prime Minister, the Earl of Aberdeen. Besides its availability, the principal advantage of the Ranger's House over the White Lodge was its close proximity to the Royal Military Academy at Woolwich, where Prince Arthur would one day receive his military training, as his governor had before him. Howard pronounced the house 'very comfortable and very nicely fitted up'.[8] It would be his home for the next nine years.

Arthur, Elphinstone and sixteen servants duly moved into Ranger's House on 1 November 1862. While Arthur busily set about hanging his many pictures and prints, the major toured the house placing thermometers on every mantelpiece. This was a habit of the Queen, who insisted that the temperature inside all her residences be kept below 60 degrees Fahrenheit regardless of the weather outside. This anti-social idiosyncrasy, which left her staff shivering in their bedrooms, was the product of Victoria's faddish belief in the health benefits of the cold – encouraged by her influential first personal physician James Clark.

Arthur was given the principal, panelled bedroom on the first floor of Ranger's House overlooking the park. Elphinstone would sleep next door. The elegant gallery where Lord Chesterfield had once hung his Old Master paintings was converted into a gymnasium, its parquet being covered in mattresses so that 'the Prince should not jump on the hard floor'.[9] Arthur was also allocated a study and a playroom, although the major hoped that on fine days the house's extensive gardens would 'afford ample space for games, as well as for exercise on such days when the neighbourhood is crowded or otherwise objectionable'.[10] With the major's help, the prince set about creating a fort in the grounds, to rival the one they had created at Osborne. When summer arrived, a croquet lawn and a cricket pitch were laid out in the grounds, and fences built for Arthur to jump on his pony.

The day after he left home, Arthur received a long letter from his sister Louise, lamenting the loss of her playmate. 'I hope you like Blackheath,' she wrote, 'and do not feel very lonely, but you know one can not always have every thing one likes, and you are now such a big boy that you must learn a little.'[11] In fact, Arthur showed little sign of homesickness. Elphinstone reported that the prince seemed 'very happy . . . he does not as yet appear to be lonely, or even to miss the companionship of his brother, everything has still too great an interest for that'.[12] His favourite pastime was playing with his new puppy Max, a leaving present from his mother.

The prince's lessons with William Jolley, who was given lodgings nearby, resumed at once in the newly fitted-out school-room. Lessons in drill and fencing had been added to the daily timetable, together with drawing classes under the tuition of two artists from the Royal Academy. Howard took a particularly close interest in their work, regretting that they were both 'landscape painters unfortunately and do not profess "figure drawing"'.[13] An accomplished artist himself, the governor helped Arthur with his drawing and painting, organizing a series of visits to the studios of a number of highly regarded watercolourists in London, among them the artist and poet Edward Lear.

Life at Ranger's House was arduous. Sixty years later, Arthur could still recall the drudgery of his daily routine. 'I was called by my servant at 6.45 a.m and my studies began about 7.15 a.m.,' he told his biographer.

I worked till about 9 a.m. when I breakfasted, work being resumed at 10 a.m. until 1 p.m. Then I had a short walk and lunched at 2 p.m. In the afternoon I walked and twice a week boys came from various schools to play with me. We played

football, hockey etc. Lessons were again resumed at 5 p.m. until
7.30 p.m. Supper at 8 p.m. and afterwards I prepared lessons
until about 10 p.m. for the following day.[14]

Sunday, the prince remembered, 'was very strictly kept. I attended
church in the morning where there was a very lengthy and dull
service lasting for 2½ hours, and I was expected on my return to
write a description of the sermon.'[15] Furthermore, Elphinstone
had insisted that they travel some distance for the service as
their local parish church of St Alfreges, a Hawksmoor-designed
masterpiece, was 'in the middle of the dirty town of Greenwich'.[16]
Ranger's House was scarcely improved by London's 'yellow fog',
which frequently crept into its rooms, choking its inhabitants and
sometimes forcing the servants to light all the candles before
lunchtime.[17]

The prince's move prompted another review of his governor's tenure. In late November 1862 Charles Phipps gently
reminded the Queen that the arrangements put in place before the
death of the Prince Consort regarding 'that excellent young man
Major Elphinstone' would soon expire.[18] It was unthinkable that
Howard would leave his post in the current circumstances, yet
Victoria took nothing for granted. She begged him to stay for at
least another four years. 'More than ever, now, in the Queen's desolate and helpless position,' she implored, 'does she require the
assistance of such a kind and devoted friend as Major
Elphinstone.'[19] Her plea was impossible to resist, although the
major must have looked a little enviously at his fellow engineers as
they forged ahead in their own careers – especially Charles
Gordon, who had won many plaudits campaigning in China. But
in agreeing to stay, Elphinstone signalled a shift in his own view of
a role which since the death of Prince Albert had assumed a far
greater significance. Replying to the Queen, he alluded to 'the
deep gloom that this last year has cast upon all and upon everything',
and insisted that 'he thoroughly feels that what might formerly
have been supposed to be perhaps even optional, has now become

changed into absolute *duty* and he therefore unhesitantly reiterates, that so long as his humble services are of *any possible* use, they are *entirely* at Your Majesty's command'.[20]

The Prince Consort's intention had always been that Leopold and Arthur would live together under Elphinstone's care. But the major was now as anxious to separate the two boys for their own good as the Queen was to keep Leo at home, so this plan was quietly dropped. Shaken by the emergency at Reinhardtsbrunn, when it had seemed again that Leo might die, Victoria had finally accepted that her youngest son would never enjoy a normal life in the public eye. Instead, he would stay with her as 'the only Prince in our poor house!' She would shelter Leo from the physical and moral dangers which assailed his elder brothers. Rather melodramatically, she told Vicky that 'the illness of a good child is so far less trying than the sinfulness of one's sons . . . one feels that death in purity is so far preferable to life in sin and depredation'.[21] The irritation she had felt at her son's physical weakness was displaced by her new sense of bearing a sacred burden, transforming Leo, once the 'ugliest and least pleasing of the whole family', into 'our cleverest and best boy'.[22] Some purpose had been restored to Victoria's shattered life. 'SHE will not give up *Prince Leopold* as long as he learns (and that he *always* will do) he is *best* at home and he *never* can enter an active profession,' she declared. 'The Queen could not part with more children and it is a great sacrifice to part with Prince Arthur. But this the beloved Prince had decided on, it answers very well. Prince Leopold, she knows, HE contemplated (if his *health* permitted) keeping *at home.*'[23]

Now that Elphinstone was living at Ranger's House with Arthur, the day-to-day responsibility for Leo's care passed to Adolf Buff, a young academic who had been originally employed to teach German to the princes.[24] 'His knowledge is great,' the Queen reported, 'but he is very shy.'[25] Buff was close in temperament to Ernst Becker and Carl Ruland, and he suffered accordingly at the hands of the overbearing English courtiers. Louisa Bowater thought him 'ill-used . . . his extreme shyness makes him unpopular here, and they take so little notice of him, I think it makes him worse'.[26] Although Howard had feared leaving Leo in the hands of 'a complete stranger', Buff's quiet nature and scholarly interests clearly suited the invalid prince.[27]

Despite Buff's appointment, the influence of the Queen's German staff sharply declined after the death of Baron Stockmar in July 1863. 'His loss will be greatly lamented by all who knew him, but especially must it be so by Your Majesty,' Howard wrote in sympathy.

> So wise and disinterested a councillor and one so thoroughly frank and upright will not be easily found, and the greater part of his life was so intimately associated with that of the dear Prince, that his loss cannot but affect Your Majesty far more deeply than could any other loss but that of a close relation or of a dear friend . . . There is consolation, however, in Your Majesty's most true remark that the loss is but for a while; until the reunion with those whom you most truly love.[28]

Within weeks of Stockmar's death, Ernst Becker left court to join Princess Alice's staff in Darmstadt, officially as her secretary but possibly also to keep a wary eye on the Hessian court for the Queen back at Windsor. Becker was followed out of the palace by Dr Theodore Günther who, undermined by the persistent rumours regarding his competence, resigned his position as Leopold's medical attendant and made an improbable career move to take up the post of Keeper of Zoology at the British Museum. The most startling departure came in October 1863, when Carl Ruland, who had enjoyed the Queen's closest confidence since Albert's death, abruptly left the court and returned to Germany – supposedly to care for his ageing parents in Frankfurt. It has been suggested that he was becoming over-familiar with the Queen's seventeen-year-old daughter Helena – a hazard which threatened the careers of many young men in the claustrophobic world of a court populated by teenage princesses.[29] However, a more likely explanation for Ruland's resignation is contained in a letter from Charles Grey to Charles Phipps, written in June, which suggests that the two courtiers had engineered his dismissal. In his letter the secretary praised the Keeper of the Privy Purse for pointedly alluding 'to the number of people that the Queen treated confidentially' in a recent note to Ruland. As Phipps and Grey had anticipated, Ruland, clearly affronted by the accusation of favouritism, showed Phipps's letter to the Queen, unintentionally opening an awkward debate on the exact nature of his position. Ruland's heated reaction to Phipps's casual remark sowed a seed of doubt in Victoria's mind as to the librarian's integrity. Grey was quick to exploit this misgiving when Augusta Stanley was sent by the Queen to seek his opinion on the matter. 'I supported your opinion most strenuously,' Grey assured Phipps, 'and implored her to stress upon the Queen the imprudence, not to use a stronger term, of ever continuing in her employment, any one who in the most trifling degree has been found guilty of deception or dishonesty . . . you know how unwillingly the Queen ever parts with a person to whom she is accustomed.'

With Ruland, Becker and Günther gone and Stockmar dead, there remained only Rudolf Löhlein to deal with before Grey and Phipps could assume full control over the Queen. Grey had freely admitted that Löhlein's access to Victoria 'often frightens me'.

> He *may* be perfectly to be depended upon, but we know how
> often old servants, supposed to have been paragons of honesty and
> fidelity, have been proved to be rogues at Court. But all this is a
> long subject which it is better to talk over and in fact I know little
> of it all for my duties, *fortunately*, seldom bring me in contact with
> domestic quarters.[30]

In fact, Löhlein would survive several attempts to unseat him before Grey was distracted by a quite unexpected and far more formidable rival for the ear of the Queen.

Away from home and the japes of his siblings, Arthur's

behaviour started to improve. Soon Howard could report that the 'old system of *punishments* formerly of daily occurrence' had ceased, to be replaced with rewards such as trips to the theatre in London.[31] In January 1863 Bertie lent them his box at the Adelphi for the pantomime. 'The French clowns are by far the cleverest I ever saw,' he told Elphinstone, 'and do the most wonderful things. Unfortunately the Pantomime is the last piece, which makes it very late. I did not get away till past 12 o'clock, so that you will return to Greenwich in the "early hours".'[32]

By far the best local attraction to Ranger's House was the Crystal Palace, which had been re-erected at nearby Sydenham after the Great Exhibition in 1851. At first Howard was reluctant to take the prince to it, on grounds less of safety than of propriety. But after judging the 'class of people' at the Crystal Palace to be respectable during a surreptitious tour of inspection, he relented. He even allowed the prince onto a merry-go-round with other children.[33] The Queen was delighted. Far from disapproving, she 'rejoiced that our dear little Darling was so much amused at the Crystal Palace, as she knows how much the beloved Prince would rejoice at his dear children being happy'.[34] One popular highlight within the Palace's sparkling halls was Louis Desanges's now completed 'Gallery of Victoria Cross Pictures': an artistic Valhalla devoted to the nation's military heroes. Arthur cannot have failed to be impressed as he stood in front of the dramatic image of his governor saving the lives of the wounded before Sevastopol. Meanwhile, Howard might have pondered how much his life had changed since that fateful night.

16

'The most gorgeous sight I ever witnessed'

WINDSOR CASTLE, 1863

IN JANUARY 1863, after spending Christmas quietly at Osborne House – Victoria's preferred location for the festive season following Albert's death at Windsor – Elphinstone and Arthur returned to London in company with the Prince of Wales. Bertie was on his way to Sandringham, his recently purchased estate in Norfolk, to prepare for his marriage to Princess Alexandra of Denmark. Despite his protestations, the Queen had decreed that her son's wedding should take place within the seclusion of St George's Chapel, rather than at Westminster Abbey with all the panoply of a state occasion. Her decision was bitterly disappointing: the whole country longed for a glamorous royal event after so many months of silence from the shuttered palace. Denied the full spectacle of a royal wedding, the people of London instead gave Alix a rousing reception when she was driven through the city after landing in England on 7 March. The diarist Arthur Munby, who witnessed the procession, described how the princess's carriage became 'imbedded in eager human faces' as it slowly inched its way through the vast throng. 'She meanwhile, a fair haired graceful girl, in a white bonnet and blush roses, sat by her mother, with "Bertie" and her father opposite, smiling sweetly and bowing on all sides; astounded, as she well might be, but self possessed; until the crowd parted at length.'[1]

Alix eventually reached Windsor that evening, where she was warmly embraced on the steps of the castle by the Queen. Victoria was moved by the significance of the current Queen of England greeting the future one, but she was also wracked with guilt at her instinctive happiness. 'It seemed so dreadful that all this must take place,' she wrote that evening in her journal, 'and he, my beloved one, not be here!'[2]

Despite the Queen's desire for restraint, the royal nuptials were celebrated with a pomp not seen since the Prince Consort's death. The castle was thronged with visitors, many of them from overseas, and many of those confused by its myriad passages. One privileged guest was William Russell of *The Times*, who had been given exclusive behind-the-scenes access to the event. As he wandered the castle corridors Russell, who was better used to observing and recording the gore of battle, fell back on military metaphor to describe the lavishness of it all. 'The vast suites of kitchens, confectionary-rooms and chambers, sacred to gastronomy, were crowded with battalions of white-capped and aproned cooks and maids,' he marvelled; 'the tables were loaded with made-dishes, ornaments and plate, so that all the kings of the earth might have feasted there.'[3]

The day before the wedding, Howard took Arthur and Leopold to see the preparations inside the chapel. Regardless of the best efforts of their mother to dampen down their enthusiasm, both the boys were very excited and 'great was the laughing and talking' when Louisa Bowater met them all on the lawn outside.[4] After the princes had gone to bed, Howard attended a state banquet held in honour of the bride and groom in St George's Hall. The Queen had dreaded the evening – though she was secretly amused when Alix's elderly father muddled Elphinstone's name with that of *Elfin*, the paddle-wheel steam yacht which conveyed the royal family and its guests to and from the Isle of Wight – so as soon as she could she slipped away, leaving her guests to watch a firework display from the windows of the White Drawing Room. Then they too drifted off to their bedrooms or to the billiard room for a final cigar before retiring. Yet 'all through the long night, toil and labour ceased not,' Russell informed his rapt readers, 'for there remained much to do. Within and without the castle, heads were working and fingers were busy.'[5]

After several days of rain, 10 March dawned crisp and clear. As the sun rose, the royal standard was 'flung to the frosty air' above the Round Tower at the heart of the castle, signalling the start to the celebrations.[6] By eight, the sound of pealing bells could be heard in the town below, and the first troops began filing into the Lower Ward, their boots ringing on the cobbles. By half-past eleven, the nave of the ancient chapel was crammed with 'nearly every person of eminence in the metropolis'. Among them was the famed artist William Powell Frith, who had been commissioned by the Queen to paint the colourful scene. Frith had been given a place close to the altar, and there he stood, busily sketching 'in the midst of a little crowd of ladies, all desperately coquetting to ensure their portraits figuring on his picture'.[7] After the wedding Howard would accompany the princes to Frith's studio in Bayswater for more extended sittings, his attendance ensuring his own prominent inclusion in the artist's finished work.

The gentlemen in the congregation wore morning dress while the ladies, trilled the court correspondent for the *Illustrated London News*,

> displayed their freshest and most brilliant toilets. Innumerable marvels in the way of bonnets, and unapproachable triumphs as regards lace and flowers. It must be admitted, however, and to the very great credit of the ladies, that exaggerated crinoline was remarkable more for its rarity than for its profusion, and that gigantic hoops were throughout the day more honoured in the breach than in the observance.[8]

Few of them were aware that ahead of them the Queen had already taken up her position in the Royal Pew, where she had sat for her mother's funeral. Eventually, as was possibly intended, this highly

Bertie and Alix photographed on their wedding day in March 1863.
The Queen maintained a doleful gaze on a bust of her dead husband
throughout the proceedings.

theatrical position would attract more attention to Victoria than she would have commanded had she simply joined her family in the choir below. As it was, she sat framed in medieval trelliswork, looking 'profoundly melancholy' as she fiddled with the streamers trailing from her widow's cap and touched the miniature of Albert pinned to her chest.[9] From her vantage point, however, the Queen could surreptitiously scan the chapel. Brave or foolhardy were those, like Benjamin Disraeli, who caught her steely eye.

A blast of trumpets heralded the carriage processions conveying the royal wedding guests. The first to arrive delivered the Danish royal family and the Maharajah Duleep Singh, the King of the Sikhs and ruler of the Punjab, whose state had been annexed by the British in 1849. Following his exile to England, the young Maharajah, who was a great favourite of the Queen's, had adopted English manners and dress. Today, however, he wore his most dazzling Indian costume – though not the magnificent Koh-i-Noor diamond, which he had surrendered to the Queen when he lost his kingdom. The carriages then returned to the Upper Ward to collect the royal family and household guests. Howard took his place beside Adolf Buff in the eighth carriage, sitting opposite Arthur and Leopold. 'There was a good cheer' from the excited crowd lining the route to the chapel when they saw 'the bright, intelligent faces of the two lads'.[10]

It had been impossible to rehearse the processions into the chapel, causing some confusion on the day. The chaotic entrance of the 'gouty purple-mantled' Knights of the Garter was considered particularly unseemly.[11] Howard walked slowly up the aisle behind 'Gold Stick': Field Marshal Viscount Combermere, a 94-year-old veteran of the siege of Seringapatam and the Peninsular War. When the royal procession reached the choir, Vicky – now Crown Princess of Prussia, following her father-in-law's accession to the throne in Berlin – glanced up at her mother and made 'a very low curtsey, with an inexpressible look of love and respect'. The princess's gesture removed any doubt as to who was the real star of the elaborate spectacle. Vicky then ushered her four-year-old son Prince Wilhelm of Prussia to a seat beside Arthur and Leopold. Willy 'looked the most compact little manikin that was ever seen out of a doll's house', according to the *Illustrated London News*. But his look of innocence betrayed a deep-seated ill-discipline, and soon the future Kaiser of Germany was irritating his uncles by biting their legs. 'When my uncle Leopold . . . told me not to fidget,' recalled Wilhelm from exile sixty years later, 'I drew the little dirk belonging to my Highland outfit, an incident about which I was greatly teased in later years.'[12] Typically, the Kaiser forgot to mention that he had then unpicked the cairngorm in the dirk and hurled it across the chapel's stone floor. Wilhelm's family, and tragically the world, would eventually grow wearily used to such violent antics.

Howard followed proceedings from a narrow wooden stall in the choir, which was now awash with vividly coloured foreign uniforms, 'picked out with English scarlet'.[13] Opposite him was William Gladstone – who considered the scene 'the most gorgeous sight I ever witnessed'[14] – while behind sat Benjamin Disraeli, 'attired in a rich, but not very tasteful, uniform coat profusely plastered with gold'.[15] Meanwhile, despite being nearly eighty, the current Prime Minister, Lord Palmerston, 'stepped lightly up to his seat and looked around him with a brisk joviality'.[16]

At half-past twelve, heralded by Mendelssohn's *Wedding March*, the bridegroom arrived, looking pale and nervous. 'Then came a long pause' as 'the Prince looked anxiously at the door'.[17] Finally a trumpet fanfare announced the entrance of the bride, wearing a silver gown decorated with orange blossom 'like the vision of a Princess in a Fairy Tale'.[18] The service was short and moving, the exchange of vows being greeted by the pealing of bells and the crash of guns out in the park. The formalities over, the Queen disappeared from view, vanishing as soundlessly as she had appeared. Her departure lifted the mood in the chapel, and the prince and his princess smiled happily as they swept back through the congregation to their waiting carriage. After signing the register in a private ceremony in the castle, Bertie and Alix hosted a lavish wedding breakfast while the Queen dined quietly elsewhere with her youngest daughter, fifteen-year-old Beatrice. Afterwards the guests marvelled at a display of the sumptuous wedding presents, which included the lavish silver-gilt toilet service presented to the newlyweds by the household. While they did so, Alix and Bertie posed for their wedding photographs – the Queen ignoring the happy couple throughout to gaze mournfully at a bust of her husband. Late in the afternoon, amid chaotic scenes on the streets of Windsor, Bertie and Alix gratefully departed on honeymoon, leaving Victoria alone to pray beside her husband's tomb.

Howard tentatively hoped that the 'reaction consequent upon all the excitement and the scenes of the past week, will not oppress Your Majesty too severely, and that you will receive strength to bear the painful associations which it must call forth';[19] but the hope that this joyous event might have marked the beginning of a gradual lifting of her mourning soon ebbed away. If anything, Victoria now sank further into her depression, bitterly complaining to Howard about the 'overwhelming amount of work which *quite* overpowers her'.[20] She took no comfort from her people, she told him; it was only from the '*personal* and *daily* contact' with those, '*high* and *low*', who evinced 'a *true* sympathy and appreciation of his sufferings (*these* are *not* always properly understood by the public) that the Queen experiences . . . soothing effect'.[21] In turning her back on her country, however, Victoria was giving dangerous succour to her republican enemies. She had also paved the way for the irruption in her court of a highly personal and potentially devastating new crisis.

'Oh vanity, how much it detracts from really good fine qualities'

1864

THE MOVE TO THE vicinity of the Royal Military Academy at Woolwich brought Howard close again to the life he had left behind when he joined court. Many of his old friends from the army came to the dinner parties he hosted at Ranger's House for Arthur, including his own mentors Sir John Burgoyne and Sir Harry Jones. One frequent later visitor would be Charles Gordon, whose exploits in China, where he had put down a rebellion with an irregular force called the 'Ever Victorious Army', had captivated the public. On his return from the east in 1865, Gordon was placed in command of the Royal Engineers at Gravesend, within easy distance of Greenwich and Ranger's House. Henry Ponsonby reported that both Elphinstone and John Cowell were 'immensely proud' of their celebrated friend from the engineers, with his curly hair and mesmerizing blue eyes.[1] On one occasion they even invited him over for dinner at Osborne House, a rare privilege, though it seems Gordon was never presented to the Queen.

Arthur was in awe of 'Chinese' Gordon, marvelling, in a letter to his mother, that such a young officer – Gordon was three years younger than Elphinstone – could already have 'commanded such a number of troops'.[2] Curiously, Ranger's House provided the setting for one of the defining moments in Gordon's troubled and ultimately tragic life. One evening in September 1866, while 'rather listlessly' dressing at the house before dining with Elphinstone, Gordon's eye fell upon his Bible, which was open at 1 John 4:15: 'Whosoever shall confess that Jesus is the Son of God, God dwelleth in him, and he in God.' 'Something broke in my heart,' Gordon wrote later to a friend, 'a palpable feeling and I knew God lived in me.'[3] In the wake of this revelation, which was to set Gordon on his path to martyrdom twenty years later in the sands of the Sudan, he was no doubt rather distracted when he later joined Howard for dinner.

One noticeably tardy caller to the house was the Queen, who delayed a year before making the short journey from Windsor to see her son in November 1863. Elphinstone thought the occasion a great success, as did the delighted local community. But Victoria confessed that she had found it 'a *very trying visit*' and that it had 'made her *very* sad for she felt that the beloved father who *ought* to have been there, and who *would* have been so pleased, was *not* there, though surely he was in spirit'.[4] Other members of Arthur's family were less reluctant visitors. Most beat a path to his door over the coming years, their royal carriages becoming a familiar site in the lanes surrounding Blackheath.

The prince's enforced separation from his mother heralded a series of steadily more ambitious expeditions with his governor. Within a year of moving to Greenwich they had completed tours of the Lake District, Midlands and Wales. These excursions were principally designed for educational purposes and to prepare the prince for his future life in the public eye. Yet it was events in Germany which increasingly occupied Howard's time; the result of a shift in sentiment towards that country by the Queen after her husband's death at the expense of the country she ruled. In particular, Victoria wanted Howard's help in solving a crisis over the succession to the dukedom of Saxe-Coburg-Gotha, a position currently occupied by the Prince Consort's childless elder brother Ernest. Strictly speaking, on Albert's death Bertie became heir to the duchy. But as Bertie's higher

Charles 'Chinese' Gordon in mandarin robes after his return from the east in 1865. Gordon was a close friend of Howard's from their days together in the trenches of the Crimea, and each would have a decisive effect on the career of the other.

calling to the throne of England ruled him out of the role, the position had devolved to Affie. Yet Victoria believed that Affie's rabid jingoism – which Howard, with the prejudice of a soldier, blamed on the prince's 'peculiar education on board a man of war'[5] – made her second son an unsuitable ruler of the German duchy, or indeed of anywhere. Moreover, tensions were developing between Affie and his governor John Cowell, whose intense religiosity grated on the worldly young prince. The Queen was anxious to avoid a damaging row between Affie and Cowell, which could leave her son as dangerously adrift as Bertie had been after General Bruce died. She implored Howard to 'take an opportunity, IF HE *can*, to urge Major Cowell to be as cordial with Prince Alfred as he can and to hint if he can to Haig [Affie's equerry] to try and do *all* to bring Prince Alfred a proper sense of *all* he owes to Major Cowell'.[6] In strictest confidence, she also asked him for advice on the Coburg succession.

The Prince of Wales's interesting suggestion that Leo should be considered for the German dukedom instead of Affie was quickly dismissed. 'A *sickly* heir would never do,' Victoria exclaimed to Elphinstone; 'we want . . . one whose health and strength will enable him to take an active part in *all* that is of importance, in military affairs, in sports, and if God spares our precious little Leopold, it will never be for any *active* bodily exertions the Queen must fear.'[7] With Bertie, Affie and Leo all apparently ruled out for the dukedom, there remained only Arthur to consider. So despite her desire to see the prince fulfil his destiny and join the army, the Queen instructed Howard to train 'our darling boy, as it were imperceptibly, for the very probable position he may have to fill'.[8]

In fact, Howard had foreseen just such an eventuality. Days before the Prince Consort died in December 1861, he had written a memo summarizing the three principal objectives of Arthur's education. These were that the prince should be trained for a career in the army; that he should be prepared for the 'distant chance' of inheriting the throne; and finally, that 'he might perhaps have to succeed his brother at Coburg'.[9] Accordingly, Elphinstone already insisted that German should be spoken three days a week at Ranger's House, while Jolley had been ordered to focus on German history in the schoolroom. In addition, the governor – by birth a German Lutheran, like the Prince Consort – did his utmost 'to exclude all that could give a bigoted Anglican tendency' to Arthur's education (despite the glaring fact that the prince's mother was head of the Anglican Church). By January 1864 Elphinstone was able to report with satisfaction that Arthur's 'natural tendencies lean more toward that expressive and characteristic German "Gemüthlichkeit"'* than towards the abruptness and reserve of the Englishman'.[10] He hastily assured the Queen that nothing would be done to give Arthur a '*special* love for Germany'. Yet he hoped to nurture in the prince a 'special liking to the localities which might eventually become his' by taking him there on holiday.[11] Contrasting the dullness of Arthur's life at Ranger's House with the excitement of travel was a similar strategy to the one the governor used to enhance the prince's longing for home. Howard assured the Queen that his own 'long residence abroad and early education have made him take a strong bias in favour of Germany, which consequently assists him greatly in carrying out the prescribed course'.[12]

In the winter of 1863–4 the vexed issue of the Coburg succession was thrown into sharper relief by the outbreak of war between Denmark and Prussia over the disputed territories of Schleswig and Holstein. The reasons for the conflict – a potent mixture of nationalism, broken treaties and territorial ambition – were notoriously complex. Lord Palmerston, the exasperated British Prime Minister, shared the almost universal confusion over the *casus belli*. 'Only three people ever understood the question of Schleswig-Holstein,' he declared. 'One was Prince Albert, who is dead. The second was a German professor who became mad. I am

---

* Cosiness, informality.

the third and I have forgotten all about it.'[13] Regardless of its origin, the war stretched family loyalties to the limit at Windsor as it pitched Alix's father, King Christian IX of Denmark, against Vicky's father-in-law, King Wilhelm I of Prussia. The Prince of Wales naturally sided with his wife, while the fervently pro-German Queen Victoria backed Berlin. In addition to the family turmoil, the war risked damaging Victoria's relationship with her people, who instinctively supported the Danes as underdogs. 'It is grievous and painful to see *how* ignorant the British *public*, especially the press, are upon the subject,' Victoria stormed in a letter to Howard, 'and then *how* unjust, unfair and, to say the least, impertinent they are towards a great nation like Germany . . . The bitter feelings which this must engender in Germany towards England is a deep sorrow to the Queen to whom Germany is a 2nd *Country*, a 2nd "Heimath" * .'[14]

Victoria's exasperation with the press was set against a backdrop of rising criticism at her prolonged seclusion following her husband's death. Like many people living close to the Queen, Elphinstone underestimated the strength of feeling in the country against her, and the dangers such discontent could pose to the monarchy. Instead he told her to ignore the 'foolish remarks [made] by a "press" that has its own petty objects to attain . . . i.e. an increased sale of its numbers!'.[15] He sympathized with Victoria over that 'most painful' conflict between Denmark and Prussia, seeing how it placed her in an invidious position. 'Even a speedy solution of all its difficulties', he predicted, 'will not be without its unpleasantness and personal concern.'[16] Like many in the military establishment, Elphinstone probably felt uneasy at the blatant aggression of the Prussians and their new 'blood and iron' Prime Minister, Otto von Bismarck. But the Queen, furious at the pro-Danish stance of her predominantly English court, forced him onto her side. 'She has not a doubt that he will take care to prevent Prince Arthur's taking a Danish view of the Schleswig-

* Homeland.

Holstein question,' she insisted; 'indeed if anyone studies the question, as the Queen knows Major Elphinstone has done, they must see that *right* is *entirely* on the German side.'[17] Howard assured Victoria that he would 'do his utmost to prevent such a bias ever being created. His own knowledge of the German language, its manners and customs, its literature and country, will greatly assist him in counteracting the growth of such prejudicial opinions.'[18]

In June 1864, to spark the prince's interest in his possible future career as a German duke, Howard took Arthur on a battle-field tour of the continent. (Although the Duke of Wellington had been Arthur's godfather, Elphinstone assured the Queen that all discussion of the battle of Waterloo would be 'thoroughly unbiased and that the gallant acts of the German Legion and the Brunswickers are fully dwelt upon and the importance of Bluchers [*sic*] assistance amply done justice to'.[19]) After dutifully calling on King Leopold of Belgium in Brussels, Howard and Arthur visited Vicky's mother-in-law, Queen Augusta of Prussia, at her rambling palace in Coblenz. The daughter of the enlightened Grand Duke of Saxe-Weimar, Augusta existed uncomfortably within the ultra-conservative Prussian court, preferring the company of artists, philosophers and poets to the soldiers and politicians who domi-nated it. By 1864 she was effectively estranged from her husband and his stiff Hohenzollern relatives, spending most of the year in Coblenz or Weimar, where she had grown up. Augusta was similar to Victoria in age and temperament, and the two queens were close confidantes, sharing secrets and consoling each other on the excesses of their many mutual cousins. Howard liked her immedi-ately, and during a long conversation about politics was not at all surprised to hear that Augusta deplored her country's war against Denmark.

On 1 July they reached the Rosenau which, Howard noted gloomily in his journal, 'looks most damp'.[20] Rain had been sweeping the region for weeks. 'I don't mean showery days', Elphinstone bitterly complained to Sir Charles Phipps, 'but a continuous steady drizzling rain'.[21] It was so cold that the major ordered fires to be lit in every room, news which prompted a warning from Windsor that he risked burning the house down. William Jolley quickly retired to bed and even the prince's indomitable valet Collins fell ill, possibly with the scarlet fever which was raging through the local village. Howard tried to appear cheerful in his daily dispatches to the palace. But in an unguarded comment to Phipps he confessed that he was considering abandoning the trip altogether, 'however much it distressed the Queen'. Unfortunately, Phipps was away when Elphinstone's letter reached Windsor and it was opened instead by Charles Grey, who mischievously showed it to the Queen. Stung by the governor's implied criticism of the Rosenau – which she revered as a shrine to the Prince Consort – Victoria tetchily reminded Howard not only that her son had already had scarlet fever but that '*good* air is *good* air, whether there be *occasional disturbances* and deteriorations of it from unusual rain and cold *or* draught'. She was 'a disbeliever in the effects of climate on healthy people', she pronounced. 'It is more one's health and *living* and feelings which affect one, or great change of temperature, than mild or cold climates.'[22] They would have to stay.

So, disregarding the weather, Arthur amused himself in the castle gardens, which had been meticulously restored to the condition they had been in during his father's childhood. Meanwhile, the major sought out Prince Albert's former governor Herr Christoph Florschütz, on whom his own role had been so carefully modelled. Under Christian Stockmar's supervision, Florschütz had devised the system of lessons, exercises and punishments for the young Prince Albert which Howard himself now followed with Arthur. As a child Albert had feared his governor, yet in time they had become close companions, even friends. Still only in his mid-sixties, Florschütz was a councillor in Coburg and a figure of considerable local stature.

Howard wanted to see Florschütz to discuss a tour of the Swiss Alps he was planning for Arthur, as he knew that

Albert had undertaken a similar expedition in 1837. After checking a battered journal, Florschütz prepared a route which closely matched the one he had taken with Albert nearly thirty years before. The Queen felt '*heart-sick*' at the thought of her son retracing his father's footsteps. Nevertheless she added some suggestions of her own to the itinerary, all gleaned from 'a little book with views which the dear Prince collected'.[23] But she absolutely forbade 'any *dangerous* expeditions being undertaken; *nothing whatever* which could be running any risk as Prince Arthur can *see quite* enough that is BEAUTIFUL without doing this'.[24]

The walking party set out from Lucerne on 23 July. Within days it was apparent that the expedition was beyond the capability of Arthur's stout tutor, the Reverend Mr Jolley. 'So complete a change of diet and habits of life have proved too much for him,' fumed Elphinstone; 'he is suffering in consequence and therefore [is] quite unable to assist in taking charge of the Prince.'[25] In contrast, a clearly irritated Jolley claimed that living so closely beside his royal pupil lowered his authority. On 3 August the disgruntled tutor abandoned the tour altogether – 'Exhausted', Howard wrote disdainfully in his journal, 'and out of spirits'.[26] One of the Queen's favoured equerries, Francis Seymour, was promptly dispatched from Windsor to replace Jolley. As a young officer, Colonel Seymour had accompanied Albert on his tour of the Alps in 1837 'and therefore can talk to Arthur about his dear father'. 'Though he may have a little peculiarity of manner,' Victoria added ominously, '[Seymour] is thoroughly refined in feeling and tone.' Howard would have much preferred his friend Colonel Du Plat as a travelling companion, but Du Plat had been ruled out as 'his manner and tone are not quite those which her beloved Prince liked'.[27]

Life in the mountains was necessarily austere and still treacherous, despite – to the major's dismay – handrails having been erected on many of the paths he had followed in his own youth to cater for the rising numbers of English tourists. Days passed in rigorous exercise were followed by nights in barren, often foul-smelling, huts. The young prince was unperturbed by these spartan conditions and, as Howard intended, revelled in the freedom from his dreary routine at Ranger's House with its stiff collars and kilts. When Seymour joined the party at Chamonix, he found Arthur 'dressed in a coloured shirt, without coat, waistcoat or neck cloth, his trousers turned up at the bottom, showing a pair of strong laced boots studded with sharp nails to prevent his falling in the snow. A wide awake [hat] with a gauze veil and a long "Alpenstock" in his hand completed his costume.'[28] Lady Augusta Bruce, honeymooning in Switzerland following her marriage to Arthur Stanley, the Dean of Westminster, marvelled at the change in the prince. 'I cannot express the pleasure it gave us to see such healthful looks and good spirits,' she exclaimed after running into Arthur and his governor outside the English Church at Berne: 'in every way one sees that the exertions made and the feats accomplished have agreed.'[29]

Howard loved being in the mountains again, yet their immense scale and beauty merely impressed upon him the loneliness of his own position. One warm evening, after carefully checking that Arthur was asleep and his lodgings secure, he 'could not resist wandering out' to experience them alone. Gazing up at the stars, he 'thought how intensely pleasant if here now with one to care for, to pour out ones heart'.[30] It would be many more years before he found such a person. To make matters worse, Francis Seymour was riling him intensely. At the age of fifty-two, the colonel was as unfit and ponderous as Jolley, while his 'peculiarity of manner', caused by a head wound from the Crimea, was deeply irritating. The walking party's previously rapid progress slowed considerably, as Elphinstone had to post guides on each side of Seymour, not only 'to pull him up' the steeper paths, but to prevent the colonel from falling as 'his short-sightedness prevented his distinguishing a hollow from an elevation'.[31] Howard might have forgiven the colonel his physical faults, but his haughty manner made his blood boil. After hearing, yet again, over the

General Francis Seymour, once a close friend of the Prince Consort's but,
replacing William Jolley on the Alpine tour of 1864, considered by
Howard an interfering and pompous old fool.

campfire how the colonel had won the *Légion d'honneur* during the war, Howard, the holder of both the *Légion d'honneur* and the Victoria Cross, exclaimed in his journal: 'Oh vanity, how much it detracts from really good fine qualities'.[32] Furthermore, Seymour's clumsy attempts 'to effect many little improvements' in Prince Arthur's behaviour during the expedition struck at the governor's authority. Clearly affronted, though confident that Seymour had 'little hope' of success, the major acted swiftly. He wrote to the Queen, before Seymour could, telling her 'that there is no defect of Prince Arthur which Major Elphinstone does not only know, but likewise is constantly trying to remedy. What *he* cannot do at once, he feels quite sure that a stranger cannot.'[33]

Howard rejected the gentle approach favoured by Seymour in handling Arthur. He steadfastly maintained that 'severity alone' would cure the prince of the 'worst qualities of his character'. 'He says so advisedly,' he persisted in an aggrieved letter to Victoria,

> and after a careful study of Prince Arthur's character of nearly five years experience, for in justice to himself and the great pains and trouble he had taken, it is but right to tell Your Majesty that during the whole course of that long period, Prince Arthur has not even on *any single one occasion* done *anything* which was recommended to him *kindly* by Major Elphinstone, unless he expected to derive some advantages by it. By firmness alone and that of an unintermittant and most trying kind, has any improvement ever been obtained. Major Elphinstone could wish it were otherwise, for it would, if nothing else, at all events save him individually, a vast amount of mental pain and anxiety.[34]

Howard suspected, rightly, that Seymour was reporting back to the Queen. He would have been surprised to learn, however, that the colonel's principal complaint was not about Elphinstone's method of managing the prince, but his insistence that they all speak French at mealtimes (presumably as he himself was unable to). Moreover, Seymour was unequivocal in his praise for the major, telling the Queen that he was 'an excellent and devoted servant' who was 'firm but kind and most patient' with her son.[35] 'In the evenings when Prince A and Major E. draw, I read aloud,' the colonel wrote from Lausanne on 22 August. 'Prince Arthur has his piano and I am glad to find has his dear father's taste for music. He cares less for drawing but Major E. encourages him as much as possible and as he draws very well himself, I trust his example will induce Prince A. to persevere.'[36]

After a month in the mountains, the exhausted party wound their way home by rail, Howard hoping that Switzerland had 'infused a more poetical tone, a more delicate taste' in the young prince.[37] During the journey, diversions were made to Darmstadt to see Princess Alice and to Amorbach to inspect the Duchess of Kent's former home with its affecting collection of family memorabilia. There was even time to call on Howard's ageing parents at Wiesbaden, where Alexander and Amelia Elphinstone now resided to avoid the high cost of living in England and 'the damp climate of Devonshire'.[38] But sensitivity over the Schleswig-Holstein War, which had recently ended in complete victory for Prussia, caused Vicky to cancel their planned visit to Berlin. Indeed, anti-English feeling was running so high in Prussia, as a consequence of official attitudes during the conflict, that the major was even prevented by the owner – 'a "Manufacturer"', he noted with disdain – from showing Arthur around Prince Albert's former lodgings at Bonn University. 'Such things', Howard observed sadly, 'have occurred more than once, but only in Prussia . . . he can only fancy that this feeling must have been caused by the violent language of our press.'[39]

They reached England on 3 October 1864. After resting for a time at Ranger's House, Arthur continued to Balmoral with Seymour to be reunited with his mother, while Elphinstone returned to the continent to holiday with his parents. Despite their differences, Elphinstone and Seymour parted on good terms, each praising the other. Like Augusta Bruce, the Queen was amazed at her son's transformation. He was 'very much improved and decidedly grown', she commented: 'as childlike, "kindlich" as ever, but not near as childish and gentle and docile'.[40] In fact, he was old enough to take a rifle and go stalking the hills with John Brown, as his father would have wanted.

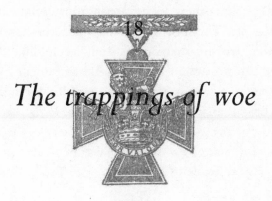

18

The trappings of woe

1865

THREE YEARS AFTER THE Prince Consort's death, the Queen still remained in deepest mourning. Her steadfast refusal to fulfil the normal functions of the monarch – even routine duties like opening Parliament – was not only causing rumblings in the press but alarming the government, who feared an upsurge in republican activity. How to rid Victoria of her '"trappings" of woe', in Charles Grey's memorable phrase, had become the principal topic of debate behind the closed doors of the palace.[1]

James Clark, the elderly royal physician who had known his wilful patient since her childhood, thought that drawing Victoria out of her seclusion 'can only be affected by a judiciously combined action of those persons about the Queen in whom she has confidence, and to whose counsel she may feel inclined to listen'. 'Whatever is decided on', he cautioned,

> should . . . be made known to the persons who are in the habit of
> having interviews with the Queen, to whom, as you no doubt
> know she frequently mentions her views, citing, at the same time,
> the opinions of others in support of her own, and in such a way as
> renders it very difficult not to agree with her or at least appear to
> do so.[2]

Grey himself knew better than most how obdurate the Queen could be. 'The more I think upon it,' he confessed to Sir Charles Phipps in January 1865,

the less I see my way over it. It is quite certain that if you or I joined in any pressure on the Queen we should simply lose any little power we may now possess of doing good . . . The Queen is already *perfectly* aware of what her subjects wish, nor can she be ignorant of what her position requires.[3]

Only one man seemed capable of dragging Victoria out of her depression – and he was in Scotland. Therefore, encouraged by Princess Alice and with the connivance of Dr Jenner, Grey and Phipps, John Brown, the Queen's 'particular ghilley', was summoned to England in the hope that his mere rugged presence might succeed where Grey's gentle wheedling had failed. The move delighted Victoria, but had little effect on her desire to resume any of her public duties. She made Brown 'The Queen's Highland Servant', a position second only in confidence – and that not for long – to that held by her 'Principal Personal Servant', Rudolf Löhlein. 'He comes to my room after breakfast and luncheon to get his orders and everything is always right,' the Queen trilled in a letter to Vicky. 'He is so quiet, has such an excellent head and memory, and is besides so devoted, and attached and clever and so wonderfully able to interpret one's wishes. He is a real treasure to me now, and I only wish higher people had his sense and discretion, and that I had as good a maid.'[4]

Victoria had always romanticized, some might say patronized, her Scottish servants. She saw them all as 'excellent honest people', untrammelled by the worldliness which she feared had corrupted her eldest sons.[5] They were held in the same esteem as her German staff. During his lifetime, Albert had even labelled Brown his personal *Jäger*, or huntsman, a term which had baffled the Scot but given him unrivalled influence among the other servants at Balmoral. When Albert died, Brown, like a squire who has

Dr James Clark, the Queen's long-time and most trusted physician who prescribed fresh air and exercise for almost every ailment and failed to diagnose the Prince Consort's final illness.

lost his knight, had drawn a protective wall around Victoria, indulging her melancholy and courting her affection. It was in this role of unofficial bodyguard that Brown had accompanied the Queen on the royal family's pilgrimage to the Rosenau in 1862. Unlike Ruland or Löhlein, however, Brown was not yet seen as a threat to the equilibrium of the household; otherwise Charles Grey would never have sanctioned his transfer to England. The secretary may even have hoped that Brown would weaken Löhlein's hold over the Queen. He could hardly have expected that the Queen would feel encouraged to bring more of her Highlanders south; nor that the ostensible reason for doing so would be Prince Leopold, whose hopes of joining Arthur at Ranger's House had finally been extinguished.

Although Howard Elphinstone remained officially in charge of Leo, such an arrangement was clearly impractical now that he was living in Greenwich with Arthur. In his absence, Howard's responsibilities as Leo's governor had fallen upon the prince's tutor, Adolf Buff. But this was equally unsatisfactory, so the Queen had begun casting about for a permanent replacement. Max Müller, a professor at Oxford University, was recruited to enquire after

> a young man of about 24 to 28, of great intelligence, with plenty of observation and knowledge of different countries and a good deal of learning and especially good knowledge of different countries and languages. He should have a very even temper and like children but plenty of firmness. He should be either a German or Swiss of good manners and deportment or an Englishman, devoid of all prejudices and peculiarities of his nation and of the young men of the present day.[6]

These qualifications so closely match those of Elphinstone that he probably drafted the description himself.

When Müller inevitably failed in his exacting task, the Queen proposed a candidate herself. In October 1864 she wrote triumphantly to Howard to tell him that 'she *has* succeeded in finding a person to take charge of Prince Leopold when Mr Buff leaves him, and this person is – Major Cowell!'[7] It seemed an ideal solution. Cowell's governorship of Prince Alfred would end soon, when Affie came of age, and despite their frequent clashes he had proved that he could cope with an awkward young prince. The appointment would also keep Cowell at court, thus assuaging the Queen's extreme reluctance ever to allow any of her husband's appointees to leave her. 'Under these circumstances naturally Major Elphinstone would *not* continue Governor to Prince Leopold,' she reasoned, 'as he would then be entirely under the care of Major Cowell, but she thinks it will be (in part) more satisfactory to Major Elphinstone himself.' Realizing that the notoriously sensitive Howard might feel offended at being supplanted by Cowell, Victoria assured him that she knew 'how fond Major Elphinstone is of dear Prince Leopold and [now] he will perhaps feel being *no* longer personally connected with him, but as Major Elphinstone is so much away with Prince Arthur he could hardly have been *more* than a *nominal* Governor to Prince Leopold. She believes he anticipated this result sooner or later.'[8]

Thus, when Alfred duly reached the age of twenty-one in August 1865, Cowell resigned his existing post and took up his new position beside Prince Leopold. He was also promptly knighted by the Queen. 'At the same time', Victoria informed the Prime Minister, Lord Palmerston,

> she would wish to give the civil *Companionship of the Bath* to *Major Elphinstone*, Governor to Prince Arthur, of whose services to our other dear boy she can likewise never speak in too high terms, and who is a very accomplished and distinguished officer. He received the Victoria Cross for his conduct in the Crimea. Since God deprived our poor dear children of their beloved father, it is impossible to overrate the value of two such excellent devoted young men as Major Cowell and Major Elphinstone.[9]

Despite the Queen's warm endorsement, Cowell's knighthood caused outrage within the upper reaches of the royal household, where position was jealously guarded and rank vigorously defended. Responding to the concerned enquiry of Phipps, Charles Grey stormed that

> however important Cowell's duties were, they were those of a tutor or Preceptor for which an honourable distinction of this sort was not the proper reward, particularly as neither his civil position nor his rank in the army qualified him for it. Both in civil position, in military rank and in the nature of our duties, you and I are in a perfectly different position, we have, I may say, *very* confidential *political* functions to perform. Our duties, though personal to the Queen, are all of a public nature and I hold that not one word could *quietly* be said against the bestowal of the order, even in its highest clasp, upon either of us. You cannot rate our duties as less important than those of many of H.M.'s Ministers both at home and abroad. Cowell was in a *very* different position and even Biddulph's duties were hardly such to justify his nomination to this distinction. If it is given in this manner to all members of the Household who have confidential duties to perform, the value of the order will soon be lowered. What better proof of this can you have than that every one agrees with me that I could not properly accept it after the manner in which it had been already bestowed? . . . It will be impossible in a very few years not to give it also to Elphinstone, whom I believe to be infinitely the superior man of the two. To *you* I cannot help saying, I have *not* the opinion of 'Sir John' that you have.[10]

Cowell's appointment as Leo's governor coincided with an unexpected change below stairs at the palace. During the summer, Arthur's loyal valet Collins announced that he was engaged to be married. Astonished that a servant should even contemplate marriage, let alone desert his post, the Queen told Elphinstone 'to speak to him on the subject and to tell him that till Prince Arthur has another servant besides, this cannot be allowed'.[11] But she soon realized that Collins had given her a heaven-sent opportunity to bring another of her beloved Scottish servants down to England. She proposed replacing Collins with Leo's valet Ben Bovington, leaving Bovington's place in turn to be taken by John Brown's younger brother Archie. 'He is 25,' she told Howard,

> as tall as his brother John, strong and healthy and would therefore be able at any time to carry and lift Prince Leopold . . . If Archie Brown is only half as attentive . . . and devoted, as his excellent brother, he will prove invaluable to Prince Leopold . . . If not too much trouble the Queen would ask Major Elphinstone to send her a copy of this letter with his answer. Löhlein, whom the Queen consulted on the subject and who knows Prince Leopold's requirements . . . is strongly of the opinion that Archie Brown would be particularly well suited for the place. The Queen has *not* mentioned it to his brother.[12]

Attitudes towards the Queen's Highland servants had, however, hardened considerably in the six months since John Brown's introduction to the English court. The household were growing weary of the Scot's overweening manner and his intimidating presence. Sensing opposition to her plan, Victoria sought the support of William Jenner, who agreed to share the details of Leo's medical condition with Archie Brown. With the backing of her sycophant doctor, she pressed on with Archie's appointment even after Collins announced that he had broken off his engagement, rendering the moves unnecessary. Elphinstone's appeal for caution was brushed aside. She had spoken with the Master of the Household Thomas Biddulph, she told him loftily, and both of them had decided that Bovington was '*vulgar*' and should be replaced by 'a nice, intelligent, steady simple and unspoilt Highlander with the "*Gentlemanly*" bearing and independent feelings they *all* have'.[13] By August 1865, Archie Brown had joined his brother John at Osborne House in rugged contrast to the predominantly English household.

On 10 November, Sir John Cowell drove over to Ranger's House with the 'strictly confidential' and surprising news that Princess Helena, the Queen's third daughter and her most stoic companion, was engaged. The princess's fiancé was Prince Christian of Schleswig-Holstein, a mild-mannered, chain-smoking, prematurely ageing man of thirty-four whose motives aroused the deepest suspicions in Helena's brothers and sisters. They suspected that, displaced by the recent war, Christian simply wanted to scrounge off the British royal family now that his own inheritance had been plundered by the Prussians. Alice saw another ulterior motive behind the engagement, stirring up trouble by accusing her mother of consigning Helena to an unhappy marriage solely to keep her daughter by her side in England. 'Very artful but the Queen sees through it,' exclaimed Lady Caroline Barrington, the lady superintendent of the nursery, when she heard of Alice's allegation. She could remember the princess's scheming from the schoolroom and suspected Alice had other reasons for trying to scupper the match.[14]

After absorbing the startling news of Helena's engagement, the two governors discussed 'many subjects relating to Prince Leopold's education'.[15] They agreed that Herr Sahl, who had replaced Becker as the Queen's librarian, should teach the prince German. Less certain was the future role of William Jolley, who had been teaching both princes before Arthur's move to Greenwich. As this was now impractical, a new tutor would have to be engaged at Windsor. Nothing further was said about Archie Brown's controversial appointment until Christmas, when Leo was yet again confined to bed following a bad fall. Writing to the Queen, Howard cautiously queried Archie's competence, particularly the Highlander's ability to carry Leopold safely over the tiled floors of Osborne House – a suggestion that he suspected drunkenness. As he was no longer Leo's governor, Howard, who enjoyed better access to the Queen, was obviously acting on Cowell's behalf in raising the sensitive issue of Archie's ability. Victoria, however, was not fooled by their collusion. 'Sir John Cowell', she stormed in reply, should know that he can *perfectly* trust Archie in *every thing*; he is an excellent young man and as conscientious as his excellent elder brother though he has not naturally his expression and remarkable strength of character. If at *any time* Sir John has any remarks to make about Archie of any general nature, he had best send for his brother John and tell *him*, for he is always giving Archie good advice and watching over him.[16]

Within weeks the sudden death at Windsor of Sir Charles Phipps altered everything. The court was stunned. Princess Helena told Elphinstone that the news had 'brought back to us our own great loss'. 'The Queen', she continued, 'begs me say that she feels sure she can ever look to you as a kind and devoted friend, for as one by one she loses her old friends, she looks more closely to those who are left her and feels she needs their help doubly.'[17] Phipps's untimely death precipitated a series of radical changes inside the household. Thomas Biddulph was promoted to the vacant post of Keeper of the Privy Purse, while Sir John Cowell, who had been Leopold's governor for barely six months, replaced Biddulph as Master of the Household. Cowell took advantage of his move to launch an extraordinary valedictory attack on Archie Brown. He accused the Scotsman of forgetfulness, poor time-keeping and malingering – further coded warnings of his drunkenness. The Queen was 'much annoyed' by this fresh criticism of Archie. 'Sir John Cowell seems to imagine he will never become a good valet,' she complained in a letter to Elphinstone. Nevertheless, forced to take Cowell's accusations seriously, she asked Howard to look into them '*quite confidentially*'. 'She *relies*', she wrote, 'on Major Elphinstone setting this right with Sir John Cowell.'[18] In his subsequent report, Howard stated tactfully that in his opinion Archie's 'deficiency is not from want of will or anxiety, but from want of knowledge'.[19] But his eminently sensible suggestion that Collins could perhaps mentor the untrained Archie as a valet was utterly rejected by the Queen. 'He will learn things gradually, better,' she snapped, 'as he does now.'[20]

Before beginning his new duties as Master of the Household, Cowell was asked to find his own replacement as Leopold's governor. Disregarding Leo's medical needs, Cowell turned to the army for suggestions, as the Prince Consort had done ahead of Elphinstone's appointment in 1858. He returned with the name of Walter Stirling, a 26-year-old lieutenant in the Royal Artillery and, like himself and Elphinstone, a graduate of the Royal Military Academy. Better still, from the Queen's point of view, Stirling was Scottish, so might be considered immune from the arrogance which, in her opinion, afflicted so many of the English officers in her army. However, in a telling and, for the candidate, ominous move, the Queen asked Howard to be present when Stirling took up his post, as he could 'easily understand *what* a trial it will be for the Queen to *begin* with a total stranger, unknown to the beloved Prince'.[21] Despite her misgivings, the Queen was initially impressed with Leo's new governor, his third in as many years. Stirling was given a room beside Leo's in the castle and allocated his own Scottish servant called Robertson, one of Archie Brown's cronies from Balmoral.

Stirling was not a man to suffer fools, and inevitably he soon clashed with the Highlanders attached to his suite. Unlike Cowell, he would not tolerate their sullen belligerence to protect his own position, treating them instead as he would insubordinate soldiers. He might also have discovered, as Elphinstone possibly suspected, that John Brown and the other Scottish servants were taunting and physically abusing the prince behind his back. Leo later complained to Stirling that '"J.B." is fearfully insolent to me, so is his brother; hitting me on the face with spoons for fun, etc.'[22]

The Queen was as blind to the faults of her Highlanders as she was ignorant of their cruelty. Hearing about the rows, she merely ordered Stirling to ensure that 'Prince Leopold behaves civilly to the servants, more especially to those constantly about him'.[23] In May 1866, after yet another heated confrontation with Robertson, Stirling confided his concerns to Elphinstone, who delicately raised the matter with the Queen, as he had previously done for Cowell. Victoria refused to listen. Instead she blamed Stirling's brusque military manner for the problems he was experiencing with Robertson. She then rebuked Howard for taking 'the part of the stronger against the *weaker* especially when the latter was *totally* ignorant of his duties as valet to a young officer'. 'If he had been kindly spoken to,' she continued, warming to her theme, 'instead of being from the first moment treated by a complete stranger as *no* royal or any servant *ought* to be, and what *no* high-spirited Highlander *could* stand, this would *never* have occurred.'

The Queen's uncritical defence of the Highlanders, even in the face of opposition from trusted courtiers like Elphinstone, was informed both by her sentimentalizing of them and by the trust apparently placed in their ability by Dr Jenner, whose opinion she never doubted. The dispute also touched upon the highly sensitive issue of how people of rank should treat their servants. In this matter, as in so many, the Queen took an unconventional view. 'It is *not* a good quality', she stormed at Elphinstone, 'to be unkind and sharp towards your *inferiors* and does not show superiority, and the Queen can not say that she ever thinks it speaks for those who *do* treat them so. This is over and the Queen will not again recur to it, but watch how matters go.'[24] As his journal testifies, since joining court Howard had, in striving to secure his position, tried strenuously to shed any appearance of arrogance himself, endearing himself to the Queen in the process.

A convenient excuse to discard Stirling presented itself to the Queen soon afterwards when Leopold began suffering what Elphinstone described as 'unfortunate attacks' – possibly epileptic fits linked to his haemophilia.[25] Binding Howard to secrecy, Victoria revealed that she had decided to replace Stirling with 'a *sort* of physician'. 'It is absolutely necessary', she insisted, 'that the person who has charge of Leopold should be perfectly competent to watch over him in a *medical* point of view.' Dr Jenner naturally agreed, although he was now rightly blamed for keeping the Queen in the dark on the severity of her son's condition for so long. 'If the Queen *had* known *what* the Doctors *really* thought of these attacks, at the time Mr Stirling was looked for,' she protested, 'and of the *extreme* care required in the treatment and watching of Leopold, the Queen *never* would have looked for a young officer who *cannot* be *expected* to understand *any thing* about health and *medicine*.'[26]

Victoria had never disguised her dislike for a man who had so provoked her Highland servants. Nor did she try to pretend that the obvious need for a medical attendant for Leo was anything other than the 'ostensible' reason for dismissing Stirling.[27] 'In strict *confidence*', she confessed,

> she may however tell Major Elphinstone, that she does *not* think that Mr Stirling was *suited* for that post; he has not enlarged views or knowledge, enough to lead and develop so clever a boy as Leopold, *without a father*, nor has he softness and kindliness of manner and character . . . the Queen must likewise own that there is *that* in Mr Stirling's manner which (and she *felt* it, though she did *not* admit it, from the *very first*) which would make it *very* difficult for *her* to get on with him.[28]

The Queen was anxious to avoid giving the impression that the crisis in her household had been caused by the Highlanders whose presence at court was now causing widespread comment in the papers. The gossip focused on John Brown, who within months of arriving in England had superseded Löhlein as the Queen's most confidential servant. The publication in 1865 of prints after Edwin Landseer's striking oil painting (now at Osborne House) of John Brown holding the Queen's pony as she read official papers heightened scurrilous interest in their relationship. Victoria herself was delighted with the picture, telling Howard that 'it is beautifully engraved and the likeness of herself (rather a portly elderly lady) and her good faithful attendant and friend are both she thinks *very* good'.[29] But the suggested intimacy of the scene fuelled the gossip, leading to some scandalous allegations.

One report in the foreign press, hotly denied by the palace,

The governor and his royal charge: Howard Elphinstone and Prince Arthur photographed at Windsor in May 1860.

The Last Moments of HRH the Prince Consort, oil painting by an unknown artist c.1862. According to the key which accompanied a later lithograph of the painting, the Queen sits at her husband's bedside clutching the hand of Princess Alice. Behind them stand Prince Arthur and Sir Charles Phipps. Princess Louise sits far right. On the other side of the bed, the Prince of Wales leans towards his father in front of, from right to left, General Bruce; the Dean of Windsor; Major Du Plat; General Bentinck; the Duke of Cambridge; and Lord Alfred Paget. Princess Helena sits tearfully on the settee with her sister Beatrice kneeling beside her. Behind the settee is a cluster of by now redundant doctors led by, second from left, Sir James Clark.

ABOVE: *John Brown, the Queen's 'particular ghilley',
whose influence at court unsettled the household.*

RIGHT: *Rare photograph of the Queen and royal family with members of the household at Balmoral on 25 May 1868. Howard is standing second from left on the terrace.*

Watercolour of Deeside painted by Howard Elphinstone while staying at Balmoral c.1860.

The Marriage of the Prince of Wales,
*oil painting by William Powell Frith completed
in 1864. Howard escorted Leopold and Arthur
to two sittings at the artist's studio, ensuring his
own inclusion in the finished work (see detail).*

Arthur and Leopold posing in the grounds at Balmoral in about 1867 with their German tutor Herr Sahl (second from left) and Leo's kindly governor the Reverend Robinson Duckworth (second from right).

suggested that the Queen had secretly married John Brown; another that she had borne his child. Both claims would have provoked complaints, and possibly legal action, if published in the British papers, which preferred instead to rely on wit and innuendo. Similar titillating speculation now dominated the after-dinner discussion in the equerries' room at the palace. Edgar Boehm, an artist summoned to court in 1867 to prepare a bust of John Brown, revealed that 'it was the talk of all the Household that he was "the Queen's stallion"'.[30] Such rumours inevitably flourished in the vacuum left by Victoria's self-imposed exile. Yet they should be treated with great caution, fed as they were by jealousy, snobbery and resentment at Brown's high-handed approach towards the household. Perhaps only the Queen's dressers were in a position to know the truth, and they said nothing. The gossips also misunderstood the Queen's lifelong need for attachment to a strong male presence, a role denied to her in childhood by the early death of her father but successively occupied since by Albert, Ruland, Löhlein and now John Brown. In reality, betraying her husband's memory in any physical sense would have revolted her.

Elphinstone liked Stirling and tried to save the governor's position by proposing that he become an equerry to Prince Arthur. The Queen dismissed such a suggestion out of hand, citing Stirling's 'peculiarities'. Fearing the loucher elements of the army, she wanted to prevent Arthur becoming intimate with any officer 'belonging to a corps connected with *much* riding' (Stirling was in the artillery), and besides 'it would *not* be fair to Lieutenant Stirling himself and a SECOND failure would be very painful'. The real reason for her opposition to the idea was Stirling's hostility towards the Highlanders. Setting out the grounds for her objection, Victoria made a remark to Elphinstone suggestive of that intimacy and understanding which had existed between them since the death of the Prince Consort. 'Having suffered so *severely* in the Prince of Wales' case from notions of *so-called "manliness"* (*falsely called*) being *forced* into him,' she wrote,

[she] feels it a *duty* to *herself* and to Arthur (who has no father to watch and counteract any of those effects which unfortunately *are* English ones as Major Elphinstone *himself* knows) not to make a *trial* even, when there is *something* in a person which does *not* inspire the Queen with *that* confidence or rather more with *that* feeling of *sympathy* which would make her *wish* him to be much with our son.[31]

Sir John Cowell was given the unpleasant task of sacking Stirling, his own standing with the Queen having fallen dramatically since his promotion to Master of the Household. Elphinstone, meanwhile, was ordered to break the news to Arthur 'in the right way'.[32] Relieved that she had avoided a painful dispute which might have brought the Highlanders into further disrepute, the Queen reported that Stirling 'wisely intends to *accept* the *only* ostensible (and very painful) reason for his departure viz: Prince Leopold's health'.[33] Anxious to cover up the real reason for his dismissal, she asked Elphinstone whether he thought Stirling could be trusted not to gossip about his short career at the palace. Howard assured her that he considered Stirling to be entirely trustworthy. A month later, he revealed that he had seen the former governor twice since his departure and on neither occasion had the Browns even been mentioned. 'Mr Stirling has evidently taken the advise [*sic*] given him, and has found it to be to his own advantage if he remains perfectly silent,' he reported.[34] That 'advantage' included a comfortable sinecure at court as an 'extra groom' – essentially a backhander from the Queen to prevent Stirling 'trying to throw blame on that excellent, devoted and trustworthy young man Archie B'.[35]

Walter Stirling's unceremonious sacking, for speaking his mind and resisting the Highlanders, deeply unsettled the court. The Queen had backed the word of a servant against that of an officer, challenging the accepted order of things. Everyone now dreaded going to Balmoral, where the influence of the Highlanders was felt most keenly. Visiting the castle a year after

Stirling's dismissal, Arthur complained about the 'constant squalls and squabbles which give rise to a great deal of bad feeling and jealousy'.[36] But the problem would not go away while the Highlanders enjoyed the Queen's confidence. When he was older and more self-assured, Prince Arthur, like his brothers and sisters, began cutting Brown, refusing even to acknowledge him when they met. Arriving at the castle in September 1874, for instance, his mother noticed, to her fury, how Arthur had shaken 'hands with ALL the highland keepers and *not* with *Brown*, who was standing by and who *ranks far higher* than them . . . [as] he is the Queen's constant attendant *every where* and one whose *extreme devotion* and faithfulness and confidential position . . . entitle him to at LEAST the *same* consideration as others!'[37]

Ten years after John Brown's first introduction to the English court, Victoria was still beseeching Elphinstone to persuade her children of the superior qualities of her Scottish servants, as compared to her effete English household. 'They are independent and free . . . [and] have a higher sense of *real* respect and of what is gentlemanlike than the most over polished and cringing Englishman' – here Victoria paused, and, as an afterthought, replaced 'man' with 'servant'. 'But', she continued in the same vein, 'young men and especially officers don't always understand and appreciate this and sometimes carry into private life the tone they *must* often employ to the soldiers under them, which is not right or liked!'[38] When her anger had cooled a little, the Queen wrote to Howard again to clarify her 'little hint' regarding her sons' treatment of her servants. This, she now emphasized, '*only applied* to Brown and the Keepers, *not* to *lower people*'.[39]

Howard sympathized with Stirling, and the officer remained a welcome guest at Ranger's House. But Stirling had lacked the blessing of the Prince Consort, an essential component for a successful career at court, regardless of ability. Leopold was devastated at losing his governor, dreading retribution from his 'dreadful scotch servants' for having taken Stirling's side in their disputes.[40] His fears were not misplaced. John Legg, the

Prince Leopold and his beloved dog Waldi, who was banished outdoors by Archie Brown.

fresh-faced young doctor appointed by Jenner to act as the prince's medical attendant, was unable, or unwilling, to protect him from the Highlanders. When Leo's staunchest ally, his equerry Colonel Du Plat, was then spitefully redeployed within the household as a punishment for defending Stirling, the prince was left almost entirely defenceless. The Queen tried to justify Du Plat's move by telling Elphinstone that the colonel's '*style* and manner were what the beloved Prince did not like'.[41] In fact, Du Plat was probably demoted on the say-so of John Brown. Now firmly back in control, the Browns and Robertson stepped up their malicious campaign against Leo, acting far beyond their authority. Within weeks the prince complained that he was being 'scolded from morning till night'. He was kept apart from the other children while even his dog, his constant companion, was banished out of doors 'because Brown does not like him'.[42] In December 1866 his sister Louise glimpsed the depth of her brother's despair. 'Loosy,' he cried, 'I don't know what would happen to me if you ever went away. All would be over for me then.'[43] His mother's misguided love was killing him as surely as the haemophilia which drained his blood.

PART THREE

Around
the World

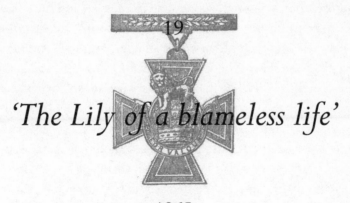

19

'The Lily of a blameless life'

1865

BEFORE THE PREPARATIONS for Arthur's entrance examination for the Royal Military Academy began in earnest, Elphinstone took the prince away for a cruise in the Mediterranean. Robert Bruce had done the same with Bertie in 1862, although the fever he had collected on that trip had cost the general his life. On 27 March 1865, before sailing for the continent, Howard was summoned to dine with the Queen at Windsor (forcing him to cancel an engagement with Charles Gordon at their club, the United Services in Pall Mall). By now, the major had dined with Victoria countless times, yet the occasion still apparently made him nervous. Afterwards he noted: 'I only gentleman, rather afraid, but everything went charmingly.' Victoria had been 'so nice and cheerful' that 'I really enjoyed this dinner' – a suggestion that they usually made him feel uncomfortable and awkward.

'I hope that you will take care of yourself,' Victoria said as they parted the next morning on the steps of the castle, 'and not overwork yourself. Goodbye Major Elphinstone.'[1]

Three days later, a damp tour of Paris concluded at the Tuileries where the prince and his governor were formally greeted by Emperor Napoleon III and Empress Eugénie. Howard had met the French Emperor once before, when he visited Paris to receive his *Légion d'honneur* in 1857. Then he had marvelled at the grandiose improvements being made to the city, and the splendour of the Second Empire. Stripped of all the pomp and ceremony of that day, he found Napoleon 'most affable'; although Arthur whispered that the Emperor had grown fat since his state visit to England in 1855.[2] The British visitors were received at the palace door by the Prince Imperial, eleven-year-old Louis Napoleon. 'A delicate child,' Howard informed the Queen, '[with] fair skin without a particle of colour, dark hair, resembling in features neither his father nor mother. He is very small for his age, but has a very intelligent pleasing face, a face that would gain upon one, for it has a sweet expression.'[3] In fact, in many ways, Louis looked like Arthur.

But the two young princes had more in common than simply a passing physical resemblance. For instance, they shared a passion for the military which was fitting for the godson of the Duke of Wellington and the great-nephew of Napoleon Bonaparte. And Louis, like Arthur, had his own military governor, the formidable General Frossard of whom it was said that he 'had that military air from which it was impossible not to recognise the officer in mufti . . . Everything in his speech, in his look, in his gesture, breathed authority; everything savoured of the Governor.'[4] Although Louis's daily routine was similar to Arthur's – long hours of study interspersed with chaperoned walks – the unpopularity of his father's regime made excursions further afield than the palace grounds too dangerous for the French prince. As he was also an only child with few friends to play with, Elphinstone thought him 'very shy [and] evidently too much by himself'.[5] But he did not know that, compelled to entertain himself for hours on end, Louis had developed a distinctly daredevil streak, courting danger 'willingly and deliberately' in the words of his horrified tutor.[6]

On his last trip to Paris, Howard had stayed in a cramped room at L'Hôtel des Deux Mondes, dining for less than three francs a night and going to the vaudeville theatre. Now he was lodged amid the elegant surroundings of the British Embassy as a guest of the ambassador Lord Cowley and his '*most* charming' wife Olivia.[7] Before dinner, the Prince Imperial made an unexpected appearance to exchange photographs with Arthur, a courtly ritual which the boys had copied from their parents. They then stood in the hallway discussing military matters under the watchful gaze of their respective governors. There was no time to make a better acquaintance, as early the following morning Arthur and the major continued by train to Marseilles, where they embarked in *Enchantress*, a comfortably sized steam yacht requisitioned from the Admiralty for their cruise. For the next ten weeks, they toured the Mediterranean clutching their history books and sketchpads. After calling at Naples, Tunis and Malta they reached Palestine and the Holy Land, the spiritual climax and overall purpose of the expedition. Following a route carefully mapped out for them by Dean Stanley, they bathed in the river Jordan, peered down Jacob's well and climbed the Mount of Olives: all essential elements of the biblical experience enjoyed by the many English tourists who flocked to the region.

From Palestine they continued to Greece, clambering over the ruins of Ephesus, Troy, Parnassus and Thermopylae to collect fragments of antiquities for the museum at Osborne House. At Gallipoli they gazed at the lines which the Royal Engineers had constructed in 1854 to protect the Dardanelles at the outset of the Crimean War. The major noted, with regret, that barely ten years on they were 'much injured and no longer serviceable as a means of defence'.[8] Every evening throughout the tour, regardless of the weather or his own often indifferent health, Howard wrote up a journal for the Queen, sending it back to Windsor in instalments. Victoria found his account 'so interesting' and 'so *beautifully* written' that she had copies made for distribution among her other children and 'our intelligent servants' – presumably the Highlanders – who, she insisted, 'take fully *as much* interest if not more as *higher* people in such things'.[9] Finally, on 14 May, *Enchantress* moored off Venice, where Arthur and the major disembarked to return home by rail. Behind them trailed trunkloads of souvenirs and folios packed with their drawings and watercolour paintings.

Back in England, Howard received news from the continent that his father's health was failing. During the summer Amelia Elphinstone brought the captain back to Livonia Cottage, where he died 'quite peacefully and quietly' on 26 September, aged seventy-six.[10] 'We were all prepared for it,' wrote Howard, who had hurried down to Devon just in time. He told the Queen that his mother had 'borne this trial with a calmness and fortitude which alone can be derived by looking to a higher source'.[11] He revealed little of his own feelings, yet he plainly took his father's loss badly. Just months before his own death, Charles Phipps spoke of Howard's 'heavy affliction' in a letter to the Queen: 'it is very touching to see how this devoted servant, in the midst of his sorrow, seems to think chiefly of his duty to Your Majesty'.[12]

Born in the year of the French Revolution, Alexander Elphinstone had fought through the Napoleonic Wars, wrung pensions and titles from the Russian government, and seen his sons embark on successful careers in the East India Company, the military and latterly at court. After a life spent pursuing his own dreams by land and by sea, this difficult, impassioned man was finally laid to rest in a quiet English country churchyard, beside his beloved daughter Rosalie. Alexander died a Russian noble, but he had failed in his long-nurtured ambition to be recognized as the seventh Lord Balmerino. Indeed, within a year of his death the Elphinstones quietly dropped their claim to the Scottish title, exhausted by its complexity and crippling expense. They were also embarrassed by a damaging row with their rival Lord Elphinstone caused by the unfortunate publication in 1862, at Howard's instigation, of their assertions in Lodge's Peerage. In his final letter to Lord Elphinstone on his family's claim, Howard defiantly declared that 'the data we have are sufficient to establish it morally, although insufficient to prove it legally'.[13] Only Howard's elder brother Nicolai still persisted in the matter, now seeking to be recognized as heir to another abeyant Elphinstone baronetcy. Eventually Nicolai simply assumed the title, launching several more decades of costly litigation for his descendants.

The death of his father and the collapse of the Balmerino case prompted Howard to press harder for promotion in the army. His fear that by taking a position at court he would hamper his military career had been realized. After trawling through the records of other engineers and artillery officers he noted with dismay that 'no less than 22 officers, all my juniors as captains have been made senior to me in the army'.[14] He could find only one other officer who had suffered such a slow progress through the ranks, and that was John Cowell. He also discovered that not one of the artillery officers on his list had been mentioned in dispatches, let alone decorated for gallantry, during the Crimean War, whereas his own record was unsurpassed. Furious at being so overlooked, Howard sought Charles Grey's help in drafting a strongly worded appeal to the War Office. When this failed to work, he personally lobbied the Duke of Cambridge, who was the commander-in-chief of the army and a cousin of the Queen. Within months a correction was issued. In August 1867 his promotion to major was backdated from January 1859 to December 1856, redressing the balance and enhancing his pay, pension and prospects for future promotion.

Prince Arthur's confirmation on 26 April 1866, shortly before his sixteenth birthday, was a significant milestone in his life, as it was for all the royal children. 'You are *now* responsible to God,' his mother lectured him:

> remember that Life is a hard battle, and that we must always be on
> our guard: ever be watchful, and ever honest, truthful, coura-
> geous, and *loving to* ALL as adored Papa was. You have a great
> position to maintain, as the son of such a Father, and the Godson
> of so Great a man, both of whom had an unflinching sense of duty.
> To be without a Father, and *such* a Father – is a misfortune which
> you will feel more and more the older you grow; But you have a
> Mother who loves you tenderly, dearly . . . You have also the bless-
> ing of having a kind, true and wise friend in Major. You never can
> repay all you owe to him![15]

To mark his symbolic transition from childhood to adulthood, Arthur was allowed to discard his detested kilt for the ceremony at Whippingham Church on the Isle of Wight, wearing instead a black tailcoat and top hat for the first time. Writing to Howard after the service, Victoria thanked him for being 'a *father* to our fatherless precious boy . . . Major Elphinstone has more than anyone, she knows, understood *her* and her beloved husband's *views* respecting boys and young men.' She finished her letter by misquoting a line from Lord Tennyson: citing the Poet Laureate's dedication of his Arthurian epic *The Idylls of the King* to the Prince Consort, the Queen prayed 'that our dear boy may ever wear "The Lily of a blameless life" '.[16] To steer Arthur towards this lofty ideal the Queen proceeded to bombard her son, by means of Elphinstone, with a series of grave warnings about the perils of smoking; racing; polo; hunting; sailing; walking around with his hands in his pockets (or even having pockets); and his affectation of saying 'what!' 'This,' his mother cautioned sternly, 'in the first place [is] not civil, and is besides to be guarded against as being a defect in the old Royal Family.'[17]

The prince's confirmation had been a happy family occasion which had ended with a lavish tea on the croquet lawn at Osborne. But the day was overshadowed by the threat of war between Austria and Prussia. Such a conflict would again cast members of the Queen's family against one another as Princess Alice's husband Prince Ludwig of Hesse and by Rhine was an ally of Austria, while his brother Henry was serving in the Prussian army beside Vicky's husband Fritz. 'Things look very bad,' Louise told Arthur on 10 May; 'fancy how dreadful one brother fighting against the other. Alice is in a dreadful state.'[18] Alice and Vicky both rallied behind their husbands, setting up field hospitals in Darmstadt and Berlin. But the conflict, essentially a struggle for control of the German states engineered by Bismarck, placed a great strain on the royal family. Elphinstone regretted the 'sad, antagonistic attitude of so many of Your Majesty's relations'.[19] Yet he took a keen professional interest in the progress of the war, unrolling maps of Europe at

Ranger's House to show Arthur the ebb and flow of the opposing armies. By carefully plotting troop movements in this way, he even correctly predicted the decisive battle of Königgrätz, near the Bohemian town of Sadowa, on 3 July 1866 – but not its result. In anticipating victory for the numerically superior Austrian force, he had forgotten his conversation with Fritz at Windsor in 1859, when the prince had patiently explained to him the advantages of the Prussians' revolutionary breech-loading rifle over the out-dated musket. The difference proved decisive at Königgrätz, and under Fritz's personal leadership the Prussians scored a crushing victory, though at an appalling cost. Colonel Walker, the British military attaché in Berlin and veteran of the Crimean War, claimed he had never witnessed such a ferocious fire-fight. 'In fact a great artillery duel, with interludes of infantry storming villages and cavalry fights in the open . . . sad work at best this trade of ours,' he wrote later.[20] By nightfall, almost ten thousand Prussians had been killed or wounded while the Austrians suffered casualties twice as high.

Although distracted by Helena's marriage to Prince Christian – which took place in St George's Chapel just two days after the battle – the royal family were nevertheless shocked by the carnage and alarmed at the Prussian aggression which had caused it. The Queen loyally congratulated Vicky on Fritz's victory but she bitterly regretted that it had been achieved 'against brother Germans'.[21] Howard, who had experienced the horrors of war at first hand, deplored 'the shedding of so much innocent blood, the wanton destruction of the homes of thousands of poor and starv-ing, for the sole purpose of establishing the most unscrupulous principles'.[22] His comments prompted Princess Alice, who was devastated by the great loss of life and the humiliation of her hus-band, to exclaim to him that only 'those who have seen [it] nearby know *what* war is!'[23]

In the autumn, the search began for a young officer to act as Arthur's companion when he entered the Royal Military Academy at Woolwich. 'The duties of this officer do not, of necessity, oblige him to be constantly with the Prince,' his governor hastily assured the Queen, knowing of her aversion to a certain breed of officer,

> or even to speak to him often in a familiar way, yet if this officer be one in whom *thorough* confidence can be placed . . . then his closer intimacy with Prince Arthur might be of immense advantage to the latter, who would feel far more inclined to follow intuitively the manner etc, etc, of one so much moreover his own age, than all the precepts and advice that Major Elphinstone could possibly give.[24]

It was the clearest signal yet that Howard felt his own position beside the prince drawing to an inevitable and natural end.

Several candidates for the post were summarily rejected by Victoria after being compared to the unfortunate Walter Stirling before Sir John Cowell mentioned the name of Arthur Pickard, a 25-year-old lieutenant in the Royal Artillery. In early November 1866 Elphinstone was sent to meet Pickard at Shoeburyness, the Royal Artillery's firing range near Gravesend. He was introduced to a tall, angular young man with light hair and a pale, freckled face. 'One cannot say good looking but pleasing,' reported Elphinstone, 'very quiet and gentlemanly, decidedly intelligent and active minded but rather silent and serious. He does not draw, nor is he musical, but is fond of all kinds of games, etc.' Pickard's serious demeanour was of some concern, as Howard feared 'there may be some doubt how far such a temperament would agree with Prince Arthur's bright merry nature'. But he came from 'an old family' and 'morally he bears the highest possible character'.[25] Pickard had also won a Victoria Cross fighting the Maoris in New Zealand, placing him in that elite band of men who so fascinated and entranced the Queen. As instructed, Elphinstone dispatched a photograph of Pickard to Windsor, although he warned 'that it is a flattering one'.[26] Happily it passed the close scrutiny of the Queen, who approved the lieutenant's appointment as her son's first equerry. Pickard would remain in this post until his early death from tuberculosis in 1880.

Lieutenant Arthur Pickard, whose Victoria Cross was recommendation enough for the post of equerry to Prince Arthur.

Arthur's entrance examination to the Royal Military Academy took place over six days in January 1867. Unlike the other candidates, who were all tested at Woolwich, the prince was examined in private at the offices of the Council of Military Education in Whitehall. Moreover, to prevent any unseemly comparison, his papers were different from those sat by the other boys, a decision which prompted accusations in the press of favouritism. Despite such privileged conditions, Elphinstone complained that the bitter cold, the 'London fog which pervaded the room' and the noise of the traffic in the streets below all combined to distract the prince.[27]

Naturally Arthur's place at the academy was assured, unlike the other one hundred and thirty candidates, who had to fight over the forty available places. Nevertheless, according to Elphinstone (for the results were never released), the prince performed with merit in his test, comfortably achieving his nominal pass mark. In a letter to the author Charles Kingsley, who had once taught the Prince of Wales and retained a close interest in the education of the royal children, Howard declared that although the result was 'excellent, I look upon it altogether as [of] minor importance. The mental as well as moral training through which the Prince has gone, in order to prepare him for so difficult an examination, and that without the advantages of emulation, competition with others etc, which forms the great incentive to action, this to my mind is of far greater importance.'[28]

Elphinstone gave the much-maligned William Jolley the 'highest possible credit' for the result, 'considering the difficulties there have been to contend with in the Prince's tuition: from his frequent change of residence, the excitement consequent upon his peculiar position, [and] the deference always shown to him by others'.[29] But the tutor was studiously ignored amid the flurry of royal congratulations which greeted news of Arthur's success, as he had recently disgraced himself at Balmoral by refusing to dine with Leo's new medical attendant. 'For Mr Jolley to pretend that he IS too good to dine with Mr Legg who *frequently* dines with the

Household is *too* much,' the Queen had stormed. 'He is *not* acting like a gentleman or a clergyman ought to do.'[30] The row highlighted the tension which existed between those inside the elite household – such as the equerries, grooms and ladies in waiting – and those marooned outside, such as the tutors, doctors and librarians. 'The whole affair is so strange and uncalled for,' despaired Princess Helena in a letter to Howard, 'and I fear Mr Jolly [*sic*] will find he has got himself in great dilemma through his want of good sense and proper feeling.'[31] Jolley's offer to resign went unheeded.

Like the rest of her family, therefore, Vicky insisted that her brother's success, the first by any English prince in a public exam, was entirely due to his governor, not to the man who had taught him. 'This success is your merit,' she pronounced; 'your care and perseverance in carrying through wise and judicious plans has led to this happy result. I feel proud and happy, and grateful to *you*.'[32] The Crown Princess of Prussia only wished that she had found an equally sympathetic mentor for her ill-disciplined son Wilhelm. Vicky told Arthur that she often wished she had Elphinstone in Berlin 'now that Willie's education has begun in earnest'.[33] In Darmstadt, Princess Alice likewise paid tribute to the 'good Major, who has spared no pains'.[34] Unsurprisingly, the most fulsome praise came from Windsor, where Victoria declared that she '*never, never can* thank Major Elphinstone *enough* for his kind, devoted and judicious care of our darling Arthur. But her gratitude *is* deep and lasting.'[35]

The prince entered the academy on 11 February 1867, exchanging his tailcoat for the simple blue uniform of a 'gentleman cadet'. At his medical it was noted that he was small for his age at entry, under five feet six and only eight stone (although, as Louisa Bowater observed, Arthur was already nearly as tall as his diminutive governor).[36] Ahead of the prince's much-vaunted arrival, Elphinstone had met the lieutenant-governor of the academy to discuss the special provisions which would be required during Arthur's year-long course. It had been agreed, for instance, that Arthur would return to Ranger's House each evening after his classes. He would also be given his own room at the academy where he could study, change his clothes and eat in private (to enable him to drink wine sent from Windsor with his meals rather than the beer given to the other cadets). Pickard would be posted outside the room at all times to guard the prince against unwelcome visitors.

Conditions at the academy were substantially better than they had been in Howard's day, the consequence of reforms triggered by the cadet riots he had witnessed in the 1840s. The introduction of organized games, such as rugby, had substantially reduced the bullying, while rigorously enforced church parade had raised the moral tone. The cadets also came from a broader range of family backgrounds than before: 'some decidedly vulgar', in Elphinstone's opinion. With Pickard's help, he therefore made every effort to keep the prince apart from his fellow cadets, to preserve his royal rank and the dignity of his position. Protecting Arthur's 'purity and innocence of mind' among so many teenage boys was far more demanding and required great 'care and judgement'.[37]

Despite his isolation, the prince's lofty status ensured he became 'the universal favourite . . . even from those who in thoughts and words are ultra democrats'.[38] It was difficult for Arthur to form close personal friendships at the academy, given the conditions of his entry. But two names stand out among his fellow cadets; names the prince would encounter frequently in later life. One was Arthur Bigge, later Lord Stamfordham, a future private secretary to the Queen and, subsequently, to King George V. The other was Herbert Kitchener, later a field marshal and the talismanic icon of empire, whom Arthur recalled as 'a tall lanky young man, very quiet and amusing.'[39] (Elphinstone, who later commanded Kitchener at Aldershot, found him 'a most zealous and promising officer'.[40]) Kitchener and Bigge were among the handful of privileged students who received invitations to dinner at Ranger's House, both departing starry-eyed at the lavish lifestyle of their royal classmate.

Prince Arthur followed his governor into the Royal Military Academy as a gentleman cadet.

But the prince's popularity soon spread beyond the other cadets and the confines of the academy. At the end-of-term ball in June, several girls 'accidentally' dropped their cards and pocket handkerchiefs near him, in the hope of an introduction. For the first time, the spectre of sex appeared in the young prince's life. Educating her children in the facts of life was a subject 'full of difficulty' for the Queen, as she admitted to Elphinstone – even though after bearing nine children she was far better qualified to do so than he was. No prude in her youth, Victoria became unusually reticent when the subject loomed up. She felt 'very anxious' to talk to him about it, she confessed, 'yet she somehow *could* not'.[41] For months she skirted around the issue, unsure 'whether Prince Arthur's *eyes are open*, or partially so, [and] to what alas!'

With no husband to advise her, the Queen agonized over whether it was better

> to *open* young boys eyes or not. Whether in either case you do not
> run the *risk* of doing more harm than good. If ignorance were
> *capable* of being *long maintained* then *that* would be best; and the
> Queen would cling to it; on the *other hand* you run the risk of his
> eyes being opened by unhallowed lips [and] by coarse jokes.

Unable to decide what to do, the Queen did nothing. Instead she left the matter entirely to Arthur's governor, enigmatically referring him to '*those* confidential letters' found among the Prince Consort's papers, presumably letters of instruction on the facts of life composed by Albert before his death.[42]

There were few reliable texts to which Howard could turn. Sex education in the 1860s was generally confused and contradictory, if not downright barmy. The extreme prudery of much of the literature contrasted with the blatancy with which hordes of prostitutes openly plied their trade on the streets of London. On one sensitive subject, however, there was almost universal agreement within the medical profession: masturbation was seen not only as debilitating and probably physically harmful to boys but also as a serious dereliction of manhood. It seems likely, therefore, that Arthur was sternly lectured by his governor on its perils. The success, or otherwise, of the approach taken by Elphinstone in this sensitive area can only be gauged by Arthur's later sexual behaviour, which by and large was moderate and well disciplined; certainly when compared to the excesses of his elder brothers. Or perhaps he was simply more discreet.

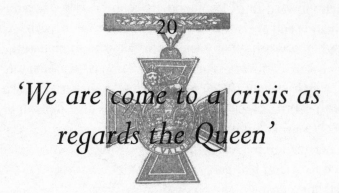

20

'We are come to a crisis as regards the Queen'

1867

FOR THE ACADEMY'S SUMMER vacation in 1867, Arthur and Elphinstone returned to Paris to attend the opening of the *Exposition Universelle*, Napoleon III's attempt to rival London's Great Exhibition of 1851. The city was jammed with royalty. Most of the crowned heads of Europe were attending, from King Wilhelm I of Prussia, King Leopold II of Belgium and the Emperor of Austria to the Tsar of Russia (who was shot at while driving in the Bois de Boulogne). Of Arthur's own family, Vicky, Alice and Affie had already made the trip, while Bertie would soon follow. They all came to celebrate the glories of the Second Empire, studiously ignoring the many cracks which were already appearing in its glittering edifice. Henry Cole, the architect who had worked with Prince Albert on the Great Exhibition, personally escorted the prince and the major around the packed exhibition halls, explaining everything to them 'in a very amusing manner'.[1] At the Pasha of Egypt's stand they bumped into the Empress Eugénie and the Prince Imperial who 'does not appear to have grown much since 1865'.[2] Arthur flatly refused to try 'a few whiffs at the Turkish Pipe', although Louis was forced to by his mother.[3]

After an inspection of the military camp at Châlons, a hurried tour of some castles and a trip to see the Bayeux Tapestry (which Howard thought 'one of the most extraordinary sights in Normandy and perhaps anywhere so far as English people are concerned'[4]), it was back to Windsor in time for the visit of the Sultan Abd-el-Aziz of Turkey. The Sultan was seen as a vital ally in the cold war to prevent Russian domination in the east, so his visit was planned as the most lavish state occasion in England since the Prince Consort's death. Even the Queen was encouraging. She gave permission for her band to play for the first time since 1861; agreed to attend a military review in Hyde Park; and promised to invest her guest in person with the Order of the Garter (the insignia for which had to be hastily borrowed from Arthur). These few actions were seized upon by her people and government as confirmation that the Queen was finally emerging from her long isolation. Victoria herself admitted that her husband's memory was fading at last. 'It seems so dreadful to feel *how* time takes you farther and farther away from that happy time and how difficult it is to *realise even how one* felt formerly!' she guiltily confessed to Howard. 'The *blessed* influence is felt and the thoughts are constantly recurring to *what* he would admire and be interested in *but* the present sad, altered life becomes a reality and that is what is often *very trying* to the *Queen*.'[5]

Victoria's apparent change of heart came not a moment too soon. Only days before the Sultan's arrival, Charles Grey warned the Prime Minister Lord Derby that 'we are come to a crisis as regards the Queen'.[6] Resentment at Victoria's long isolation had merged with the stories about John Brown to produce a potentially explosive situation. Grey had heard rumours that a crowd were 'getting up to hoot J.B. if he should appear on the box of the Queen's carriage at the Review in Hyde Park'. Derby calmly suggested that, with the help of a strategically placed bottle of whisky, the Highlander might be encouraged to suffer '*some slight ailment*' beforehand.[7] In the event, the problem did not arise, for the review was cancelled when reports reached England that the Emperor of Mexico, a cousin of the Queen by marriage, had been executed by rebels. The shocking news plunged Victoria straight back into deepest mourning. She may have briefly reached out to her people, but she was still not ready to rule.

The Queen had first broached the idea of a prolonged holiday overseas to recover her zest for life two years before. But at the time she had still been bound to her husband's memory, and when the Austro-Prussian War then broke out the plan was quietly abandoned. No such obstacle existed now; so, after the Sultan had gone, she quietly asked Elphinstone to find 'a nice place for me to go to'.[8] She longed to be away from her realm, her ministers and her people. Any doubts about the wisdom of such a move in the current political climate were swept aside when Dr Jenner assured the Queen that such a trip would be good for her health. A number of destinations for the proposed holiday were discussed and dismissed as either too hot or too remote, before the Queen settled – perhaps inevitably, considering the country's ties to Albert – on Switzerland. In the autumn of 1867 Elphinstone was instructed to go out there 'to find a *quiet* spot in true mountain scenery with fine, *bracing* air!' Victoria's vision of a quiet holiday, however, was rather different from that of most other people. 'She would put up with a *few small* houses,' she decided, 'supposing *only* she and her children, maids and two or three men servants lived *in one*, the ladies and gentlemen in another and so on; that would do *perfectly* well, indeed she would *like* THAT *best*.'[9]

But Elphinstone's reconnaissance trip was forgotten when Arthur fell dangerously ill with smallpox at Ranger's House. The illness reached a crisis on 9 October, when Howard counted thirty boils on the face of the stricken prince, who 'showed a slight symptom of wandering in his mind' – an alarming echo of the last hours of the Prince Consort.[10] As in December 1861, the court circulars steadfastly refused to acknowledge the gravity of the illness, dismissing the prince's condition as no more than a 'mild attack of modified chicken pox'.[11] Dr Jenner, who remained in Scotland with the Queen throughout the emergency, was also typically reassuring. But the situation was grave. 'God grant that the dear boy may get over it,' exclaimed Alice in Darmstadt after reading Howard's more candid report to her, 'and that his dear handsome face be not marked!'[12] Against royal protocol, the major summoned a female nurse to sit with Arthur, while he took turns with Pickard to read aloud to the prince (the governor read in German from Schiller; the equerry in English from an 'expunged' edition of Shakespeare's plays). All the letters Arthur wrote to his mother were 'literally toasted before the fire' before leaving for Balmoral to avoid the spread of infection.[13] Eventually, nothing more elaborate than a diet of rest, beef tea and claret pulled the prince around. In early November, after leaving orders to fumigate and entirely redecorate Ranger's House to prevent reinfection, Elphinstone at last sped to the continent to find a property for the Queen.

But it was not easy meeting Victoria's exacting standards. The need for secrecy meant Howard had to act incognito, making it more difficult for him to gain access to potential royal holiday homes. He returned with nothing more concrete than the radical suggestion that the Queen take rooms in a *pension*. Fortunately the holiday itself was delayed when Victoria became beset by political trouble at home. A bitter and divisive argument over the right of the Anglican Church to collect tithes from the impoverished Catholic population in Ireland had cast damaging new light on the Queen's exile from her constitutional duties, which included her position as Defender of the Faith. William Gladstone tried to defuse the political row by sponsoring a bill – bitterly opposed by the Queen – to disestablish the church in Ireland, while Victoria tried to deflect the personal criticism of herself by publishing an account of her family's holidays in Scotland, which she entitled *Leaves from the Journal of Our Life in the Highlands*. The aristocracy sneered at the Queen's modest literary endeavours and her children feared the outcome of publication. But the book proved a marketing masterstroke for the monarchy. It became an instant bestseller and produced – as Elphinstone had almost alone predicted when the idea was mooted – 'a most beneficial effect throughout all classes'.[14] Unfortunately, the book also stirred up fresh interest in the Queen's peculiar relationship with John Brown, whose brooding presence stalked through its pages, and a fresh crop of titillating stories appeared in the papers.

Charles Grey, who was still struggling to cope with the Scottish genie he had unwittingly uncorked, saw the gossip as a symptom of a more intractable problem. 'If the seclusion is persisted, as it *will* be,' he told the Home Secretary forcefully, 'unless some body can speak to the Queen with *authority*, and really sense her *fears* as to the consequences, it is impossible to foresee how the discontent will find expression . . . Every hour added to the period of her seclusion increases the danger. I cannot see my way. *No one* here can speak with the slightest chance of being listened to.'[15] Grey had tried countless times to tackle the problem himself, but had only undermined his own position, forcing a terminal breach in his relationship with the Queen. Elphinstone was as well placed as the secretary, but more cautious and tactful. As late as 1872, the Queen was still rebuking Arthur for raising the matter. 'She is distressed to see him harping upon *the old story* of *her* appearing MORE!!' the Queen raged at Howard afterwards.[16] 'Prince Arthur penned his letter with the kindest possible intentions,' Elphinstone soothingly replied; 'any expressions or sentiments he used about Your Majesty "*doing more*" were simply the result of his newspaper readings.'[17] Arthur had been spurred into action after hearing 'disagreeable things' said about his mother in front of him at his club.[18] He could not know that such comments were more typical of the gentlemen's clubs he patronized than the public houses frequented by the majority of his mother's subjects, where affection for the Queen was more resilient – as the sales of her book proved.

Unknown to her critics, against the backdrop of the constitutional crisis a very private tragedy was unfolding at the heart of the Queen's family. Leopold's bleeding attacks began again in earnest in 1867, draining the last of his mother's shattered spirits as surely they did his young veins. The prince had sunk into a depression after the dismissal of Walter Stirling, seeking solace in reading and collecting the autographs of the famous people who came to the palace. A crumb of comfort had come with the appointment of the Reverend Robinson Duckworth as his new tutor in June 1866. Duckworth was recommended to court by Henry Liddell, the Dean of Christ Church, Oxford. He was also a good friend of Charles Dodgson – better known as the author Lewis Carroll – whose affectionate homage to Liddell's daughter entitled *Alice's Adventures in Wonderland* had been a runaway success the year before.* Duckworth was a gentle, sympathetic man who encouraged Leopold's literary interests and shielded him from the frequent rows which rocked the palace. When Leo's medical attendant John Legg abruptly left the palace in July 1867, Duckworth was promoted governor, his liberal outlook overcoming the Queen's reservations about appointing a clergyman to such a position.

Early in the New Year of 1868, Elphinstone and Arthur attended a shooting party at Knowsley, the Cheshire seat of the Prime Minister Lord Derby, causing mild rumblings in the press about royal bias towards the ruling Conservatives. On 19 January Arthur rejoined his family on the Isle of Wight, where they had spent Christmas as usual, while Elphinstone returned to Greenwich to arrange matters before the prince resumed his military studies at the academy. A week later, after a happy evening playing charades at Osborne House, Leopold anxiously confided to Arthur that 'he felt something sticky in his drawers and on opening them he found several drops of blood'. Calling for Duckworth, Arthur helped his brother into bed, while the doctors were urgently summoned from the mainland. 'He was incessantly vomiting,' a badly shaken Arthur wrote to Elphinstone in the morning,

> and some milk he had taken with his arrowroot that evening for supper came out in the shape of cheeses and he went several times

---

* Dodgson portrayed Duckworth as the Duck in the Pool of Tears.

during the night to the stool, but all that passed out of him were streams of blood . . . It is fearful to see him, he looks like a corpse already, his face is ashy pale, and his eyes are so sunken. His mind has wandered occasionally but not for any length of time.

Even the normally ebullient William Jenner feared for Leo's life. Arthur overheard the doctor admitting that 'if the bleeding should commence again with as *much violence* as yesterday there is no hope for him'.[19] For a few dreadful minutes, Jenner could find no pulse at all, the words already forming in his mind as to what to tell the Queen. Arthur stayed at his brother's side throughout the crisis, making drinks, holding bowls for him to vomit into, and arranging his bedding. Soon he was so exhausted that he became ill himself, sleeping fitfully in the room next door while Jenner tended Leopold. Slowly things improved. By 31 January, Leo could keep down some beef tea, though he still vomited when given milk. The next day there was a significant improvement. 'I believe that we may consider him out of danger,' Arthur told Elphinstone. 'He still suffers a good deal from the griping pains in his bowels but that one must expect for he *must* get rid of all the bad blood that still remains in his bowel.'[20] Leo's mother marvelled at his narrow escape. 'Henceforth', she wrote in her journal, 'this dear child, who as it were, has been given back to me from the brink of the grave, must be the chief object in life.'[21] The Queen's continued seclusion should be seen in this context.

The misery caused by Leo's illness faded in the spring amid excitement at Arthur's forthcoming graduation from the Royal Military Academy. The prince's final marks were not published, but the Duke of Cambridge had been confident enough of success to sign his cousin's commission in the Royal Engineers before the examinations concluded – even though he would have preferred to see the young prince enter one of the aristocratic Guards or Cavalry regiments rather than his governor's corps. He had told Howard rather tetchily that 'I do not think that an exclusively Engineer or Artillery officer would be as well versed in the requirements of colonial command, for which I look upon Arthur as ultimately destined, as he would be when serving in the line.'[22] But as this was the route into the army that the Prince Consort had mapped out for his son, there was little the duke could do except to console himself that, over time, Arthur would be appointed to a series of regiments.

Despite a bout of ill-health, Elphinstone attended Arthur's graduation ceremony at Woolwich on 19 June. He rarely spoke of his own achievement at steering the prince through his education; yet he felt rightly proud that Arthur was 'the first Prince of England whose education has been carried on at a public school and who has been submitted at his age to public examinations of considerable severity'. No longer was the prince his pupil and charge; now he was 'an officer and therefore far more his own master'.[23] With excellent timing, the prince's commission as second lieutenant coincided with his governor's long-awaited promotion to lieutenant-colonel. But if Howard's thoughts had turned again towards resuming his own career in the army, he would once more be disappointed. His frustration was surely sharpened with the victorious conclusion that summer of yet another imperial military adventure without his participation, this time in Abyssinia under the command of General Robert Napier.

Victoria marked her son's graduation by raising his allowance to £500 a year. This was enough to buy his own clothes and to entertain his fellow officers modestly, but not to get into trouble by overindulging. She also took the opportunity to give Arthur another long lecture on the perils of growing up. On the day of his passing-out ceremony, she reminded him to

> *fight a good fight* as your beloved and spotless father did . . . you
> have two great positions to maintain *viz* that of your father's *son* to
> be worthy of him, and as a *soldier* and a subject to be worthy of
> the name of your *great* godfather *whose* name you bear. No greater
> soldier ever lived and no sovereign ever had a more devoted sub-
> ject! Let *duty* always go before pleasure and *self* and you will be

sure to succeed. Life is a *fearful* battle! Temptations will surround you in every shape and you will require *all* the courage and firmness and self denial which exists in the soul of man to *resist* them.[24]

Yet no sooner had Arthur begun his career in the army than disaster struck. During manoeuvres at Chatham that August, a troop of soldiers fell into a seventeen-foot-deep ditch when a bridge constructed under the prince's command suddenly collapsed. One soldier was killed and fourteen more seriously injured as the men tumbled onto their bayonets. Fearing another royal scandal, the Duke of Cambridge immediately asked Elphinstone to inquire into the incident. In his confidential report, Howard assured the duke, and the equally anxious Queen, that 'no blame whatsoever' could be attached to the prince.[25] The fault lay with the officers who had ordered so many soldiers over the bridge. Only when he had received this assurance did the duke's thoughts turn to the devastated young prince. 'I am only sorry for the lad himself,' he told the colonel; 'we must do all we can not to discourage him, and I look to you for this.'[26]

The Queen heard of the tragic accident in Switzerland, where she had finally travelled to recover her strength and to evade the attention of the British newspapers. She had crossed Europe officially incognita under the pseudonym of the Countess of Kent – not to escape recognition (which was impossible) but to avoid the royal protocol of having to pay formal respects to the countries through which she passed. For a woman who loved the theatre it may also have given her the thrill of subterfuge.

Remarkably, given his failure the year before, Howard had finally found Victoria a holiday home which met most of her exacting requirements. The Pension Wallis belonged to Robert Wallis, a wealthy engraver of landscape paintings who had retired to Switzerland to open a new business catering to the booming new tourist industry in the Alps. The house was a picture-perfect, three-floor property, with covered veranda and look-out towers, perched high on a hill above Lucerne. Writing to Howard, Princess Louise gushed that the view from her window was 'beyond all our expectations'.[27] More restrained in her praise, but equally pleased, Victoria described it all as 'very snug'.[28] Yet the house was still substantial enough to absorb most of her retinue of courtiers, maids and dressers. A reduced household of five – 'including Jenner' – were lodged in an adjoining chalet.[29] John Brown, who had travelled with the royal party from England ('as the Queen would not feel safe if she had *not* Brown *with* her'), was given his own apartment close to Victoria in the *pension*.

Elphinstone and the prince, who travelled as Lieutenant the Hon. Arthur Kent RE, reached the Pension Wallis on 23 August. As Pickard was ill, his place on the trip had been taken by a friend of Howard's: Major Richard Harrison, the adjutant at the Royal Engineers school of engineering at Chatham and a man from whom, Howard assured the Queen, 'the Prince would hear nothing but what was good'.[30] The Queen was delighted to see them all, yet she informed Elphinstone quite firmly that 'we have no room to *spare* for a *mouse* so that neither Prince Arthur or any one should STOP *here* (in the House) for *above* an hour or *two* and excepting for breakfast certainly *not* to *meals*'.[31] So they returned to Lausanne, taking rooms at the Schweitzerhof, a small hotel in the town where Arthur and Howard had lodged in 1865.

After a week spent sketching and sightseeing with the Queen, during which an ascent was made of the Rigi, the three men departed on a walking tour through the Tyrol to the Italian lakes. But a planned assault on 'one of the big mountains' near Zermatt had to be abandoned when Elphinstone suddenly collapsed at their hotel. 'It was only then', Harrison recalled, 'I discovered that the manager of our trip, who had walked with us the whole way, was suffering from an old illness that he had contracted in the Crimea. Although often in pain, he had never said a word, but had borne it because he did not wish to spoil our pleasure.'[32] The exact nature of Howard's medical condition, which had dogged him since the war, is unknown. With the passage of time and the scarcity of definite recorded symptoms, it is now impossible to diagnose with any certainty. Howard rarely mentions it in his letters, although Victoria's concern is often palpable in her replies. It may have been connected to his head wound or even to psychiatric damage inflicted by shell shock. More likely, given Harrison's remark about 'an old illness . . . contracted in the Crimea', Howard was suffering the effects of an intermittent disease which afflicted many veterans of the war. This was variously known as 'Crimean', 'Mediterranean' or 'Malta' fever, but is now identified as brucellosis. As the bacterium which causes brucellosis is carried by animals, the likely source of infection for the soldiers was the milk they drank: specifically, goat's milk from Malta, where many troopships paused on their way to the Crimea. (Howard stayed on the island in March 1854 before sailing for the Dardanelles, describing the men he encountered there as 'swarthy, Italian in appearance and dress, shoes and stocking very scarce. Women, with no exception that I could see, ugly and shrivelled up.'[33])

The flu-like symptoms of the sudden-onset, chronic form of the illness – fever, lethargy, severe joint pain, headache and general malaise – broadly accord with the sketchy details of Howard's attacks. They have also been discerned in the mystifying condition which affected Florence Nightingale following her return from the Crimea, after which she lived for many years as an invalid and virtual recluse.[34] Intriguingly, one significant symptom of brucellosis which Howard may have shared with Florence Nightingale was the severe depression it caused, leading to periods of emotional instability and neurosis. In Nightingale this was characterized by her often tyrannical behaviour towards both her own family and those in authority. In Howard's case it may have accounted for the feeling of worthlessness which assailed him when he entered court and his occasional harsh treatment of Prince Arthur. By 1880, twenty-five years after the war, Florence Nightingale was said to have fully recovered from her distressing condition, resuming normal relations with her friends and relations. It may have taken a similarly long time for Howard's symptoms finally to lift. Certainly, towards the end of his life his personality was unrecognizable as that of the fraught, irritable young man who had first met the Queen. Eventually he would fully recover the quiet humour and 'calm and collected way' so beloved by his sister Rosalie and later recalled with fondness by his children. For the time being, however, he was forced to suffer, consoled only by the opinion of the teenage Princess Louise, who concluded, after this latest bout of ill-health, that 'You do too much and work too hard, that is the fact.'[35]

21

'The strange
impressionable Irish'

1869

B Y 1867, ALMOST EXACTLY midway through her long reign, the Queen had visited Ireland, that most troublesome and needy quarter of her realm, just three times, most recently in 1861. In the face of an upsurge in Irish nationalism – simmering resentment at the British government's heartless response to the country's famine in the 1840s having been fed by the crisis over the church in Ireland – she was urged to return to inspire loyalty in her Irish subjects. It was even suggested that she might establish a residence in Ireland to rival Balmoral. Lady Augusta Stanley later mused that 'if it had been Ireland she had visited and settled on, instead of Aberdeenshire the ecstasies and interests that would have grown up would have been just as great, and Fenianism* would never have existed'.[1] The Queen herself marvelled at such a preposterous idea. 'For health and relaxation', she told her political intimate Benjamin Disraeli, 'no one would go to Ireland, and people only go who have their estates to attend to.'[2]

On the other hand, with fears mounting of a republican outrage to coincide with an impending high-profile Fenian trial in Manchester, it seemed foolhardy to contemplate sending any

---

*The Fenians were members of a secret society bent on liberating Ireland from British rule.

member of the royal family to Ireland. Alarming rumours were already circulating of plots to kidnap or kill the Queen and her children. The police were inundated with reports of wild-eyed Fenians roaming the countryside, and of conspiracies to blow up the Houses of Parliament. In October 1867, in response to well-sourced intelligence that a gang of Fenians was planning to seize Victoria from Balmoral, a squad of undercover police officers were sent from Scotland Yard to Deeside armed with cutlasses and revolvers. The officers were posted in a cordon around the castle with strict instructions from the Metropolitan Police Commissioner Sir Richard Mayne to watch out for 'persons of suspicious appearance (or Fenians)'.[3]

The Queen was sanguine about the danger, grumbling in a letter to Howard about such 'really *absurd* precautions'.[4] She had already survived half a dozen botched attempts on her life during her reign, so was undaunted by this new crop of rumours of kidnap and assassination. Howard took an equally robust view. 'The wild exaggerated nature of these stories quite surpasses belief,' he wrote, 'and one cannot understand how even the maddest of Irishmen could possibly have come to such an idea.'[5] It was 'abominable', he told the Queen, that her 'only peaceful retreat should thus be disturbed'.[6] But the Queen's overworked secretary Charles Grey had to take every threat seriously. He extracted a promise from Victoria that she would return to the castle each evening before nightfall from her wanderings around the estate. He also arranged for security passes to be issued to servants and family alike. 'Who ever took a pass out on a ride?' exclaimed Princess Louise to Howard when she heard of this latest security measure.[7]

As the royal family's annual holiday at Balmoral drew to a close, Grey started to fret about how to get the Queen safely back to Windsor, particularly as her train would have to travel through 'the manufactory districts where the Irishmen are most thickly congregated'.[8] Fearing hijack, the overwrought secretary suggested that the Queen travel with a squad of armed policemen: '12 at the front of the train and 6 behind'.[9] He also insisted that the train's driver take the longer, cross-country route south and proceed by daylight, advice which irritated the Queen as she liked to travel at night so that she could sleep. The government's offer of a detachment of troops to safeguard the train was declined on the basis that it might give the public an impression of panic. In the event the journey passed off peacefully, although Grey was unsettled to hear on arriving at Windsor that 'a man speaking with an Irish accent' had been seen near the castle.[10]

Fears of a terrorist attack on the royal family reached fever pitch in December, when an explosion in Clerkenwell killed twelve people during an attempt by a Fenian gang to spring a republican gun-runner from prison. Visiting the scene of devastation with Arthur two days afterwards, Elphinstone marvelled 'that the loss of life was so small. One woman was blown out of her house into the prison yard, a distance of more than 150 yards.'[11] Such an unprecedented outrage stoked the rumour-mill still further. On 17 December the Home Secretary forwarded to Grey a well-sourced report that 'a sworn band' of Irish assassins had sailed from New York intent on killing the Queen at Osborne House.[12] Two hundred troops were immediately sent to the Isle of Wight ahead of the royal family's annual visit there for Christmas. Writing to Elphinstone, Victoria railed against such 'extraordinary and really absurd precautions'.[13] Yet they seemed very prudent to the Master of the Household Sir John Cowell who, after touring the Osborne estate with the local inspector of police, had gloomily reported to Grey that there was 'nothing to prevent any number of ill-disposed persons coming in at night, notwithstanding all our watching and lying in the woods, till they find an opportunity of perpetrating their crime'.[14]

The panic peaked on 20 December, the day of the expected assault by the Irish terrorists. 'Everyone lost their heads and seemed to think the whole Island teemed with danger,' exclaimed Victoria, 'excepting herself, her children, the Ladies, and one or two other men!'[15] Even Arthur and Howard were briefly detained by the police after landing on the island for their Christmas holiday. But the Fenians failed to appear, and by 11 January 1868 the Queen could happily state that her country 'was never more loyal or sound. I would throw myself amongst my English and dear Scotch subjects alone (London excepted as it is so enormous and full of Irish) and I should be as safe as in my own room.'[16]

Grey and Commissioner Mayne had hardly begun to relax when word reached England that Prince Alfred had been shot and wounded while on tour in Australia. His assailant had apparently been bent on avenging the recent execution in England of three Irish nationalists. The news badly shook the complacency at the palace. Elphinstone, who was recovering at Ranger's House from another bout of illness, called the assault 'so atrocious that it is impossible even to speak of it with patience'.[17] Affie had been shot in the back at point-blank range while attending a garden party in Sydney, his life saved only by his thick leather braces, which had lessened the bullet's impact. To allay fears of a worldwide Fenian conspiracy, it was made known that Affie's would-be assassin – the son of an immigrant Irish butcher called James O'Farrell – had a history of mental illness and was acting alone. Yet he was not treated accordingly. Even before news of his attack had reached England, O'Farrell had been condemned to death and hanged, curtailing closer inquiry into his motives. As the guardian of another royal prince, however, Elphinstone had to be told the truth. In a private letter to him, the Secretary of State for the Colonies, the Duke of Buckingham, revealed, '*Entre nous*', that O'Farrell had been 'sent with others from England and they drew lots, but this must be *kept secret*'.[18] It was a warning that Elphinstone had a new enemy to contend with as he guided the prince through life.

The Queen's sympathy for her son was short-lived. 'I am not as proud of Affie as you may think,' she told Vicky when Affie returned home in triumph to convalesce, 'for he is so conceited himself and at the present moment receives ovations as if he had done something, instead of God's mercy having spared his life.'[19]

Yet recent events – and the cajoling of her new Prime Minister Benjamin Disraeli, who assured Victoria that her Irish subjects 'yearned for the occasional presence and inspiration of Royalty'[20] – had finally persuaded her of the urgent need for a royal tour of Ireland. Plans were laid for Arthur to visit the following summer, Victoria reminding Elphinstone that as one of the prince's fore-names was Patrick, his appearance there would 'gratify the strange impressionable Irish very much. The very idea of *his* being, as they think, specially their *own* Prince must do good.'[21] But when Gladstone replaced Disraeli as Prime Minister in December 1868, he – who had originally so energetically promoted the idea of an Irish tour – tried to block the plan, citing security concerns. In fact, Gladstone was probably more concerned about the delicate progress through Parliament of his controversial bill disestablish-ing the Irish church. In any event, the Lord Lieutenant of Ireland, Earl Spencer, resisted every attempt to cancel the long-awaited visit. 'The Prince will get an admirable reception,' he assured Elphinstone. 'Many say that no Royal visitor will come at a more propitious time.' Any delay, Spencer added, 'when all is expecta-tion for the Prince's arrival would be most unfortunate'.[22] Elphinstone referred the matter to the Queen, who bypassed Gladstone and sought a confidential report on the security situa-tion in Ireland from the Home Secretary, Henry Bruce. Except for occasional 'agrarian outrages', Bruce declared, the country was safe. The Fenians in Ireland were a spent force, undermined by internecine warfare and a lack of money, despite their radical comrades in the United States exercising 'a mischievous influence on great numbers of their ignorant kinsmen'.[23] Armed with this assurance, Victoria happily overruled Gladstone and Arthur's tour was given the go-ahead. Nevertheless, before Howard sailed with the prince on 5 April 1869, she extracted his promise that '*no risk should be run* by *sea* or *land*'.[24]

As Lord Spencer had predicted, Arthur was politely received in Dublin. He told his mother excitedly that 'I heard more than one say "och sure he's a real Paddie, sure he is".'[25] Sir

Joseph Napier, who was travelling with the prince on behalf of the government, was more sober in his assessment. 'The reception he met with was extremely favourable and *cordial* throughout,' he reported to Henry Bruce; 'not enthusiastic but that just now could hardly be expected.' Napier was critical, however, of the heavy-handed security which surrounded the prince:

> There is no more danger here than there would be in England of
> his being shot at and I think the precaution and suspicion which
> those about him show, will do harm, whereas if he went about
> freely and trustfully his prepossessing manner would do a great
> deal to dissipate the remains of Fenianism and bring back a better
> tone.[26]

The Queen was more concerned about the company her son was keeping in Ireland than the risk posed by Fenian terrorists. Howard assured her that he had not detected the 'slightest approach to anything "fast"' in the company assembled at the Vice Regal Lodge, a fact he considered noteworthy 'in the present day'.[27] He also diligently compiled lists of all the people the prince and he encountered at the various house parties to which they were invited, where possible listing their professions or family connections. For instance, among the names of the guests at Shane's Castle, the seat of Baron O'Neill in Antrim where they stayed on 30 April, was twelve-year-old Annie Cole, the daughter of a wealthy English industrialist whose brother was courting an Irish heiress. Little could this shy, red-headed girl have imagined how her life would one day become entwined with that of the serious-minded forty-year-old colonel who accompanied the royal prince.

Elphinstone was not very impressed by the Irish people, viewing them with that detached curiosity he reserved for most foreigners. On a later visit he dismissed them as 'queer people . . . a mixture of childishness with all the cruelty and hardness of childhood'.[28] He was thankful, therefore, when Arthur's carriage wound into the more loyal northern counties, where the 'face and language' of the people were reassuringly 'more scotch'. 'The welcome too has been very different,' he discerned, 'the wild Irish yell has been replaced by a more sober, but far deeper feeling.'[29] So it was ironic that the only trouble the royal party encountered on the whole tour of Ireland was in Londonderry, where rioting erupted outside the prince's hotel. Two men were shot dead by the police in the ensuing struggle and several more were seriously wounded. Despite hastily assuring Victoria that the disturbance had nothing to do with her son's visit, Elphinstone conceded that Arthur's appearance in the town had 'probably excited them and brought matters to a climax'. He blamed the trouble on the 'Irish Church question' – the disestablishment of the Anglican Church in Ireland – reporting that 'Dissenters as well as Presbyterians appear strongly opposed to the measure'.[30] As a precaution, two detectives were sent ahead to ensure the tour ended peacefully in Belfast, which it did on 4 May. Only when he reached the safety of Ranger's House did Elphinstone admit how stressful he had found the whole experience. 'On more than one occasion he felt rather anxious,' he confessed, 'even for the personal safety of the Prince; and there were many difficulties in the way; more especially from the party spirit which was everywhere strong, and which had to be smoothed.'[31]

Ireland having been safely navigated, plans were now advanced for an even more ambitious exercise in royal promotion. As part of his military training it was proposed that Arthur should join the Rifle Brigade in Montreal, from where he could tour Canada and, perhaps even, the United States. The Prince of Wales had made a similar trip with General Bruce in 1860 to universal acclaim. The Queen strongly encouraged the idea. She now saw Arthur as a useful roving ambassador whose youthful good looks and stainless reputation could shore up flagging loyalist morale in the remoter regions of her empire while deflecting criticism of her isolation at home.

But the mood in both Canada and the United States had

altered considerably since Bertie's visit nearly ten years earlier, and it was far from certain that another royal prince would be so welcome in either country. Relations between London and Washington were at a low ebb. President Ulysses Grant's administration was highly suspicious of Britain's stance during America's recent civil war, believing London had covertly supported the defeated Confederates. Moreover, the large immigrant Irish population in the United States, many of them originally refugees from the famine, had been fertile ground for the growth of the Fenian Brotherhood. North of the border, too, the situation was markedly different. Canada had been proclaimed a dominion in 1867, and many of its inhabitants were torn between their abiding loyalty to the Crown and a nagging desire for complete separation from Britain. There was even talk of Canada joining the United States. Charles Grey, who had served in Canada with the army, pooh-poohed the idea, trusting in the nation's loyalty. '*Virtual* self-government', he countered in a letter to Elphinstone, gave the Canadians 'all the advantages of English connection without interfering with their independence'.[32] Victoria herself, in conversation with Gladstone, even floated the idea of turning Canada into a kingdom, with Arthur as its monarch. New York's *Journal of Commerce* greeted rumours of this suggestion with disdain. 'Fancy so shrewd a statesman as Mr Gladstone', the paper declared, 'contemplating the medieval absurdity of erecting a throne on this free Western continent, when the ultimate drift of his modern progressive policy is to rid England of the one that now encumbers her.'[33]

The man best placed to judge the wisdom of another royal tour to North America was less complacent than Charles Grey. Sir John Young, the Governor General of Canada, thought there was a considerable risk to the prince's safety from rogue Fenian elements entering the country from the United States. Riven by splits, riddled with informers, drained of resources and smarting from the shambolic failure of a bold attempt to invade Canada in 1866, the brotherhood was in no position to mount a large-scale operation. Yet, in Sir John's opinion, this made it still 'more likely that resort may be had to assassination by the more obscure and violent members of the league'. Sir John was used to talk of Fenian plots, but following the recent murder of Thomas D'Arcy McGee, a leading politician and journalist gunned down in broad daylight in April, he felt unable to dismiss all of them as 'merely idle expressions'. Writing in strict confidence to the Colonial Secretary Earl Granville, Sir John admitted it was impossible to know for sure whether 'the light regard for human life which obtains among the Celtic races, and especially amongst Fenians, the lowest and least reasoning type of those races, might not take some such direction as that indicated'. He reluctantly concluded therefore that in spite of 'good intelligence' from 'an excellent body of police and some very clever detectives in Montreal', there was 'a certain amount of risk attending HRH's visit'.[34]

Lord Alexander Russell, who commanded the Rifle Brigade in Canada, was equally nervous. He declared that he could not guarantee the prince's safety during his stay in the country (and clearly did not want to, feeling unhappy with the responsibility). A government insider had warned him that Arthur could suffer the same fate as his brother Affie in Australia. 'It is quite on the cards,' Russell had been told by his source; 'he must take his chance of that, one thing is certain he must not go into the States or they will kidnap him to a certainty.' Russell then quoted a conversation which an undercover police agent had overheard between two notorious Fenians in an Illinois bar:

'I see a Prince is coming to join the Royal Canadian Rifles,' one had said; 'well if he does, he will want all his regiment to take care of him, we don't want any Princes in these parts.'

'I wonder Queen Victoria sending her son out here after the warning she got at Sydney,' the other had replied, darkly.[35]

Unease at the proposed royal tour quickly reached the highest levels of government in London. Granville passed Russell's alarmist report to the Foreign Secretary, Lord Clarendon, who asked the British minister in Washington, Sir Edward Thornton, for his opinion. Thornton, a level-headed man with excellent contacts in the security services, was relaxed about the threat. He conceded that 'plots for such purposes may easily exist in this extensive country without my being able to obtain any clue to them'. Yet he dismissed Russell's reported gossip as 'constantly in the mouths of blustering Americans and still more blustering Irishmen in this country . . . I do not think they mean much.' He suggested employing a private detective from Pilkington's to investigate the threat, although he warned that 'one could not place entire confidence in the detective's honesty [as] everything entrusted to his charge would be made known to the United States Government and he would claim a high price for his service'.[36]

Regardless of Thornton's breezy nonchalance, Clarendon felt unable to authorize the trip. On 29 July 1869, just days before the prince was scheduled to sail with Elphinstone, the minister plucked up the courage to tell the Queen that 'Prince Arthur should not go to Canada at the present moment.'[37] Yet he had underestimated Victoria's determination to see the tour go ahead. Ignoring Clarendon's advice, she asked the Prime Minister to intervene personally to save the trip. After meeting Elphinstone and Granville to discuss the matter in private, Gladstone suggested a compromise. The prince could sail for Canada as planned, but before he reached Montreal he would be recalled to Europe 'for some other suitable and adequate purpose', such as attending the opening of the Suez Canal.[38] Recalling the dangers he had faced attending the prince in Ireland, Elphinstone agreed with Gladstone's proposal. From Gladstone's office he dictated a telegram which was sent to the Queen in cipher outlining 'the general idea of the scheme'. When he reached Ranger's House later that evening, he wrote more fully to Victoria, aware that she might respond badly to having her plans thwarted. The Prime Minister, he promised her, ' is quite convinced himself that it is the only proper course to follow, and one by which all risks are avoided'.[39]

But Victoria was as reluctant to accept Gladstone's advice on this matter as on any other. 'The Queen cannot make out that anything new has occurred to cause this,' she countered, not unreasonably.

> If it is thought better for Prince Arthur not to remain as was
> intended, that may be done. But, it must be remembered that
> Prince Arthur's military career will suffer severely if what has
> been carefully planned and worked out for him for months, not to
> say years, is at a moment's notice to be completely upset, and this
> idea of sending him to the opening of the Suez canal is not one of
> use to his profession, or good for him in any way. A young Prince
> should be made to work hard and not to be always representing at
> great ceremonies.[40]

As the Queen refused to cancel the prince's tour of Canada, attention shifted to the means of securing his safety while he was there. On 23 August, Sir John Young wrote to the new Prime Minister of Canada, Sir John Macdonald, seeking his opinion on the security threat and an assurance that everything would be done to safeguard the prince during his stay in Montreal. Yet a further two months passed before Macdonald asked Charles Coursol, the police commissioner in Quebec, for a security report – by which time Arthur was already touring the eastern provinces. Like Thornton in Washington, Macdonald was unconcerned about the risk posed to the prince by renegade Fenians. He was also mildly irritated by the consternation the issue had caused in London and the high-handed attitude of Sir John Young. 'I do not participate in the fear,' he confided to Coursol, 'yet we must show particular vigilance in order to satisfy Her Majesty. Please write me an official letter, stating what you have done and prepare doing, during Prince Arthur's residence in Montreal with respect to guarding his house and person.'[41]

Unlike the politicians, Coursol took the threat very seriously indeed. He shared responsibility for national security with Gilbert McMicken, the police commissioner in Ontario, and together they ran a network of undercover agents along the border with the United States. Both men were being inundated with intelligence suggesting that the Fenians were planning to kill or seize the royal visitor, much of which emanated directly from Fenian headquarters in New York. First, credible reports emerged of a plot to poison the prince. Then in October the New York paper *Universal News* reported that at a recent meeting of the Fenian high command 'every member of the committee' had endorsed a plan to kidnap Arthur. 'It is very significant', the report continued, ominously, 'that some half-dozen of the very smartest of their men . . . left this city suddenly at a late hour last night for Buffalo.'[42] Even more alarming, a Fenian terrorist cell had been identified close to Rose Mount, the prince's intended residence in Montreal. The leader of the cell was John Murphy, the brother of the 'notorious Mike Murphy', a much feared Canadian Fenian who had died on the run a year before.[43]

To defend against attack, Coursol placed a watch not only on all the ports and railway stations in Montreal, but on 'all persons in the city tainted ever so slightly with disloyalty'. 'I feel sure', he confidently reported to Sir John Macdonald, 'that nothing in the way of a plot or intrigue of any kind, can go on, or even be initiated, without my being duly apprised of it.'[44] Yet no-one knew for certain what might happen when the prince arrived in North America, or whether he would ever return safely to his mother.

'We are constantly thinking of you'

MONTREAL, 1869

IN THE GREY LIGHT of dawn on 12 August 1869 Prince Arthur, Howard Elphinstone and Lieutenant Pickard slipped away from the Isle of Wight to begin their long journey to Canada. Before parting with them all the evening before, the Queen had stressed to the colonel 'the necessity of taking every possible precaution against any possible evil intention and to avoid anything of a *foolhardy* nature'. In a moving gesture, as he said goodbye, the prince had cut off a lock of his hair as a keepsake for his mother. Then Victoria's thoughts had turned to Elphinstone. She gave him a jewelled tie pin, pleading that he 'take as much care of his own health, which is so valuable, as he can'.[1] The scene had painful overtones of Leo's departure for France in 1861, an event for ever associated with the death of the Prince Consort.

Later that morning, on the quayside at Southampton, the colonel was handed a note. 'The carriage came to the wrong door,' the Queen had telegraphed, clearly flustered, after he left Osborne House, 'and I was unable to wish you goodbye as I was most anxious to do. I am much distressed at this. God bless you.'[2] On 14 August, after travelling up to Liverpool, the prince and the colonel embarked in the *City of Paris*, a passenger steamer bound for Canada. 'We are constantly thinking of you,' Victoria wrote in her last letter to Howard before he sailed. She then declared –

more for her benefit than for his – that she was 'really *not* alarmed' by the Fenian threat in America.[3] The colonel calmly assured her that he was 'alive to every eventuality [and] *perfectly* prepared'.[4] Among the sixty trunks of royal luggage, he had remembered to pack his revolver.

During the eight-day crossing, the prince 'mixed freely' with the other passengers in the ship – 'People from almost every grade of Society,' reported Elphinstone, including several 'radical Americans' and three hundred 'well-behaved' Irish emigrants.[5] Writing to his sister Louise, Arthur described his fellow passengers as 'a very motley set . . . most of them Americans, some of whom are most amusing. I cannot say very much for the ladies on board. There are really only one or two that can be called *ladies* . . .'[6]

The royal party was greeted at Halifax by Sir John Young, who immediately announced that he saw no reason why the prince should not remain in Canada for the full length of his tour. Indeed, now that the prince had arrived, the subject of his returning early to Europe was barely mentioned and soon forgotten. The Governor General simply advised Elphinstone to delay arriving in Montreal, where Arthur would join the Rifle Brigade, until the security situation there could be better assessed. The town had a large Irish population so, as Elphinstone patiently explained to the Queen, it was 'the only place about which there can be any doubt'.[7] Pending this assessment, to kill time the royal party embarked on a series of lengthy sporting expeditions into the Canadian wilderness (confirming for many the suspicion that this was the real reason for the high-profile royal visit to North America).

In late September they finally headed towards London in Ontario, where the prince had agreed to open an agricultural show. Six police officers were assigned to accompany them on the train journey from Quebec City, although the colonel insisted that the guard be reduced to two ahead of their arrival, presumably for better effect.[8] Nevertheless, this was a risky decision. Gilbert McMicken had received a well-sourced report from one of his agents that four Fenians from New York were in London specifically 'to see what the Prince is like'. The agent did not know what the Fenians were planning, if anything; but on the basis of 'several remarks I have heard them make', he urged his chief to place a 'strict watch' on Arthur.[9] McMicken immediately assigned extra bodyguards to the prince, while the exhibition halls were ringed with armed troops. For the first time Howard was not in sole charge of Arthur, or of events.

Despite McMicken's fears, the opening ceremony passed off without incident. The only threat to the young prince's safety, the *Toronto Globe* reported, was 'a stout Irish matron [who] surcharged with loyalty . . . exclaimed "God Bless the son of her gracious Majesty" and made to get at His Highness, when Colonel Elphinstone good humouredly checked her progress'.[10] Howard took satisfaction in having persevered with the engagement, giving McMicken no credit for securing the prince's safety as he believed the precautions excessive. 'Some people had expressed uneasiness about this visit to London,' he wrote in the journal he kept for the Queen,

> in consequence of the immense crowd and the proximity of the
> place to the American frontier. I confess however, that I felt no
> apprehension whatsoever . . . I consider that there is less chance
> of harm in a crowd than anywhere else . . . the more one knows
> the people one sees that this feeling is not on the surface, like in
> Ireland, but deep and true.[11]

Everywhere they went, the colonel was impressed by the warmth of the Canadian welcome, which dispelled any lingering doubts that the tour might have been ill-conceived. He was convinced that the prince's presence in Canada would demonstrate Britain's firm commitment to its former colony. Rumours of troop cuts and ill-advised remarks by Gladstone in London had brought insecurity to the new dominion, encouraging talk of independence or merger with the United States. But, he observed, 'Prince Arthur's sudden appearance at this critical moment arrested this feeling and gradually revived the dormant loyalty, which increased day by day, until it assumed that loud universal expression to which it has now attained.'[12] Given the crisis of confidence in the monarchy in England, however, the Queen could be forgiven if she had ignored Howard's observation that 'The receptions the prince has received out here . . . are far more loyal and hearty than anything that I have ever seen . . . given at home even to Your Majesty.'[13]

Arthur was equally anxious to cheer up his mother, knowing how deeply the persistent criticism at home affected her. 'I am sure it must please you', he wrote,

> to hear how thoroughly loyal all the Canadian people are, their great pride is that they are Englishmen, and that they are under your rule. They abhor the idea of annexation to the States, they almost hate the Americans, and I feel certain that if there were any chance of either a Fenian or American invasion the whole population would rise to a man.[14]

Emboldened by their success in London, Elphinstone now took the audacious step of accepting an invitation to visit Buffalo, a fast-growing city on the American side of the border and also a well-known Fenian haunt. An American army officer had accosted the prince during the recent agricultural show and, in 'crude' language, had assured him that he would be a welcome visitor. 'Now Sir, we don't know *you*, but we do your Mother right well,' he had said, 'and we guess Sir, there is no woman like Her. Yes Sir, we admire Her and we are anxious to see you, because we think that a son of such a mother is worth knowing.'[15] Gladstone would certainly have blocked such a dangerous sally into American territory. But Gladstone was thousands of miles away in London; so it was the colonel's decision.

Despite the secrecy surrounding the trip, a large crowd gathered to watch as the prince and Elphinstone were escorted around the muddy streets of Buffalo by its most distinguished citizen, Millard Fillmore, a former President of the United States. Fillmore was an amiable, cultivated man with a mane of thick white hair who enjoyed showing the prince the many institutions he had founded in his home town. Elphinstone found him 'most agreeable, well informed, and apparently most able'.[16] Fillmore's warm welcome, however, stood in marked contrast to the mood of the majority of the people, who came out to stare coldly at the prince, their suspicion palpable. In its scathing report of the visit, the *Buffalo Express* described the royal tourist as 'a slim-breasted youth of nineteen with dainty side whiskers; very light hair, parted three inches above his left ear; and with the royal nose and shelving forehead of the Georges'.[17] After a quick lunch in a local hotel they returned to Canada, Elphinstone nevertheless pronouncing their foray into 'the very centre of Fenianism' a 'complete success'.[18] The *Buffalo Express* took a different line. 'He made no remarks to us,' complained its reporter,

> did not ask us to dinner; walked right by us just the same as if he
> didn't see us; never inquired our opinion about any subject under
> the sun; and when his luncheon was over got into his carriage and
> drove off in the coolest way in the world, without ever saying a
> word . . . It was *Veni, Vidi, Vici*, with him. He came, he saw that
> lunch, he conquered it . . . Time on American soil, four hours and
> a half . . . It is usual for Princes to 'express themselves well
> pleased with their visit.' No doubt this one did, but not to us.[19]

Most of the American press were deeply suspicious of the motives for the royal tour of Canada. The *Journal of Commerce* in New York was more charitable than some: it spied the reason in the many fishing rods and guns packed into the prince's extensive luggage. 'To come to the point, the royal boy is out for a little vacation, and a little sport,' it pronounced:

> the English Princesses can be married off, and thus happily
> disposed of, but the best possible use that can be made of the

Princes, since no thrones are vacant for them, is to bundle them off to see the world and life, and keep them in good health, and stop John Bull from growling, as he is apt to do, over the spectacle of a palace full of costly and idle Kinglings . . . The Canadians go into no loyal ecstasies over his advent. They turn out . . . and give him dinners and balls, and flock to see and cheer him wherever he goes. He is a curiosity, a sensation. This pleases them, and it does not greatly bore the Prince, who has not yet been surfeited with lionising.[20]

The *Journal of Commerce* was wrong to downplay the significance of the royal visit quite so far, however. As Elphinstone's correspondence with the Queen reveals, the tour was a deliberate attempt to improve the image of the royal family in Canada and to restore ties loosened by the granting of its dominion status.

The American press might try to dismiss the prince's travels in Canada as an irrelevant distraction, but it took a very close interest in their progress. No fewer than three journalists from New York trailed the royal party wherever it went. Howard soon complained that they seemed determined to find fault with the prince solely 'in order to suit the Fenian tastes'. Sensibly, however, instead of ignoring the reporters, he tried to win their trust, developing such a rapport with one correspondent that he was fed Fenian intelligence from New York. 'This man attends their meetings,' the colonel told the Queen, 'and has given more accurate information . . . than that received by the Government.' The journalist revealed that 'no attempt against the Prince had ever been contemplated and had in fact been forbidden by the chiefs, as it might embroil them with the United States Government, which they would not do, and that moreover, they themselves could not possibly gain anything by it'. It was probably the most accurate report of the many Howard read every day throughout the tour.[21]

Despite the generally dismissive tone of its piece, the *Journal of Commerce* was right to describe the prince as 'a curiosity, a sensation'. Crowds flocked to his carefully staged public appearances.

Juliana Ewing, the wife of a British officer stationed in Canada and later a famous children's author, described waiting for hours simply to catch sight of Arthur when he visited Fredericton. She was not disappointed, describing him as a 'very nice looking young man with a very dignified graceful manner'.[22] Women queued up to dance with the prince at the many lavish balls held in his honour. Accordingly, as Howard remarked, Arthur was forced to endure more than his 'very fair share of ugliness as well as age'.[23]

One of the more remarkable events in his frantic itinerary was Arthur's induction into the Iroquois tribe on 1 October 1869. The ceremony took place on the Six Nations' reserve near Brantford, with the press relishing the stark contrast between the 'pale' faces of the well-dressed spectators and the 'dusky'-coloured, near-naked warriors. During the initiation rituals Arthur was dressed in a red robe, draped in beads and led around a circle of 'Indian braves, in a most gorgeous display of paint and feathers'.[24] The prince was christened Karaghkantye, or 'flying sun': the name given to the daily course of the sun from east to west, but also symbolic of his journey from Europe to America. Howard was fascinated by the experience, judging the war dance 'curious rather than pretty'.[25]

A week later Arthur and the colonel finally entered Montreal, where they would reside for the remainder of their stay in Canada. A crowd estimated at over thirty thousand gathered to see the prince's carefully choreographed approach by steamer, cheering wildly as he stepped onto the quayside. He was there greeted by the mayor of the town and by the commanding officer of the British forces in Canada, General Sir Charles Windham, whose dramatic exploits during the final assault on Sevastopol on 8 September 1855 had earned him the sobriquet 'Windham of the Redan'. With mild disappointment, the *Montreal Evening Star* noted that the prince 'was dressed in mufti', rather than in uniform, and that he was wearing a tight-fitting coat with velvet collar, check trousers and lavender-coloured gloves.[26] But it was the prince's startling habit of wearing his collar turned down that attracted the most attention. Within hours of his landing, Rice Brothers, the leading gentlemen's outfitters in the town, were advertising *Prince Arthur Collars: The Greatest Novelty of the Day*. The normally imperturbable Elphinstone was slightly overwhelmed by the reception, which far surpassed anything he had so far encountered with the prince. He was also pleasantly surprised by the beauty of the town, declaring it, after driving through its packed streets to their residence, 'the finest' he had seen in America, capable of comparing 'even in architecture . . . with many of our best at home'.[27]

Rose Mount stood in a commanding position above Montreal, a handsome two-storey residence surrounded by extensive grounds. Ahead of the royal party's arrival, a journalist from the *Montreal Evening Star* was granted exclusive access to the house, enabling him to give his readers a gushing account of its interior. A substantial portico on the front of the house, he had written, revealed a hall 'gaily decorated with flags and branching antlers' and dominated by the double flight of stairs leading to the bedrooms. To the left of the hall was an oak-panelled library; to the right, the dining room: 'a gorgeous display of silver and crystal'. The large drawing room was equally sumptuous, being furnished in 'the richest brocatelle' and hung with 'a choice collection of pictures'.[28] The house was named for its owner John Rose, a prominent politician and wealthy businessman who had vacated the property ahead of a lengthy business trip to Europe. The Prince of Wales had stayed at the house with General Bruce in 1860, so its many servants were familiar with the peculiar demands of a royal guest.

Howard reported to the Queen that 'both Mr and Mrs Rose have done everything in their power' to make Arthur 'as comfortable as possible' during his stay.[29] Security was provided by Commissioner Coursol who, after meeting the colonel to discuss his requirements, posted four armed policemen around the house, day and night. More officers were detailed to follow the prince wherever he went out, 'in such a manner as to attract no attention'.[30] 'Even on the shooting expeditions,' the colonel assured the

Pickard, Elphinstone and Prince Arthur on the steps of Rose Mount, their snowbound residence in Montreal.

Queen, 'where safety is ensured by the large number of armed sportsmen, a detective in disguise has never been absent.'[31] The final line of defence was provided by a St Bernard dog which Arthur had been given on landing in Canada. Elphinstone confidently predicted that this huge beast 'would not allow anyone to touch the Prince'.[32]

The Queen praised Elphinstone's 'wonderfully judicious' care. Her ministers, she reported, had told her she was 'most fortunate' in having such a man at her son's side.[33] Such a sentiment, Victoria continued, 'is nothing new to the Queen but it is *very* gratifying to her to see how he is appreciated by her government'.[34] She delighted in hearing how her son had passed Christmas shivering under canvas on a moose hunt. 'Prince Arthur and I had to cook our own dinner,' Elphinstone recounted. 'We were a long time about it and tried many experiments, we succeeded in making some very good pea-soup, and an excellent dish of beef from the preserved meats. Our second course was biscuits and marmalade, a little sherry and tea completed the Bill of fare for Christmas day 1869.'[35] It was all a very long way from the sumptuous banquets they could remember from the Christmases at Windsor during the Prince Consort's lifetime.

23

'No end of queer Yankee expressions'

NEW YORK, 1870

ELPHINSTONE FOUND THE WARM autumnal air of Canada much to his liking. 'There is a freshness and clearness about it that is most invigorating and charming,' he told Victoria. He claimed to have 'never felt better in his life': an indication that, like Florence Nightingale, he was at last sensing the symptoms of the illness he had suffered since the Crimean War beginning to lift.[1] He was less impressed by Montreal society, which, 'with the exception of the officers quartered here . . . appears to be composed almost entirely of business men, and a sprinkling of old French noblesse; all very jealous of each other and especially of their relative social position'.[2] Arthur pitied his companion's heavy workload: an endless round of security meetings and hours of correspondence. There was little time for Howard to paint, but he found some respite from work playing his violin, and there were plenty of old friends from the army at the garrison, such as Garnet Wolseley, who had been by his side during the attack on the Quarries in June 1855.

After the mild autumn, the onset of winter came as a shock, the drop in temperature dramatic even for a man who had experienced a winter in the trenches. 'From 43° degrees Fahrenheit . . . to 21° degrees *below* zero,' Elphinstone marvelled. When the snows came, it was often difficult to leave Rose Mount at all.

When the prince did venture out, it was so cold that his pocket watch froze up and the air so dry that, as Howard related, 'after being rubbed on the back for a few times with a fur glove, [he] was able to light the gas with the electric spark discharged from his fingers!'[3]

Among the deluge of invitations with which the colonel had to deal on behalf of the prince were countless requests from the United States for an official visit. Unable to decide on such an important matter himself, the colonel referred the matter to Windsor. Without consulting Gladstone, who would certainly have cautioned against such a move, the Queen gave Howard her permission to take her son there 'whenever it is thought advisable'.[4] When Edward Thornton, the British minister in Washington, then sought confirmation of the proposed visit through official channels, a plainly aggrieved Foreign Secretary asked the Queen to telegraph her approval, 'as it appears from Major Elphinstone's letter [*sic*] that Prince Arthur already has Your Majesty's permission to go to the United States'.[5] In allowing her favourite son to visit the United States, Victoria was overcoming a prejudice against a country which had not only broken the heart of her grandfather George III, but had caused her husband so much anxiety in the last days of his life.

Elphinstone and the prince travelled south by train, reaching New York on 21 January 1870. Arthur was dressed in a beaver fur hat, a tight-fitting double-breasted coat and the same lavender-coloured kid gloves which had caught the eye of the press in Montreal. At the Hudson River railway depot they were greeted by Edward Thornton, who led them through a curious but polite crowd to their waiting carriage. The American papers affected indifference to the royal visit, a reflection of their readers' disenchantment with the British since the Civil War. Nevertheless, one correspondent could not resist penning vivid portraits of the city's guests, providing a memorable image of Elphinstone at the time. 'This gentleman is about forty years of age,' the journalist wrote, though he does not look it, and is somewhat shorter than the Prince . . . He has black piercing eyes, wears a full beard and moustache, except that he has his chin shaved. He watches the Prince with a care and assiduity which is surprising . . . He forgets nothing and even the most trivial circumstance never escapes his attention. He is pronounced by those who have known him one of the most pleasant and courteous gentlemen to be met with. He is an elegant dancer, much better than Prince Arthur or Lieutenant Pickard and many a fine gentleman might well envy his exaggerated good appearance in the ball-room.[6]

After settling into Breevort's Hotel on Fifth Avenue, Elphinstone and Arthur went for a drive in the park before leaving their carriage to walk down Broadway. Everywhere they went, they were escorted by a plain-clothes detective and five armed police officers: 'One on each side of the Prince and three behind,' the colonel assured Sir John Cowell back at Windsor, 'this guards all possibility.'[7] On the face of it such precautions seemed unnecessary, for the royal walkabout attracted little interest. At least two hundred thousand people were reported to have lined the same pavements to welcome the Prince of Wales in 1860. Ten years later his younger brother could stroll down the street unmolested, although he was still 'recognised by most people'.[8] Arthur was 'amused with the bustle and life of New York', the colonel reported. He found it 'full of enterprise and energy, but as regards architecture could not for a moment be compared to Montreal'.[9] That evening they went to the theatre, before returning to their apartments at Breevort's which, the colonel sensibly omitted to tell the Queen, had been intentionally furnished by the owner with busts of Richard Cobden, the English radical politician, and George Washington, the first President of the United States.

The next morning the royal party left early for Washington and an official visit to the White House, the highlight of the short tour. They were both unimpressed by the American capital. Elphinstone called it 'miserable', simply 'two and three splendid buildings separated by a wilderness of mud';[10] Arthur complained about the 'abominably paved' streets and the 'rather deserted' feel to the place.[11] Rather grudgingly, they conceded that the Capitol building with its glistening new dome and white marble façade was quite 'handsome', while the White House seemed 'not unlike Frogmore, but much larger'.[12] A brisk walk to the military cemetery at Arlington, which as a consequence of the recent war was already covered with 'several thousand . . . white marble tablets', revived their spirits, preparing them for the ordeal of an audience with the US President, Ulysses Grant.[13]

As anticipated in London, the welcome they received at the White House was decidedly cool. After being kept waiting for a few minutes in the Blue Room they were greeted coldly by the President, 'a man of small stature, square built and . . . very silent'.[14] In a letter to the Queen, Elphinstone attributed Grant's hostility towards his English guests to 'the "gaucherie" natural to a man unused to society'.[15] To Cowell he reasoned that, on account of the fragile relations between their two countries, the president felt 'bound to keep up a little unfriendliness'.[16] However, as Howard confided, there was little doubt that the youthful prince was being deliberately given the 'cold shoulder' by a government in thrall to 'the Irish element which has likewise been kind enough to threaten the Prince's life while here'.[17] In fact, Grant had initially refused to see Arthur at all, despite protracted negotiations involving Edward Thornton and Hamilton Fish, the American Secretary of State. The President saw no reason to show any respect to a fresh-faced nineteen-year-old English boy, especially as Britain and America were currently at loggerheads over reparations arising from the Civil War. Eventually, after the personal intervention of Baron Gerolt, the Prussian minister in Washington, it was agreed that Grant would meet the prince – but only on condition that both men would remain standing throughout their conversation, enabling the President to maintain his rank.

After their awkward conversation with the President, Arthur and Howard were taken to the Red Room to meet the

President Ulysses S. Grant, hero of the Civil War in America but considered by the British minister in Washington to be 'the most uncouth man I ever met with'. Howard would have agreed.

First Lady, Julia Grant, and her elderly father. Julia, with her provincial manner, twitching eye and poor figure, was seen as a figure of fun by her husband's opponents. 'Pretty she certainly is not,' the colonel acknowledged, 'but apparently an honest good-natured and simple minded little body.'[18] The atmosphere improved somewhat over the official dinner which followed, during which the prince gallantly toasted his hosts for their robust handling of the Fenians. Hamilton Fish, a large, amiable man, responded in kind with Elphinstone noting that the Secretary of State seemed 'anxious to overcome that studied stiffness of the President'.[19] General Sherman, the commander-in-chief of the US army, was also 'particularly agreeable and amusing', his affability further easing the awkwardness of the occasion.[20]

In London, Gladstone diplomatically tried to brush aside news of the President's treatment of the prince. 'As Your Majesty will remember in Tennyson's Guinever,' he grandiloquently told the Queen, 'scorn was allowed as part of his defect.'[21] Edward Thornton was more direct. Writing to the Foreign Secretary, Thornton called the US President 'the most uncouth man I ever met with, [who] has on this occasion intentionally . . . endeavoured to show by his conduct to the Prince that the people of the United States consider themselves aggrieved by us'.[22]

The prince's snubbing by the President drew little sympathy from the *New York Times*. In an editorial, ironically entitled 'Pity a Poor Prince', the paper mocked the discomfort of this 'representative of a bloated aristocracy'. 'Royalty ought to have some drawbacks,' the paper pronounced, 'otherwise we should all wish that a Queen had been our mother and an ever-to-be-lamented Prince Consort our father.'[23] But the *Times* misjudged the changing public mood. Reports of President Grant's insulting behaviour towards his royal guest caused embarrassment in New York, and when they returned to the city Elphinstone found they had to fend off countless invitations to dances and dinners. 'I hear that even Washington feels a little ashamed of itself,' he told Cowell with a hint of smugness. Only the mayor of New York still steadfastly cold-shouldered the prince, an attitude which Thornton blamed on the influence of the 'low Irish population' which had elected him.[24] But society was now 'dying to talk and dance with the Prince': even republicans, the colonel wryly noted.[25]

The upsurge in public interest in the royal tour was matched by the increased attentions of the Fenians, who had been tracking the prince's every step. Even the normally composed colonel now felt that the usual threatening letters were arriving 'too frequently to disregard them altogether, especially as they showed an intimate knowledge of one's movements'.[26] Despite Howard's best efforts, some of these threats even reached the ears of the prince, although Thornton reported that 'he does not seem to care much about them'.[27] Elphinstone put up a 'bold front' to counter the danger, meanwhile anxiously counting down the days until they could return to the relative safety of Canada.[28]

The moment of greatest danger came on the last night in New York, when the prince and colonel were invited to a reception at a mansion on Fifth Avenue. They had planned to leave at ten o'clock, yet the crush at the party was so great that the colonel took the prince away early, narrowly avoiding a gang of armed Fenians waiting for them outside. It was uncertain whether the men wanted to abduct or kill the prince, but there was no doubt, as Thornton put it in his report for London, that 'these fellows meant mischief'.[29] The New York Times, however, doggedly sceptical to the end, dismissed the whole affair as 'a wicked canard, which is already proven to have had no foundation whatever in fact'.[30]

The alarm caused by the episode to already jangled nerves hastened the royal party's retreat to Canada. After a brief detour to Boston to attend the funeral of the Anglophile philanthropist George Peabody, they reached Rose Mount on 9 February 1870. Summing up the tour of the United States for the Queen, Elphinstone observed that although the Americans quite obviously 'hate and despise monarchy', they were generally 'extremely civil' and displayed 'a strongly expressed love towards Your Majesty's person and character'. However, he did not hide from Victoria the 'constant anxiety' the trip had caused him, which he admitted had been worse even than that he had felt in Ireland.[31] Only Edward Thornton's tact and diplomacy had saved the whole tour from disaster. The colonel was even more candid about his feelings towards the United States in a letter to John Cowell. 'It is a curious country,' he reflected, 'and as a study still more so. But defend me from living in it.' He had to concede, however, that there was a 'very remarkable' amount of 'vitality and energy' in the United States, 'far greater than in Canada'.[32] In his own report on the tour, Edward Thornton tactfully singled out Arthur's conduct for praise. He told the prince's mother that 'his amiable and agreeable conversation' had particularly impressed the Americans 'as it is a rare quality among themselves'.[33] Thornton's own contribution in steering the tour to a safe conclusion was recognized with a knighthood.

Arthur was the most generous in his opinion of his hosts in America, possibly because he had been shielded from the worse of their threats and insults. 'I do not suppose there is a more hospitable people in this world than the Americans,' he told his mother; 'they are rough and vulgar with a total absence of modesty or manners, but they have a good and kind heart and do not care how much trouble they give themselves in order to please one, and as regards expense they never give that a second thought.'[34] He was particularly struck by the girls he had encountered. Not only, he told his sister Louise, were they 'very pretty and extremely well dressed', they were also much more fun than their reserved cousins back in England, amusing him, for instance, 'with no end of queer Yankee expressions'.[35] The prince's fascination with America, and American women in particular, would blossom both figuratively and – in a later close friendship with socialite Léonie Leslie (Winston Churchill's aunt) – literally into a lifelong love affair with the country.

As winter eased in Montreal, fresh rumours began to circulate that the Fenians were planning a raid on Canada from the United States. Undercover agents along the border relayed sightings of training camps and, according to Elphinstone, 'serious reports of Fenian movements'.[36] The militia were called out in readiness for an attack and Arthur's regiment, the Rifle Brigade, was placed on high alert. In England, the heavily cosseted Prince Leopold sorely envied his brother, bemoaning in a letter to Louise that 'Arthur will have an opportunity of sniffing powder, happy boy!'[37]

The state of emergency in Canada was complicated by an insurrection by settlers in the Red River valley, a sprawling territory in the north-western provinces of the country recently transferred to the dominion government by the Hudson's Bay Company. Garnet Wolseley was ordered to lead an expedition to subdue the unrest, denuding Montreal of troops at a critical time. Nevertheless, Elphinstone was supremely confident that a raid could be resisted. Canada would obviously be defeated if the United States declared all-out war, he asserted, but 'I would confidently back it were it only 2 to 3 in numbers. There is greater stamina, more real courage in the English Canadian than in the American.'[38]

As time passed and the threat of invasion remained just that, even the colonel grew apprehensive. On 2 April, he complained to Commissioner McMicken that 'the worst of these fellows is that they only talk of coming, instead of actually appearing. If we could only get them to come somewhere in force, I think they would regret it and cease bothering the country.'[39] He told Victoria that the Canadians – who were losing a fortune in trade during the crisis – were the 'unfortunate sufferers' of 'a purely Imperial question . . . done to avenge Ireland's supposed wrongs'.[40] Another six weeks of fevered anticipation passed before it was finally confirmed that a force of American Fenians, estimated to be in the thousands, had mustered near the border with Canada, about sixty miles south-east of Montreal. The prince was at a ball to celebrate his mother's birthday when the order came through to report at once to his regiment. Hours later, before dawn on 25 May 1870, he departed by special train for the front, leaving the colonel to hurry back to Rose Mount to settle matters before joining him later in the day.

The climax to the affair came quicker than anyone had anticipated. At eleven that same morning, the hastily assembled Canadian troops engaged no more than a few hundred Fenians – not the thousands as feared – at Eccles Hill, near St John. The Fenians were all young and inexperienced – one Canadian journalist described them as 'the scum of American cities'[41] – and, despite their pristine green and blue uniforms, shamrocks and tricolour flags, poorly armed. After a brief fire-fight the Fenians fell back, leaving a handful of dead and wounded on the ground. The battle continued in a desultory fashion for several more hours but by six, with the Fenian leader captured and his men routed, it was all over. After such a tense build-up, the invasion itself had been an anti-climax. Arthur 'unluckily' arrived too late to witness the battle (though he placed himself in the thick of the action in his recollections sixty years later).[42] On 28 May he returned disconsolately to Rose Mount, clutching several trophies given to him from the battlefield, including the bloodstained uniform of one of the Fenians killed in the action.

At Balmoral, the Queen paid surprisingly scant attention to her son's 'little expedition to the frontier'.[43] As she explained to Howard, she was reeling from a far worse domestic disaster. The Prince of Wales had been embroiled in 'one of the *most disgusting* and *scandalous* trials *on record*!' Sir Charles Mordaunt, one of Bertie's least savoury acquaintances, had sensationally cited him in his divorce case after his wife Harriet admitted she had committed adultery 'often and in open day' with several men.[44] Evidence of the prince's involvement was flimsy and based on nothing more than a handful of fairly innocuous letters and Harriet Mordaunt's vivid imagination. Nevertheless, he was forced to defend himself in open court, to the glee of his mother's enemies. Victoria implored Howard to hide the details of the trial from Arthur, 'for they are such as *hardly* to be readable for any one and make *every one shudder* that the world *should* be *fed* with such *scandal*!'[45]

The Queen's bleak mood was further depressed by a series of deaths at court. In April, Charles Grey died suddenly, his loss casting 'a great gloom over us!' 'He had his failings and crochets and a difficult temper,' Victoria wrote, when she broke the news to Howard, 'but he was so clever, very honest, kind hearted and most agreeable when in good spirits, and few people will be more missed.'[46] In truth, Grey's relationship with his mistress, never an easy one, had deteriorated badly in the last months of his life, hastened by his criticism of John Brown and his grim, and ultimately hopeless, determination to see the Queen resume her public life. In one of his last letters to his wife, Grey had wearily revealed how his once all-powerful position had been reduced to no more than that of a clerk copying letters and dispatches. 'I . . . never hear a *syllable* from her of what passes between her and Gladstone,' he moaned,

> and I know *nothing* of what communications may have passed on
> the subject of the relief of the Fenians, even the Irish land
> question. I tell you fairly, I am *much* dissatisfied. Her manner
> when I dined with her last night, was anything but gracious and if
> confidence is withheld, it takes from one even the feeling of being
> useful, which alone reconciles me to going on with my slavery
> . . . I have promised you to endure this wretched life as long as I
> can, for *your* sake. Thank God I have kept clear of all the *miseries* of
> the Palace. I know, for Lady Ely told me so, that the quarrels in
> certain quarters are of daily occurrence.[47]

Within weeks, Grey was followed to the grave by three of the Queen's closest friends: her confidante Countess Blücher; her long-time personal physician Sir James Clark; and her political intimate Lord Clarendon. 'How many are gone,' she cried to Elphinstone, 'since you left in August last!'[48] On top of the earlier deaths of Sir Charles Phipps and General Bruce, these losses reduced the dwindling number of courtiers who had once known the Prince Consort yet further, sharpening the significance to the

Queen of those few left behind – men such as Elphinstone and Cowell. Grey's place as private secretary was taken by Henry Ponsonby, whose modern, liberal views aroused suspicion in the Queen's family while his artful bonhomie irritated Elphinstone.

In spite of all its attendant dangers and possible pitfalls, the prince's tour of North America was overall judged a success. Writing to Elphinstone, Sir George Cartier, who had replaced Macdonald as Prime Minister of Canada, described it as 'un *succès complet*'. 'Mais dans ce succès,' Cartier declared, 'chacun dira avec moi que vous y avez un part. Vous avez contribué à former ce Prince si accompli, et dans le succès de l'illustre Pupille on ne peut oublier celui qui l'a guidé depuis plusieurs années . . . vous devez être fier de votre *Royal Pupil*.'[49] Apologizing for the 'personal comments about himself', the colonel forwarded Cartier's compliments to the Queen together with his own personal summary of their adventure.[50] 'It has been in every way an immense success,' he wrote on 15 June, shortly before embarking for the long voyage home.

The Prince came here at a time when discontent was still rife; people were talking of independence and demagogues were preaching annexation to the States; while rumours were afloat, as Your Majesty knows, that his life would be in danger. He leaves universally esteemed and beloved; the cry of annexation has not only died out, but dare not be raised now; and every member who has attempted 'independence' has been entirely frustrated at the hustings.

'There appears a general wish', the colonel concluded, 'that he will soon come again, not as a simple officer of the "Line" but as "Governor General".'[51] It would take another forty years, but this desire would eventually be realized when Arthur returned to Canada as commander-in-chief of the army and Governor General in 1911, posts he would hold for five difficult years.

The American tour took a heavy toll on Elphinstone's

fragile health. Apart from the constant worry over the prince's safety, he complained that the endless correspondence had kept him up into the early hours every night. He freely admitted he craved rest – glancing uneasily perhaps towards the fate which had befallen Bruce, Phipps and now Grey, all of whom had died prematurely serving the Queen. Seeing Wolseley head off to glory on the Red River expedition had also reminded him, yet again, of the damage his position at court was causing to his army career. His request for leave was granted, but any hope that he might soon be able to hand over his onerous duties to a younger man like Pickard were dashed when the Foreign Secretary told the Queen that he trusted 'that the rest which Colonel Elphinstone requires is only of a temporary character. He seems to be a most valuable servant to Your Majesty.'[52] Victoria rarely relinquished valuable servants. Indeed, it would not be too long before the colonel was pitched into a fresh crisis at the palace.

24

'This frightful War'

1871

WHEN ELPHINSTONE AND ARTHUR arrived back in Europe in July 1870 they found Prussia and France at war. An arcane debate over succession to the vacant Spanish throne had spiralled into a bitter struggle between King Wilhelm I and Emperor Napoleon III for ascendancy on the continent. It was another war – the third in six years – engineered by Otto von Bismarck, now Chancellor of Prussia, to advance his country's influence and its territorial possessions. Once again the branches of Europe's royal houses were pitted against each other and family loyalties stretched to breaking point. Victoria despaired at the turn of events. 'God knows!' she complained to the colonel, 'this frightful War and the utter *uselessness* as regards National interests or Assistance to one's *own*, of these foreign alliances, certainly confirms all the Queen's feelings, and views on this subject.'[1] While the British government remained officially neutral throughout the conflict, the Queen unashamedly encouraged the Prussians while the Prince of Wales urged on the French from Marlborough House. The royal household was as divided as the royal family, splitting along its old fault-line, the English at court supporting the French and the Germans backing the Prussians.

Elphinstone had a closer interest than most in the conflict. His elder brother Nicolai (or Sir Nicholas Elphinstone, as he now preferred to be known) was living in France, having retired from a civil service position in India a few years before. When war came, Nicolai and his wife Georgina had volunteered to join the 'National Society for Giving Aid to the Sick and Wounded' – the forerunner of the British Red Cross Society. Together the Elphinstones had set up a field hospital at Tours to deal with the thousands of casualties flooding into the town from both sides of the conflict. Colonel Robert Loyd-Lindsay, later Lord Wantage, a founder of the society and a former equerry to the Prince of Wales, described the horrific scene. 'Wounded men', he wrote, '[arrive] every night by hundreds at the station where they are carried in, or hobble along themselves, a terrible array of martyrs without arms or legs, or their hands bandaged up, mostly French, but a good many Germans. Colonel Elphinstone [has] been at the station every evening with hot soup, coffee and bread.'[2] Deeply affected by what she witnessed, Georgina Elphinstone said that it was 'impossible to conceive the gratitude the poor fellows feel and express for all their comforts'.[3]

Dreams of past glories were not enough to save the Emperor of the French from disaster. With awesome efficiency and cold ruthlessness, the Prussians crushed Napoleon's army at the battle of Sedan on 1–2 September 1870. The Emperor was taken into captivity while Empress Eugénie escaped to England, her getaway aided by the elderly Sir John Burgoyne whose pleasure yacht happened to be moored at Trouville. On 6 September Eugénie was reunited with her son the Prince Imperial at a hotel in Hastings, Louis having been smuggled out of France separately by loyal Bonapartists. A month later, Howard and Arthur visited the unhappy exiles at Camden House, a mansion in Kent rented by the Empress for what she hoped would be a short stay. 'The future of France seemed to cause her great anxiety,' Elphinstone reported afterwards, 'and she earnestly hoped that peace would be declared. She spoke a good deal of the excited state of Paris just before she left, and that she herself had saved nothing excepting some of her jewels . . . her present separation from the Emperor seemed to cause her more pain than anything.' The colonel noted that the Prince Imperial, whom he had not seen since the grandiose events surrounding the Paris *Exposition* in 1867, still appeared '*far* younger than his years, but curiously inquisitive. His presence with the army has rather spoilt him, and made him very conceited. But this may probably wear off.' [4]

Even though its Emperor was incarcerated, its Empress exiled, its capital under siege and its imperial army shattered, France refused to yield to the Prussians. Pockets of armed resistance sprang up around the country to harass the occupying army. As the paper's most celebrated war correspondent, William Russell, was embedded at Prussian army headquarters in Versailles, the editor of *The Times* in London invited Nicolai Elphinstone to report on the resistance in his region. Dogged perseverance and bare-faced effrontery eventually secured Nicolai access to General Chanzy, the French military commander at Le Mans, 'who, though of course overwhelmed with important work, received me most cordially'.[5] Unlike the newspaper-savvy Prussians, before his capture the Emperor had refused to allow journalists anywhere near his army, leaving his people with a catastrophically false impression of their ability to defend the country.

Encouraged by his editor, who wanted to scoop his rivals in London, Nicolai began filing reports to *The Times* without first submitting them to the French censor, as he was bound to do. On 11 January 1871 he was arrested as a Prussian spy and thrown into prison. Fearing imminent death by firing squad, Nicolai wrote a series of final messages to his wife on his whitewashed cell wall – unadvisedly using German. Then, before dawn two days later, his cell door was opened and he was given a cigar and a tumbler of brandy, a sure sign of his impending doom. 'I need hardly say that this collation by no means overjoyed me,' Nicolai recalled dryly.[6] He was saved from summary execution only by the sudden fall of the town that very morning and by the timely arrival of the fearsome 'Red Prince', Prince Friedrich Carl of Prussia, who may have recognized the prisoner's distinctive surname from those among the court at Windsor. Released into Prussian hands, Nicolai was allowed to return to Tours, marvelling at his narrow escape. As he travelled slowly through the war-torn landscape, Nicolai was unaware that hundreds of miles away, at a glittering ceremony orchestrated by Bismarck at the palace of Versailles, King Wilhelm I of Prussia was being acclaimed Kaiser of a new, unified Germany or Second Reich.*

Howard evinced no anxiety about his brother's fate, being ignorant of the gravity of his situation until it had passed and he read Nicolai's colourful account of his adventures in *The Times*. Moreover, he was distracted by a mundane debate with the Queen about how Arthur should be addressed after the prince turned twenty-one in May. Arthur was determined to be made a duke, like Affie who had been created Duke of Edinburgh at a similar age. Despite this glaring precedent, Victoria was reluctant to agree to her son's request, telling Elphinstone that, on reflection, she now thought a dukedom was 'rather lowering' for 'a Prince of the Royal Blood'.[7] Recalling the lessons taught her by Baron Stockmar, Victoria also feared any of her sons taking a seat in the House of Lords to dabble in politics, a habit which had tarnished the reputations of earlier royal dukes. She emphasized 'the extreme *necessity* for Prince Arthur *not* to speak about the *present state of affairs*. The two elder Princes are unfortunately *known* to be *il*liberal, which the Queen considers very unfortunate in these days, for the dear Prince always used to say that the *Princes (wherever they were)* ought to be *very liberal*, and the country, or people, conservative.'[8]

Egged on by his impatient young charge, however, Howard boldly pressed further. 'Colonel Elphinstone is aware of the objections that have been raised,' he responded; 'nevertheless as these were overruled in the case of Prince Alfred, they could not well be now applied to Prince Arthur . . . The name to which Prince Arthur has taken special fancy is that of "York" but as an Irish title

---

*The first was the Holy Roman Empire (962–1806).

would be desirable there is "Connaught". He might be made a Duke of each.'[9] Still Victoria prevaricated. York was out of the question, as it was traditionally reserved for the second son of the monarch; and Connaught, a region in Ireland, was unpalatable as 'the Queen does *not like* the idea of one of her sons bearing a title of that disaffected and unreliable country'.[10] Nevertheless, after a great deal of soul-searching and protracted consultation with heraldic experts, Howard's idea was eventually taken up. In 1874 Arthur was officially recognized as the first Duke of Connaught, still his more familiar name today. (The full title was actually Duke of Connaught and of Strathearn, the latter element presumably added in deference to Victoria's devotion to Scotland and to soften the blow of conferring an Irish title on her favourite son.)

The turbulence on the continent was echoed in another pro-longed bout of unrest at court. While Howard was in Canada, Robinson Duckworth, Leo's likeable young governor, had been dismissed by the Queen on suspicion of flirting with 21-year-old Princess Louise, a fate similar to the one which may have befallen Carl Ruland. Knowing how popular Duckworth was at court, Victoria applied the same ploy she had used with Stirling, citing Leo's health as an excuse for sacking him, again claiming that her son needed a medical attendant, not a governor. A young doctor called George Poore was employed to replace Duckworth. 'Which *ought* always to *have been*,' the Queen told Elphinstone tri-umphantly; 'when Doctor Legg left, the Queen wished him to be succeeded [by a] medical man but she was *not* listened to as the Doctors thought he was better, and this was a terrible mistake . . . It is what would be, and is, done in every private family with a del-icate boy.'[11] Yet again, Leo was left bewildered by the abrupt departure of a much-loved friend, and more than ever now at the mercy of his bullying Scottish servants.

Poore had been employed on the recommendation of his mentor William Jenner, but the two men soon found themselves in conflict over the prince's care. The younger man found the emi-nent Queen's physician much changed from the doctor he had admired in general practice. 'The difficulty arises I think', Poore told his mother, 'from a reluctance on Jenner's part (from feelings of jealousy) to give me any medical standing here. Jenner the Professor and Jenner the Courtier are I find two different people the one honourable the other slightly contemptible.'[12]

Princess Louise was aghast at Duckworth's dismissal, blaming herself for it yet condemning her mother's decision as utterly 'misjudged'. 'Fancy what an existence for the boy,' she confided to Howard who she referred to as 'my dear Col.':

> perpetually with a doctor. He is to be nothing but his keeper, not his Governor. It is unfair toward him always to be changing. He never has had anyone more than four years with him and when there is someone who does understand him and try to make him happy and contented, with his many trials; it does seem hard. Arthur would, I am sure, never have turned out what he has had you left him . . . Mr Duckworth himself, of course, will gain by this and will be able to lead an active and independent life.[13]

The princess was currently embroiled in her own tussle with her mother regarding the identity of her future husband. Several names gleaned from the *Almanach de Gotha*, the essential guide to European royalty, were considered and rejected before the Queen, urged on by Vicky, settled on Prince Albrecht of Prussia, a nephew of Kaiser Wilhelm I. However, as Albrecht bluntly refused to live in England and the Queen was equally anxious to avoid losing a third daughter to a foreign court, his name was unceremoniously dropped, causing consternation in Berlin. Ignoring the protests of the Hohenzollerns, the Prussian ruling family, Victoria had made it known that she would even consider marrying Louise to a titled commoner to keep her in England. This startling proposition flew in the face of everything that Victoria had ever said on the matter of royalty consorting with the nobility. It had also infuriated her other married children, all of whom had dutifully taken royal partners. Undaunted by the howls of protest, the Queen had shamelessly launched a lengthy beauty contest on Louise's behalf, submitting several eligible young aristocrats to her careful scrutiny. Appalled by the wrangling over her future, Louise had poured out her heart in a series of highly charged letters to Elphinstone shortly before he returned from Canada with her brother.

'I think you may perhaps like to hear from me,' she had written in April 1870, 'and know that my thoughts are very often at Rosemount with dear Arthur, and yourself. I hope you will believe how much I still miss you, and wish for you back.' She continued:

> I think you know this Prussian affair has been entirely forbidden, and the only way of putting a stop to it has been that the Queen should have no objection to a subject. I have been for the last year most cruelly placed in consequence. You know *how* much Vicky and the King wished the other. The few people I should have cared for here are just married, so I do not know what is going to happen. Mean whiles every one is speaking, either for or against this, and it is most uncommonly unpleasant, and I am to decide without a proper chance of knowing anyone, so I leave it to you to judge what a delightful position I am in. I hope you will not think me very forward in telling you these things but you have, since I am a child, always been so kind to me, that I have been bold in writing to you.[14]

The colonel's reply is lost, but it was clearly reassuring as Louise replied straight away:

> Let me tell you how much I feel your kind interest in me, and in my future. But *I* want you to know that I am in *no* hurry or wish for another life. But it is that I *am* hurried on all sides which is painful. We must all of us have some disagreements, so I must not mind I know, and I try not to. Please consider all I have ever told you as only between us. When you come back we must see how things stand.[15]

Yet by July little had changed, though the outbreak of war on the continent had pushed the issue to one side. Louise tried to concentrate instead on making bandages for the wounded, some of which may have made their way to Nicolai Elphinstone at his field hospital in Tours. She suffered headaches and watched disconsolately as the royal household settled into its familiar factions. Then in the autumn her mother invited a fresh batch of suitors to Balmoral, on the pretence of entertaining Arthur on his return from Canada. Among them was the Marquess of Lorne, heir to the Duke of Argyll, whom the princess had already discarded once before. But there was much to love in this handsome young lord with his blue eyes and mop of blond hair; and, despite her previous reservations, this time Louise was smitten. On 3 October Lorne, confident of the Queen's blessing but boldly proceeding without her knowledge, proposed to Louise during a walk around the estate. News of the engagement was kept secret a while longer to prepare the royal family for the shock of its announcement. But those, like Elphinstone, who attended that evening's royal dinner party might have guessed at it by catching the knowing glances between the couple across the table. Victoria alone 'knew all', having spoken with her daughter privately before the meal.[16] When the news was finally made public it was celebrated with a ball in the Servants' Hall at the castle, presided over by the delighted Queen. Afterwards George Poore, still new to the strange routines of Victorian court life, complained that 'the room was hot, dusty and as odorous as a sailor's chapel'.[17]

Howard was '*most* favourably impressed' by Lorne. 'No one', he told the Queen, 'can help being struck with his remarkable intelligence, the extent and accuracy of his information, and his sound and clear judgement.' Indeed, the two men struck up such a rapport that Victoria charged Howard with minding her future son-in-law before his wedding to prevent his compromising the engagement. When the young lovers were thrown together at Osborne House at Christmas, for instance, the colonel received a curt note instructing him to ensure 'that Lord Lorne is not brought across to the Princesses corridor'. Arthur, meanwhile, was severely reprimanded for driving 'his still unmarried sister through Cowes' without a lady in attendance.[18]

Louise and Lorne were married in St George's Chapel on 21 March 1871. Most of the royal half of the congregation in the chapel were still seething that the Queen had approved such an unequal match, the first between an English princess and a commoner for centuries. Louise's elder brothers and sisters considered her rank undermined by the marriage. The Prince of Wales, in particular, was 'very unkind about his sister's marriage', the Queen complained.[19] Yet their disapproval was as nothing compared to the dismay of the Hohenzollerns, who boycotted the ceremony altogether, shaking their heads in bewilderment at its indecency. Victoria blithely ignored them all. At the service she looked 'positively radiant, her whole face beaming with smiles'.[20] Ten years after Albert's death, she had finally rediscovered the art of ruling.

25

The Queen's Knight

1871

WITH LOUISE SAFELY DISPATCHED on her honeymoon, the Queen began to search for a wife for Arthur. On 1 May 1871 the prince marked his twenty-first birthday with a lavish tea party on the lawn at Osborne House for his family, the royal household and servants. For Victoria the occasion was not one of celebration but of regret that a third son now stood on the threshold of 'his *Manhood* and Independence'.[1] Of her nine children, only Leopold and Beatrice still lived at home, and she would fight tooth and nail to ensure they remained so. A recurrence of that chronic illness prevented Elphinstone attending the party. But the prince sent him a porcelain tea service as a memento while the Queen, her heart 'very full' with emotion, wrote to him twice that evening. She told him all about the party and of her feelings on a day 'on which *he* must feel proud and thankful; for to *his* care, unceasing devotion and watchfulness, our dear Boy owes *much more* than he or the *Queen can ever* express, or repay'.[2]

For his birthday, Arthur received more framed photographs of his dead father, the addition of a Highland servant to his retinue and another stern lecture from his mother on his future conduct. As always, the prince listened dutifully, even when his fashionable oversized collars were criticized by his mother as being '*too hideous* . . . They really look like the old gentlemen of a former generation.'[3]

*Watercolour of the entrance front of
Ranger's House, Greenwich, painted by
Howard for the Queen in January 1863.*

Watercolour of the Mount of Temptation near Jericho, with royal encampment in the foreground, painted by Howard during his tour of the Holy Land with Arthur in March 1865.

Photograph of Howard and Arthur in camp with their entourage.

Watercolour painted by Howard during his climbing tour of the Alps with Arthur and a distinctly hippy Major Harrison in 1868 (see inset). In a unique self-portrait, Howard has marked his own figure in red with his initials: 'H.C.E.'

LEFT: *Lady Augusta Stanley, who marvelled at the opulence of the Russian court and the 'peculiar characters' who populated it.*

Marie 1874
Petersburg

Watercolour of the Kremlin painted by Howard during the
festivities in Moscow celebrating the marriage of Prince Alfred
(above right) to Grand Duchess Marie Alexandrovna, daughter
of Tsar Alexander II (above left), in January 1874.

Princess Louise, the Queen's most spirited and attractive daughter, who poured her heart out to Howard during the tortuous process leading to her betrothal to the Marquess of Lorne.

He gravely promised the Queen that he understood the responsibilities of a prince of the blood. 'Of course I know that a young man of my age is open to the greatest temptations,' he wrote,

> but I hope that my previous education and training and dear Papa's good and noble example will always support me in the hour of difficulty and temptation, I have had a great advantage in having so good and kind an adviser as the Colonel . . . I trust that the good feeling that has always existed between the Colonel and myself (which has not existed always with other people like for instance dear Affie & Sir John) will be a slight guarantee of my desire to follow good examples.[4]

Barely days later, a bizarre accident at Buckingham Palace almost claimed the prince's life. Before dressing for a ball, Arthur and the colonel had slipped away for a game of billiards with Prince Christian. It was a warm evening, and during the game Arthur had leaned back against a blind – falling through an open window and into the courtyard some eight feet below. Two nearby policemen rushed to the scene while the colonel hurried around the maze of palace corridors to reach the courtyard, a thousand terrifying thoughts rushing through his head. When he eventually reached the stricken prince, he found him conscious but shaking violently, having suffered a severe head injury. As the guests started arriving for the ball, Arthur was bundled off to his room, leaving the colonel to compose a 'carefully worded telegram' for the Queen, who remained at Balmoral. Once she had been reassured that her son would survive his fall, Victoria sympathized with Elphinstone. 'The Queen', she wrote, 'can hardly imagine *what* the kind and devoted Colonel must have felt . . . on seeing darling Arthur vanish. Even now the Queen can hardly dare to think of it. It causes her to shudder.'[5] 'These falls often leave *traces* behind,' she then warned him, 'which *must* be *very carefully* watched, often for *months* if *not years*.'[6]

By July, Elphinstone had recovered sufficiently from the

shock of the accident, and Arthur from the fall itself, to organize a coming-of-age dance for the prince in the grounds of Ranger's House. Yet this event too was overshadowed by a potentially catastrophic mishap when the tent caught fire after a lantern fell over. While the party continued unabated inside, Howard broke the news of the accident to the Queen, casually assuring her that the fire 'had been put out without any damage done beyond the destruction of the entire tent, a passage and the seats it contained'.[7] Although 'shaken' by Howard's account, Victoria was more alarmed to hear from another source that her son had been seen cavorting with Lady Rosamond Spencer-Churchill, the beautiful teenage daughter of the seventh Duke of Marlborough (and, like Léonie Leslie, later an aunt of Winston Churchill). The Queen was horrified, exclaiming that she 'would have no objection whatever to his marrying a *subject* but would *not* like this connection as there is so *much madness* in the Duke of Marlborough's family'.[8] The report confirmed the urgent need to find Arthur a bride. So the Queen dusted off her copy of the *Almanach de Gotha*, discarded during the fraught process of finding a husband for Louise, and once again settled down to view the options.

The colonel naturally envisaged the prince's coming of age as the conclusion to his employment at court. Victoria saw things differently. She recalled Affie's 'great loss' when John Cowell left him, and how Bertie had suffered when General Bruce died.[9] She urged Elphinstone to remain 'in some manner' with Arthur, 'at least at the Head of his Household'.[10] But the colonel was resolute. After twelve years' attendance on the prince, he was anxious to resume his army career, to savour life outside the suffocating world of the palace, even perhaps to find a wife. He was also certain that his continued presence would become 'decidedly irksome' to the now adult Arthur. His mind was set. Sir Thomas Biddulph, the Keeper of the Privy Purse who handled the delicate negotiations, was certain Elphinstone would resign this time. Hearing of this, the Foreign Secretary discreetly approached the colonel with the offer of a diplomatic post in Vienna, an excellent and sensitive location in which to exploit Howard's wide-ranging royal connections.

Victoria was bitterly disappointed at the colonel's reply, but she was equally determined to keep him at court. Howard was one of the few remaining links to the world before her husband died: that world of children's parties, music and laughter. He had shared in her happiness and felt her sorrow. He could not go. She therefore proposed a period of reflection while she devised 'some honorary title which would not prevent him returning to his profession' but which would still keep him close to her.[11] Taken aback by the force of the Queen's argument – and by six highly emotive letters from her within forty-eight hours – Elphinstone agreed to listen. He was 'perfectly prepared', he replied equably, 'to do all that he possibly can so long as it does not seriously mar all his future prospects'.[12]

With Biddulph's help, a deal was brokered whereby Elphinstone would remain at court for one more year as controller and treasurer of Prince Arthur's growing household. As it was expected that his new duties would be less onerous than formerly, this compromise would enable Howard to resume at least some military duties before returning to the army full-time. To avoid the 'pecuniary loss' Howard feared accepting the post might cause him, the Queen agreed to match his salary as a controller to his current generous palace pay of £600 a year. As he would also be able to resume his full pay of approximately £400 a year as a colonel in the engineers, this would give Howard a comfortable annual income of about £1,000.[13] In addition, Victoria promised him a handsome pension, an issue which had been another sticking-point. These arrangements, intended to last for only one year, stayed in place until Howard's death twenty years later.

The Queen was delighted with the outcome. 'You will I am sure', she pressed Arthur, 'express *yourself* your gratitude to the Colonel, for it is not without a sacrifice to his own convenience that he undertakes this.'[14] But one other delicate matter remained unresolved. During his initial meeting with Biddulph to discuss his retirement from royal service, the colonel had requested 'some public token of approval' before returning to his regiment. 'Otherwise', Biddulph had tactfully explained to the Queen, 'if he was entirely dissociated with Your Majesty it might appear as if he had not given satisfaction.'[15] The colonel 'did not appear particularly to wish for the KCB*', he added hastily.[16] Nevertheless, Howard had rather pointedly compared his twelve-year stint as Arthur's governor to the mere eight years John Cowell had completed with Prince Alfred before he received a knighthood.

The issue of reward was not mentioned again until June 1871, when Henry Ponsonby reported to the Queen that the colonel now seemed 'very anxious to obtain the honour of the KCB'.[17] Ponsonby and Elphinstone were never close friends, so the secretary's comment may simply have been mischievous. But the changed circumstances since April, and his agreement to stay at court a while longer, may have genuinely altered Howard's opinion on the matter. Initially he may have baulked at the prospect of receiving a KCB in the Civil Division, traditionally the reward of time-servers and back-scratchers. He would have much preferred a knighthood linked to military service, as his great-uncle and namesake Major-General Sir Howard Elphinstone had received on the Duke of Wellington's recommendation following the Peninsular War. In the close-knit worlds of the army and court, such fine distinctions were very closely scrutinized. In May, however, to mark Arthur's birthday, the Queen had raised the Commander of the Bath in the Civil Division which Howard had received in 1865 (when Cowell's knighthood so upset Charles Grey) to the more prestigious rank of Military Division, paving the way to the higher-status knighthood. Confirmation that he had been right to attach so much importance to the exact definition of his award came in the letter of congratulation he received from Lord Napier, the conqueror of Abyssinia, who praised Howard's knighthood as 'well earned in war and peace'.[18]

---

* Knight Commander of the Bath.

Victoria was as uninterested in such minutiae as she was in Ponsonby's pompous suggestion that handing out too many knighthoods was 'dangerous to the dignity of the Order'.[19] She pronounced that Cowell's earlier award had set a precedent for knighting the governors of all her sons and that, if anything, Elphinstone had an even 'stronger claim' to the decoration than Cowell.[20] Moreover, she wanted the award to be seen specifically as her personal gift and not one of simple entitlement, further increasing its prestige. Writing to the colonel to confirm his knighthood in the sought-after Military Division, she explained that this was her way of showing

> publicly her deep sense of the very valuable and devoted service which *Sir Howard Elphinstone* has rendered to her beloved son Arthur, and thereby to herself . . . the great responsibility of Sir Howard's position, particularly in distant parts, like in Canada, as well as his almost constant presence with Arthur, must have been very trying to him and has, the Queen fears, told upon his health.[21]

In a very personal sense, Howard was now the Queen's knight.

The colonel described his new role at the palace as Prince Arthur's '"adviser" and . . . friend, but not as . . . authorised guide or monitor'.[22] He took a military post at Aldershot camp – his first with the army since the 1850s – confident that the long hours at court were finally behind him. He also began to hanker after a wife, a family and a home of his own. The Queen, however, had other ideas. Disregarding the terms of his re-engagement, she began bombarding him with the names of potential brides for Arthur, all gleaned from her well-thumbed copy of the *Almanach de Gotha*. The matter had been given added urgency by the pro-tracted negotiations over Prince Alfred's projected marriage to Grand Duchess Marie Alexandrovna, the daughter of the Russian Tsar, Alexander II. Wary of the showy Romanov court and uncom-fortable at the prospect of an English prince marrying into the

Russian Orthodox Church, the Queen had dragged her heels over the match. Affie was 'bent' on marrying the grand duchess, but the diplomatic ramifications were such that, as Victoria confessed to Howard, he was 'by no means *sure* of obtaining' her.[23] The Germans were aghast that such a high-profile match between two of their rival nations was being made over their heads. Even the Russians were cooling a little, fearing the damage the marriage could cause to their relations with Berlin.

In these delicate circumstances, Vicky and Alice again conspired to persuade their mother that quickly identifying a wife for Arthur who was amenable to the Germans would ease the problem. Such an outcome would also bolster their own fragile positions on the continent and calm Prussian tempers frayed by Louise's recent marriage to the Marquess of Lorne. The Queen concurred and in January 1872 dispatched Elphinstone and the prince on a reconnaissance mission to Berlin, for 'it is well he should look about, for else these Princesses may get snapped up'.[24] Arthur 'may, and in fact SHOULD, *try* and *look* at *several Princesses*', she instructed. The colonel was also told to keep an eye open for an alternative bride for Prince Alfred, just in case negotiations collapsed in St Petersburg.[25] In fact, Victoria was glad to be rid of Arthur for a while, as he had shown scant sympathy for the Prince of Wales, currently laid up with typhoid at Sandringham. Both Arthur and Affie had been reprimanded for their behaviour during their brother's '*death struggle*'.[26] 'There was too much giggling and too much liveliness of manner,' their mother had complained, 'and the way in which you both *listened* to poor Bertie's wanderings grieved me.'[27]

Before sailing for Germany, Elphinstone assured the Queen that 'the Princesses which Your Majesty mentions are all down on his private list'. He would 'take every opportunity of seeing the various Princesses that are likely to suit, and either encourage or discourage acquaintance, as may seem advisable, taking care however that the reason of his so doing, does not become apparent to Prince Arthur'.[28] He knew, however, that he had to be very careful, less to avoid embarrassing Arthur than for fear of upsetting the delicate political situation on the continent. Memories of the war between Prussia and France were still painfully fresh, and the ink on the new map of Europe was barely dry. Moreover, the English were viewed with the greatest suspicion in Berlin, where they were accused not only of clandestinely backing the losing side during the war but also of giving refuge to the French imperial family after it. Arthur's choice of bride would therefore be closely watched by the other royal houses of Europe as a demonstration of current English sympathies. An ill-advised match could jeopardize fragile alliances, confirm prejudices and set the tone for future conflict. And no-one would follow events more intently than Otto von Bismarck, made a prince himself after Prussia's triumph against France and the unification of Germany.

Despite general hostility, the Machiavellian German Chancellor was keen to exploit the visit of one of Queen Victoria's sons to Berlin. He ensured that Arthur was fêted everywhere he went, including at the countless balls and dinners held in the Prince's honour. 'Fortunately', Elphinstone reported, 'the hours here are very early so that there is not much fatigue . . . Everybody dines at 5, and the theatres are over by 9 pm.'[29] Moreover, he was astonished at 'the modest behaviour of the Prussian officers', fully expecting to find them boastful and overbearing after their recent victories. He also perceived 'a strong touch of sadness' in Queen Augusta of Prussia, now Kaiserin of Germany, whose liberal sympathies had been assaulted by the aggressively nationalistic pact struck between her estranged husband and his predatory chancellor.[30]

Despite all the pageantry, Elphinstone never forgot the purpose behind his visit to Berlin. Arthur's sister Vicky, the Crown Princess of Prussia, gleefully connived in Howard's subterfuge, relishing the company of a familiar and friendly face from home. She invited several of the titled girls on his secret list to tea at the royal palace so that he could discreetly appraise them. While the cakes were passed around, the colonel, as he rashly revealed in a letter to Windsor, was 'asked to come in and look at some of the paintings in the room, so that no suspicion of the object of the visit should get about'.[31] Victoria, however, was furious to hear that her daughter was meddling in such a delicate matter. 'The Crown Princess has a mania for matchmaking,' she warned Elphinstone.[32] He was firmly ordered 'to keep the Crown Prince and Princess *out* of any matrimonial prospects for Prince Arthur'.[33] The Queen feared that, if discovered, Vicky's involvement in Howard's ruse would further undermine her reputation in the Prussian court. Slightly disingenuously, Howard assured the Queen that 'although the Crown Princess was consulted, she was certainly not made a "Confidant" in the matter'.[34]

The Queen also abruptly informed Elphinstone that she had now cooled on the idea of marrying Arthur to a German princess. Instead, she wanted a report on Princess Thyra, the daughter of the King of Denmark and younger sister of the Princess of Wales. The Queen's quixotic change of heart was probably influenced by a fleeting respect for the opinion of the Prince of Wales, whose near-miraculous recovery from his illness was the cause of national celebration. Bertie strongly promoted another Danish match. Not only was Thyra his sister-in-law, but he believed such a marriage would act – like his own – as a bulwark against growing German influence on the continent. 'To see the German element die out of our family would grieve the Queen *very much*,' Victoria reflected sadly in February 1872; 'still *peace* in the family . . . was the *great thing*.'[35]

Princess Alice's enthusiasm in the matter of Arthur's marriage had also been undermined as it appeared linked to her own demands for financial support. After visiting her sick brother at Sandringham, the princess had returned to Darmstadt trailing indefinite accusations of '*mischief* and *intrigue*'. Alice's 'greediness for money is terrible', Victoria exclaimed in a letter to Howard, and she strongly advised him against calling on her on the way back from Berlin.[36] The Duchy of Hesse was indeed relatively impoverished when compared to the lavish courts enjoyed by the rest of the royal family, so to some extent Alice's complaints were justified. For this very reason, however, Howard would not be dissuaded from visiting her, afterwards declaring that the relaxed and slightly ramshackle Hessian court had produced a good effect in Arthur, having 'smoothed down some of the angularity acquired by the military spirit of Berlin'.[37] It was a clever remark, as the colonel knew that Victoria recoiled from the bellicose tone and 'snobbish style' of many of her own army officers – an attitude she termed 'John Bullism' and had detected in the unfortunate Walter Stirling.[38] So his comment produced an impassioned reply from the Queen and a reprieve for Alice. 'The military angularity of Berlin', she stormed, her daughter's behaviour quite forgotten, 'would *never do* HERE.'[39]

'Magnitude and magnificence which is impossible to surpass'

St Petersburg, 1874

O N 27 February 1872, beneath leaden skies, nine carriages swept out of the gates of Buckingham Palace. They were heading to St Paul's Cathedral for a Service of National Thanksgiving to mark the miraculous recovery of the Prince of Wales from typhoid. Ultimately, when countless appeals from her courtiers and government had failed, it had taken this very private and unexpected crisis to drag the Queen from her seclusion. Nevertheless, she had still dreaded the event. 'She is not feeling strong *or equal* to the *dreadful* day of Tuesday,' she confided to Elphinstone beforehand, 'though she is anxious to show her sense of the loyalty and sympathy shown by her people ... she is most anxious that Sir Howard should go with us in the carriage procession.'[1]

So he did, travelling in the leading carriage with Arthur. The Queen followed them, her appearance eagerly anticipated by the vast crowd which thronged the route to the cathedral. As usual, John Brown sat on the box seat of her landau, impervious to the cheers and occasional ribald jeers. Everyone was curious to see their monarch after so many years of obscurity. *The Times*, which had often criticized the Queen in the past, reported that she appeared happy and in 'excellent health'. Victoria was amazed by her reception, calling it 'a day of triumph, really most marvellous!'[2] Unlike her ministers, she had never – or so, at least, she claimed – doubted the loyalty of her subjects.

Two days after the service, Howard saw Arthur join the Queen, Prince Leopold and Lady Jane Churchill for a drive in the park. They were back within the hour, their arrival being greeted by a polite round of applause from the small crowd gathered at the palace's garden gate. In the inner courtyard of the palace, Brown jumped off his seat to lower the carriage steps, while Lady Churchill rose to get out. It was then that a lanky, sallow-faced boy wearing a battered black hat suddenly appeared beside the Queen. At first, she thought he was a footman come to lift the travelling rug from her knees. 'Then I perceived that it was someone unknown, peering above the carriage door, with an uplifted hand and a strange voice.' The next moment, Arthur, who was sitting opposite their mother, shouted a warning and, jumping up, shoved the interloper away with his hand before tumbling after him out of the carriage. Screaming, Victoria threw herself across Lady Churchill. When she looked up, she saw Brown grasping the boy around the neck while Arthur and Leopold struggled to wrestle him to the ground. Only when he was fully restrained did they all notice the pistol 'shining on the ground' beside the carriage. Everyone turned 'as white as sheets'. Jane Churchill began to cry softly while 'Leopold looked as if he were going to faint'.[3] A rapid search of the boy's pockets subsequently revealed a knife and a badly worded petition seeking the release of Fenian prisoners. All the old fears of an Irish terrorist attack came rushing back.

At his committal hearing, however, it was made known that the Queen's would-be assassin – a seventeen-year-old clerk called Arthur O'Connor – was a deluded young man acting alone, rather than a hit man from a terrorist cell. The story was given out that, far from having been confronted by a Fenian fanatic, Victoria had come into rude contact with nothing more sinister than London's oppressed poor. It was said that O'Connor, well-educated and bookish by nature, had fallen into mental ill-health after a road accident and a decline in his family circumstances. He had dabbled in Fenian politics but had been thrown out of the brotherhood for his erratic behaviour. At the time of the assault he had been working in a paint factory in south London. His mother spoke movingly of the changes in her son. He had destroyed all his writing, she sobbed, missed work and spent whole nights simply wandering the empty streets. She had no idea he had taken an interest in Irish politics. It also emerged at the hearing that O'Connor had originally intended to accost the Queen before the service at St Paul's, but had been scared off by the large police presence. Under cross-examination, he swore that his plan had been only to frighten the Queen, not to kill her, as he knew that the Prince of Wales was unlikely to be any more sympathetic than his mother to the cause of Irish republicanism if he became king; in fact, of course, given the circumstances of his sudden accession, he would be a lot less so. A police officer then testified that the pistol O'Connor had brandished was 'old and broken' and primed only with 'a piece of greasy red rag'.[4]

Finally, and sensationally, John Brown and Prince Leopold were summoned as witnesses. The prince was greeted with cheers and applause. But it was the appearance of the brooding Highlander which caused the greatest interest in the court's packed and expectant gallery. In what the *News of the World* described as 'genuine *Aberdeen-awa* Scotch of the most undiluted character', Brown steadily recalled how he had spotted O'Connor running round the back of the carriage as it drew up beside the palace entrance. 'I gied him a bit shove back,' Brown continued, his voice booming around the hushed courtroom, 'I took hold o' him with one of my hauns and I grippit him with the other by the scruff o' the neck . . . 'till half a dizzen had a grip o' him, grooms, equerries, I kenna how mony there was, so then I tocht it time to gie up.'[5]

The facts of the case against O'Connor – his insanity, his expulsion from radical politics, the confirmation that he had acted alone – all strangely echoed the evidence produced at the trial of Prince Alfred's assailant in Australia five years earlier. As Howard knew, the truth had been covered up then, so it seems likely that it was now too. Revelations about a Fenian conspiracy might have destabilized the government, rocked the throne and given renewed hope to republicans in Ireland and elsewhere. Unlike Affie's attack, however, this latest incident had sparked a mass of publicity, so there was no opportunity for a swift judgment and the summary execution of its perpetrator. There would have to be a proper trial.

The Queen was furious that Leopold had given the impression in his testimony to the court, which the press had then repeated, that it was his brother Arthur and not John Brown who had saved the day. 'You tried to push the wretch's hand back,' she wrote forcefully to Arthur, 'but you did not take it [the pistol] from him, as it fell to the ground when Brown seized him by the throat . . . one must be so careful for fear that one witness should contradict another.'[6] But any suspicion that Leo, who had suffered years of ill-treatment at the hands of the Highlanders, might have understandably sidelined Brown's role in the affair was undermined by the statement of the defendant himself. O'Connor clearly recalled that it was 'the gentleman who sat opposite the Queen [i.e. Arthur] [who] knocked the pistol out of my hand'.[7] The Queen steadfastly refused to believe this version of events, declaring that Brown 'alone saw the boy rush round and followed him'.[8] She then used her position to take exquisite revenge on the Scotsman's detractors. 'You will see in tomorrow's papers what I have done to mark good Brown's admirable conduct on the occasion,' she declared triumphantly in a letter to Arthur on 5 March.[9] With no precedent for the decoration of faithful royal servants, she had instigated 'The Devoted Service Medal', awarding its inaugural (and to date only) example to John Brown for 'his devotion on the occasion of the attack made upon Her Majesty in Buckingham Palace Gardens on the 29th February 1872'.[10] As she explained to Vicky, the Queen was delighted finally to have the opportunity to give public recognition to her Highland servant, as 'my good Brown is far too simple and modest ever to think much of any service he has rendered me, and this is only one of many, many for which I can never be grateful enough'.[11]

In contrast to Brown's highly public reward for apparently saving the Queen's life, Arthur was given a tiepin while Leopold received nothing at all. The Prince of Wales was furious at these slights, complaining bitterly about them in a long letter to his mother. He also refused point-blank to acknowledge Brown's actions. Enraged, Victoria flung Bertie's complaint at Elphinstone, 'as he knows all', requesting him to reply, as 'a few words from Sir Howard Elphinstone to the Prince of Wales (who she *knows likes* to hear from Sir Howard sometimes) saying *he had heard* the Prince of Wales had said something of the kind to the Queen, would do *more* good *even* than what *she proposes* to write'.[12] Uneasy at becoming involved in the family spat, Howard tactfully suggested a meeting between mother and son to clear the air. But Victoria wanted to register her anger in writing. 'A *few short* words', she declared, 'would be most useful and better written AT ONCE.' In his letter to Bertie, the colonel was to dispel the impression that Arthur 'should have been also rewarded and more have been said about him in the papers . . . which did not exist in Arthur's mind, nor she believes in anyone else's'.[13] After their recent *rapprochement*, it was obvious that Bertie and his mother were once again in open conflict.

O'Connor offered no defence when he appeared at the Old Bailey in April, denying the public a proper explanation for his actions. But in spite of his assumed insanity, the court doctor declared the defendant fit to plead, so O'Connor's silence was taken as an admission of guilt. On 11 April, watched from the public gallery by Prince Leopold, he was sentenced to one year in prison with hard labour. The judge also ordered that he was to be whipped twenty times with a birch rod. The Queen was outraged by this leniency. 'Only one flogging with merely a year's imprisonment and hard labour!' she exclaimed to Vicky.[14] She pressed the Prime Minister to review the case, arguing, not unreasonably, that as O'Connor was sane enough to stand trial he should receive the usual tariff of seven years. Given the sensitive nature of the trial, its outcome suggests that O'Connor may have benefited from a plea bargain, gaining a reduced sentence in return for his silence on the motives behind his attack.

With Bertie again in disgrace, the Queen rapidly lost enthusiasm for his suggestion that Arthur should marry his wife's sister Thyra. She had also recently heard that the Danish princess was 'not at all pretty, her mouth being so very ugly with projecting teeth'.[15] Yet courtly realpolitik demanded that the Queen should at least examine the possibility of such a match; and so eventually, in July 1873, Howard was sent to Trondheim to appraise Thyra at the coronation of the King of Norway. Afterwards, the colonel declared himself

> much pleased with what he saw . . . She is far taller than either of her sisters and more strongly built, but still very graceful in figure. Her eyes are very large and fine . . . So far as one could judge after so short an acquaintance nothing could be nicer than either her manner or her character. She is decidedly clever and most sensible and agreeable.[16]

In fact, she was nothing like the Queen's description.

Despite the subterfuge, the palace's interest in the Danish princess soon reached the London papers; some even suggested that she was already secretly engaged to Arthur. Even the prince expressed some mild interest in Thyra, remembering her from childhood parties. Amid mounting press speculation, and the rising hopes of the Danish royal family that they might land a second English prince, Victoria was forced to reconsider her opposition to the match. She could not deny that Thyra possessed all those graceful qualities which had made the Princess of Wales so popular in England, while 'a strange, stiffly brought up German Princess with *airs* . . . would *never* do'.[17] Yet she fretted that Thyra, '*not* being German', would diminish still further the 'German element' in the British royal family, 'to the Queen's great sorrow'.[18]

The princess would also inevitably ally herself with the so-called Marlborough House Set, luring Arthur into the louche crowd which clung to the Prince and Princess of Wales. Moreover, Thyra's mother was beginning to behave oddly: first zealously pressing her daughter's cause, then becoming distant and 'rather cool', apparently after the hoped-for offer of marriage from Arthur had failed to appear during his recent visit.[19] This settled it. 'We must be firm and explicit in all we say,' Victoria told Howard, fearing a Danish ploy, for 'the Queen of Denmark is a sly woman'.[20] All talk of marriage between Arthur and Thyra was to end at once and exploration of other avenues be resumed.

After an uncertain start, Affie's matrimonial plans were now proceeding rather better than his brother's. Overcoming her prejudices against the Romanovs, the Queen was resigned to his marriage to Grand Duchess Marie Alexandrovna, despite the couple's religious differences and the degeneracy of the Russian court. She had even accepted the Tsar's demand that the wedding take place in Russia, although she insisted that a separate Anglican ceremony should immediately follow the Orthodox rituals. In January 1874, Arthur Stanley, the Dean of Westminster, was duly dispatched to St Petersburg to conduct the English service. The dean led a party which included his wife Augusta, the Prince and Princess of Wales, Prince Arthur, Sir Howard Elphinstone, and the bridegroom's former governor Sir John Cowell. Elphinstone and Cowell both had their own reasons for attending the ceremony. As Master of the Queen's Household, Cowell wanted to see how the Romanov court entertained its guests on such a grand state occasion, while Elphinstone was again scouting for a bride for Arthur. Before he left Windsor, the Queen gave him a photograph of one particular wedding guest she wanted him to view: fifteen-year-old Princess Hélène of Mecklenburg-Strelitz who, Victoria had earlier noted, was said 'to be very charming and well brought up and will be *rich!*'[21]

There was a warm reception in Berlin from the crown princess when the royal party paused in the city during their long journey to St Petersburg. Officially, Germany frowned on the marriage between the Russian grand duchess and the English prince, as Bismarck feared a hostile alliance between their two countries. But Vicky, at odds with her adopted country as usual, looked forward to welcoming Marie into her family and planned to travel to the ceremony alone if her husband Fritz felt he could not. In the meantime, she delighted in seeing 'so many English faces' in Berlin, organizing skating and shooting parties for her guests.[22] The Kaiserin Augusta was equally 'most kind and affable, and discussed in her usual way the different political "situations" on the continent'. In contrast, the 76-year-old Kaiser Wilhelm I was 'much depressed in spirits'.[23] Augusta confided to Elphinstone that her husband had recently suffered an 'apparent entire loss of memory' which had left him still further in thrall to his rapacious Chancellor.[24] With Wilhelm apparently fast fading, Fritz's succession to the throne seemed imminent: a prospect as eagerly anticipated by the liberals at the Prussian court as it was dreaded by the reactionary faction led by Bismarck.

One evening in Berlin, the Chancellor joined the English visitors for dinner, stalking across the room like 'a giant amongst them all in look and stature'.[25] Despite his fearsome reputation, Bismarck struck Dean Stanley as an 'amiable and gracious' man who talked 'in a perfectly easy manner on England, Shakespeare etc'.[26] Augusta Stanley was more interested in the domestic arrangements in the city. After passing so many years shivering in her room at Balmoral, Osborne or Windsor, she reported excitedly to her sister that the guest rooms at the palace in Berlin were 'all warmed, and with blazing fires, real open fireplaces'.[27]

After attending a wild boar hunt organized by Fritz, the wedding guests continued to St Petersburg by rail. Vicky vowed to follow a few days later, steadfastly refusing to be cowed by Bismarck into boycotting her brother's marriage. With his eye for detail, Elphinstone noted that the train sent by the Tsar to collect them at the Russian border was exactly 1,050 feet long, 'with separate sleeping cabins for each person, a large saloon of assembly and a still larger dining-room, at which we sat down 27 people'.[28] Early on 15 January 1874 they crossed into Russia, a land which had figured large in Howard's imagination ever since his childhood. His ancestors had fought, and died, for the Russian empire; yet, born under tsarist rule himself, and with Russian blood in his veins, he had almost lost his life fighting against it. Now he would experience the Russian court for himself; would see the milieu, and the life, which had dazzled and maddened his ancestors.

Tsar Alexander II himself was waiting at St Petersburg station to greet his guests. After the formalities, they were ushered into a fleet of waiting carriages to be wrapped in furs and 'whirled' through the snow-covered streets to the Winter Palace.[29] Augusta Stanley was overwhelmed by the scale and the riches of the Imperial Palace, marvelling at its 'miles of gallery' and 'acres of Halls' hung with 'lines and lines of frowning old Czars'.[30] Yet beneath the grandeur, the palace was absolutely filthy, while the 'smells, natural and artificial, are past all belief'.[31] Above all, Augusta was amazed by the strange customs of the colourful population of 'peculiar characters' who occupied the palace's corridors, some of whom harboured surprising desires. One beautiful young Russian woman even declared that 'she had lost her heart to me and had asked Sir Howard Elphinstone at dinner whether he thought I would be offended if she proposed to kiss me? How should Sir Howard know I ask?'[32]

Conditioned to the clockwork routine (and spartan temperatures) of the English court, the colonel found the Winter Palace disorganized and unbearably hot. Yet he could not deny that everything was 'done on a scale of magnitude and magnificence which is impossible to surpass and which could not be equalled in any but such huge palaces'.[33] When Howard's great-grandfather Admiral John Elphinstone had walked those same corridors a century before, he had remarked on the 'air of ease and freedom' inside the Imperial Palace; how Catherine II had been able to wander its rooms and corridors without ceremony or armed guards. After a century of revolutions in Europe, the palace, as Augusta Stanley observed, now contained 'a little army of soldiers of all Regiments with drawn swords'.[34] Such precautions were wise, but ultimately fruitless. Seven years later, the Tsar was killed by a nihilist's bomb on the streets of the city.

One morning, the English guests watched, fascinated, as Alexander led his family in the traditional ceremony of the blessing of the River Neva. Elphinstone noted how a hole was first broken in the thick ice to allow a cup of water to be raised and blessed by an Orthodox priest. 'Holy water was then sprinkled over the bystanders and the Emperor and all his family underwent the process of kissing the crucifix, and likewise the hand of the Patriarch of the Church.' Howard was struck by the dignity of the event and the Tsar's great humility. Everyone stood bareheaded throughout the rituals; fortunately the weather was unusually mild, otherwise 'serious consequences must have followed of standing there uncovered in their uniforms'.[35]

The evening before the wedding ceremony, disaster threatened to overwhelm the English contingent. Augusta Stanley suddenly realized that she had forgotten to arrange a bouquet for the bride, as she had faithfully promised the Queen before leaving Windsor. While Augusta 'ran right and left' in a panic, Howard calmly volunteered to 'ransack the town' for flowers. As revealed by Arthur Stanley, apart from the extreme short notice, one difficulty the colonel faced was his inability to speak Russian: evidence that despite his upbringing in Livonia he had never learned the language of its rulers. Undeterred by this handicap, he returned in triumph, having conjured up a bunch of white roses from a florist with the help of a translator and £7.[36]

The two marriage services then proceeded without another hitch, Augusta marvelling at the 'exactness' with which everything was carried out 'down to the minutest detail'.[37] The first part of the ceremony followed the rites of the Orthodox Church and took place in the Winter Palace's magnificent private chapel. 'The deep tone of the choir,' recalled Augustus Loftus, the British ambassador to St Petersburg, 'the thrilling force of the chants mingled

with the grand voices of the clergy, the magnificent dress and jewelled ornaments of the priesthood, and the impressive forms of
the Greek service, gave an imposing and solemn effect to the ceremony.'[38] The Tsar was deeply moved by the occasion but his
estranged wife remained icy cool throughout, an impression
heightened by her white satin gown and spectacular diamond
jewels. As Affie's sponsor at the service, Arthur stood behind the
bride and bridegroom during their vows, holding above them a
gold crown. As the service reached its climax, a ray of sunshine lit
up the darkened chapel, 'appearing as a ray of heavenly light beto-
kening a divine benediction on the happy couple'.[39] When the
Orthodox ritual concluded, the guests made their stately way to
the gilded magnificence of the Alexander Hall for the short
Anglican service. They then retired to a sumptuous wedding banquet, dining off the finest Sèvres porcelain using gold cutlery in a
scene, according to the ambassador, of quite 'indescribable' opulence.[40] Yet this was just the beginning of the week-long
celebrations, which quickly exhausted the English visitors.
Howard, who would have preferred to wander the exotic city with
his sketchbook and pen, found the constant changing of clothes all
rather 'monotonous and wearisome'.[41] Even Augusta grew tired of
seeing so many diamonds.

The Crown Princess of Prussia found the endless socializing
almost unbearable. 'I cut a sorry figure at Balls,' Vicky once confessed to her mother, 'as my eyes invariably close with fatigue and
I have to make such faces to keep them open!'[42] She sought refuge
in touring the astonishing artworks which filled the Romanov
palaces or in sneaking out of the palace with Howard to sketch in
the city. The princess was unaware of – or perhaps simply ignored
– the Russian secret service agents who tracked her every move.
But the colonel sensed sharply the menace lurking behind the
gloss of the state occasion. 'Every word one says', he told the
Queen, 'or any act one does is watched. Your Majesty will understand that one cannot say all that one wishes, and that the letters
sent by post must therefore be guarded.'[43] The cause of the

colonel's unease lay thousands of miles away in Central Asia, where Russian ambitions to extend their borders east met British determination to protect India. After decades of diplomatic skirmishing and occasional regional bloodshed, the so-called 'Great Game' was entering its most aggressive phase yet, with recent Russian incursions into Samarkand, Bukhara and Khiva, all of which lay on the doorstep of India. Howard's own family had a long history of playing the game. Mountstuart Elphinstone, brother of the twelfth Lord Elphinstone, had charted the strategically vital kingdom of Afghanistan for the British as early as 1808, while General William Elphinstone, grandson of the tenth Lord Elphinstone, later led – and died during – the disastrous retreat from Kabul in 1842. So Howard understood perfectly well the stakes the British were playing for.

The gruelling wedding festivities continued in Moscow, which the English guests reached after a 300-mile railway journey in the Tsar's opulent train. 'Moscow is very curious, quite peculiar in its way, and quite different to St Petersburg,' Howard reported from his rooms at the Kremlin; 'here the streets are narrow, and the houses have all an Eastern character, interspersed with churches innumerable, all adorned with gilt cupolas. The effect is most picturesque.'[44] After a week of sightseeing in the city, it was back to St Petersburg and then home, the colonel breaking the journey for a tour of the naval port of Kronstadt where his grandfather Samuel Elphinstone had lived, fought and died. Another sad reminder of his family life was waiting for him at the German border, where he received word that his mother Amelia was dying in Switzerland. Leaving the others to continue to England without him, Howard rushed to her bedside in Montreux, but arrived just too late to see her alive.

Arthur revealed that the colonel had been 'nervous' about his mother's health for some time, but that the suddenness of her death had shaken him badly. Much of Howard's adult life had been spent apart from his family, but now, with the death of both parents and little communication with his brothers and sisters, he felt entirely bereft. 'The loss of a mother is indeed a hard trial,' he lamented unhappily, 'and felt more severely even in later life than in youth.'[45] He could not know that salvation from his loneliness was imminent; for it arrived totally unexpected.

PART FOUR
Berlin

27

'My dear little darling'

1876

BY 1875 ELPHINSTONE SEEMED resigned to a solitary life, sharing his time between court and army. The Queen had assured him that his duties would lessen when Prince Arthur was twenty-one; in fact they scarcely reduced at all, merely changing in nature. His role as controller to the prince's household was all-encompassing, conferring on him responsibilities from managing the large staff to overseeing the accounts. He was also placed in charge of the project to build Arthur a suitable new residence at Bagshot, a small village in Surrey close to Windsor. An existing grace-and-favour house, once the home of the Queen's physician Sir James Clark, was pulled down and a rambling red-brick edifice in mock-gothic style with Arts and Crafts flourishes was erected in its place. After Osborne, Balmoral and Sandringham, Bagshot Park completed the quartet of great houses built by the Queen during her reign. The prince's mother was unimpressed, however, with her son's vast new property when she eventually visited it in 1880. It appeared, she conceded in a letter to Howard, to be 'very comfortable but excepting the dining room and drawing room she thinks *all* too *dark*; the windows too small and the furniture too dark. This [is] the fashion the Queen hears.'[1] She made no mention of the house's billiard room, in the design for which Howard had recruited the talents of

285

the architect Lockwood Kipling, the professor of architecture at Bombay University and father of Rudyard. Yet its exuberant decoration undoubtedly influenced her later choices in commissioning the famous Durbar Room at Osborne House.

On his return to military duty, Elphinstone had been placed in charge of the Royal Engineer units at Aldershot camp, his first real position of command after nearly thirty years in the army. During the summer of 1875 he was joined there by the French Prince Imperial, who had been posted to the camp with the Royal Horse Artillery. After a period living quietly in exile with his parents in Kent, Louis had followed Prince Arthur into the Royal Military Academy, a military education being thought essential for the Bonaparte heir to the French throne. After the death of his broken-hearted father in January 1873, the idealistic young prince had become the focus of the Bonapartists' fading hopes, this apparent destiny spurring him on in his quest for military glory. Officially, Louis's awkward constitutional status and foreign nationality ruled him out of a commission in the British army; but some string-pulling at the palace eventually secured him a position with the artillery, a fitting situation for the great-nephew of France's greatest ever gunner: Napoleon Bonaparte.

After the Emperor's death, Victoria had taken a keen maternal interest in the young Prince Imperial, like many romanticizing his role and situation. So she was horrified to discover, as she exclaimed to Howard, that Louis was entering the British army 'quite alone and without even a confidential valet, which *she* thinks a mistake and what she herself would never have done'. She charged the colonel with the task of watching over the French prince at Aldershot, to ensure he was 'in *good hands*, [and] with a good set'.[2] The moral peril into which the Prince Imperial had been thrust was dramatically illustrated by a scandal which erupted at the camp soon after his arrival. The *cause célèbre* concerned the assistant quartermaster-general at Aldershot, a man well known to Howard but described by the Queen as the 'bad notorious' Valentine Baker.[3] On 17 June 1875 Baker, a highly distinguished officer who had served in the Crimea, India and Afghanistan, was arrested on suspicion of raping a girl in a train. Worse still, Baker was a close intimate of the Prince of Wales and at the time of the alleged assault had been travelling to London to dine with the Duke of Cambridge. To cap it all, the girl's brother was an engineer serving under Elphinstone's command at Aldershot.

'One's heart sinks within,' the Queen told Elphinstone, 'when one thinks of young Princes or indeed any young men, being exposed to the contact of such men.'[4] The accusation seemed to confirm all her prejudices against the army. To her fury, Arthur tried to exonerate Colonel Baker, as indeed did most of the officers who knew him. Quoting her son's defence of Baker to Howard, Victoria complained that Arthur had protested 'as to his *not having fair play*, and *not* having a bad character and she is very anxious Sir Howard should *warn* him *against* joining in *such* remarks which would do *him* harm, especially when it is coupled with the ATTEMPT to blacken the poor defenceless girl's character!'[5]

Throughout his sensational trial on 2 August 1875, Baker made no attempt to deny the charge, believing such a course of action to be ungentlemanly against the word of a lady. Even so, the testimony of several high-ranking officers ensured that he was cleared of attempted rape. But it was not enough to save Baker from conviction for the lesser offence of indecent assault. Before he was led away to prison, the disgraced colonel sent a letter resigning his commission to Horse Guards, a copy of which was forwarded to the Queen the same day by Elphinstone. She found it 'very satisfactory', but also totally inadequate.[6] Against the entreaties of the Duke of Cambridge, the Prince of Wales and the entire military establishment, she cashiered Baker, throwing him out of her army in disgrace. Such unprecedented public humiliation was sweet revenge for a woman who for years had distrusted and despised the type of officer represented by Baker.

The drama of Baker's arrest and imprisonment had unfolded during one of the wettest summers on record. Conditions at Aldershot had quickly deteriorated. From his modest wooden hut, the only accommodation available to officers at the time, Elphinstone could see only a 'mass of black mud and wet tents'. One of these sheltered the young Prince Imperial, who was camped 'in a dismal place called "Colony Bog"'. Louis himself was cheerfully unconcerned by his living conditions and took charge of the cooking while his men dug trenches, explaining to Howard that 'being a Frenchman it was his *métier* to look after the cuisine'.[7] (The gunners apparently found Louis's soup 'first rate'.[8]) A further reminder of how far the Bonapartes had fallen since the glories of the Second Empire came in August, when the colonel left the mire of Aldershot to escort Arthur to Germany for a family wedding. Passing through Paris, they visited the palace of St Cloud, which lay in 'utter' ruins after its destruction during the revolutionary Commune which followed the Franco-Prussian War.[9] It was a bleak reminder of the perils of monarchy.

Howard never travelled now without the code book which enabled him to cable Windsor in secret. Such caution was essential as the political situation on the continent was deteriorating fast and, as the Queen discreetly put it, 'there might be questions and *certainly* information to be imparted' during the colonel's forthcoming visit to Berlin.[10] The slow disintegration of the Ottoman Empire, the so-called 'Sick Man of Europe', had triggered a series of uprisings in the Balkans, fuelling antagonisms among the major powers as they jostled for supremacy in that strategically important area.

It was the English crown princess who bore the brunt of the rising feeling in Germany against her native country (and the corresponding animus against Germans when she was in England). Before he died, the Prince Consort had instilled in his daughter a lively interest in contemporary affairs, a curiosity which agitated painfully against the traditionally supine nature of her role in Prussia. A love of gossip was expected in a princess, but Vicky's unfeminine taste for politics merely exacerbated the hostility of her Hohenzollern in-laws, who resented her meddling and her liberal outlook. It also undermined her husband's valiant but hopeless efforts to resist Bismarck's iron grip on his enfeebled father.

Isolated and vulnerable on all sides, Vicky warmly welcomed Howard to Berlin. She invited him to stay at the Neues Palais in Potsdam as her personal guest – twenty years after he had explored the then deserted palace as a tourist. Together they sketched and talked, each perhaps sensing the other's loneliness. '*Emboldened*', as she later confessed, by his 'kindness at Potsdam', by the time he left the palace Vicky considered Howard her sworn confidant and friend.[11] He was now one of the few people outside her large and bickering family to whom she could pour out her heart without fear of exposure or reprisal.

Within just weeks the crown princess sought Howard's advice on a personal matter. Her sister Alice had unsettled Vicky with reports that a clique was operating against her in England. 'There is a strange feeling of dislike and distrust (*all* ABOUT *me*) prevalent at Windsor in highest quarters,' she complained bitterly to Howard.

> Somebody has been interpreting simple facts in a very mischie-vous way. We cannot quite afford that, as I fear we are not over popular at home! I trust to *your* wisdom *and* discretion in *this* delicate matter, that is SHOULD *you* be in the way of dispelling this *impression* in high quarters. I hope you will try as it will be a great thing for me! There is always some *mischief being* made between *this* House and Windsor, and *I* am the sufferer and NEVER there to defend myself and explain things, as you know![12]

Egged on by Alice, Vicky came to suspect that their brother Bertie, with his Danish wife and well-known anti-German views, was behind the intrigue. Howard downplayed this fear, assuring Vicky that no-one at Windsor meant her any harm and that all the stories of plots and conspiracies were exaggerated; news which 'greatly relieved' her.[13] He had already proved himself a better friend to the crown princess than her sister, whose motives for so upsetting her are unclear.

Howard used his visits to Germany this year and the next to make fresh attempts to locate a bride for Arthur. After the fiasco over the Danish match, the Queen had drawn up a new list of eligible princesses which the colonel was to examine *'without betraying* anything'.[14] This time, Victoria was especially keen to know more about the youngest daughter of the King of Hanover, whose family had very close ties to her own. (The current king was her first cousin; only the Salic law, which prohibited female inheritance, had prevented Victoria from becoming the ruler of Hanover herself.) Howard's assessment of the princess was a model of discretion. 'To a *severe* critic,' he reported cautiously, 'it is very likely that the hands and feet of Princess Mary would appear large. But then she herself *is* very tall and consequently it does not strike one. Very thin she is not.'[15] Ignoring Howard's less than flattering opinion, the Queen pursued the idea for a while, attracted by the thought of reuniting the separated crowns in marriage. But the idea was doomed from the start. The Hanoverians were sworn enemies of the Hohenzollerns, which complicated matters considerably; and Princess Mary bravely declared that as she did not love Arthur, she could never marry him. The Queen despaired, petulantly declaring that she had now 'exhausted all those families from whom any Princess is to be obtained'.[16] None the less, the last thing she expected was that the colonel would find a wife for himself before he found one for her son.

The young girl Howard had barely acknowledged while staying with Lord O'Neill at Shane's Castle in 1869 had since grown into a striking beauty. Born after the Crimean War, Annie Cole was one of five children from a rumbustious family living in a handsome town house in London's Portland Place. Her father had made a fortune trading in quinine – the new wonder drug –

while her mother was the daughter of the founder of Justerini & Brooks, the celebrated West End wine merchants. Still only nineteen, in the spring of 1876 Annie was introduced more formally to Howard by Sir John Cowell's wife Georgina, whose sister was an old schoolfriend of Annie's mother. Despite an age difference of twenty-seven years, they were strongly attracted to each other, perhaps drawn by their shared love of painting and of music. Within weeks they were engaged.

According to convention, the colonel broke this startling news to the Queen through her lady in waiting, Lady Ely. It was an anxious moment. Howard knew that Victoria took a dim view of any of her staff marrying, believing it to be an unnecessary, even disloyal, move. She had been aghast when Lady Augusta Bruce, her most faithful companion, married Dean Stanley in 1863, afterwards insisting that they both remain at court. The same ploy was now used on Elphinstone. In her muted letter of congratulation, Victoria expressed her confidence that Howard was 'far too conscientious ever to let his private affairs interfere with his services to herself and her dear son'.[17] To secure his allegiance, within a year of his engagement the Queen made Elphinstone her personal aide-de-camp, a highly prestigious position which would keep him at her side regardless of the path his future career took.

Howard's relief at the Queen's reaction is evident in the letter he wrote to his 'dear little darling' on 1 July 1876, the day their engagement was announced. He assured Annie, who had waited anxiously for news at home with her parents, that Victoria was 'most kindly disposed towards you'. The Queen had been 'very nice and gracious' at dinner that evening, and 'she will be so for my sake on first meeting you, but afterwards I know this will increase from a better knowledge of yourself'. Prince Leopold had been less diplomatic. He had expressed his amazement at the announcement, quizzing the colonel closely on Annie 'because he thought I never would have married being so frightfully particular. When I told him that the chief cause was your complete unselfishness and bright nature, he said, "I don't believe in a truly unselfish woman, but if she is so indeed, as you say, you are a very lucky fellow."' The royal household were equally astonished. 'Questions of all kinds were asked,' he continued, rather gravely, 'which however I was determined not to answer, as I do not choose to gratify simple idle curiosity. Your own worth they will find out when they know you.'[18]

Howard and Annie were married quietly in London on 5 December 1876. Georgina Cowell, who, with her husband and Major Pickard, was one of only a handful of guests to attend the wedding, informed the Queen that 'it was a most wretched day and that the church had to be lit with gas'. But the bride had 'looked so nice and pleasing' that nothing could dampen the joy of the occasion. Victoria sent five silver gilt fruit baskets as a wedding present and an invitation for Annie, now that she was married, to visit her at Windsor. It was a daunting prospect for the new Lady Elphinstone. But, as Howard had assured her would be the case, the Queen was very friendly and, after driving around the park with Annie, pronounced her a 'very pleasing, bright little thing'.[19]

After a short honeymoon in Corsica, the Elphinstones returned to No. 2 Hut, K lines, North Camp, the colonel's unprepossessing residence at Aldershot. Together they transformed its drab interior into a comfortable home, filling it with the eclectic collection of treasures which Howard had gleaned on his travels with Arthur. The walls were panelled with medieval oak salvaged from a cathedral, while their guests sat on chairs made by French prisoners during the Franco-Prussian war. Among their friends at the camp was Juliana Ewing, the children's author who had waited hours to catch sight of Prince Arthur in Canada in 1869. With her husband, now a major in the pay department at Aldershot, Juliana was a regular visitor to the hut, giving an intriguing glimpse of its exotic interior in a letter to her sister. 'In the matter of pictures I do not always agree with Sir Howard', she wrote, 'but his decorative taste is very good, and the things he has picked up in all parts of the world are delightful . . . He is so very ingenious, and has made a dado over the mantelpiece, with a white or coloured border on which he puts pictures and photographs.'[20]

Later Juliana would pen an equally vivid portrait of Howard himself for her novella *The Story of a Short Life*, which was published in 1885 as a celebration of military valour in the context of a Christian life. In the book Juliana used Elphinstone as her inspiration for the character 'V.C.', a heroic young officer at Aldershot who represents the chivalric ideal to a dying child. 'V.C. did not look like a bloodthirsty warrior', she wrote.

> He was not very big, and he was absolutely unpretending. Before the campaign in which he won his cross he was most distinctively known in society as having a very beautiful voice and a very charming way of singing, and yet as giving himself no airs on the subject of an accomplishment which makes some men almost intolerable by their fellow men. He was a favourite with ladies on several accounts, large and small.[21]

Beyond their own circle of friends, the Elphinstones played a full part in the many social activities at the camp. Their lasting contribution was the small theatre they established for the soldiers, painting the scenery themselves and directing a series of light-hearted plays. 'The acting was exceptionally good and the music too,' recalled Agnes Carey, a member of Empress Eugénie's household who attended a performance in 1886. 'It was a nice little theatre, very well arranged and managed entirely by Sir Howard. The combination of officers' uniforms and ladies evening dresses was very pretty.'[22] But this was no ordinary troop show. Before the performance, Agnes had noticed Prince Albert Victor, or Prince 'Eddy', the eldest son of the Prince of Wales, being led into the little theatre by Annie Elphinstone. Other members of the royal family were also frequent visitors, all drawn by their friendship with the colonel and his wife.

This happy period in Howard's life was soon threatened by war. In April 1877 the fraught 'Eastern Question' – essentially a

Victoria Alexandrina Elphinstone, the Queen's god-daughter, whose naming caused minor confusion.

struggle for supremacy in the Balkans – sparked conflict between Russia and Turkey. For a time it seemed that Britain would be pitched into a repeat of the Crimean War. The army was mobilized and troopships once again sailed for the Dardanelles. Annie, who had returned from honeymoon pregnant, soon grew anxious. 'Do not bother yourself about the War,' her husband assured her, 'there is no chance whatsoever of my going out at present . . . not until we actually go to war, would there be any chance of *my* moving, and there is not the slightest chance of that for a long time to come.'[23] Howard's confidence was well grounded. Britain kept out of the war, stepping in with threats of retaliation only when Russia threatened Constantinople itself. With the Royal Navy hovering on his doorstep, the Tsar tactfully withdrew, leaving behind a puppet state in the Balkans called Bulgaria and simmering resentment at Russian domination in the region.

On 7 September 1877 Annie retired early, euphemistically feeling 'not quite the thing'.[24] At quarter to four the next morning she gave birth to a healthy baby girl. Two days later, her husband received a telegram from Balmoral expressing the Queen's delight at his news and her hope 'that baby may bear my name'.[25] Deeply '*flattered*' by such an honour, the colonel nevertheless took the trouble to check which form of her name the Queen wanted his daughter to take: her given name or the name she had assumed on ascending to the throne. Slightly confused, Lady Ely replied that the Queen wished the Elphinstones' child to 'be called by both her names, Alexandrina Victoria; I suppose Victoria first'.*[26] Howard and Annie followed their instructions precisely, and on 18 October the little girl was christened with her godmother's name in a short ceremony at the garrison church in Aldershot. The Queen sent a gold christening mug for the baby

---

*The Queen's baptismal first name of 'Alexandrina' was proposed by the Prince Regent, later George IV, in tribute to her godfather Tsar Alexander I of Russia. Her only other name of 'Victoria' was taken from her mother the Duchess of Kent. Known as 'Drina' in childhood, upon her accession the new Queen insisted that her first name, with its provocative Russian overtone, be dropped, and it was never used again (Longford, *Victoria RI*, 27–8, 89).

and motherly advice to Annie on recovering from childbirth. From now on, however, little Victoria Alexandrina Elphinstone would be known to her family more simply as Viva – or, as Howard joked, Viva Elphinstone: Long live Elphinstone.

'Strange people these Germans'

POTSDAM, 1878

IN MAY 1878 ELPHINSTONE returned to Berlin, carrying a bundle of important letters from the Queen. Before sailing, he told Annie to engage a German – rather than French – nurse for Viva, 'as the latter as a rule are flighty and hot tempered, both bad qualities with a child'. He also tentatively approached the Queen about renting a plot of land near Prince Arthur's new residence at Bagshot on which to build a house of his own. The eventual outcome was a substantial mansion in modish Arts and Crafts style which the Elphinstones called Pinewood. Howard placed his initials above the door beside the carved stone model of a bird's nest in which a family of chicks sheltered. It was the first house he could call his own, and he saw himself growing old there surrounded by his wife and children.

After trawling through the courts of Europe for years, Arthur had finally found himself a bride. Princess Louise of Prussia was the youngest daughter of Prince Friedrich Carl of Prussia, a nephew of the Kaiser and the unlikely saviour of Nicolai Elphinstone during the Franco-Prussian War. Friedrich Carl's fondness for his favourite Hussars uniform had earned him the nickname 'Red Prince', but the epithet applied equally to his temperament, which was brutish and bullying. All his children lived in fear of him. When Louise was born in 1860 Friedrich Carl had beaten his wife so severely for producing another girl that he had permanently destroyed her hearing.

Although she hated the 'Red Prince' for his stupidity and his violence and for conspiring with Bismarck against her, the Crown Princess of Prussia had always been fond of his three daughters. Indeed, Vicky had proposed the eldest girl, Mary, as a possible bride for her brother Arthur as early as 1872. But the Franco-Prussian War had then intervened, making further integration between the English and Prussian royal families politically undesirable, even provocative. Five years later, Victoria still cited 'the extreme unpopularity of Prince Friedrich Carl and Prussia' as an objection to marrying her son to any of his daughters. She also suspected the Red Prince would divorce his wife when the Kaiser eventually died, leaving a moral stain on his children.[1] Moreover, from the photographs Vicky had so assiduously sent her over the years, she judged Louise to be 'ugly' and so an unsuitable consort for her favourite son (no beauty herself, Victoria always prized good looks). Even Arthur, who was smitten by the romantic notion of rescuing Louise from her miserable existence at home, admitted she had 'bad teeth'.[2]

Nevertheless, the idea had quickly gathered momentum. Vicky eagerly pressed the match, keen to bolster her own fragile position in Germany with another tie between her mother's court and the Kaiser's. To her surprise, she could count on the support of the Prince of Wales, whose antagonism towards the Prussians had eased in proportion to the rising threat of conflict with Russia in the Balkans. The Queen's concern that her son was being steam-rolled into marrying the Prussian princess by his brothers and sisters was eased by Elphinstone. He assured her that Arthur 'did certainly not intend to fall in love, or be "talked" into it. The young lady must have something pleasing in her character or manner; else this could not have happened.'[3]

Indeed, though the initial idea was Vicky's, after meeting Louise over dinner in Berlin in January 1878 Arthur himself had taken the initiative. By May 1878, faced with almost universal enthusiasm for the match and touched by the stories of Louise's unhappiness, the Queen had relented and given her consent, setting aside her qualms about marrying another of her children to the Hohenzollerns. Disregarding the drawn-out saga behind the engagement, she declared that she would never have prevented her favourite son 'from making his own choice'.[4] The only thing she regretted, she announced loftily, 'is that no one gave me a hint of this as I had so particularly wished Arthur to see others before he engaged himself to anyone. However there it is and the only thing is to do everything we can to make all work well and comfortably in the family.'[5] Despite shamelessly telling the colonel that she had never been in a hurry to marry Arthur off, she now urged him to complete the formalities as quickly as possible. She freely admitted that a firm commitment would secure Arthur a substantial grant from Parliament before the long summer recess; otherwise, with disillusionment with the monarchy reaching a peak, a protracted and bruising battle for public money might ensue.

Thus Elphinstone had been speedily dispatched to Berlin; and the letters he carried were those for the Kaiser and Louise's parents, detailing the royal marriage terms. These included the Queen's demand that the wedding take place in England. 'Arthur is my son,' she reminded the crown princess, 'and I am a woman unable to travel any distances for festivities like those at your Court which I could not ever go through.'[6] Affie's marriage to the Grand Duchess Marie would remain the only wedding of her nine children that Victoria failed to attend. (Outside the royal family, this was a feat possibly rivalled only by Elphinstone, who missed Vicky's and Fritz's wedding in 1858 but eventually attended all eight others.)

After a 'not unpleasant' journey, during which he sketched the passing scenery and read a novel, the colonel reached Berlin late on 7 May, checking into the Hotel de Russie on Schinkel-Platz. In the morning, encased in full dress uniform, he called on the Kaiser at the Schloss, the sprawling baroque headquarters of

the Prussian royal family in the city. The last time Howard had seen
Wilhelm he had described him as 'much depressed in spirits'. Four
years on, he thought the 83-year-old Kaiser looked in 'splendid
health and spirits, with plenty of fresh colour in his cheeks, and
sparkling eyes'.[7] The liberals clustered around Fritz and Vicky
viewed the Kaiser's apparent indestructibility with mounting
dismay, as every day he remained alive delayed the dawn of a more
enlightened regime.

The colonel reported that Wilhelm was 'very pleased
indeed at this fresh matrimonial alliance between England and
Germany'. He had happily agreed to the Queen's request that
his niece's wedding take place in England, as this would 'silence'
suggestions that there was any breach between their two countries. Prince Friedrich Carl barely concealed his delight at
having secured such a prestigious prize for his daughter. Howard
wryly commented that he 'never before saw so truly joyful an
expression on his face'.[8] But this satisfaction did not prevent
the Red Prince from raising a whole series of 'little hitches',
principally issues concerning his daughter's future rank, title and
income.[9]

On his first full evening in Berlin, Elphinstone dined at the
British Embassy with the ambassador, Lord Odo Russell, and his
wife Emily. Russell was a stocky man, with a large head, bushy
beard, and eyes which sparkled mischievously behind his small
round spectacles. A highly experienced diplomat, who had been
envoy to Rome before landing the plum job in Berlin, Russell had
a reputation for 'tact, judgement and quick wit and repartee'.
Exceptionally for an Englishman in Germany, he could also count
Otto von Bismarck among his friends. Emily Russell, the daughter
of the former Foreign Secretary Lord Clarendon, was much
younger than her husband but, like him, 'very nice and clever'.
Howard was instantly drawn to them both and abandoned his
'usual silent mood' over dinner to quiz his hosts about the Prussian
princess, whom he had yet to meet. Like everyone else, the
Russells described Louise as 'not pretty, but very nice and

King Wilhelm I of Prussia, proclaimed first Kaiser of Germany in 1871: indomitable, reactionary and apparently indestructible.

amiable', and although 'dreadfully shy', possessed of a most 'charming manner . . . which wins people'. The Russells also considered her 'decidedly English in her predilection', with a passion for reading and drawing.[10]

Three days later, on 11 May, as he sat writing letters in his hotel room – 'in fact I am doing nothing else all day long'[11] – Howard received news of a 'most dreadful occurrence'.[12] The Kaiser had been shot at 'by some fanatic' while out driving. In the initial confusion Elphinstone heard that the bullet had hit Wilhelm's helmet, and feared the worst. It was some hours before it was confirmed that it had gone 'nowhere near the Emperor', who appeared 'as calm as possible' that evening at dinner.[13] To reassure the Queen in England that Germany was not on the verge of revolution, the colonel sent her a telegram describing the 'great demonstration' of support for the Kaiser which built up outside the Schloss during the meal.[14] The sound of 'tremendous cheering' even reached into the ornate dining room where Howard sat with the Prussian royal family. Bismarck's press roundly blamed the socialists for the attack: '*i.e.*', the colonel patiently explained to Annie, offering an insight into his own politically conservative views, 'the ultra democratic party that wishes for entire equality in everything. Like the communists in Paris it is a large growing class and most dangerous to every government and love of order. They hate work.'[15] Having levelled the blame, Bismarck was anxious to scotch rumours of a wider conspiracy or damaging speculation on the political motivation for the shooting. So, pursuing the strategy used by the British government after the Fenian-inspired attacks on the Queen and Prince Alfred, he made it known that the Kaiser's would-be assassin was an unemployed plumber who had acted alone after being expelled from the Socialist Party for his eccentric behaviour. With public confidence restored, Bismarck then felt emboldened to launch a vicious clandestine crackdown on socialist activity.

The next day, with Berlin still abuzz over the failed

assassination attempt, Elphinstone called on Princess Louise to introduce himself formally as the Queen's envoy in the matter of her marriage. As the Russells had suggested, he found her a 'very sweet and pleasing' girl with 'a decidedly high-minded, upright, truthful character'.[16] He was less impressed with her physical attributes, describing the Prussian princess to Annie as 'certainly not pretty [with] a regular German face, rather square protruding forehead, bad nose and large mouth, but good fine eyes. I thought her very badly dressed, and her hair cut short in front which looks very bad and widened her forehead all the more.'[17] As expected, there were many issues to resolve with Louise's father regarding the royal wedding. Howard had already gloomily reported that 'much wants smoothing down', and he now foresaw many more late nights of correspondence before the negotiations were safely concluded.[18]

Meeting Arthur's future bride had merely sharpened the colonel's longing for his own young wife back in England. From his hotel room, he pronounced himself 'heartily sick' of the crippling protocol and suffocating atmosphere of Prussian court life. With meals at inconsiderate hours – lunch was at twelve and dinner at five – 'half the time of the men is spent in dressing and undressing'.[19] The colonel found that he was forever running back to his hotel to change into 'full dress, plain clothes, evening clothes, etc etc etc'.[20] His journey home was then delayed by the Kaiser's inconsiderate decision to hold a dinner at the Schloss in honour of his niece's engagement. 'Don't fret please about my prolonged absence,' the colonel wrote despondently to Annie, 'it can't be helped as you know, with a thousand kisses, ever your own H.E.'[21] But his delicate mission to Germany did not pass entirely without personal reward. Before he left on 18 May, he was invested by the Kaiser with the Order of the Red Eagle, Prussia's second highest decoration for gallantry and one usually restricted to nobles or officials who had rendered special service to the state. Once the Queen had given her permission for Howard to accept this prestigious award, the

Foreign Secretary Lord Salisbury drew up the 'requisite instrument' allowing the colonel to wear the order – a white enamelled cross decorated with the Prussian eagle – on his British army uniform.[22]

No sooner had Elphinstone reached home than he was asked to return to Germany with Arthur. Prince Friedrich Carl, eager to exploit his valuable new connection, had invited his future son-in-law to stay at Gleinicke, his country retreat near Potsdam. The trip had a less than auspicious start. Shortly before the prince and the colonel sailed, they heard that the Kaiser had again been targeted by an assassin, this time to far more devastating effect. Lead shot had hit Wilhelm in the cheek, throat, shoulder and right hand. He had survived the attack, but it was thought that he was severely, probably terminally, incapacitated. Power devolved to Fritz as the crown prince; yet Bismarck resisted calls for a formal regency, believing that while the Kaiser still lived there was hope of preserving the reactionary status quo.

Yet when the colonel arrived back in Berlin on 9 June, his mind was far from the constitutional crisis affecting Germany. He had lost his trunk at Calais, and with it the correct clothes to wear at Gleinicke – 'which to a German is horrific, showing want of respect, etc'. Still worse, they had been greeted at the station by the entire Prussian royal family, all attired in court dress or full uniform. 'A strange contrast', Howard observed, 'to our soiled shooting costume and dirty state.'[23] Gleinicke itself offered few comforts. The colonel found there was no soap in his room, while the only bathtub in the entire castle had accompanied Arthur down to the cottage on the estate to which the prince had been dispatched, etiquette preventing him from sleeping beneath the same roof as his fiancée. 'Strange people these Germans,' Howard wearily concluded as he finally fell exhausted into bed.[24]

Despite the castle's glorious setting, perched high above a lake some two miles from Potsdam, this was a very dull assignment. 'My life in the country', the colonel soon complained to Annie, 'is a most melancholy one as there is nothing whatever to do excepting the ceremonial meals . . . but although thoroughly idle, our time is taken up in the most ridiculous manner.'[25] Apart from the merry-go-round of dressing for meals, hours passed simply smoking cigarettes beneath the trees. 'I am getting woefully bored,' Howard wrote again two days later. 'I long to have my little woman next to me. For you little naughty, you know well enough that I love you *very* dearly.'[26] He found that he was slowly warming to Arthur's fiancée, however. 'The more I see of her, the more I like her,' he decided. 'She ought to make him happy.'[27]

While the colonel kicked his heels at Gleinicke, the future shape of Europe was being decided some twenty miles away in Berlin. Eager to strut on the world stage, Bismarck had convened a congress to resolve the 'Eastern Question' or, more specifically, to untangle the mess left behind in the Balkans following the recent war between Russia and Turkey. On 16 June, Elphinstone and Arthur took the train to the city to dine with Vicky and Fritz, and to attend a reception at the British Embassy. Following the attacks on Wilhelm, the atmosphere in Berlin was very jittery. Arthur described the palace which harboured the stricken Kaiser as in a 'state of siege', surrounded as it was by a cordon of nervous-looking armed police officers.[28] Inside, Wilhelm sat strapped to a chair, looking 'terribly feeble', with ice packs on his swollen arms and his head heavily bandaged. 'I am afraid that if the Emperor ever recovers he will *never* be himself again,' Arthur told his mother dolefully.[29] The colonel was struck more by the appearance of the women at court. The Kaiser's wife Augusta looked 'far from well and exhausted after so long a trial', while the Tsarina of Russia, who was in Berlin with her husband for the congress, 'likewise appears seriously ill'. 'We are therefore in the midst of illness,' Howard glumly reported to Annie.[30] Even the indefatigable crown princess seemed depressed, worn down by the constant fear of assassination and the enervating political uncertainty. Vicky admitted to Howard that 'the state of feeling is not nice and that even she herself has received several threatening letters that if she appeared in public she would be shot'.[31]

The embassy reception was a hot, crowded and very formal affair, with the gentlemen in full uniform and the ladies in ball gowns. The only black frock coats in the room belonged to the Americans, who were not officially represented at the congress but whose legation in the city had been invited anyway. Among them was former President Ulysses Grant, who was touring Europe with his wife and son Jesse. Grant had already visited England, where he was received by the Queen at Windsor with a great deal more warmth than he had shown to Prince Arthur at the White House in 1870. Victoria had considered Julia Grant 'civil and complimentary in her funny American way'. But Jesse was branded a 'very ill-mannered young Yankee' for insisting that he dine with the Queen and his parents rather than with the royal household as directed.[32] Bismarck bore no such grudge, and at the reception everyone noticed how he made a beeline to the Grants and blatantly courted them.

Another guest at the reception was the British Prime Minister Benjamin Disraeli, who had insisted on travelling to Germany for the congress, despite his age and increasingly fragile health. According to Elphinstone, Disraeli was 'immensely looked up to by all the diplomatic circle in Berlin'. His keynote address to the delegates had 'created a great sensation', saving the day by silencing the doomsayers who predicted all-out war.[33] The colonel had previously been rather wary of Disraeli's colourful blandishments – describing them on one occasion to the Queen as overly 'sarcastic'[34] – yet he now conceded to Annie that the old roué was indeed 'most amusing', while his grasp of the complex situation affecting the Balkans was second to none.[35] Even Bismarck had fallen under the Prime Minister's spell, drinking late into the night with him to discuss the crisis. Such intimacy with the insatiable Chancellor was exhausting, but it helped Disraeli to secure a good settlement for his country while deftly clipping the wings of the Tsar in the Balkans. By the terms of the treaty concluded at the Congress of Berlin, Serbia, Romania and Montenegro were given independence from Turkey; Austria was allowed to occupy Bosnia and Herzegovina; Cyprus was handed to England; and control of Tunis passed to France. Bulgaria, which the Tsar had seen as his puppet and a valuable locus of Russian influence in the region, was arbitrarily split in two. The southern half became a Turkish province called Eastern Rumelia, while the remnant kept the name Bulgaria but became a principality under Russian control ruled by an obscure 22-year-old German prince called Alexander of Battenberg. Amid all the backslapping of the congress, only Disraeli was prepared to admit that such an artificial arrangement was bound to fail.

When the congress concluded, the colonel was invited to stay with the crown princess as her private guest at the Neues Palais while Arthur courted Louise at nearby Gleinicke. With the Kaiser still incapacitated and her husband Fritz, nominally at least, holding the reins of power, Vicky should have been relishing her altered position in Berlin. But Bismarck, fearing the liberal influence of the English princess and seeing her as a rival for Fritz's attention, had stepped up his vituperative campaign against her, forcing her to retreat to Potsdam with her paintbox, her children and Count Götz von Seckendorff, her faithful court chamberlain. Seckendorff was a tall, rake-thin man with a dandyish dress sense who shared both his mistress's political outlook and her passion for painting. More importantly, he shielded Vicky from the worse insults of her Hohenzollern in-laws, steadfastly refusing to be drawn into the intrigues which encircled her at the Prussian court. Odo Russell thought him 'one of the most amiable and agreeable Prussians I know'.[36] In contrast, Bismarck hated Seckendorff. When attempts to supplant the chamberlain with his own henchman failed, the Chancellor spread rumours that Seckendorff was corrupt, even that he was having an affair with the princess.

Each morning, when Arthur had left for Gleinicke, Elphinstone and Vicky sketched and painted together, critically appraising each other's work. The colonel had always admired the princess's 'quiet perception and excellent taste' in matters of art.

He now tried to imitate her style in his own pictures, although he still used watercolour and not the oil paints she boldly preferred. The princess urged him to be patient, and to persevere. 'You ought not to attempt so many sketches,' she told him; 'far better to spend three weeks at a drawing and do your best.'[37] This sound advice prompted the colonel to retort, not unreasonably, that he was never in one place long enough to enjoy such a luxury. Nevertheless, he forced himself to draw more carefully and, encouraged by Seckendorff, an accomplished artist himself, he completed several large paintings.

On rainy days the princess and the colonel toured picture galleries or the other royal palaces at Potsdam. In the warm evenings they drank hock together, dined on 'baked beef with pickled cucumbers' in the cool shadow of the palace colonnades and talked about the past. Sometimes there were recitals or visits to the opera. In fact, it seemed to Howard that in her own loneliness the princess was 'determined to do her utmost to please me, and certainly it is most kind of her to lionise me in this way'. Yet for all the pleasant 'artistic taste and talk' he was not immune to the tension that existed in the palace, or to the 'the wheels within wheels' at the Prussian court.[38]

His sojourn at the Neues Palais also gave Howard the chance to study Vicky's eldest son Wilhelm at close quarters. Now aged nineteen and a student at Bonn University, the prince still displayed the childish impetuosity which had marked his noisy attendance at the wedding of the Prince and Princess of Wales back in 1863. Slow to learn but quick to take offence, Wilhelm was prone to furious tantrums. His outbursts echoed through the corridors of the palace, or around the park as he stormed off the tennis court after losing. Like some others in the royal family (such as his late grandfather the Prince Consort), the prince also had an unpredictable and irritating sense of humour, though his was streaked with cruelty. As James Rodd, a British diplomat in Berlin and occasional visitor to the palace, once remarked: 'It might gratify a certain mentality to be smitten from behind with a tennis racquet by a future emperor, but on the other hand such gratification was qualified by the fact that the blow could not be returned.'[39]

Painfully aware of an accident at birth (roundly blamed on his mother's English doctors) which had left him with a withered left arm, Wilhelm had embraced all the trappings of his elevated position to bolster his confidence and disguise his handicap. Even in the heat of August, he preferred wearing full military uniform to the cotton clothes worn by his brothers and sisters. His relationship with his mother was also difficult and complex. Long periods of bitter estrangement were punctuated by intimate episodes of almost oedipal intensity. Easily influenced, Wilhelm had willingly fallen under Bismarck's spell, hysterically blaming his own mother not only for his disability, but for all the woes currently affecting Germany.

All of Wilhelm's worst traits – and more – surfaced at Potsdam that summer, when discussion over his future wife reached fever pitch. For once a bystander, Howard merely observed that 'in feeling he is still a boy, full of life and the desire to amuse himself. Marriage under these circumstances would be foolish.'[40] By no means a romantic, Wilhelm was nevertheless already smitten by Princess Elisabeth of Hesse-Darmstadt, the daughter of his aunt Alice. However, Ella, as she was known, steadfastly refused to reciprocate her cousin's stilted attentions, recalling the cruel tricks he had played on her as a child. Her unwillingness to respond to her first cousin's clumsy advances bemused the Prussian court. It has been suggested, however, that Vicky may secretly have been relieved at Ella's obduracy.[41] Knowing that Ella's younger brother, like her own, was a haemophiliac, Vicky might have guessed that her sister Alice was a carrier of the condition, as their mother had been (while she herself was not). In these circumstances, marrying her son to any of her sister's daughters would be an unacceptable risk for Vicky's future grandchildren, and for the preservation of the Hohenzollern bloodline.

Vicky energetically promoted a match instead with the unsullied Holsteins, into whose family another of her sisters, Helena, had married. On 30 August, as she had arranged, the Duke and Duchess of Schleswig-Holstein-Sonderburg-Augustenburg arrived 'unannounced' at the Neues Palais with their two eldest daughters: Augusta Victoria, or 'Dona', and Elisabeth. A few days later they were opportunely joined at the palace by Helena and her husband Prince Christian. Still sulking over Ella, Wilhelm rightly suspected that his mother was actively conspiring with one of his English aunts to thwart his unrequited love for the daughter of another. Howard, who had rarely seen Helena since her wedding in 1866, thought the princess had 'grown *very* stout' and looked about ten years older than her sister Vicky (she was in fact six years younger). After seeing the Holstein princesses shamelessly paraded before Wilhelm, the colonel was also thankful that Arthur had already made his choice of wife. 'They are both young, fresh, ladylike,' he reported to Annie, 'thorough little ladies, speak English perfectly. But there is not sufficient character to suit him. They are too soft and womanly, whereas he wants someone who will lead him.'[42]

Even fifty years later, the events of that long hot summer, when he felt forced to abandon his love for Ella out of duty to his country, still rankled with the ex-Kaiser Wilhelm II. Writing from exile, he told his grandson that 'few sovereigns in the world are lucky enough to be able to marry the object of their first love'.[43] Yet, as so often, the old man was deluding himself. He forgot to mention that during his cousins' short stay at Potsdam he switched his affections from Ella of Hesse to Dona of Holstein with, in the words of his astonished father, 'outrageous rapidity'.[44] Within two years they were married at a lavish ceremony in Berlin, during which it was said that Wilhelm seemed 'more concerned with the appearance of the Guard than of the bride'.[45]

On 6 September 1878 the colonel scrawled a quick line to Annie as his portmanteau was being packed for the long journey home. 'My stay here has been very pleasant,' he wrote, 'entirely due however to the Crown Princess. She has been most kind, and put herself out to oblige me. Her object has been to make one feel welcome and that is a very pleasant feeling, more especially when coming from one in her position.'[46] He little expected that a tragedy elsewhere would force his return to Berlin within just a few weeks.

29

'Those horrid Zulus'

1879

H OWARD'S SECOND DAUGHTER, IRENE, was born at a quarter
past ten on 11 December 1878. Thousands of miles away
that same morning, on the banks of the Thukela River in southern
Africa – the demarcation line between British-administered Natal,
and Zululand – the King of the Zulus, Cetshwayo KaMpande, was
presented with an impossible ultimatum. He was ordered to dis-
band his army, dismantle the military system which kept him in
power and hand over those of his warriors guilty of harassing the
British along the border – or face attack. The demands were an ill-
disguised attempt by the British governor of the Cape, Sir Bartle
Frere, to provoke war between the Zulus and the British. Frere
had been secretly tasked by London with the confederation of
South Africa: an imperial goal frustrated, in his opinion, by the
obdurately proud and warlike Zulu king. As the governor had
hoped, Cetshwayo could not meet his demands; so on 11 January
1879 a formidable invasion army commanded by Lord
Chelmsford crossed into Zululand. The main force was supported
by a large contingent of native soldiers raised and led by Colonel
Anthony Durnford, Howard's friend from their days together as
young subalterns in Edinburgh. (As Durnford chaired the bound-
ary commission used by Frere to justify the offensive, he is also
considered in large part responsible for the war.)

Three days after the Zulu king received his challenge, the Queen in England mourned the loss of a child. Yet it was not Leopold who succumbed first, as had been expected for years; it was Princess Alice who died, after catching diphtheria while nursing her children through the disease. Alice died on 14 December 1878 – the seventeenth anniversary of her father's death: a coincidence which seemed to her devastated mother (who dabbled in spiritualism) 'almost incredible, and most mysterious'.[1] Yet to the end, Victoria understood, and trusted, the serious-minded Alice the least of all her children.

One consequence of the tragedy was the postponement of Arthur's marriage from February to March 1879. On 6 January, therefore, Elphinstone left for Berlin in haste to reorganize the complicated arrangements. He returned to Germany very reluctantly, loath to leave Annie again so soon. 'Give my love to Viva,' he wrote despondently when he reached Calais, 'and say I hope she will be good. The mite I suppose will have changed immensely by the time I get back. A thousand kisses, you little woman, from ever your own H.E.'[2] After a bitterly cold rail journey through drifts of deep snow, he reached Berlin 'enveloped in my fur bag and coat'.[3] The events of the previous summer at Potsdam, when he had been fêted by Vicky, seemed no more than a distant memory. Instead Howard was condemned to hours 'shut up' in the gloomy splendour of his suite of rooms at the imperial Schloss.[4] Here he waited for a summons to see the Kaiser; desultorily sketching, reading and thinking 'all the time' of home.[5] Three times a day he wrote to Annie.

> As I have not you by me, I like to read my dear little woman's thoughts. It is the only way of being near her and I do like that, for you know I am very, *very* fond of you. I begin to think far more so than I ought to be after two years! But somehow my love increases for you, you wicked woman . . . It is far *far* deeper and fuller than it was even six months ago. I suppose it is a sign of age creeping on! I ought, as a married man, assume the staid, instead of caressing that dear little duck of mine and giving her such a lot of kisses.[6]

As the Prussian court was in mourning for Princess Alice, and the crown princess in bed with a heavy cold, most evenings he ate alone, which was 'fearfully dull'. The food was 'cooked somewhere or other in this huge palace and then at 5pm portions are sent up to different people living here'.[7] After several visits to the city in recent months, he knew a 'fair number of people' in Berlin. But with the exception of Vicky, Count Seckendorff and the Russells, there was 'not one whom one cares for. Their habits, their thoughts, their manners are so different that one cannot possibly care to become intimate.'[8] The bruised, snow-swollen skies matched his mood. The skaters he watched in the park 'went simply backwards and forwards without attempts at any figures'.[9] He was equally dismissive of the German paintings he saw at an exhibition; and there was 'not a shop that contains a thing of taste or that one would care about'.[10] To pass the time, he sat for his portrait with Reichard & Lindner, the imperial photographers on Unter den Linden. But he complained that the result showed up his wrinkles too clearly: a stark reminder that he had entered his fiftieth year.

When Vicky recovered, she invited Howard to a 'regular family dinner' with Fritz and their children.[11] The crown prince's sham regency had ended in December with the unexpected recovery of his father, destroying any hope of an early liberal renaissance in Germany. This probably accounted for the sourness the colonel noticed in Vicky when they met. Over the meal, she 'spoke in a most disparaging tone of the German people', complaining that she had no friends and was 'generally unpopular in consequence of the free thinking tone she took up'.[12] She had even been forbidden from attending her sister's funeral in Darmstadt from the fear of infection; a well-intentioned command which merely embittered her still further. Vicky blamed Augusta for this 'cruel' order, seeing her mother-in-law as her greatest enemy within the corridors of the claustrophobic Prussian court. She accused the Kaiserin of undermining her own position by casting aspersions on her fitness to be Crown Princess of Prussia.[13] A stickler for rigid etiquette,

*Howard photographed by Reichard & Lindner in Berlin in January 1879:
'they seem very good [at] bringing out my wrinkles well', he lamented to
Annie.*

the ageing Kaiserin was certainly now a terrifying sight – particularly, as one palace guest observed, 'when she appeared in her war-paint, her diamonds, laces, tiaras and, last but not least, her wonderful wigs'.[14]

Howard was more generous towards Augusta than her highly charged daughter-in-law. 'She has always been most open to me,' he admitted to Annie, 'and never attempted to hide either the faults or the difficulties of the situation here in Germany.' During a 'long interview' with Elphinstone on 11 January, the Kaiserin candidly expressed her fears for the 'lamentable' state of her country, which she revealed was suffering 'very great' poverty after three wars in rapid succession. It also seemed 'incredible' to her that Arthur – who she claimed was her favourite English cousin – should want to marry Princess Louise of Prussia: 'as there was neither beauty nor great social qualities to attract him'. The colonel uncharitably replied that he thought 'pity was the motive power' behind the prince's decision. He claimed that the princess's 'cruel position at home, coupled with her English education were the elements which roused him'.[15]

An invitation to dine with the Russells at the British Embassy was warmly welcomed. But just as he was 'looking forward at last to English ways and English people', Howard was summoned to tea at the Schloss. This was a great honour, as tea, presided over by the Kaiserin in person, was the principal social event of the imperial day. After an interminable lecture on chemistry, the handful of privileged guests sat down to a stomach-churning meal of pâté de foie gras, oranges and ice cream. 'I need not tell you', the colonel admitted queasily to his wife, 'that I did not take of this wholesome mixture.' The old Kaiser, who had seemed close to death six months before, 'was looking wonderfully well and as cheerful as possible'.[16] One arm remained in a sling from the shooting, and Wilhelm complained that he could still feel the pellets in his neck and shoulder. Otherwise he seemed none the worse for his experience.

Although he tolerated Augusta's eccentricities, Howard

nevertheless deplored the jealous atmosphere she encouraged within her court, which was worse even than that at Windsor. 'There is no doubt the society here is made up of very small "sets",' he told Annie wearily. 'Each set is quite exclusive, and will not even look at the other. The aristocracy as such is not to my liking, being very vain, small minded and decidedly dull. Of politics they are afraid to talk, of art and literature they know little. Consequently, bitter tittle-tattle is their element, in which they excel.'[17] He especially hated the way the men humiliated their wives in public. 'Not in a chaffy way, for a German does not understand that,' he reported, 'but openly and with great cruelty.' As an example, the colonel recalled his acute embarrassment at seeing a woman being 'outrageously' snubbed by her husband over dinner; behaviour which would never have been tolerated in England. He could only conclude that among the German aristocracy the '"love" part' of a marriage 'cools down very soon', if it had ever existed in the first place. The German sense of humour – or lack of it – came in for equally strong criticism. 'How little idea they have what wit is,' Elphinstone exclaimed, after hearing some 'savants' declare that comedy should always be 'sarcastic and biting'. 'They are too serious and probably too vain to enter into it,' he decided bluntly.[18]

Unlike Vicky, Elphinstone could escape from Berlin and the numbing effects of Prussian society. Back in his hotel room, he counted down the days until he would 'be back to my little woman, and kiss her dear little face, and neck and chin; in fact squeeze her to death, at least nearly, so often have I wished that you were near me and help me to pass my dreary evenings'.[19] 'Never before,' he wrote two days later, on 21 January 1879, 'have I felt so utterly oppressed with my stay as this time.'[20] His mood was about to darken further. Hours later and thousands of miles away on the baking plains of Africa, Lord Chelmsford's army was slaughtered by the Zulus at Isandhlwana. Among the last to die a hero's death that day was his friend Anthony Durnford, perforated by *assegai* stabs as he made a last desperate stand. The defeat was the greatest humiliation for the British army in living memory, perhaps ever. Afterwards, Durnford was posthumously castigated for failing to defend the camp; an impression the culpable Lord Chelmsford was more than happy to encourage. Even the Queen wondered how it was that Durnford had 'been enticed away' during the action.[21]

News of the massacre at Isandhlwana, and of the heroic stand of a company of the 24th Foot at Rorke's Drift later the same day, was waiting for Howard when he reached London. 'I can't tell you how shocked I was at the terrible news from the Cape,' Prince Arthur wrote to the Queen when he heard. 'It is indeed a great disaster and one which the whole country will feel most deeply . . . The Zulus are not to be despised as enemies and I am afraid that they will be over bold now after this success. Let us however hope that all will yet go well and that the poor 24th Regiment will be fully avenged.'[22] In the frantic effort to exact that revenge, thousands of troops were hastily dispatched to Natal. Among those following events closely from his mother's house in Kent was Louis Napoleon, the exiled Prince Imperial who, following his father's death in 1873, was now emperor-in-waiting of France. Brim-full with romantic notions of chivalry since his childhood, Louis begged the commander-in-chief of the British army, the Duke of Cambridge, to be allowed to join the expedition. 'When one belongs to a race of soldiers,' he theatrically declared, 'it is only sword in hand that one gains recognition.'[23] The Empress was appalled by the prospect of her son fighting for the British in Zululand, tearfully reminding him that the hopes of a Bonapartist restoration in France rested squarely on his shoulders. But Louis was adamant. Many of his comrades from the Royal Artillery were already on their way to the Cape, and others would soon follow. 'How could I show myself again at Aldershot,' the prince confided desperately to a friend, 'when they will all be out there?'[24]

Yet Louis's grandiose dream of glory appeared doomed to frustration, for the Duke of Cambridge, realizing the folly of sending the claimant to the French throne on a perilous mission to

Africa with the British army, dismissed the idea out of hand. But Louis refused to give up. After recruiting the powerful support of the Prince of Wales, he drafted an emotive response to the duke's refusal. 'When at Woolwich and, later, at Aldershot, I had the honour of wearing the English uniform,' Louis wrote, 'I hoped that it would be in the ranks of our allies that I should first take up arms. Losing this hope, I lose one of the consolations of my exile.'[25]

Exasperated, the duke passed the prince's plea to the palace for the Queen to consider. She was 'touched at the kind and gratifying expressions he makes use of, and cannot but admire his desire to go out and serve with my brave troops. But I am glad I am not his mother at this moment.'[26] Victoria's ambiguous comment gave the duke implicit approval to change his mind. He therefore agreed to let the prince go; but only as a 'spectator', not as a soldier on active duty. The U-turn caused consternation in official circles. Benjamin Disraeli, who saw the danger of the decision more clearly than most, was appalled. 'I am quite mystified about that little abortion, the Prince Imperial,' he stormed at Lord Salisbury. 'I thought we had agreed not to sanction his adventure? Instead of that he has royal audiences previous to his departure . . . What am I to say on this? H.M. knows my little sympathy with the Bonapartes.'[27]

Louis sailed for Africa on 27 February 1879, exchanging the civilian clothes he had agreed to wear for his army uniform as soon as he was out of sight of land. He therefore missed Prince Arthur's wedding on 13 March, although St George's Chapel was so packed with Germans that there was scarcely room for another guest. Elphinstone, who was in charge of the event, complained that every room at Windsor Castle was occupied, down to the gun room and children's playrooms. Managing so many dignitaries was a daunting challenge, particularly as so many of them had fragile tempers. 'In fact,' Howard complained wearily to Annie, 'one's whole time is taken up with writing, and deputations, and arrangements.' The colonel could barely disguise his irritation with Henry Ponsonby, the Queen's private secretary, who found it difficult coping with the foreign invasion. 'Very fortunate I was here,' he sourly remarked on one occasion, '[as] Ponsonby would otherwise have interfered most unpleasantly as regards presents for the Germans.'[28]

As they had planned, early on the morning of the wedding Howard slipped away from the castle to secure a good seat for Annie in the chapel. Glimpsing them together in the still-deserted choir, the court correspondent from the *Daily Telegraph* made a note of the 'lady in white satin, ostrich plumes and diamonds . . . chatting familiarly with an elderly gentleman in court dress' – 'The first time', the colonel wrote proudly to his wife when he read it afterwards, 'you have figured thus in print.'[29] After taking her prime seat, Annie watched her husband lead the prince down the aisle to the altar, where he was joined by the equally nervous bride. The Queen appeared at the service wearing the gargantuan Koh-i-Noor diamond, the first time she had done so in public since her husband's death. It was a sign of her especial regard for Arthur and confirmation that the deep mourning for her husband was finally at an end. After the wedding breakfast, feeling exhausted and 'much against my will', the colonel was obliged to take Louise's father Prince Friedrich Carl on a tour of his daughter's future residence at Bagshot. The Red Prince's complaint that the rambling new house had too few bedrooms was swiftly silenced by the colonel's tart reply that 'the money was wanting for more'.[30] When the 'very cross' Prussian prince then tried to raise the matter again over dinner the Queen, with a note of triumph, 'assured him I had just the same at Osborne!'[31]

On 26 March, Arthur and his wife left for the continent, Howard and Annie joining them at Bordeaux to accompany the newlyweds on their honeymoon cruise in the royal steam yacht *Osborne*. For Annie, recently appointed lady in waiting to the teenage princess, this was her first taste of living with the royals. Over the next three months, as *Osborne* wandered around the Mediterranean, she sent a series of wide-eyed letters back to her

Prince Arthur with Princess Louise of Prussia, daughter of the brutish 'Red Prince'. Howard thought 'pity was the motive power' behind Arthur's surprising choice of bride.

mother in England. Up to twenty people came on board each evening for dinner, she recounted, with Howard and the prince 'dodging about the cabin arranging where everybody is to sit'.[32] Guests ranged from the King of Portugal – 'who is very dull and stupid like a drowsy bumble bee' – to Doctor Schliemann, the famous archaeologist who had recently discovered the site of Troy. Despite the luxury of their vessel, the whole party was frequently seasick: 'Howard, of course, excepted; for the worse we all get the better he is'.[33] Even the colonel was forced to admit, however, with tragic prescience, that 'there was considerable motion' in the Bay of Biscay 'and the heavy swell of the Atlantic was felt unpleasantly during the three days run'.[34]

They arrived home in June to some shocking news concerning the Prince Imperial, who had never intended to stand idly by in Britain's African war. Instead, on landing in the Cape he had secured a place on Lord Chelmsford's staff and was soon making intelligence-gathering forays into Zululand. He did so under the watchful eye of Richard Harrison, the Assistant Adjutant-General of Surveying and the officer who had accompanied Elphinstone and Prince Arthur on their walking tour of the Alps in 1869. Colonel Harrison should have known better, therefore, than to allow the prince to join a dangerous patrol into enemy territory, as Louis did on 1 June, escorted only by a small detachment of troops. At about three-thirty that afternoon, the men were attacked by Zulu warriors as they watered their horses at a deserted homestead. The prince was caught as he tried to flee, fighting gallantly for a minute or so before falling beneath the repeated blows of the Zulus' *assegais*. For the *coup de grâce* he was stabbed through his right eye. When the warriors had finished, they stripped Louis's body and sliced open the stomach to perform a purification ritual. Then, as twilight gathered over the bloodstained plain, they abandoned the torn, eviscerated body to the vultures.

The survivors of the attack stumbled back into camp an hour later to tell their grim tale. Archibald Forbes, a war correspondent embedded with Chelmsford's army, later recalled how he was chatting with some officers when Harrison 'put his head inside the tent door, and called out in a strange voice, "Good God! The Prince Imperial is killed!"' Harrison had a reputation for jesting, so for a moment his awful announcement was not taken seriously. 'But,' Forbes continued, 'sitting by the door, I discerned in the faint light of the dying day the horror in Harrison's face, and sprang to my feet instinctively.'[35]

At Windsor it was John Brown who broke the news, which he must have gleaned from the telegraph office at the castle, to the Queen. 'The young French Prince is killed,' he announced solemnly.[36] Then the telegram itself arrived and, with a 'thrill of horror', Victoria read the details. The news was her worst night-mare, as it was to every mother with a son serving in the army. Haunted by 'those horrid Zulus' and unable to sleep, she sat up until dawn writing her journal. 'To die in such an awful way is too shocking!' she wrote. 'Poor dear Empress! Her only child, her all, gone! I am really in despair. He was such an amiable, good young man, who would have made such a good Emperor for France one day. The more one thinks of it, the worse it becomes.'[37]

Howard, too, was deeply shocked by the 'horrible death', having known Louis since the prince's childhood.[38] Arthur voiced the concerns of many in questioning why his friend had been allowed to 'go out on such a dangerous expedition with so few fel-lows. I suppose he begged very hard to be sent out on some such adventurous business.'[39] The outrage caused by the Prince Imperial's death and the accusation that his escort had bolted, leaving him to his fate, led to the prosecution of the senior officer on the patrol, Harrison's deputy Lieutenant Carey. Nor did Harrison himself escape censure. 'I was attacked because the duties of the Prince when he went out were not defined with greater clear-ness,' Harrison wrote thirty years later in self-justification. 'Naturally I saw nothing of these Press criticisms until long after-wards, and, even then, I did not think it my duty to answer them; and so blame rested on me until I returned to England.'[40] Harrison

Louis Napoleon, Prince Imperial of France, photographed in British uniform shortly before his violent death at the hands of the Zulus.

was eventually cleared of direct blame, but the report into the Prince Imperial's death nevertheless highlighted his 'defective' orders and lack of 'firmness and foresight'.[41] For the second time in six months, Howard was forced to watch a friend being tried by the newspapers and dragged through an official inquiry. Unlike the luckless Durnford, however, Harrison recovered his reputation and prospered. He returned to duty as Howard's second-in-command at Aldershot, rising eventually to become a full general.

On 29 June, Elphinstone travelled to Kent with Arthur and Louise to pay their respects to the devastated French Empress. Eugénie's hysterical reaction to their news that her son's body would soon be landed in England was '*most* violent', according to Arthur.[42] They returned for the funeral on 12 July, when a crowd estimated at over thirty thousand collected in the narrow lanes around Camden Place to watch as the Prince Imperial's coffin, draped with the fleur-de-lis of France, was carried to St Mary's Roman Catholic Church in Chislehurst. There Louis was gently laid to rest beside the tomb of his father, Emperor Napoleon III. By a quirk of fate, the ceremony took place almost a hundred years to the day since Louis's great-uncle had left the island of Corsica to begin the remarkable story of the Bonapartes. This was its final chapter.

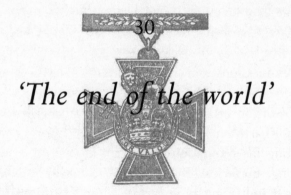

30

'The end of the world'

1881

EARLY IN 1881 HOWARD ELPHINSTONE heard that he was in line to command the Royal Engineers on Mauritius, and that he was to travel there as soon as possible. This abrupt order, apparently caused by illness elsewhere in the corps, took the colonel 'quite aback'.[1] Apart from the miserable prospect of a lengthy separation from his growing family – a sweltering, disease-ridden island in the Indian Ocean being no place for young children – there was also the small matter of seeking leave from the Queen. At a meeting in London on 30 April, the colonel confided these concerns to a friend called Cooke at the War Office. During their conversation, it became apparent that the only means by which Howard could avoid the unwelcome assignment were either to find a substitute for the post or to resign his commission in the army, which was an unthinkable prospect. Twenty years of royal service had already seriously disrupted his army career, so he was loath to abandon it now, 'if I can help it, as eventually I may be able to do some good if I remain'.[2] Yet the chances of finding an officer not only willing, but able, to replace him at short notice seemed slim. 'I doubt my being able to obtain one,' Howard confided miserably to Cooke.[3] After checking through his files, the official came back with the name of the one officer who he thought might consider an exchange. 'I don't know that he will,' he warned

Elphinstone, 'but he might, as he has nothing to do at present.'[4]

In fact, Charles Gordon had already enjoyed such an eventful career that he was surely entitled to a lengthy break. Following his exploits in China and a spell commanding the engineers at Gravesend – from where he had often visited Ranger's House for dinner – Gordon had been appointed governor general of the Sudan. In Khartoum he had suppressed the local slave trade, consolidating his reputation back in Whitehall as a useful, but exasperating, maverick. By April 1881, however, Gordon was unemployed and facing an uncertain future. His offer to assist in subduing an insurgency in Basutoland had been ignored, while the War Office had refused him extended leave to explore the Holy Land. Otherwise he might not have read Elphinstone's cautiously worded letter so closely. 'My dear Gordon,' Howard wrote, 'Pray forgive me writing to you as I now intend to do; but as it is by the advice of so sensible a man as Cooke, I venture to suggest what otherwise I would not have dared to do.'[5] In fact, Elphinstone's anxious enquiry could not have been better timed: Gordon accepted by return telegram, brushing aside his friend's offer of payment for doing so.

Bitter disappointment over the Holy Land tour certainly influenced Gordon's decision to take the 'thankless and insignificant post' on Mauritius, as Lytton Strachey later described it in *Eminent Victorians*.[6] But there is also a suggestion that he was set up for it by someone in power. Certainly it suited the War Office to dispatch this awkward officer, who already enjoyed cult status among the public, to a remote backwater. Equally, there was alarm in the palace at the prospect of losing Elphinstone. Even before the transfer was officially confirmed, Henry Ponsonby confidentially advised the Queen (his letter revealing Victoria's close interest in the matter) that 'Sir Howard Elphinstone has found an engineer officer, Colonel Gordon ("Chinese Gordon") to take his place at the Mauritius so that he now remains as before at Aldershot.'[7] Whatever the truth of the exchange, his friendship with Elphinstone had now been instrumental on two occasions in significantly changing the course of Gordon's life. In 1866 he had experienced a profound religious revelation while dressing for dinner at Ranger's House. Now 'Elphin', as he had called Howard since the Crimea, had altered his career by practical means. Both events contributed to Gordon's eventual martyrdom.

On 2 May, Howard returned to the War Office to sort out the necessary paperwork. The same day, he confirmed to Gordon that 'everything is "en train"; but as you know red tape requires lots of signatures and countersignatures etc'. The Duke of Cambridge, he reported, was 'very glad to hear that you were going to rejoin and do regular R.E. work'. Elphinstone promised to bring the papers down to Southampton in person as he looked forward to 'a long chat upon all kinds of topics. You and I talking together reminds one of olden times again.'[8]

Gordon soon came to regret his hasty decision, and Elphinstone to be even more grateful for it. Within days of landing on Mauritius – believing it 'only fair to let you know what you escaped' – Gordon wrote a long letter to 'dear Elphin' revealing the confusion and maladministration which existed on the remote, but strategically important, island. 'Oh! This place is the end of the world,' he exclaimed. 'Had Lady E. come out what would she not have suffered.' After quickly surveying the island, Gordon had concluded that its defences were virtually non-existent. 'And yet,' he fulminated, 'Childers [the Secretary of State for War] and all those Ministers are perfectly content and wrapped up in their ignorance as happy as larks, with their flippant answers in the House of Commons . . . I suppose however that my report will be considered factious, and so things will go on.'

In his depressed mood, it slowly dawned on Gordon himself that his appointment might have been rigged. 'A Colonel R.E. here is a farce,' he complained; 'there is ¾ of a battery, 3 companies of the 58ᵗʰ Regt. and 5 sappers!' His appearance had come as 'a sort of thunderbolt' to the other officers stationed on the island. They suggested to him that the Duke of Cambridge, who had often clashed with Gordon, had engineered the move to be rid of him. 'They say', Gordon miserably confided to Howard, 'that H.R.H., in one of his furies with someone, said to the Adjutant-General "send him to Hell". That the Adjutant-General said, "we have no station there, your Royal Highness", on which His Royal Highness said: "Send him to Mauritius".'[9]

As Gordon despondently hacked his way through the Mauritian undergrowth, he had no idea that thousands of miles away in Egypt events were unfolding which would seal his fate and secure his legendary status. On 1 February 1881, a little-known colonel in the Egyptian army called Sayed Ahmed Bey Arabi – or, more commonly, Arabi Pasha – mounted a nationalist coup against the Khedive. The Khedive, an appointee of the ruling Ottoman Empire, had been weakened by Egypt's massive debt and an ill-conceived military adventure in Abyssinia. He was, however, a vital ally to the British as the Suez Canal, the lifeline to India, ran through his territory. Fearing that the security of the canal would be compromised by Arabi's rebellion, in 1882 William Gladstone's government made plans to send an expeditionary force to Egypt to secure the canal and restore the Khedive's authority. Inevitably Garnet Wolseley, who since the Red River expedition in Canada had cemented his reputation for daring leadership with further victories in the Ashanti and Zulu wars, was summoned to lead it. News of the mission soon reached Aldershot, where Prince Arthur, now the proud father of a baby girl, commanded a brigade of Guards. Despite a bout of ill-health from which he was only just recovering, he begged his mother to be allowed to join the force. Keenly aware that he was sometimes accused of simply enjoying the trappings of his artificially elevated rank in the army – he had been made a general at thirty – Arthur knew that only by experiencing active service would he ever earn the genuine respect of his men.

The prince's eagerness to see action, however, raised before his mother's eyes the awful spectre of the Prince Imperial's body lying bloodied and torn beneath an African sun. She did her utmost to frustrate his objective, insisting that he submit to a rigorous medical examination before volunteering, a test she expected him to fail following his recent illness. To her horror he passed, demolishing her principal obstacle and forcing her, with tears in her eyes, to give her consent. 'He will do splendidly,' Elphinstone assured the Queen, although he deeply regretted being unable to accompany Arthur on his adventure – 'the first time', he lamented, 'that this has happened'.[10] From the depths of despondency, Victoria sympathized with Elphinstone, 'knowing what he must feel and have felt at seeing his beloved Prince go out on active service exposed to peril, without him, who had so carefully watched over and guarded him and kept *all* dangers (as much as he could) from him'.[11]

Arthur sailed from Woolwich on 30 July 1882. As soon as the troopship was lost to sight, and the 'tremendous cheers' of the watching crowds had died away, a clearly upset Elphinstone telegraphed confirmation of his departure to Osborne.[12] Reading the telegram, Victoria felt as if 'her heart were torn in two', fear mingling with pride to exhaust her. She now entered another 'great trial', telling Howard that all she could think of by day was Arthur, while she was 'haunted by *terrors* at night'.[13] 'My nerves were strained to such a pitch by the intensity of my anxiety and suspense,' she wrote in her journal, 'that they seemed to feel as though they were all alive.'[14]

The anxiety was very great, but the waiting was mercifully short. Before dawn on 13 September, Wolseley's force attacked Arabi's camp at Tel-el-Kebir, about forty miles north-east of Cairo. Arthur was in the thick of the short, bloody action which ensued, emerging physically unscathed but deeply affected by the cries of the wounded and the piles of Egyptian dead. Accounts of the victory reached London by telegram the same day. 'Your Majesty's troops seem to have behaved in a most brilliant manner,' Elphinstone proclaimed, 'and were led with a dash and gallantry which it is impossible to surpass.'[15] He was 'so thankful' that the Prince was safe.[16] 'Now that all risks of danger are over,' he wrote, 'you cannot but rejoice that he has undergone the true test of a soldier's capability, and come out of it with such brilliant success.'[17] Wolseley inevitably eulogized Arthur's conduct during the battle, although he admitted to the Duke of Cambridge that he had been terrified throughout the action that the prince would be killed.[18] No-one could forget the disgrace heaped on the officers who had failed to protect the Prince Imperial in Africa three years before.

The Queen 'felt unbounded joy and gratitude' at the news of the battle and her son's survival.[19] She ordered a bonfire to be lit on Craig Gowan, 'just where there had been one in 1856 [*sic*] after the fall of Sevastopol, when dearest Albert went up to it at night with Bertie and Affie. That was on September 10, very nearly the same time twenty-six years ago!'[20] As before, John Brown organized the celebrations, arranging the beacon and proposing toasts in whisky. Public scrutiny and official concern at the Highlander's access to the Queen had eased since the fraught 1860s, when the whiff of revolution had been in the air. Yet he still remained a deeply divisive figure in the palace. Cowell, in particular, found it almost impossible to fulfil his duties as Master of the Household properly while Brown stalked the corridors drunkenly countermanding his orders. Few sympathized, therefore, when Brown took to his bed with a cold in March 1883; most, as usual, blamed the effects of his chronic drinking. Only on 25 March, when Dr James Reid, the Queen's young new physician, diagnosed erysipelas, a dangerous bacterial infection which had been aggravated by the patient's delirium tremens, did Victoria express any alarm. So she was devastated when Prince Leopold, who bravely volunteered for the task, called on her two days later towards midnight to tell her that Brown had died. The 'irreparable loss of her dear, devoted attendant and friend' prompted an emotional outpouring from the Queen not seen since the demise of her husband. She penned an announcement of the death for the papers herself, and gave orders that Brown's body should lie in state at Windsor before being conveyed to Scotland for burial. 'The void, daily, nay hourly, seems only to *increase* as time goes on!' she wailed to Elphinstone more than two months later. 'She prays God to make her patient and resigned, which she fears as yet she *cannot* say she really is!'[21]

The intensity of the Queen's reaction to Brown's death, and her publication the following year of *More Leaves from the Journal of a Life in the Highlands*, a further series of extracts from her Scottish journals which she dedicated to his memory, raked up speculation on the exact nature of her relationship with her servant. The copy Victoria sent Elphinstone – which she inscribed 'in recollection of former days' – came with a letter extolling the 'perfect servant' whose death had left 'a blank never to be filled up'.[22] Brown's passing was a further stark reminder to her of how few people remained at court who had known the Prince Consort and herself in former happier times. Death and (more rarely) retirement had cut a swathe through the household which Elphinstone had joined in 1859. Sir Charles Grey, Sir Thomas Biddulph, Sir James Clark, Sir Charles Phipps and Lady Augusta Stanley had all gone, to be replaced by a new breed of post-Crimean War courtiers: men like Reid, Arthur Bigge (appointed assistant private secretary in 1882) and the new Dean of Windsor Randall Davidson, all of whom were still in their thirties. The views of this modern generation were best expressed by Davidson, who dismissed Sir John Cowell, a palace stalwart, as 'essentially something of a martinet [who] strangely lacked adaptability or ingenuity in effecting his excellent purposes for and in the Royal Household. His splendidly high tone and serious views of life were appreciated by the Queen, although she came personally to be tired of him and certainly did not follow his advice.'[23] Cowell's observation that the household 'gets on better since John Brown's disappearance from the scene' would scarcely have endeared him any further to Victoria.[24]

The slow evolution within the court was reflected by technological change in the wider world. In 1878, Elphinstone had seen Alexander Graham Bell demonstrate the telephone to the Queen at Osborne. 'Wires were connected with Cowes,' he had reported to Annie, but somehow the first wire failed and consequently the Queen did not hear the quartet singing which had been purposely got up for her at Cowes. But at midnight the fault in the wire was found and the connection completed. The singing sounded charming, and we likewise heard a bugle played at Southampton and an organ in London but the latter was very weak.[25]

The Queen was receptive to such newfangled inventions. Later she even allowed her voice to be recorded on Thomas Edison's phonograph.* (She steadfastly refused, however, to fit her residences with gas lighting, fearing fire.)

Changes to her household were of far less interest to Victoria than the swelling size of her family. In 1879 her numerous grandchildren – eventually thirty-six in all – were joined by her first great-grandchild (born to Vicky's eldest daughter Charlotte). Of the Queen's nine children, only Princess Beatrice still remained unmarried and living at home by 1884. To her surprise, even Leopold had survived long enough to take a wife, though his choice, a princess from the obscure German principality of Waldeck-Pyrmont, provoked renewed scorn among the Hohenzollerns. Fearing the spread of his illness through her family, Victoria admitted privately to feeling 'anxious' at Leo's marriage. Yet within ten months his wife delivered him a daughter with no apparent ill-effects,† and for a time it seemed that Leo, created Duke of Albany in 1881, might enjoy a normal family life at Claremont, the house in Surrey gifted to him by the Queen.

But by 1884 the prince was again suffering from severe swelling in his joints, a side-effect of the haemophilia which had plagued him since childhood. In February he travelled incognito to the South of France to recuperate at a friend's villa near Cannes. The warm weather and peaceful surroundings once again worked

---

*The recording is now lost.
† Princess Alice, who died in 1981. As the Queen had feared, Alice was a carrier of haemophilia, passing it to her son Rupert who was a sufferer (another son died in infancy). Prince Leopold also had a son posthumously, who was healthy.

their spell and Leo was soon visiting sites along the coast, determined to purchase a house in the region for his new family. But on 27 March he fell heavily while hurrying into the yacht club in Nice to change for a function. He remained conscious but the fall triggered a series of seizures, culminating, it is thought, in the brain haemorrhage which killed him the next day. The prince had escaped death so often before that it was hard for his family to understand that he had finally gone. Victoria was 'stunned, bewildered, and wretched'. 'I am a poor, desolate old woman,' she wept, 'and my cup of sorrows overflows.'[26]

Sir John Cowell was sent to France to collect Leopold's body, which was laid to rest in the chapel dedicated to his father's memory at St George's Chapel on 5 April. Elphinstone, who had so carefully watched over Leo during his childhood, was devastated at his death, despite its long inevitability, at the young age of thirty-one. 'He could not have believed that he would have been so affected by it,' he admitted to the Queen. Yet he now had three children of his own – the latest, another daughter named Olive, having been born in 1882 – so he could well imagine the pain of a parent losing a son. Visiting Balmoral some weeks after the funeral, he confessed that 'seeing again places so associated with old memories of the past has been so overwhelming that yesterday he did not dare speak with Your Majesty, for fear of breaking down himself'.[27]

Arthur, who was in India with his regiment at the time, was 'crushed' by his brother's death. 'I am sure that you will feel for and with me,' he wrote to Howard, 'for you know how devoted we were to each other and how much we had been together from our earliest childhood . . . His life had been so full of illness and suffering and yet he always recovered so well and was so full of life and its enjoyments.' 'Life,' Arthur concluded miserably, 'is indeed terribly fickle.'[28]

31

'A museum of old-fashioned furniture'

BERLIN, 1884

MEETING THE QUEEN AT WINDSOR after the battle of Tel-el-Kebir, Garnet Wolseley had given her a warning. In her journal Victoria wrote that the general had

> supposed I had heard what alarming news had arrived from the
> Sudan, where a most serious insurrection, in favour of the so
> called false prophet, was going on. A number of Egyptian troops
> had been killed . . . and the false prophet was said to be besieging
> Khartoum. Should this be taken, the whole country would go
> with him, and the consequences might be disastrous.[1]

Whether the government in London liked it or not (and Prime Minister William Gladstone most certainly did not), the British occupation of Egypt made the Sudan, an Egyptian protectorate, unavoidably its responsibility too.

Already a popular hero, Wolseley now became Viscount Wolseley of Egypt and the most highly regarded soldier in the British army. Ambitious, ruthless and politically astute, Wolseley did not fail to exploit his elevated position. Charles Gordon, for example, revealed in a letter to Elphinstone that he thought the general was as sharp as a 'sword-fish': a man who preyed on the esteem of the army, government and public. The secret of

Wolseley's success was the clique of like-minded officers which he gathered around himself, the so-called Wolseley Ring. In return for their loyalty, these men received the benefits of the general's considerable patronage. Nor did he hesitate to use his influence elsewhere to further their careers. After Tel-el-Kebir, for instance, Wolseley was keen to exploit Elphinstone's position at court to secure reward for Colonel Sir Gerald Graham, who had served alongside both of them in the Crimea. Wolseley archly reported that Graham was 'somewhat hurt at the Queen having taken no notice of him since he returned from Egypt, where he did so well'. 'I leave the matter in your hands,' he continued meaningfully. 'It is one in which my name must not appear for I have the honour of being thought officious. Graham is a *VC* and, as you know, a very fine, brave fellow.'[2] But Elphinstone, or the Queen, resisted these blandishments. Despite Wolseley's best efforts, no further honours were forthcoming for Graham, except for an invitation to dinner at Osborne.

In January 1884, facing an escalating crisis in the Sudan and at Wolseley's personal urging, the government dispatched Charles Gordon to Khartoum to assess the situation and, if necessary, evacuate the city. After a year in Mauritius and service in Basutoland, Gordon had finally embarked on his longed-for tour of the Holy Land. At a loose end since his return to England the previous year, he had toyed with resigning his commission altogether to work for King Leopold of Belgium in the Congo; but when the call came to return to the Sudan, he barely hesitated. His orders were imprecise, but the emergency seemed to offer this deeply religious and fatalistic man an opportunity for one final transcendental personal experience. So when the Duke of Cambridge and Wolseley saw Gordon off in person at Charing Cross Station on 18 January, he probably already little expected, or even hoped, to return. Gordon was greeted in Cairo by Colonel Graham, who had returned to Egypt with the occupying army. 'It was a great sight,' recalled an eye-witness, 'as tall Graham, some inches over six feet, grasped both Gordon's hands with "Charlie, dear boy, how are you?" and "Gerald, my dear fellow, how are you?" answered the little man joyfully.'[3] Days later, Gordon headed down the Nile to Khartoum – and immortality.

No-one followed events in the Sudan more closely than the Queen at Windsor. She unfavourably compared Gladstone's ambivalence towards the country's fate with Gordon's apparently single-handed attempt to save it from disaster. 'The Queen trembles for General Gordon's safety,' she warned the Prime Minister; 'if anything befalls *him*, the result will be awful.'[4] When news reached London in March that Khartoum was besieged by the Mahdi and Gordon himself in grave danger, she pressed the government to send a relief expedition, egged on by a fiercely jingoistic press. After fatal official procrastination, Wolseley was again summoned to save the day, departing for Egypt to rescue the man he had originally embroiled in the affair.

On 1 August 1884, while Gordon checked Khartoum's dwindling food supplies, Howard hosted a lunch for the Crown Prince and Princess of Prussia at Vine Cottage, his residence at Aldershot camp as the commanding Royal Engineer. Ahead of this daunting engagement, Howard told Annie that Vicky, who was visiting her mother at Windsor, had 'always longed to see our little abode'.[5] The royal couple were accompanied to the cottage by three of their daughters and by their court chamberlain, Count von Seckendorff. If the eldest of the girls, eighteen-year-old Victoria, or 'Moretta', looked forlorn it was probably on account of Prince Alexander of Battenberg, the ruler of Bulgaria since the Congress of Berlin. Described by Mary Ponsonby as a girl with 'much of her mother's impetuosity and her eldest brother's eccentricity', Moretta had fallen passionately in love with 'Sandro' during his recent visit to Berlin.[6] Believing her feelings reciprocated, the princess had declared her love and after Sandro returned to Sofia considered herself secretly engaged to the dashing prince. Moretta's mother – and her grandmother at Windsor – encouraged the love match. But Fritz frowned upon it, citing Sandro's lack of breeding. As Sandro's father had married

337

a commoner out of love, rather than a royal out of duty, his children were considered *personae non gratae* by the fastidious Hohenzollerns. Moreover, Sandro's support for the growing nationalistic movement in Bulgaria had so irritated his Russian masters that official approval of his marriage to a Prussian princess might threaten a security pact between Berlin and St Petersburg. 'We were living in a fool's paradise,' Moretta bitterly recalled fifty years later, 'for what seemed to us a simple thing soon became hedged in with difficulties.'[7] Nevertheless, the subject had occupied Vicky's thoughts all through the summer. Despite the deep hostility towards Sandro, she was determined to fight her daughter's cause; secretly if necessary.

Lunch over, the Elphinstones escorted the royal party to nearby Farnborough, where the Empress Eugénie had recently settled in a sprawling mansion. The Queen described the house as 'in the old English style'; but in truth it was more an extravagance of eccentric Swiss design, with heavily carved wooden gables and steeply tiled roofs. At its heart was a museum of Napoleonic relics which the Empress had formed around the pitiful handful of belongings she had personally recovered from the site of her son's death in Africa. Indeed, five years after his death, the lingering shadow of the Prince Imperial was still unavoidable. In one room was a marble statue of Louis as a child, while another had been built as an exact replica of his bedroom at Camden Place, complete with clothes and sword. But it was the bay window in the sitting room which revealed the reason behind the Empress's move from Kent to Hampshire. This overlooked a neighbouring hill where a still-to-be-completed church in late gothic, distinctively French style could be glimpsed through the trees. The church had been commissioned by the Empress to house the bodies of her husband, son and one day (it would not be until 1920) herself.

After taking tea on porcelain marked with the letter 'N' and the Imperial crown, Vicky, Fritz and the children returned to Windsor. Annie Elphinstone meanwhile departed for a seaside holiday in Deauville with the children. Howard remained on duty at Aldershot, promising to meet up with his family at the end of the month at West Woodhay House, the handsome Jacobean mansion in Berkshire recently purchased by Annie's wealthy father; until then any holiday for him was impossible, as the whole camp was frantically preparing the expedition to the Sudan. Gordon's situation inevitably dominated the conversation a few days later when Howard dined with General Sir Archibald Alison, the commander of the Aldershot Division and a veteran of Tel-el-Kebir. Another guest was the explorer Henry Stanley, whom the colonel found a 'very interesting little man; with a funny mixture of broad Scotch and American'. Stanley, who had been engaged by the King of the Belgians to work with Gordon in the Congo before the crisis in the Sudan broke, said he had 'never met Gordon . . . but wherever he went he heard wonderful tales of him'.[8]

On 30 August, Elphinstone travelled to Osborne to dine with Vicky and Fritz for one last time before they returned to Germany. His visit, however, was overshadowed by reports from Berlin of the sudden death of the British ambassador, Lord Odo Russell. Vicky was distraught at the news, sobbing to Howard that Russell had been 'of immense use, even personally to her, in smoothing difficulties of family matters'. Elphinstone, too, was deeply 'grieved'; Russell had been an avuncular host during his otherwise dreary visits to Berlin and one of the few friendly faces at the forbidding Prussian court. 'In the political sense', Russell's untimely death was 'an immense calamity'.[9] The ambassador had acted as a vital diplomatic bulwark against Bismarck's vaulting ambitions, managing to maintain the Chancellor's respect despite the differences between their countries. Russell's experience and equanimity would be sorely missed in Berlin, particularly as Germany was entering an aggressive phase of colonial expansion – a policy which, the diplomat James Rodd admitted with typical restraint, was 'ruffling' relations with Britain.[10]

Wolseley was overwhelmed by applications to join his

swashbuckling mission to save Gordon. One of the lucky officers to be handpicked was Colonel Leopold Swaine, the British military attaché in Berlin, who had also served on the general's staff during the campaign against Arabi Pasha. Before Wolseley sailed on 1 September 1884, he sent Swaine a telegram inviting him to join the expedition at Cairo. Swaine did not hesitate. He packed his bags and headed for Africa, eager to be a part of the great adventure. With the British legation in Berlin already seriously weakened by Russell's death, a temporary replacement for Swaine had to be found quickly. On 31 August, the day Wolseley took his leave of the Queen at Osborne, the Duke of Cambridge telegraphed Howard at West Woodhay House offering him the post. 'The Duke', the colonel informed Victoria, 'said it was very important that they should have now at Berlin someone who was very well acquainted with Germany.'[11] The proposal to send Elphinstone back to Germany on official business was encouraged both by the Queen at Windsor and by the crown princess in Berlin. To Howard, who received the request just as he was greeting Annie and the children on their return home from France, it was rather less welcome. But, given the highly charged circumstances of the moment, it was impossible for him to refuse.

So, as Howard had once done to him, Gordon now inadvertently intervened in his friend's career. After attending Odo Russell's funeral, Howard set off again for Berlin, a city he disliked and had hoped never to see again. It was arranged that Annie would follow as soon as things were settled. There was no knowing how long his assignment would last, or even whether Swaine would return alive from the Sudan. Howard was ill-prepared for his new role, complaining to his wife in his first letter home that his dress uniform, battered by years of court functions, was finally 'giving way'. Finding decent lodgings for them both in the crowded city was also difficult.[12] 'Mrs Swaine is remaining in Berlin so we can't have her house,' he wrote despondently, after trudging around various hotels and boarding houses.[13] His task in the city was not made any easier by the secret which he carried from the Queen. 'It is that he should know that Princess Victoria of Prussia is very much attached to the Prince of Bulgaria and vice versa. The Crown Princess favours the project and the Crown Prince is now not disinclined to it, but the Emperor and Empress are violently against it, and they are very unkind.' Declaring herself 'strongly in favour' of the match, the Queen cajoled Howard into putting in 'a friendly word' on the matter with the Kaiser when they met.[14] At the same time, he was to watch developments closely and report them back to Windsor in cipher.

By coincidence, as Elphinstone took up his diplomatic post in Germany, an investigative French journalist called Juliette Adam published a series of letters addressed to a fictitious friend who had 'entered the Diplomatic Service and become an *attaché* at Berlin'. These give a vivid and entertaining insight into the life Elphinstone faced in the city, and the difficulties he would encounter. 'The first half of your news is good,' she wrote; 'I cannot say so much for the second. Berlin Society does not welcome strangers; men of high position are exceedingly reserved; the women are either prudes or dissolute . . . there is little intellectual conversation [and] Gossip and scandal are more than usually prevalent.'[15]

There were at least some friendly, if not altogether familiar, faces at the British Chancery, which was located near the Brandenburg Gate. These included James Rodd, third secretary Charles Cadogan, and Charles Scott, the chargé d'affaires since Russell's untimely death. In October 1884 a new ambassador arrived to take up residence down the road in the British Embassy on Wilhelmstrasse, which was 'upside down' after the recent upheavals.[16] Sir Edward Malet was a genial man with long experience of the diplomatic service, most recently in Cairo at the time of Tel-el-Kebir. He was also very determined and energetic, and one of his first actions was to move the isolated chancery into the embassy's former stables, instantly improving communication and *esprit de corps* among the British delegation. It was sorely needed.

Almost as soon as the new ambassador arrived, the city hosted an international conference to discuss Germany's colonial ambitions in Africa. James Rodd later complained that in all his years as a diplomat he had 'seldom experienced a more strenuous period than the three months during which it sat'.[17] The conference led to Britain formally acknowledging Germany's suzerainty in Cameroon and Tanganyika, while agreeing to share control of New Guinea. Aside from the conference, Elphinstone was charged with the normal activity of any attaché in a foreign country, which is to spy on his host for his own government. The War Office in London, for instance, asked him to provide details on a 'new infantry projectile' secretly developed by the Prussians and to gather intelligence on their *Kriegspiel*, or war games.[18]

Apart from the thrill of his undercover work, life in Berlin was as constricting as it had always been. The court was also more decrepit: Juliette Adam compared it to 'a museum of old-fashioned furniture'. Kaiser Wilhelm, who had miraculously survived into his late eighties, was preceded everywhere by a 'limping *cortège* and followed by people who try to efface the irreparable ravages of time by the aid of art'.[19] The Kaiser himself looked 'in excellent health' when Howard dined at the Schloss on 15 December. Meanwhile Augusta, who was now confined to a bathchair, still retained her sharp interest in current affairs, quizzing the colonel closely on Gordon's predicament. 'No family matters of any kind were touched upon,' a clearly relieved Howard assured the Queen in England afterwards;[20] so he had been spared the awkward task of raising the question of Moretta's proposed marriage to the Prince of Battenberg with his Prussian hosts. Victoria replied that she was 'glad that the Empress did not enter upon ticklish ground', complaining that her once close confidante now sent her only 'stiff and not very amiable letters'.[21] The colonel's intimacy with the crown princess was so well known, however, that it is highly unlikely that Augusta, a fierce opponent of the engagement, would have revealed her own efforts to frustrate it.

Juliette Adam further cautioned the new attaché about the looseness of Prussian morals. 'Adultery flourishes like a plant in a favourable soil,' she warned, 'It ripens in the sunshine, and its fruits are displayed, gathered, and eaten without scruple.'[22] Betraying his young wife was inconceivable to a man of Elphinstone's moral rigour, so the sight of others disregarding their marriage vows quite openly must have appalled him. He was overjoyed, therefore, when Annie, after leaving the children with her parents at West Woodhay, joined him in his cramped rooms at the Hotel de Russie on 5 November. But Annie clearly found Prussian society even more trying than her husband (there is no evidence that she even spoke German). The entries in her journal, formerly crowded with descriptions of her busy family life at Aldershot, quickly dwindle to a bare record of events. With Howard occupied all day with his work at the conference, Annie was left with little to do; so the opening of the Reichstag on 20 November came as a welcome distraction, offering Annie the opportunity to meet the infamous German Chancellor for the first time. Life improved greatly with the ending of the West African Conference and the easing of Howard's workload. Encouraged by Sir Edward Malet, the Elphinstones set up a theatre at the embassy – as they had at Aldershot – painting the scenery and producing a series of entertainments for the staff.

There was also the crown princess. The evening after the opening of the Reichstag, the Elphinstones had attended Vicky's forty-fourth birthday party, pressing into the packed ballroom at the Schloss with the rest of Berlin society. They were then invited to spend Christmas Eve with the royal family, to avoid passing a miserable evening missing their own children back in England. 'It was rather a big affair,' Annie told her mother modestly: 'all their own family, and the whole household. Howard and I however were the only outsiders.' After a lavish dinner, Vicky led her guests into the drawing room where a long table was decorated with Christmas trees and loaded with presents and platefuls of 'apples, nuts and different kinds of gingerbread'. Everyone came in for their share. The Elphinstones received some prints; an antique brass bowl decorated with an image of St George and the Dragon; and 'some little gold pins from the little Princesses'. There were also 'a lot of toys' for their own children, including a musical box – still owned by their descendants – 'which when you play sets a bell ringing and a woman dancing and a water wheel turning'. Over the years, Howard had spent many Christmases with the royal family at Windsor, in happy times and in sad. But Annie found it all slightly overwhelming, though she appreciated the generous gesture: 'I think it was very good of them having us in like that,' she exclaimed.[23] It was not, however, altogether without purpose.

32

'*Air Castles*'

BERLIN, 1885

IN JANUARY 1885, WORD filtered back to England that Wolseley's force had won a fierce battle against the Mahdi's dervishes at Abu Klea, only a hundred miles downriver from Khartoum. Relief of the city, and Gordon's salvation, seemed close at hand. The *Times* correspondent in Berlin noticed the crown princess take Howard aside to discuss the dramatic news while they were skating together in the Tiergarten.[1] 'The brilliant result obtained against such large odds', the colonel then confidently informed the Queen, 'ought practically to close the campaign, and must be a source of universal satisfaction. Communication with Gordon is no doubt by this time re-established and the Mahdi's power will be completely overthrown.'[2] But he spoke too soon. The next fragment of information from the Sudan brought the horrific confirmation that Khartoum had been taken and Gordon killed, just two days before the vanguard of Wolseley's forces reached the city. 'The heart breaking news from Khartoum has caused great sorrow here,' reported Sir Edward Malet from Berlin.[3] Everyone at the embassy was deeply shocked; none more so than Howard, who had known Gordon for more than thirty years.

Victoria was told at Osborne House. A potent mixture of anger at Gladstone's government, humiliation at her country's defeat and sorrow for Gordon fuelled a fusillade of furious

telegrams from the Isle of Wight to Whitehall, many sent deliberately *en clair* to be read by anyone handling them down the line.
For the Queen, this disaster was the culmination of years of
sparring with her 'terrible' Prime Minister.[4] Overnight William
Gladstone, the 'G.O.M.' (Grand Old Man) of British politics,
became the 'M.O.G.' (Murderer of Gordon). She may have met
Gordon only once – when Elphinstone and Cowell invited him to
dinner at Osborne in December 1872 – but his brutal death had
come to symbolize for her all the ills of her country. Sir John
Cowell, the Queen's harbinger of doom, was dispatched to
Southampton to sympathize with Gordon's grieving sister. In
return, she gave her brother's tattered and worn Bible to the
Queen, who encased it in crystal and gold before placing it in a
prominent position at Windsor Castle as a lasting rebuke to the
men who had failed Gordon in his hour of need.

Arthur admitted to Elphinstone that Gordon's death made
his 'blood boil' with grief and anger. The colonel's own sorrow
mingled with his outrage at the military disaster. Wolseley, whose
bombastic style he and Gordon had once gently mocked, had
failed his friend catastrophically. When he returned to England,
Howard volunteered for the committee, patronized by the Queen,
that was set up to establish a boys' school in Gordon's name. As a
token of his friendship, he was also given a facsimile copy of the
general's heavily annotated edition of Cardinal Newman's inspira-
tional *Dream of Gerontius*, which Gordon had sent back from the
Sudan before he was killed.

While her mother's thoughts were concentrated on the loss
of one man in a remote desert, the Crown Princess of Prussia's
were on matters closer to home. The announcement in December
that her youngest sister Princess Beatrice was going to marry the
Prince of Bulgaria's brother Henry of Battenberg had redoubled
her clandestine efforts to secure Sandro's hand for her own daughter Moretta. The Queen did not share the Hohenzollerns'
intemperate dislike of the Battenbergs and had brushed aside their
dynastic concerns as irrelevant in giving her daughter permission

to marry Henry. But hostility towards Sandro was greater than ever in Berlin. With the exception of Vicky, the Prussian royal family was unusually united in its opposition to his proposed marriage to Moretta, fearing the dilution of Hohenzollern blood by an impure 'Battenberger'. Even Fritz found it impossible to shrug off his innate prejudices. Vicky admitted to her mother that her husband 'was unusually touchy' on the 'question of rank and position'.[5] Henry of Battenberg's engagement to Princess Beatrice was therefore greeted with incredulity in Berlin. 'To such depths has the Queen of an old and powerful dynasty descended to keep her daughter in the country (as a secretary),' sneered the Kaiser, whose loathing of Sandro had been further stoked by his grandson.[6] Jealous of Sandro's military prowess and dashing good looks, Prince Wilhelm, now twenty-six, had begun spying on him, sending salacious reports on his behaviour to the Kaiser as well as the Tsar, Alexander III.

Behind the Hohenzollerns' hatred of Sandro lurked Bismarck, who was quite prepared to exploit their prejudice against the Prince of Bulgaria for his own political ends. Sensing a British plot co-ordinated by the crown princess to drive a wedge between Berlin and St Petersburg, the Chancellor theatrically threatened to resign if the marriage was allowed to proceed. As Bismarck intended, the powers now ranged against the English crown princess left her isolated and, worse, appearing hostile to German interests. Achieving her romantic goal against such overwhelming odds seemed impossible. By 30 January 1885, Vicky had apparently abandoned the plan altogether, telling her mother that 'there is *nothing to be done*'. 'Poor Vicky [Moretta] sees it too,' she lamented,

and deeply as she is attached to Sandro she will *not* stand in the way of his interests! He *must* think of his country and as Prince Bismarck insists on swelling out the question to one of high political importance and has told the Emperor and Fritz it cannot be, for many highly important reasons we must think of it no more.[7]

Apparently 'in great distress', the crown princess told Elphinstone that 'all our hopes are at an end and I am quite miserable'. In fact, her comments were slyly deceptive, as Vicky now embarked on a high-risk strategy to save her daughter's love affair by subterfuge. The same day she wrote to Windsor, Vicky gave Howard a letter for Sandro, asking him to arrange its delivery to the prince in Bulgaria as 'the *Post* is not to be *trusted* and it must go SAFE'. 'Could it not go as a letter from you to the English minister at Sofia or is it not *safe?*' she queried anxiously. Then a final dreadful thought occurred to her. 'I wonder whether they watch what letters you write at your hotel?' she exclaimed, certain her own were being intercepted and read by Bismarck's agents.[8]

The colonel was becoming embroiled in a very dangerous game, as Sandro's desire for Bulgarian independence from Russian control directly challenged not only the Tsar but Germany's policy in the Balkans. If discovered, the crown princess's attempts to communicate with the prince secretly would have been construed as treason in Berlin. For his own part, Howard risked aggravating already fraught relations between Russia and England and being arrested himself as a spy. Vicky was prepared to run the risk out of love for her daughter and a stubborn desire to play a role in shaping Germany's foreign policy. Elphinstone did so out of duty to the Queen and sympathy for the princess. It is unlikely that the government in London would have approved of either motive.

Sandro's reply to the first letter the crown princess smuggled to him through Howard is lost, presumably destroyed after she read it. But her reaction to a repetition of the process some weeks later make her relief and gratitude only too plain. The prince's words had brought her 'one *little* ray of *sunshine* and of HOPE though it is *but faint*', she told Elphinstone, and emphasized:

This I owe to *you*; you would have been repaid if you had seen my poor child's tears of gratitude. *Now* ALL depends on long patience and on PERFECT silence! NO ONE of *my* FAMILY, *no one* HERE either IN or out of the House must guess, that there is the *slightest* chance, or all will again be spoilt, and *then* – for ever! NONE of HIS family must guess it either! For *them* and for the rest of the world the thing must be 'over and done with' altogether.[9]

Elphinstone was now the go-between between the crown princess and the prince of Bulgaria as they attempted to deceive Bismarck and his spies. 'You are the only person who knows this,' the princess told him, 'and I know the secret is safe with you.' The only proofs of their perilous correspondence to survive are Vicky's highly emotive letters to Howard – which, ignoring her order to burn them, he kept for his own protection – and Sandro's hurriedly scrawled notes from Sofia acknowledging the safe receipt of the colonel's parcels.

On 26 February 1885, after an exhausting round of farewells, the Elphinstones left Berlin, Colonel Swaine having returned unscathed from Egypt. 'Lots of people' came to the station to see them off: a very different scene from Annie's solitary late-night arrival in November. Too upset to see them go in person, Vicky sent a note and a painting by a favoured artist 'in remembrance' of their stay. In their luggage, the Elphinstones also carried a portrait of Howard painted by Götz von Seckendorff. The picture shows a tired man, worn down by years of underlying ill-health and the pressures of work. Nor was this about to change. Howard and Annie reached London before dawn the next day 'after a tiresome journey and very tired'.[10] The last thing they wanted to see therefore was a telegram from the Queen summoning them to Windsor for dinner that evening. She wanted to know all.

The first request for Howard to smuggle another message to Sofia came from Berlin within just a few days. 'May I ask you the favour of forwarding this letter?' the crown princess implored.

Then you could send *me* word by telegraph: 'Letter has been received'. I need hardly say that if you think there is danger of the letter getting lost or going astray, it would be better not to send

349

it! Should Prince Alexander of Bulgaria be away, you could give directions that the letter should be returned to you. Perhaps you would also let Prince Alexander have your direction *in case* he wanted to send me an answer! I ought to add that the Queen and Beatrice [and] Prince Henry of Battenberg know nothing of this note, so please do not mention it at Windsor. I am so anxious to avoid rucks and complications in our large family . . . If I could only see you, I would explain the reason of this . . . We miss you both so much! Do give dear Lady Elphinstone my love – I can just fancy you both in your dear little Home at Aldershot! . . . *Please burn this* DIRECTLY.[11]

It was not easy for the princess to smuggle her letters to Howard from Germany. The safest way was to hand them to trusted friends who were either returning to England or could deliver them in person to a British consulate overseas for onward dispatch to Elphinstone. Howard then used a variety of means to forward the letters on to Sandro. Most went by diplomatic pouch to Frank Lascelles, the British consul in Sofia. 'If *you* direct it,' Vicky had suggested to Howard, 'he cannot know that it comes from *me*!' (It is very unlikely, however, that the clever young consul did not.) Other letters were collected from Howard at Aldershot by a mysterious man sent for the purpose from Bulgaria. Sometimes opportunity, such as the funeral of Arthur's father-in-law, the unlamented Prince Friedrich Carl, at Potsdam in June, gave Vicky the chance to slip the letters to Elphinstone herself. The intimacy of her subterfuge with Howard was obviously exciting to the crown princess. She felt in control at last, outwitting her enemies in Berlin. Her strategy was simple: 'The matter *is* and *must* be looked upon by the WHOLE of MY family and HIS family, also the *Prussian family*, as quite at an *end*,' she explained. 'Then the *future* is open to us, and we can avail ourselves of changed and better times. You are the only person who knows this, and I know the secret is safe with you.'[12]

Vicky found the long interval between smuggling each letter

out of Germany to Howard and receiving a reply from Sandro almost unbearable. 'I shall live in terror and anxiety for fear of it going astray or falling into the wrong hands,' she wrote after sending one packet to Howard in April 1885.[13] Having secured the colonel's trust, and believing also that he was destroying her letters, the princess now took Howard further into her confidence. She began venting her frustration at her position in Berlin, on one occasion complaining bitterly that 'In Germany I am a good liberal, and in England a liberal *Chauviniste!*'[14] More perilously still, knowing of the colonel's close contacts at the War Office, she began to see their secret correspondence as a means of wielding real influence behind the scenes in international affairs, power denied her in Berlin. Citing a 'senior official *German* source', she revealed that Russia was utterly unprepared for war and urged Britain to attack Germany's close ally. 'I do *not know* WHY we are losing so much time in England,' she protested. 'I *quite* believe the Russian govt do *not* [want] war NOW . . . they prefer to be better prepared . . . for the fulfilment of what *they for* generations have looked upon as their *national destiny* – the *conquering of India!* . . . I *own* I do *not* like our delay AT ALL!'[15] She then freely divulged the opinion of 'a *high* military authority *here*' who had told her '(*for me* alone) that if England meant to be masters of the situation she *ought to take no time* in *forcing the Dardanelles. Pray never* mention ME, but I thought it might be of use for you to know this.'

Feeding Elphinstone intelligence gleaned from the Prussian court was unquestionably treasonable. The crown princess clearly understood the grave risk she was running, begging her accomplice to 'NEVER *betray* ME!'[16] Yet despite all the precautions the correspondents took, it is unlikely that the German Chancellor did not know of their collusion. The Queen herself had warned Elphinstone when he first became attaché in Berlin that 'Bismarck has his spies everywhere'.[17] Even Vicky spoke hysterically of telegrams being 'bought and stolen' before they reached their destinations.[18] For the time being, Bismarck seemed happy to play a waiting game while the princess compromised herself still further.

The Queen in England may not have known the exact details of her daughter's plotting, but she recognized the danger of its exposure to both their countries. Without consulting her first, she banned Vicky from attending Princess Beatrice's marriage to Henry of Battenberg on the Isle of Wight in July 1885. Sandro was expected as a guest at his brother's wedding, 'and it would never do for you to meet so soon with the excited feelings existing at headquarters'.[19] The Prussian royal family snubbed the nuptials altogether, refusing to witness the union of a Battenberg with a royal princess. Vicky was deeply hurt at her exclusion from the ceremony, the only marriage of all her siblings she missed. She reconciled herself to the disappointment by sending a packet of letters for Howard to pass surreptitiously to Sandro during the festivities. 'You need never repent of having done a kind action,' she declared, as soon as she had received confirmation of its safe delivery, 'and the service of a real friend.'[20]

In the autumn, Vicky took Moretta to Venice, a trip designed to revive the flagging spirits of both women. While staying at the Hôtel d'Europe, the crown princess heard of 'a great disturbance in B[ulgaria]'. 'I do trust there is no danger of our letters being intercepted!' she immediately wrote to Elphinstone in obvious panic.[21] In fact the people of Eastern Rumelia, the puppet state bordering Bulgaria set up after the Congress of Berlin, had finally revolted against their Russian masters. They proclaimed union with their neighbour and acclaimed Sandro as the leader of a newly unified country. The move secretly delighted the English but incensed the Tsar, who stepped up his vendetta against the Bulgarian prince. Meanwhile Bismarck watchfully bided his time.

Elphinstone sent a reassuring reply to Venice, but with Bulgaria in turmoil and Sandro's situation unclear, the crown princess feared that all of her carefully laid plans were going awry. 'I cannot help hoping that good *may* come out of all this,' she prayed, 'when Russia's rage, *fury* and disappointment has calmed down. Perhaps it may bring me lasting good too, though of course not NOW while *all* is so unsafe and unsettled. The principal thing for me is to have at hand SOME means of *communication* in case of an emergency left, and for *this* you are my only hope!'[22]

On 2 October Vicky wrote a 28-page letter to Sandro. Its survival suggests that, in all the unrest, Elphinstone was unable to get it through to Sofia, as the prince would certainly have destroyed it as usual. 'When I saw nothing but long faces one fine morning', she opened,

> and heard that Prince Alexander had annexed East Rumelia, I nearly jumped with surprise, astonishment and fear. Many people shook their heads and said, 'That will mean war'. I said and thought: the Prince is acting with courage, boldness, self-sacrifice, patriotism and wisdom like a true man . . . Thank God we were not in Berlin or Potsdam but here abroad, where we can ask questions freely and speak without being watched and spied upon . . . Vicki [Moretta] wanted to run away, disguise herself as a man and go to war with you!! [she] is so terribly frightened the Russians might make an attempt on your life. She hopes that the charm you wear will really protect you . . . My hands are tied and my lips are sealed, otherwise I would raise my voice. I love a fight and am not easily intimidated; I know how to fight for my convictions.[23]

In a state of 'feverish anxiety', the crown princess and her daughter tried to enjoy their holiday. Vicky related to Howard how they had taken tea with 'Mr Browning the poet' and spent hours sketching in Piazza San Marco. But her thoughts rarely strayed far from Sofia and she clung to the hope that, one day, she would still see Moretta and Sandro together.

One unforeseen consequence of the revolt in Eastern Rumelia was the insecurity felt by the King of Serbia at the reunification of his neighbours. On 14 November 1885 Serbia declared war and launched an invasion of Bulgaria. For a time, the crisis threatened to spark a wider conflict as the major powers in Europe took sides. 'Russia is working like a torpedo under water,' a clearly horrified crown princess told Howard.[24] However, a swift victory by the Bulgarian army, gallantly led by Sandro to the consternation of both the Tsar in St Petersburg and an envious Prince Wilhelm of Prussia in Berlin, prevented an escalation of the war. The crown princess, now back in Germany, rejoiced at the prince's unexpected triumph. 'The enthusiasm for him is *very great* here, in general amongst ALL CLASSES,' she reported. 'My parents-in-law, William, the Grand Duchess of Baden and Count Herbert Bismarck are the only exceptions, their animosity is unabated (and not a little dangerous) and kept up by Russian influence.'[25]

Yet, ironically, Sandro's success only hastened his downfall. Alexander III was now determined to topple him and restore Bulgaria to full Russian control. On the night of 20 August 1886, the prince was kidnapped by Russian agents and forced to sign a document of abdication. His abduction caused outrage across Europe. The removal of any ruler by force unsettled every royal house in Europe, even the Hohenzollerns. Fearing Russian reprisals, Germany and Austria refused to intervene in the crisis, but under pressure from the Queen the British government threatened to send a fleet to the Black Sea. The Tsar also misjudged the reaction among ordinary Bulgarians to the kidnap of their gallant prince. Within days, a nationalist counter-revolution overthrew the conspirators' junta, paving the way for the prince's triumphant return to Sofia on 29 August. But Sandro then made a fatal, and final, misjudgement. Believing that his security rested on the goodwill of the Russians, he telegraphed Alexander pledging his loyalty and grandiloquently offering to abdicate if requested. 'As Russia gave me my Crown I am prepared to give it back in the hands of its Sovereign,' he declared theatrically. Bolstered by massive public support in Bulgaria, the prince did not intend, or expect, his gesture of reconciliation to be taken seriously. But the Tsar seized upon this heaven-sent opportunity to humiliate his irritating rival, calling the prince's bluff by publishing the telegram and showily accepting the abdication. Boxed in, ultimately defeated by principle and his own political naïvety rather than force of arms, Sandro departed Sofia before dawn on 10 September 1886, never to return.

The crown princess was horrified at this unexpected outcome. 'Events go *so* fast . . . and are so sad!' she wailed, 'though the audacious and outrageous act of the Russians has not succeeded; yet the poor Prince has no support from any other Power, and to save his country a Russian military occupation (invasion) or civil war, I hear by telegram that he has voluntarily abdicated – what was he to do?'[26] Yet it also dawned on Vicky that as Sandro no longer posed any threat to German interests, Bismarck and the Kaiser might now relent and allow the prince to marry Moretta. It was a false hope. Her mother in England was not alone in appreciating that once he had lost power Sandro would no longer need to marry the lovestruck Prussian princess to secure his position. Nor had the dramatic events in the Balkans lessened the Hohenzollerns' deep-seated objections to the prince's non-royal blood. 'I can understand and admire that Moretta should remain faithful to dear Sandro,' the Queen wrote gently to Vicky, 'and now it signifies but little if he is freed or not. Two years ago his marrying would have been of use to him. But now you could not, I fear, get over the Emperor's and Empress's prejudices?'[27] Moretta wrote later of how she had 'waited and hoped' with her mother, 'while the storm raged round and about us', sending letters and telegrams to the exiled prince as he wandered around Europe.[28] It was all to no avail; for the astute Queen was right about Sandro's original motives. In 1889 he abandoned Moretta altogether and married an actress he met at the theatre in Darmstadt.

In August 1886, just as events were reaching a climax in Bulgaria, the crown princess had escaped on holiday with her younger children. Fritz remained behind in Berlin, promising to follow after the annual military manoeuvres. In her husband's absence, Vicky begged the Elphinstones to join her at the secluded villa which Lord Carnarvon had lent her above Portofino on the Italian Riviera. For three weeks the old friends walked, sketched the surrounding hills, and explored the sleepy coastline by steam launch. 'The spot is so beautiful', the crown princess wrote after Howard left, 'that a true lover of nature can never be bored, and you have not half exhausted its charms, or its treasures of beautiful views.'[29] Annie and Howard stayed in an ancient tower perched on a cliff edge high above the villa, each evening navigating the steep pathway separating the two properties by the light of a swaying lantern. Moretta remembered the holiday as among the happiest she ever spent with her family, while for Vicky they were the last few weeks of her life untouched by tragedy.

Fritz joined them all at the villa on 1 October, exhausted by the constant intrigues at the Prussian court and debilitated by a series of colds and a dry, persistent cough. Soon after he arrived, the weather changed, becoming colder and, as Annie noted in her journal, 'very showery'.[30] The Elphinstones left Italy ten days later, returning to Aldershot via Paris. The crown princess missed them badly. 'Your little tower is quite shut up,' she wrote miserably to Howard, 'and we think of Lady Elphinstone and you each time we pass it.'[31] A sense of foreboding had settled over the holiday since their departure. The villa was being buffeted by 'violent squalls of wind and rain'; Fritz felt no better; and cholera had broken out in the neighbouring town of Genoa. Elsewhere 'the political horizon looks very dark and clouded', Vicky reported unhappily. Embittered by recent events in Sofia, she still plaintively urged Britain to take military action against Russia, describing the Tsar's empire as 'a barbaric power, the representative of corruption, absolutism, lawlessness, tyranny etc'. As the rain lashed against the shuttered windows of the Villa Carnarvon, she even wildly imagined the French coming to Russia's aid, forcing their old foe Germany out into the open and onto the side of the British. This, she concluded, would 'be an inestimable advantage, as Germany's position *now* is as false as possible'.[32] But she was living in a fool's paradise. Neither Bismarck nor Lord Salisbury, the new Prime Minister in London, would ever allow Vicky to exercise influence on foreign affairs. Instead, she was reduced to fulminating on the

Annie Cole, the nineteen-year-old who captured Howard's ageing and lonely heart in 1876. Recovering from her shock at the engagement, the Queen thought Annie a 'very pleasing, bright little thing'.

ABOVE AND FAR RIGHT:
*Watercolours of the Neues
Palais at Potsdam, painted by
Howard while staying with
the Crown Princess of Prussia
in August 1878.*

RIGHT: *Vicky and Fritz, the
Crown Prince and Princess of
Prussia, whose activities were
closely monitored by Bismarck.
The couple's lives were touched
by tragedy.*

LEFT: *Prince Wilhelm of Prussia as a child, already keenly conscious of his disability and of his future destiny.*

ABOVE: *Portrait in oils of Howard, painted in 1884 during his appointment as military attaché in Berlin, by Götz von Seckendorff, Vicky's court chamberlain.*

RIGHT: *Princess Victoria of Prussia, 'Moretta', whose unrequited love for the Prince of Bulgaria embroiled Howard in a dangerous game of espionage.*

RIGHT: *The Crown Princess of Prussia, who recruited Howard as go-between between her daughter and Sandro.*

BELOW: *Wedding photograph of Princess Beatrice and Prince Henry of Battenberg, taken at Osborne House on 25 July 1885. During the celebrations, Howard surreptitiously passed Sandro (top left) a bundle of letters from Berlin.*

The silver-mounted miniature of Howard
and the envelope containing his last letter to
the Queen, found among Victoria's personal
belongings when she died in 1901.

Annie in the garden she created with Howard at Pinewood, photographed in about 1892 with the four daughters he would never see grow up. From left: Toby (the dog), Olive, Victoria, Mary, Annie and Irene.

The view from Lord Carnarvon's villa above Portofino, where the Elphinstones stayed with the Crown Prince and Princess of Prussia in August 1886.

sidelines in private letters to her few friends.

There was a valedictory air to this holiday in Italy which the crown princess caught in a remarkable letter she wrote to Howard before returning to Germany with her sick husband. 'Would that air Castles could turn into Bricks and Mortar by enchantment and without money,' she imagined wistfully, 'and that you could spend a little time each year with me perched in my castle high up on the rocks, amongst the olives and pines, over the deep blue sea, with the distant hills and their circle of bright houses and villages at their foot to look at, and the soft air blowing around one. It would be *very* nice!'[33]

In Berlin, the cause of Fritz's cough was diagnosed as nothing more than a harmless growth on his larynx – the result, the doctors said, of years of heavy smoking. In fact, Vicky's life would never be the same again.

33

'An unforgettable
moment of pride'

JUBILEE, 1887

A T FIRST THE QUEEN was reluctant to mark the fiftieth
anniversary of her reign officially. She cited the expense and,
less convincingly, the impropriety of celebrating the death of her
predecessor King William IV. Privately, she admitted that she
dreaded the 'mob of royalties' which would inevitably descend on
her from around the world.[1] However, under sustained pressure
from the press, public and, above all, from the Prince of Wales,
who relished the prospect of a lavish royal event, Victoria
conceded defeat and agreed to a service of thanksgiving at
Westminster Abbey. But she granted her permission on the strict
understanding that the event would be only a *semi*-state occasion
and that it would take place on 21 June, a day after the fiftieth
anniversary of her accession. There would be no crowns, no robes
and no brightly gilded coaches.

Her decision made, she departed for Scotland, leaving Sir
John Cowell to struggle with the sensitive problem of finding suitable accommodation for the hundreds of dignitaries expected to
converge on the capital for the celebrations. Sadly, two guests who
were not expected to attend were the Crown Prince and Princess
of Prussia, as Fritz's health was still uncertain. But on 8 June, just
two weeks before the ceremony, the Queen received a telegram
from Berlin reporting that the growth in Fritz's throat was still

considered 'perfectly healthy'.[2] Her daughter and son-in-law would be coming to London after all, to the disappointment of their son Wilhelm who had wanted to represent the Hohenzollerns himself.

The Queen was greeted on her return to Windsor by Arthur, who had sailed from India to be beside his mother on her big day. To everyone's surprise, and Cowell's horror, Arthur had been followed to England by a deputation of Indian princes, all eager to pay their respects to their Queen and Empress. Among the glittering array of gifts they carried with them were two Indian servants, Mahomet Baksh and Abdul Karim, both of whom had volunteered to remain in England to serve the Queen. Victoria was intrigued, describing them as 'fine looking men, handsomely dressed in scarlet with white turbans'.* [3]

Warm, bright sunlight greeted the day of the thanksgiving service: 'Queen's Weather', as usual. 'Troops began passing early with bands playing,' Victoria recalled later, 'and one heard constant cheering.' After breakfasting quietly at Buckingham Palace with Beatrice and Arthur, Victoria, now sixty-eight but still sprightly, climbed into a black landau for the drive to the abbey. The simplicity of the Queen's vehicle, an unintended triumph of self-promotion, matched the plainness of her dress. Her only concession to the joyous occasion was a startling white lace bonnet decorated with diamonds. Around her in the palace courtyard

---

* Karim, later known as the Munshi (or teacher), would become the Queen's especial favourite, eventually exerting a control over her not seen since the days of John Brown. He also stirred up a similar resentment in the household, who accused him of falsifying his origins to impress his mistress. In the 1890s the Munshi's claim that his father worked in the civil service in India and so was 'belonging to a good and highly respectable family', would be challenged, investigated and dismissed as a lie. Victoria refused to be persuaded, doggedly insisting that the Munshi was to be believed and hinting that the campaign against him was racist in origin. Unlike the household, she knew that the accusation was at odds with Howard Elphinstone's opinion of the Munshi's father, whom Howard had described after meeting him in Agra in April 1888 as 'a very fine, intelligent looking man [who] felt very proud of his son being about Your Majesty' (HE to QV, 14 April 1888, RA VIC/Add A 15/5081). This opinion carried more weight with Victoria than that of a clique of jealous courtiers. So it was only with the very greatest reluctance that she eventually saw the Munshi's role reduced at court.

assembled a vividly coloured cortège of mounted royalty, thirty-two princes in all, each of them drawn from the Queen's family. The most eye-catching of them was the Crown Prince of Germany, who looked distinctly Wagnerian as he sat on a towering grey charger wearing the brilliant white uniform of the Pomeranian Cuirassiers with its sparkling breastplate and eagle-crested helmet. Holding back tears of pride, Moretta thought her father looked like 'a typical knight of the fairy tale days'.[4]

As the Queen's aide-de-camp, Elphinstone rode with the princes. Promoted to major-general in January, he wore the dress uniform of the Royal Engineers; the plume on his cocked hat fluttered in the breeze as the morning sun caught the many decorations on his scarlet coat. After thirty years of royal service, he was now at the very apex of an empire which by 1887 had spread halfway around the globe. Minutes before the landau moved off, Howard trotted over to a small wooden stand erected in the courtyard for the household, where his three children – ten-year-old Viva, nine-year-old Irene and six-year-old Olive – sat with an aunt intently watching proceedings. Seeing their father with the Queen on such a day was 'an unforgettable moment of pride for them', one recalled sixty years later.[5] Their mother was already in the abbey, waiting uncomfortably for the ceremony to begin.

At half-past eleven the royal procession began to snake its way to the abbey, like 'a glittering river of liveries and trappings'.[6] The undisputed star of the cavalcade was Fritz, whose dramatic appearance awed the thousands of excited onlookers. The writer Augustus Hare, a friend of the Elphinstones who (possibly with their assistance) had secured a place inside the abbey, described seeing the prince during the service 'kneeling erect like a knight, in jackboots, but with folded hands and a simplicity of unwavering devotion'.[7] The Queen sat impassively on the chair she had used on her only previous visit to the abbey, which was for her coronation. At the conclusion of the service she gave the crown prince a very public embrace, a gesture of solidarity not missed by his son Wilhelm, who returned to Berlin feeling slighted and with a lasting hatred for England.

HUGHES & MULLINS   REGINA HOUSE, RYDE, I.W.

PHOTOGRAPHERS BY APPOINTMENT TO THE QUEEN.

An official portrait of the Queen given to Howard on the occasion of her Golden Jubilee in June 1887.

Fritz's moment of triumph was tragically short. His English doctor continued to be reassuring, but in November a new tumour was found in his throat and this time there could be no avoiding the seriousness of his condition. With his father Kaiser Wilhelm I fading fast, Fritz knew that he was finally about to ascend to the Prussian throne. But instead of preparing to lead his country into a more enlightened and liberal future, as he and Vicky had planned for years, Fritz was now plunged into a desperate battle for survival against his cancer. Given the grim circumstances, he might have reasonably expected some sympathy from the Prussian court, and indeed the German people. Instead, stoked up by Bismarck's press, they turned on the prince's English wife for ignoring his condition, and on his English doctor for failing to cure it. There were even scandalous suggestions that Vicky welcomed the prognosis, alleging that her husband's death would enable her to pursue her love affair with Count von Seckendorff. Meanwhile, Prince Wilhelm eagerly, and not so subtly, anticipated his own earlier-than-expected accession to the throne.

Elphinstone was appalled at the gravity of Fritz's illness and his likely fate. 'Everything seemed to be progressing so favourably,' he wrote to Victoria from India, where he had travelled immediately after the Jubilee with Prince Arthur,

that one felt sure almost that his perfect recovery was merely a question of a few weeks. This sudden change is therefore all the more distressing. Still all hope is not yet gone and one must trust and pray that the present alarming symptoms may entirely disappear and allay all anxiety on his account. One cannot but feel most deeply for the poor Crown Princess. To her, this doubt must be most agonising.[8]

It was unfortunate that at this time, when Vicky needed her confidant more than ever, Howard was thousands of miles away on the subcontinent. Instead, she stubbornly clung to the hope that the doctors were wrong and that her husband would recover, watching helplessly as he endured a clumsy tracheotomy. Then, on 9 March 1888, Kaiser Wilhelm died, the news reaching Elphinstone at Suez as he sailed home. His first thoughts were with Fritz as he embarked on his 'onerous' new duties.[9] But the Queen warned him that the latest reports from Berlin were 'very sad and make one very anxious'.[10] Wilhelm, now crown prince, was behaving '*outrageously*': plotting against his father and openly discrediting his mother. Howard's former colleagues at the British Embassy in Wilhelmstrasse stood appalled and powerless as events unfolded. 'There was', James Rodd later recalled, 'through all this grim period . . . a conspicuous absence of chivalry at Berlin.'[11] To Colonel Swaine it seemed that 'a curse had come over this country, leaving one bright spot and that is where stands a solitary woman doing her duty faithfully and tenderly by her sick husband against all odds. It is one of the most, if not *the* most, tragic episodes in a country and a life ever recorded in history.'[12] Kaiser Friedrich III's reign was predictably and, for his wife and his country, tragically short. While his family fought for control of his legacy and his doctors squabbled over the best treatment, Fritz's health had relentlessly declined. On 1 June, unable to speak and breathing painfully through a silver cannula, the Kaiser was moved to the Neues Palais at Potsdam, where he lingered for two more agonizing weeks. As his father lay dying, Wilhelm ringed the palace with armed guards to prevent any papers being smuggled out. When the death was announced on 15 June, the guards sprang into action, rifling through drawers for documents to incriminate Vicky. They were too late. Most of the papers had been carried in secret to England at the time of the Queen's Jubilee; others – such as Howard's letters about the prince of Bulgaria – had been burnt. Those few that remained had been handed to Colonel Swaine by the Kaiser just hours before he died. Two days later Swaine delivered them in person to the Queen at Windsor, where they remain.[13]

Fritz's funeral was arranged with unseemly haste and with none of the pomp accorded to his father barely three months before. No invitations were issued, no parades organized and no thought given to the devastated widow or to the last wishes of the deceased. Instead, after ordering an autopsy solely to establish the incompetence of his father's English doctors, the new Kaiser ordered that the funeral be concluded as quickly as possible, and away from the public gaze at Potsdam.

Fritz's English friends and relatives were not so easily thwarted, however, from paying their last respects. A special train was laid on to convey the Prince and Princess of Wales, the Marquess of Lorne, Henry Ponsonby and Howard Elphinstone to Germany in time for the funeral. They left Buckingham Palace in such a hurry that Howard had to telegraph ahead for a tailor to stitch black crepe to his uniform coat when he arrived. He left Annie nursing their newborn child, a fourth daughter whom they had named Mary. At nine on the morning of the funeral, this dejected and exhausted little party gathered in light drizzle for the short journey from Berlin to the Neues Palais, where the body of the Kaiser lay in state. 'The palace was crowded to excess,' Howard reported, with ministers and aides-de-camp all jostling to pay their final respects. After some anthems and brief prayers in the palace, he followed the hearse as it was slowly drawn to the Friedenskirche, or Church of Peace, in the park. Drums rolled and bands played a slow funeral march, but all Elphinstone could remember afterwards was the large number of troops lining the route to keep spectators away. Walking beside him, the Prince of Wales was struck by the way Fritz's chestnut horse, Worth, neighed throughout the procession, as if sharing in the grief. Howard thought the service 'very short, impressive and quiet' while, deeply moved, Bertie felt he 'had parted from the noblest and best man I had ever known, except my ever-to-be-lamented father'.[14] Vicky, her bitter grief compounded by the lack of respect shown towards her and her husband's memory, had refused to attend the ceremony. Looking up as he walked back to the palace, Elphinstone caught sight of her at a window. 'It must have been a heartrending moment for them all,' he lamented. 'The Empress is

I hear quite beside herself and will not see anyone. Poor woman, it will be a very hard life for her. What she will do or where she will live none of us can find out.'[15]

The morning after the funeral, Vicky called Elphinstone back to Potsdam for a private meeting, which he found 'a most painful affair'. Howard disclosed little of what had passed between them in a letter to Annie, except to reveal that the Dowager Kaiserin had broken down during their conversation and was 'much to be pitied'. After the meeting, Seckendorff, clearly distraught, had hinted darkly at the 'liberties' taken by 'the old noblesse' towards Vicky since her husband's death. 'I will not write further,' Howard concluded hastily, fearing Bismarck's spies, 'but say all that passed.'[16] His first report, however, had to be to the Queen, whom he met in the peaceful surroundings of the garden at Frogmore when he reached Windsor on 25 June. In that pleasant setting Elphinstone spoke quietly, as the Queen recorded in her journal, 'of the many disagreeables poor dear Vicky had to go through, which are very disgraceful and so cruel'.[17] They would not be the last her devastated daughter would have to endure.

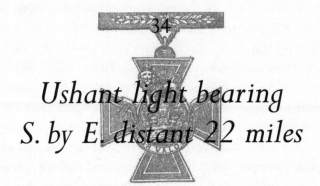

Ushant light bearing
S. by E. distant 22 miles

8 MARCH 1890

D ESPITE THE DISTRACTION of his busy life at court, Elphinstone's career in the army had prospered since his return to duty in the 1870s. In April 1889 he was given command of the Western Military District, which was centred on Devonport near Plymouth. But his health was still indifferent, an enduring legacy of the Crimean War, and after Christmas that year a severe attack of bronchitis confined him to bed for several days. Annie and the children were also unwell, suffering the effects of a flu epidemic which was sweeping the country. Irene, indeed, had been so poorly that she had been sent to convalesce in the warm air of Tenerife, where her parents promised to join her as soon as they could. On 6 March 1890, two days before the Elphinstones were scheduled to sail, the Queen summoned the general to Windsor to discuss the arrangements for her own forthcoming trip to the South of France. A fellow officer recalled that Howard 'was quite unfit for so long a journey and knew it; but said he "must go"'.[1] Even Victoria confessed that he 'was not looking well' as she said goodbye to him from the top of the stairs at the castle. 'But I hope that the trip to Tenerife . . . will do him good,' she wrote to Arthur, who was preparing to return from India after five years commanding the army in Bombay.[2] Pausing only to call on the Ponsonbys in the Norman Tower, the general then hurried back to

Devonport, arriving later the same evening after a round trip by train of several hundred miles.

On Saturday 8 March, before embarking in SS *Tongariro* at Plymouth, Howard penned a brisk letter of farewell to the Queen, enclosing some promised photographs of his four daughters. By eleven that morning he was on board with Annie, thirteen-year-old Viva and Annie's younger sister Edith Cole. Seven-year-old Olive and baby Mary would remain behind with their grandparents at West Woodhay, while Irene anxiously awaited her parents in Tenerife. Among the Elphinstones' fellow passengers in *Tongariro* was Arthur Pendarves Vivian, a former MP who had made a fortune in the Cornish copper business, now departing for a month's holiday with his second wife Jane and his son Harry, a young army officer. The previous evening, the Elphinstones and Vivians had met over dinner at the nearby mansion of the Earl of Mount Edgecumbe, an old friend of Howard's from court. Despite the gloomy, overcast sky they were all still in ebullient mood and looking forward to their voyage. At midday, in squally rain, *Tongariro* sailed.

During the afternoon, as they crossed the Channel, the Elphinstones sat with Edith Cole on the covered upper promenade deck, near the wheelhouse. The principal business of *Tongariro*, a 4,500-ton steamer owned by the New Zealand Shipping Company, was transporting frozen meat from Wellington to London. But her comfort, speed and elegant design made her a popular ship for English tourists chasing winter sun, and there were about thirty other passengers on board. The rain cleared offshore, but it remained blustery and towards evening Annie, Viva and Edith retired to their cabins, complaining of seasickness. As usual, Howard was unaffected by the heaving sea, appearing 'very cheerful' as he sat next to the captain at dinner.[3] Afterwards, loath to retire early, he invited young Harry Vivian to join him for a turn on deck. Before going out, the men briefly returned to their cabins: Harry to change his soft leather boots for rubber-soled galoshes, Howard to throw on a heavy ulster overcoat and to kiss Annie and Viva goodnight.

The two men then strolled around the lower deck enjoying their cigars, Harry no doubt slightly awed by his illustrious company. It was 'a bright moonlit night', Arthur Vivian later recalled, but as *Tongariro* entered the Bay of Biscay the sea 'increased considerably', hurling the ship to and fro and spraying the decks with water.[4] At about nine, hearing that the Ushant lighthouse was visible some twenty miles off to the port side, Howard and Harry went up to the upper deck to get a better view. There they remained chatting near the wheelhouse, clearly visible to the officers on watch and to the captain examining the charts in his cabin. Harry steadied himself by holding onto a handrail. But the general, with some bravado, simply stood with his hands in his pockets, riding the motion with his back to the sea. At about nine twenty-five, the ship suddenly 'made a heavier roll than perhaps any previous one'. For a moment, Howard stood 'perfectly still', apparently feeling quite secure as he made no attempt to grab for a rail. He was powerless therefore to stop himself sliding sharply backwards, 'as if on ice', when the roll reached its lowest point. Disastrously, where the men were standing the safety railing which ran around the deck was briefly interrupted by chains to allow a lifeboat to be lowered. Howard's back now hit the chains 'and he was hurled with great force in a complete somersault over them', disappearing into the darkness below. Harry rushed forward and for an instant saw Howard lying spread-eagled and 'quite lifeless' on an iron plate covering a port on the lower deck, some fifteen feet below. Then, with another lurch of the heaving ship, Howard slid off into the sea and was gone.

The officers on watch saw the accident and even before Harry, panic-stricken, could yell 'Man overboard!' a lifebuoy had been thrown on to the black, churning water close to the spot where Howard fell. There its phosphorus burned while the ship's engines were urgently slowed and thrown into reverse. 'The running about of the crew,' related one shocked passenger, 'the shouts of the officers giving orders, and especially those for the boat, the whistling of the boatswain and his two mates certainly made rather a wild scene.' Within just six minutes the ship was back near the buoy. A lifeboat was quickly lowered, the crew inside braving high seas to row out to the buoy. One witness described seeing the boat 'one moment almost entirely out of the water on the crest of a wave, and the next out of sight altogether'. The rescue mission was so dangerous that as soon as it was discovered that the buoy was empty, the boat was recalled to prevent further tragedy. 'But for sometime the ship was kept near the spot. Not from any hope of saving the lost man, but from a feeling, as the captain said, that it would not be decent to hurry away.'[5]

Annie was in bed when she felt the engines slowing. At first the passengers were told that something was wrong with the ship's steering gear. Some of them nervously joked that they were sinking. 'But Annie was alarmed at once,' recalled Edith Cole, 'and asked for Howard.'[6] Then Jane Vivian, her face pale and frightened, 'came to tell her the truth'. With a cry, Annie threw a shawl over her nightgown and rushed up on deck, in time to see the lifeboat lowered to the sea. 'Her suspense during the absence of the boat was painful to see,' recalled one of the passengers. But all hope was gone. She knew that Howard could not swim.

A reward of £100 was later offered for the recovery of the general's body, but it was never claimed. To comfort her, the captain told Annie that her husband's body would have sunk straight to the bottom of the sea, where the shifting sands would have soon covered it. He gave her his chart marked with the exact spot of the tragedy: *Ushant light bearing S. by E. distant 22 miles*. This was the last sighting of Major-General Sir Howard Elphinstone VC, KCB, CMG.

For four more agonizing days *Tongariro* steamed on, out of touch with the rest of the world. The accident 'cast a gloom over the ship' and there were none of the usual deck games or amusements.[7] Instead the passengers wrote a letter of condolence to Annie and collected money for the men who had risked their own lives trying to save Howard's. The captain gave Annie his cabin for the remainder of the voyage, as there was no chance of her

SS Tongariro. *Howard fell overboard close to the first lifeboat on the port side near the wheelhouse.*

boarding a homeward-bound ship before Tenerife. 'My sister has been very good,' Edith wrote while still at sea, 'but her heart is broken. Only the thought of her children and their need of her can make life seem possible . . . there is nothing to do but to think and think . . . Victoria has been so good. A real help and comfort to her mother.'[8]

Finally, at dawn on 13 March, the island was seen on the horizon. Waiting impatiently on the quayside was Irene, with her nurse. By eight Edith was in the dockyard telegraph office dictating a message for the duty clerk to send urgently to John Cowell at Buckingham Palace: 'Howard swept overboard Saturday night. Please inform Queen. Terrible news. Also inform Duke. Annie arrives Plymouth Tuesday.'[9] She then went back to Annie and the children.

Afterwards

ANNIE RETURNED TO PLYMOUTH in *Tongarira*'s sister ship
Rimutaka, arriving at dawn on 19 March, only hours before a
planned memorial service for her husband at Exeter Cathedral.
The late arrival of her ship prevented John Cowell from delivering
the letter he had been given by the Queen. Instead it was taken out
to the *Rimutaka* by the port commander in his launch. Annie barely
had time to read it before she was taken to the cathedral for the
service at noon. Representatives of every member of the royal
family were present at the service, together with seven hundred
soldiers and sailors from Howard's command at Devonport. They
had all gathered, in the words of the Dean of Exeter who delivered
the homily, 'to thank God for the memory of a great and good man
whom we had lately with us, to show sympathy with our beloved
Queen and his sorrowing relations and brother officers, and to
recall with awe and astonishment the suddenness of his removal
from us'.[1]

'I cannot write much,' Annie apologized in her reply to the
Queen,

> but I must tell Your Majesty *how* your great kindness has touched
> me in this terrible time of sorrow. The service today was *very, very*
> grand and beautiful. After those terrible ten days of utter loneliness

373

at sea, the service in the cathedral and the feeling of universal sorrow and love for him was overwhelming. God gave us thirteen years of uninterrupted happiness together and I have always that to look back upon. It is a great thing for me and for his children to know that the Queen he honoured so loyally in his life mourns for him now.[2]

Memorials were raised to Howard in Exeter Cathedral, at Aldershot camp and in the private chapel at Windsor Castle, where the Queen placed a plaque in his memory beside the altar. For the next forty-eight years Annie lived quietly at Pinewood, the mansion in Bagshot which she and Howard had built together for his retirement. Here she was surrounded by her husband's paintings and his mementoes of court life. On one wall was a case containing his Victoria Cross and other decorations. But she rarely spoke of him; the pain of her appalling loss was too great. 'The shock turned her to stone,' her youngest daughter recalled. 'Silence was her only refuge, and for years to come the very mention of his name was more than she could bear.'[3] She tended her garden and his memory, keeping her thoughts to herself. Annie died in 1938, aged eighty-two.

All four of her daughters married army officers, all of whom won Distinguished Service Orders fighting for their country. Victoria Elphinstone, the Queen's god-daughter caught up in the drama of her father's violent death, married Major Hugh Norman Cowie of the Dorset Regiment. After he was killed defending Hill 60 in the Ypres Salient in May 1915, Viva was left, like her mother before her, a widow in her thirties with four young children.

Sir John Cowell died at Osborne only four years after Howard, on 29 August 1894 – finally succumbing, like so many other courtiers, to the incessant demands of his Queen. According to Dr Reid, in the last years of his life Victoria 'came personally to be tired of him and certainly did not follow his advice'.[4] It seems she never forgave Cowell for leading the palace campaign against John Brown.

Annie Elphinstone making a point forcefully to Prince Arthur, Duke of Connaught, in about 1930. Princess Louise, Dowager Duchess of Argyll, looks on.

After a long career in the navy, Prince Alfred, Duke of Edinburgh, did after all inherit the throne of Saxe-Coburg-Gotha, sparing his brother Arthur this onerous task. But his years at sea and a chronic drink problem undermined his relationship with his Russian wife. Eventually the marriage was destroyed by the suicide of their son, shortly after which Affie himself died, succumbing to cancer of the tongue at the Rosenau in July 1900. His sister Louise survived him by thirty-nine years but, after such a bright start, her childless marriage to the Marquess of Lorne was similarly unhappy, a shadow cast over their relationship by unsubstantiated rumours of Lorne's homosexuality. Nevertheless, they were sufficiently reconciled for the princess to suffer a nervous breakdown on her husband's death in 1914. The war then provided an outlet for her charitable work and in the last years of her life she dedicated herself to benevolent and artistic causes. In contrast to Louise, Princess Beatrice enjoyed a happy, but tragically short, marriage to Prince Henry of Battenberg, who died of fever in 1896 after rashly volunteering for service on the Asante expedition in West Africa. Like her mother and sister Alice, Beatrice was a carrier of haemophilia, passing it to her son Leopold who died of the disease at the same age, thirty-one, as his eponymous uncle. Another son, Maurice, was killed in action in 1914. The marriage of Beatrice's daughter Ena to King Alfonso XIII of Spain subsequently transmitted haemophilia into the Spanish royal family. Today, Princess Beatrice is best, but unfairly, remembered for selectively transcribing, then destroying, the Queen's journals. In the process much fascinating material – including, presumably, candid remarks about John Brown and Victoria's other confidants at court – has inevitably been lost to posterity; but Beatrice felt she had fulfilled her duty to her mother and, after all, it was for her to judge. Beatrice survived until 1944: the last of Victoria's children to die.

After Fritz died, Vicky retreated to Friedrichshof, the gothic-style mansion she built in his memory at Kronberg near Frankfurt. There she rode and painted, estranged from her son

Kaiser Wilhelm II and stoically resigned to her lonely fate in Germany. In 1898 she was diagnosed with breast cancer; the disease quickly spread to her spine, and within a year she was confined to bed, where she could 'only scream and groan' as the morphine prescribed by her doctors failed to dull the terrible pain.[5] Death finally released Vicky from her agony on 5 August 1901, aged sixty. Like her husband, and to the fury of her son, she managed to smuggle her private papers to Windsor before she died.

Prince Arthur received the news of Howard's death during his voyage home from India. Although he had seen little of his childhood governor in recent years he was deeply shocked at his death, writing in his journal that 'he was my friend and confidant, and occupied a position which no-one else could ever fill'.[6] By strange coincidence, Sir Malcolm Murray, the man who replaced Howard as the prince's controller, also later drowned after capsizing his canoe in Virginia Water. As governor general of Canada at the outbreak of the First World War, Arthur volunteered to fight but age and status ruled him out of active service. Nevertheless, he visited the Western Front several times, standing beneath his cousin Wilhelm's shells as they whistled over his head. His wife Louise died in 1917 shortly before her family was swept from power in Germany. Arthur, however, lived on, visiting Annie Elphinstone regularly at Pinewood until her death, after which he retreated from public view to Bagshot Park. He died in 1942 aged ninety-one, having survived to see his country once again take up arms against Germany.

Arthur had been at the Queen's bedside when she died at Osborne House on 22 January 1901, aged eighty-one. Three days later, with the help of the Kaiser and the new King, Edward VII, he had lifted his mother's body into her coffin, marvelling at its lightness. On 2 February, following the funeral at Windsor Castle, he sent Annie a miniature of her husband mounted in a silver replica of the Victoria Cross, 'which', the prince wrote, 'belonged to the Queen and was always in her room here, at Osborne and at

Balmoral'.[7] There was also a fraying envelope with a heavy black border. This had also been found carefully preserved among the Queen's private possessions. On the envelope Victoria had inscribed: 'Last letter from dear Sir Howard Elphinstone written just before he embarked and a few hours before his death 8 March 1890'.[8] It was the final touch of her knight; cherished until the end.

Acknowledgements

I WISH TO THANK HER MAJESTY THE QUEEN for her gracious permission to consult and publish extracts and letters from the Royal Archives at Windsor Castle. Pamela Clark, the Registrar of the Royal Archives, and her staff were unfailingly courteous and cheerful in patiently guiding me through the thousands of documents necessary to complete this book. Pamela herself generously read the manuscript with scrupulous care, offering invaluable advice and help when I stumbled over Queen Victoria's often elusive handwriting.

In addition, I am indebted to Lord Ashcroft, Lady Reid, Lord Howick, Sir John and Lady Elphinstone, Dr Sally Whipple, Mark Dalton, Rebecca Cheney and the staff of the Royal Engineers Museum at Chatham; and to Michael Naxton, whose boundless enthusiasm for my task spurred me on.

Thanks are again due to Doug Young, my editor at Bantam Press, for his unfailing support; to Gillian Somerscales for once more patiently untangling my words; and to the whole team at Transworld for producing another beautiful book. My agents – Peter Robinson in London and Christy Fletcher in New York – also deserve special and heartfelt mention for keeping faith in me as I embarked on this, my second book.

The Queen's Knight follows a path brilliantly laid down by

Mary McClintock, who published a moving account of her father's life in 1945. Sixty years on, I am most grateful to Maidlie's daughter Patsy Cyriax for sharing with me her vivid memories of Annie Elphinstone; and, in particular, to her granddaughter Sylvia Wright for her ceaseless interest, practical assistance and encouragement throughout my research.

Indeed, I am indebted to all the descendants of Sir Howard Elphinstone's four daughters – Victoria Cowie, Irene Welch, Olive Jackson and Mary McClintock – for their patience and good-humoured encouragement while I raked up their past. Especial thanks are due to John Cowie, David Cowie, Julia Robb (*née* Cowie), Juliana Grose (formerly Mrs Nigel Cowie), Jan Welch, Martyn Jackson, Sarah Rogers (*née* Jackson), Pamela McClintock, Alex 'Frank' McClintock and Michael McClintock.

Finally, the greatest debt is owed as always, and with my love, to the eldest child of the eldest child of the eldest child of Sir Howard Elphinstone: my wife Sam, who shares his talent for painting, daring sense of adventure and generosity of spirit.

Picture Acknowledgements

All images have been supplied courtesy of the family collection except for the following:

In the text

Devon Library and Information Services: 26; The Royal Collection, © 2007 Her Majesty Queen Elizabeth II: 55; © Royal Photographic Society/Science & Society Picture Library: 89; Notman Photographic Archives/McCord Museum, Montreal: 236; © Corbis: 242, 301; Hulton-Deutsch Collection/Corbis: 324

First colour section

Howard Elphinstone winning the Victoria Cross: Royal Engineers Museum, Chatham

Ernst Becker; Carl Ruland; Sir Charles Phipps; Royal Household group at Osborne House: The Royal Collection, © 2007 Her Majesty Queen Elizabeth II

Second colour section

The Last Moments of H.R.H. the Prince Consort: Wellcome Library, London
John Brown: National Portrait Gallery Picture Library, London

Marriage of the Prince of Wales: The Royal Collection, © 2007 Her Majesty Queen Elizabeth II

Third colour section

The Entrance Front of the Ranger's House: The Royal Collection, © 2007 Her Majesty Queen Elizabeth II

Fourth colour section

Princess Victoria of Prussia: The Royal Collection, © 2007 Her Majesty Queen Elizabeth II

Bibliography

Periodicals and reference works

Hansard's Parliamentary Debates, 3rd series
New Dictionary of National Biography (Oxford, 2004)
Register of the Victoria Cross (Cheltenham, 1988)
Royal Engineers Journal
Royalty Digest
The Sapper

Individual works

Addresses Delivered on Different Public Occasions By His Royal Highness The Prince Albert, published by the Society of Arts (London, 1857)

Alice, Grand Duchess of Hesse, *Letters to Her Majesty the Queen* (London, 1885)

Alice, HRH Princess Countess of Athlone, *For My Grandchildren* (London, 1966)

Allingham, H. and Radford, D., *William Allingham: A Diary* (London, 1907)

Allison, R. and Riddell, S., eds, *The Royal Encyclopedia* (London, 1991)

Anon., *The Private Life of the Queen by One of Her Servants* (London, 1897)

Arengo-Jones, P., *Queen Victoria in Switzerland* (London, 1995)

Ashdown, D. M., *Queen Victoria's Mother* (London, 1974)

—— *Royal Children* (London, 1979)

Aston, Sir George, *His Royal Highness The Duke of Connaught: A Life and Intimate Study* (London, 1929)

Atkins, J. B., *The Life of Sir William Howard Russell: The First Special Correspondent*, 2 vols (London, 1911)

Bailey, J., ed., *The Diary of Lady Frederick Cavendish*, vol. 1 (1927)

Baillie, Albert, Dean of Windsor, and Bolitho, Hector, eds, *Later Letters of Lady Augusta Stanley 1864–1876* (London, 1929)

—— *Letters of Lady Augusta Stanley: A Young Lady at Court 1849–1863* (London, 1927)

Baker, A., *A Question of Honour: The Life of Lieutenant General Valentine Baker Pasha* (London, 1996)

Barnes, M., *Augustus Hare* (London, 1984)

Bennet, H. Graham, ed., *Dress worn by Gentlemen at His Majesty's Court and on Occasions of Ceremony* (London, 1903)

Bennett, D., *King without a Crown* (London, 1977)

—— *Queen Victoria's Children* (London, 1980)

—— *Vicky: Princess Royal and German Empress* (London, 1971)

Benson, A. C. and Esher, Viscount, eds, *The Letters of Queen Victoria: A Selection from Her Majesty's Correspondence between the Years 1837 and 1861*, 1st ser., 3 vols (London, 1907)

Bilmanis, A., *A History of Latvia* (Princeton, 1951)

Blom, M. H. and Blom, T. E., eds, *Canada Home: Juliana Horatia Ewing's Fredericton Letters 1867–1869* (Vancouver, 1983)

Bloomfield, Baroness Georgiana, *Reminiscences of Court and Diplomatic Life* (London, 1883)

Bolitho, H., *Albert Prince Consort* (London, 1964)

—— *My Restless Years* (London, 1962)

Bolitho, H., ed., *The Prince Consort and His Brother: Two Hundred New Letters* (London, 1933)

Boulger, D. C., ed., *General Gordon's letters from the Crimea etc.* (London, 1884)

Briggs, A., *Victorian People* (London, 1954)

Bibliography

Buckle, G. E., *The Letters of Queen Victoria: A Selection from Her Majesty's Correspondence and Journal between the Years 1886 and 1901*, 3rd ser., 3 vols (London, 1930)

Campbell, C., *Fenian Fire: The British Government Plot to Assassinate Queen Victoria* (London, 2002)

Carey, A., *The Empress Eugenie in Exile* (London, 1922)

Carlton, C., *Royal Childhoods* (London, 1988)

Carr, J., *Travels around the Baltic* (London, 1805)

Cartwright, J., ed., *The Journals of Lady Knightly of Fawsley* (London, 1915)

Chomet, S., *Helena, Princess Reclaimed: The Life and Times of Queen Victoria's Third Daughter* (New York, 1999)

Clark, R. W., *Balmoral: Queen Victoria's Highland Home* (London, 1981)

Cole, Lt-Col. H. N., *The Story of Aldershot: A History and Guide to Town and Camp* (Aldershot, 1951)

Cole, J. A., *Prince of Spies: Henri Le Caron* (London, 1984)

Collier, the Hon. E. C. F., *A Victorian Diarist: Extracts from the Journals of Mary, Lady Monkswell 1873–1895* (London, 1944)

Connolly, T. J., *History of the Royal Sappers and Miners*, vol. 2: *1848–1856* (London, 1857)

Corti, Count Egon Caesar, *Alexander von Battenberg* (London, 1954)

Courtney, N., *Royal Children* (London, 1982)

Creagh, Sir O'Moore, and Humphris, E. M., eds, *The VC and DSO*, vol. 1 (London, 1924)

Crook, M. J., *The Evolution of the Victoria Cross* (Tunbridge Wells, 1975)

Cross, A., *By the Banks of the Neva* (Cambridge, 1997)

Cullen, T., *The Empress Brown: The Story of a Royal Friendship* (London, 1969)

Dangerfield, G., *Victoria's Heir: The Education of a Prince* (London, 1941)

Dasent, A. I., *John Thadeus Delane: Editor of 'The Times'*, 2 vols (London, 1908)

David, S., *Zulu: The Heroism and Tragedy of the Zulu War of 1879* (London, 2004)

De La Noy, M., *Windsor Castle: Past and Present* (London, 1990)

Duff, D., *The Shy Princess: The Life of Her Royal Highness Princess Beatrice* (London, 1958)

Duff, D., ed., *Victoria in the Highlands* (London, 1968)

Eden, H. K. F., *Juliana Horatia Ewing and her Books* (London, 1896)

Elphinstone, Captain A. F., *Narrative of the late Admiral John Elphinstone during his service in Russia and Subsequent* (privately printed, 1838)

Elphinstone, Sir Howard Warburton, *Recollections of the Thirties and Forties of the Nineteenth Century* (privately printed, c.1915)

Elphinstone, K. V., *The Elphinstones of Blytheswood and Lopness* (privately printed, 1925)

Emden, P., *Behind the Throne* (London, 1934)

Epton, N., *Victoria and her Daughters* (London, 1971)

Erskine, Mrs S., ed., *Twenty Years at Court: From the Correspondence of the Hon. Eleanor Stanley* (London, 1916)

Ewing, J. H. E., *The Story of a Short Life* (London, c.1910)

Feuchtwanger, E., *Albert and Victoria* (London, 2006)

Filon, A., *Memoirs of the Prince Imperial (1856–1879)* (London, 1913)

Fletcher, S., *Victorian Girls: Lord Lyttelton's Daughters* (London, 1997)

Frankland, N., *Witness of a Century: The Life and Times of Prince Arthur Duke of Connaught 1850–1942* (London, 1993)

Fraser, A., *A History of Toys* (London, 1972; first publ. 1966)

French, A., *Ranger's House Blackheath* (London, 1992)

Fulford, R., *The Prince Consort* (London, 1949)

Fulford, R., ed., *Dearest Child: Letters between Queen Victoria and the Princess Royal 1858–1861* (London, 1964)

—— *Dearest Mama: Letters between Queen Victoria and the Crown Princess of Prussia 1861–1864* (London, 1968)

—— *Your Dear Letter: Private Correspondence of Queen Victoria and the Crown Princess of Prussia 1865–1871* (London, 1971)

—— *Darling Child: Private Correspondence of Queen Victoria and the Crown Princess of Prussia 1871–1878* (London, 1976)

—— *Beloved Mama: Private Correspondence of Queen Victoria and the German Crown Princess 1878–1885* (London, 1981)

Gathorne-Hardy, J., *The Rise and Fall of the British Nanny* (London, 1993; first publ. 1972)

Gernsheim, H. and Gernsheim, A., *Roger Fenton: Photographer of the Crimean War. His Photographs and Letters from the Crimea* (London, 1954)

Girouard, M., *Windsor: The Most Romantic Castle* (London, 1993)

Gordon, H. W., *Events in the Life of Charles George Gordon* (London, 1886)

Gordon-Roe, F., *The Victorian Child* (London, 1959)

Grey, Sir Charles, ed., *The Early Years of the Prince Consort* (London, 1967; first publ. 1867)

Guggisberg, F. G., *'The Shop': The Story of the Royal Military Academy* (London, 1900)

Hare, A., *The Story of My Life*, 6 vols (London, 1900)

Harrison, General Sir Richard, *Recollections of a Life in the British Army* (London, 1908)

Hartcup, A., *Children of the Great Country Houses* (London, 2000; first publ. 1982)

Haswell Miller, A. E. and Dawnay, N. P., *Military Drawings and Paintings in the Collection of Her Majesty the Queen* (London, 1966 plates; 1970 text)

Hibbert, C., *The Court at Windsor: A Domestic History* (London, 1964)

—— *The Court of St James's* (London, 1979)

—— *The Destruction of Lord Raglan* (London, 1961)

—— *Edward VII: A Portrait* (London, 1976)

—— *Queen Victoria: A Personal History* (London, 2000)

—— *Queen Victoria in her Letters and Journals* (London, 2003; first publ. 1984)

Homans, M., *Royal Representations* (Chicago, 1998)

Homans, M. and Munich, A., eds, *Remaking Queen Victoria* (Cambridge, 1997)

Hough, R., *Edward and Alexandra: Their Private and Public Lives* (London, 1992)

Hudson, D., *Munby: Man of Two Worlds* (London, 1972)

Hudson, R., *The Jubilee Years 1887–1897* (London, 1996)

Hughes, K., *The Victorian Governess* (London, 2001)

Jagow, K., ed., *Letters of the Prince Consort 1831–1861* (London, 1938)

Johnson, N. E., ed., *The Diary of Gathorne Hardy, later Lord Cranbrook, 1866–1892: Political Selections* (Oxford, 1981)

Jones, Major-General H. D., *Journal of the Operations conducted by the Corps of the Royal Engineers*, part 2 (London, 1859)

Keller, U., *Ultimate Spectacle: A Visual History of the Crimean War* (Amsterdam, 2001)

Kinglake, A. W., *The Invasion of the Crimea*, vol. 8 (Edinburgh, 1887)

Knapland, P., ed., 'Letters from the Berlin Embassy 1871–74 and 1880–85', *Annual Report of the American Historical Association for the Year 1942* (Washington DC, 1942)

Knight, I., *With his Face to the Foe: The Life and Death of Louis Napoleon, The Prince Imperial, Zululand, 1879* (Staplehurst, 2001)

Kohl, J. G., *Russia: St Petersburg, Moscow, Kharkoff, Riga, Odessa, The German Provinces on the Baltic, the Steppes, The Crimea and the interior of the Empire* (London, 1842)

Kuhn, W. H., *Life at the Court of Queen Victoria* (London, 2002)

Lamont-Brown, R., *John Brown* (Stroud, 2004; first publ. 2000)

Lant, J. L., *Insubstantial Pageant: Ceremony and Confusion at Queen Victoria's Court* (New York, 1980)

Lehmann, J. H., *All Sir Garnet: A Life of Field-Marshal Lord Wolseley* (London, 1964)

Lindsay, W. A., *The Royal Household* (London, 1898)

Loftus, Lord Augustus, *The Diplomatic Reminiscences of Lord Augustus Loftus 1862–1879*, 2nd ser., 2 vols (London, 1894)

Longford, E., *Victoria RI* (London, 1964)

Longford, E., ed., *Darling Loosy: Letters to Princess Louise 1856–1939* (London, 1991)

Luvaas, *The Education of an Army: British Military Thought, 1815–1940* (London, 1964)

Maas, J., *The Prince of Wales's Wedding: The Story of a Picture* (London, 1977)

McClintock, M. H., *The Queen Thanks Sir Howard* (London, 1945)

MacDonald, Capt. J. A., *Troublous Times in Canada: A History of the Fenian Raids of 1866 and 1870* (Toronto, 1910)

Macfarlane, L. J., *William Elphinstone and the Kingdom of Scotland 1431–1514* (Aberdeen, 1985)

McFeely, W. S., *Grant: A Biography* (New York, 1981)

MacKay, D., *The Square Mile: Merchant Princes of Montreal* (Vancouver, 1987)

Marples, M., *Princes in the Making: A Study of Royal Education* (London, 1965)

Martin, T., *The Life of His Royal Highness The Prince Consort*, 5 vols (London, 1875–80)

Matson, J., *Dear Osborne* (London, 1978)

Matthew, H. C. G., ed., *The Gladstone Diaries*, vol. 6 (Oxford, 1978)

Meyer, J., *L'Éducation des princes du XVe au XIXe siècle* (Paris, 2004)

Millar, D., *The Victorian Watercolours and Drawings in the Collection of Her Majesty The Queen*, 2 vols (London, 1995)

Miller, A., *For Your Own Good: Hidden Cruelty in Child-Rearing and the Roots of Violence* (London, 1997)

Morton, W. L., *The Critical Years: The Union of British North America 1857–1873* (Toronto, 1964)

Napier, G., *The Sapper VCs: The Story of Valour in the Royal Engineers and its Associated Corps* (London, 1998)

Ó Broin, L., *Fenian Fever: An Anglo-American Dilemma* (London, 1971)

Packard, J., *Victoria's Daughters* (Stroud, 1999)

Pakula, H., *An Uncommon Woman: The Empress Frederick* (London, 1996)

Pollock, J., *Gordon: The Man behind the Legend* (London, 1993)
—— *Kitchener* (London, 2002; first publ. 2001)

Ponsonby, A., *Henry Ponsonby, Queen Victoria's Private Secretary: His Life from his Letters* (London, 1942)

Ponsonby, Sir Frederick, *Recollections of Three Reigns* (London, 1951)
—— *Sidelights on Queen Victoria* (London, 1930)
—— ed., *Letters of the Empress Frederick* (London, 1928)
Ponsonby, M., *Mary Ponsonby: A Memoir, some Letters and a Journal* (London, 1927)
Pound, A., *Albert: A Biography of the Prince Consort* (London, 1973)
Prothero, R. E., *The Life and Correspondence of Arthur Penrhyn Stanley*, 2 vols (London, 1893)
Pryce-Jones, A., ed., *Little Innocents* (Oxford, 1986; first publ. 1932)
Quinlivan, P. and Rose, P., *The Fenians in England 1865–1872: A Sense of Insecurity* (London, 1982)
Radforth, I., *Royal Spectacle: The 1860 Visit of the Prince of Wales to Canada and the United States* (Toronto, 2004)
Radziwell, Princess Catherine, *Those I Remember* (London, 1924)
Ramm, A., *Beloved and Darling Child: Last Letters between Queen Victoria and her Eldest Daughter 1886–1901* (London, 1990)
—— *Sir Robert Morier: Envoy and Ambassador in the Age of Imperialism 1876–1893* (Oxford, 1973)
Ranken, W. B., ed., *Canada and the Crimea; or Sketches of a Soldier's Life from the Journals and Correspondence of the late Major Ranken, RE* (London, 1862)
—— *Six Months at Sebastopol; Being Selections from the Journal and Correspondence of the Late Major George Ranken, Royal Engineers* (London, 1857)
Rappaport, H., *Victoria: A Biographical Companion* (Santa Barbara, 2003)
Reid, M., *Ask Sir James* (London, 1987)
Renton, A., *Tyrant or Victim? A History of the British Governess* (London, 1991)
Rhodes James, R., *Albert, Prince Consort: A Biography* (London, 1983)
Robins, C., ed., 'The First Assault on the Redan, 18th June 1855: The Letters of Captain Fanshawe, 33rd Regiment', *The War Correspondent*, vol. 12, no. 3, October 1994, 7–10.

Rodd, Sir James Rennell, *Social and Diplomatic Memories 1884–1893* (London, 1922)

Röhl, J., *Young Wilhelm: The Kaiser's Early Life, 1859–1888* (Cambridge, 1998)

Rowell, G., *Queen Victoria Goes to the Theatre* (London, 1978)

Royle, T., *Crimea: The Great Crimean War* (London, 1999)

Russell, W. H., *The British Expedition to the Crimea* (London, 1858)

—— *A Memorial of the Marriage of HRH Albert Edward Prince of Wales and HRH Alexandra Princess of Denmark* (London, 1864)

St Aubyn, G., *Edward VII: Prince and King* (London, 1979)

—— *Queen Victoria: A Portrait* (London, 1991)

—— *The Royal George: The Life of HRH Prince George Duke of Cambridge* (London, 1963)

St John Nevill, B., ed., *Life at the Court of Queen Victoria 1861–1901* (Exeter, 1984)

Schatzman, M., *Soul Murder* (London, 1973)

Schoch, R. W., *Queen Victoria and the Theatre of her Age* (Basingstoke, 2004)

Senior, H., *The Last Invasion of Canada: The Fenian Raids, 1866–1870* (Toronto, 1991)

Smith, Sir John, *Sandhurst: The History of the Royal Military Academy, Woolwich, the Royal Military College, Sandhurst, and the Royal Military Academy Sandhurst 1741–1961* (London, 1961)

Smith, M. C., '"Missis Victorier's sons": A History of the Victoria Cross', unpublished PhD dissertation (2000)

Stockmar, Baron Ernst, *Memoirs of Baron Stockmar*, 2 vols (London, 1873)

Stoney, B. and Weltzien, H. C., eds, *My Mistress the Queen: The Letters of Frieda Arnold Dresser to the Queen 1854–9* (London, 1994)

Strachey, L., *Eminent Victorians* (London, 2002; first publ. 1918)

Swaine, Major-General Sir Leopold V., *Camp and Chancery in a Soldier's Life* (London, 1926)

Thomas, A., ed., *A New Most Excellent Dancing Master: The Journal of Joseph Lowe's Visits to Balmoral and Windsor (1852–1860) to Teach Dance to the Family of Queen Victoria* (New York, 1992)

Thompson, D., *Queen Victoria: Gender and Power* (London, 1990)

Tisdall, E. E. P., *Queen Victoria's John Brown* (London, 1938)

—— *Queen Victoria's Private Life* (London, 1961)

Tooley, S. A., *The Personal Life of Queen Victoria* (London, 1896)

Urbach, K., *Bismarck's Favourite Englishman: Lord Odo Russell's Mission to Berlin* (London, 1999)

Van der Kiste, J., *Dearest Vicky, Darling Fritz: Queen Victoria's Eldest Daughter and the German Emperor* (Stroud, 2002; first publ. 2001)

—— *Sons, Servants and Statesmen: The Men in Queen Victoria's Life* (Stroud, 2006)

Van der Kiste, J. and Jordaan, B., *Dearest Affie: Alfred, Duke of Edinburgh, Queen Victoria's Second Son* (Stroud, 1984)

Vassili, Count Paul, *Berlin Society* (London, 1885)

Vetch, Colonel R. H., ed., *Life, Letters, and Diaries of Lt General Sir Gerald Graham* (London, 1901)

Vizetelly, H., *Glances Back through Seventy Years*, 2 vols (London, 1893)

Vickers, P. H., *'A Gift so graciously bestowed': The History of the Prince Consort's Library* (Winchester, 1993)

Victoria, Queen, *Leaves from the Journal of Our Life in the Highlands, from 1848 to 1861* (London, 1868)

—— *More Leaves from the Journal of a Life in the Highlands, from 1862 to 1882* (London, 1884)

Victoria, HRH, Princess of Prussia, *My Memoirs* (London, 1929)

Wake, J., *Princess Louise: Queen Victoria's Unconventional Daughter* (London, 1988)

Walker, General Sir C. P. Beauchamp, *Days of a Soldier's Life* (London, 1894)

Wantage, Lady, *Lord Wantage, VC, KCB, A Memoir* (London, 1907)

Watson, V., *A Queen at Home* (London, 1952)

Weintraub, S., *Albert: Uncrowned King* (London, 1997)

—— *The Importance of Being Edward: King in Waiting 1841–1901* (London, 2000)

—— *Victoria* (London, 1987)

Whittle, T., *Victoria and Albert at Home* (London, 1980)

William II, Ex-Emperor of Germany, *My Early Life* (London, 1926)

Wolseley, Field-Marshal Viscount, *The Story of a Soldier's Life*, vol. 1 (London, 1903)

Wood, Evelyn, *The Crimea in 1854, and 1894* (London, 1895)

Woodham-Smith, C., *Queen Victoria: Her Life and Times 1819–1861* (London, 1972)

Wraight, J., *The Swiss and the British* (Salisbury, 1987)

Wrottesley, G., *Life and Correspondence of Sir John Fox Burgoyne*, 2 vols (London, 1873)

Wyndham, H., ed., *Correspondence of Sarah Spencer Lady Lyttelton 1787–1870* (London, 1912)

York, HRH Duchess of, with Stoney, B., *Victoria and Albert: Life at Osborne House* (London, 1991)

Zeepvat, C., *Prince Leopold* (Stroud, 1998)

Notes

Abbreviations used

Albert   Albert Francis Charles Augustus Emmanuel (1819–1861), Prince of Saxe-Coburg-Gotha; Prince Consort (1858)

Alfred   Alfred Ernest Albert (1844–1900), Prince; Duke of Edinburgh (1866), Duke of Saxe-Coburg-Gotha (1893)

Alice   Alice Maud Mary (1843–1878), Princess; Princess Ludwig of Hesse and by Rhine (1862), Grand Duchess of Hesse and by Rhine (1877)

Annie   Annie Frances Cole (1856–1938); Lady Elphinstone (1876)

Arthur   Arthur William Patrick Albert (1850–1942), Prince; Duke of Connaught and of Strathearn (1874)

Beatrice   Beatrice Mary Victoria Feodore (1857–1944), Princess; Princess Henry of Battenberg (1885)

Bertie   Albert Edward (1841–1910), Prince of Wales; King Edward VII of Great Britain and Ireland (1901)

Cambridge   George William Frederick Charles (1819–1904); Duke of Cambridge (1850), commander-in-chief of the British Army (1856), field marshal (1862)

HE	Howard Craufurd Elphinstone VC, KCB, CMG, RE (1829–1890); lieutenant (1847), captain (1856), major (1859), lieutenant-colonel (1868), knighted (1871), *aide-de-camp* to the Queen (1877), colonel (1877), major-general (1887)
Helena	Helena Augusta Victoria (1846–1923), Princess; Princess Christian of Schleswig-Holstein-Sonderburg-Augustenburg (1866)
Leopold	Leopold George Duncan Albert (1853–1884), Prince; Duke of Albany (1881)
Louise	Louise Caroline Alberta (1848–1939), Princess; Marchioness of Lorne (1871), Duchess of Argyll (1900)
QV	Alexandrina Victoria (1819–1901), Princess Victoria of Kent; Queen Victoria of Great Britain and Ireland (1837)
QVJ	Queen Victoria's Journal (Royal Archives)
RA	Royal Archives, Windsor Castle
Vicky	Victoria Adelaide Mary Louise (1840–1901), Princess Royal, Crown Princess Friedrich of Prussia (1861), Empress Friedrich of Germany (1888)

Notes to Prologue

1 RA QVJ, 13 March 1890; quoted in McClintock, *The Queen Thanks Sir Howard*, 260.

2 Journal of Dr James Reid, 13 March 1890, private collection.

3 RA QVJ, 13 March 1890; quoted in McClintock, *The Queen Thanks Sir Howard*, 260.

4 *The Times*, 15 March 1890; quoted and illustrated in McClintock, *The Queen Thanks Sir Howard*, 262–3.

5 Henry Ponsonby to QV, 13 March 1890, RA VIC/Add A 15/5436.

6 QV to Annie, 17 March 1890, family collection; quoted in

McClintock, *The Queen Thanks Sir Howard*, 260.

7 Bertie to QV, 13 March 1890; copy in family collection.
8 Helena to QV, 18 March 1890, family collection.
9 Louise to QV, 14 March 1890, family collection.
10 Vicky to QV, 15 March 1890, family collection.
11 Quoted in McClintock, *The Queen Thanks Sir Howard*, 261.

Notes to Part One

1

1 Connolly, *History*, vol. 2, 324.
2 Jones, *Journal*, part 2, 271.

2

1 Alexander Elphinstone to James Buller Elphinstone, 16 May 1853, National Archives of Scotland, GD 156/7/4.
2 *John Elphinstone Papers Relating to the Russo-Turkish War*, Box 1, Folder 6, Department of Rare Books and Special Collections, Princeton University Library.
3 A. F. Elphinstone, *Narrative of the late Admiral John Elphinstone*, 8.
4 Ibid., 18–19; quoted in McClintock, *The Queen Thanks Sir Howard*, 9.
5 A. F. Elphinstone, *Narrative of the late Admiral John Elphinstone*, 19.
6 Quoted in Cross, *By the Banks of the Neva*, 189.
7 A. F. Elphinstone, *Narrative of the late Admiral John Elphinstone*, 88–9.
8 *John Elphinstone Papers Relating to the Russo-Turkish War*, Box 1, Folder 6, Department of Rare Books and Special Collections, Princeton University Library.
9 Quoted in A. Cross, 'The Elphinstones in Catherine the Great's Navy', *The Mariner's Mirror*, vol. 84, no. 3 (Aug. 1998), 274.
10 K. V. Elphinstone, *The Elphinstones of Blytheswood*, 20.

11 Carr, *Travels around the Baltic*, 355–6.

12 K. V. Elphinstone, *The Elphinstones of Blytheswood*, 31.

13 *John Elphinstone Papers Relating to the Russo-Turkish War*, Box 2, Folder 1, Department of Rare Books and Special Collections, Princeton University Library.

14 Kohl, *Russia*, 333.

15 Petition of Alexander Elphinstone to Tsar Nicolai I (1835), *John Elphinstone Papers Relating to the Russo-Turkish War*, Box 1, Folder 5, Department of Rare Books and Special Collections, Princeton University Library.

16 Alexander Elphinstone to Andrew Scott, 23 July 1847, National Library of Scotland, MSS ACC 8924/2.

17 *John Elphinstone Papers Relating to the Russo-Turkish War*, Box 1, Folder 6, Department of Rare Books and Special Collections, Princeton University Library.

18 Mountstuart Elphinstone to Alexander Elphinstone, undated June/July 1843, National Library of Scotland, MSS ACC 8924/7.

19 Amelia Elphinstone to HE, 7 March 1850, family collection; quoted in McClintock, *The Queen Thanks Sir Howard*, 13.

20 Amelia Elphinstone to HE, 5 Oct. 1850, family collection.

21 Amelia Elphinstone to HE, 7 March 1850, family collection; quoted in McClintock, *The Queen Thanks Sir Howard*, 13.

22 Rosalie Elphinstone to HE, 22 Sept. 1851, family collection; quoted in McClintock, *The Queen Thanks Sir Howard*, 14.

23 Rosalie Elphinstone to HE, 23 March 1848, family collection.

3

1 Alexander Elphinstone to Lady Frances Elphinstone, 20 Sept. 1842, National Library of Scotland, MSS ACC 8924/7.

2 Rosalie Elphinstone to HE, 8 April 1848, family collection.

3 Amelia Elphinstone to HE, undated letter; quoted in McClintock, *The Queen Thanks Sir Howard*, 12.

4 *The Times*, 18 Dec. 1847.

5 Alexander Elphinstone to HE, 4 Dec. 1849, family collection.

6 HE Journal, 29 Oct. 1850, transcript in family collection.

7 HE Journal, 17–18 May 1850, transcript in family collection.

8 Quoted in McClintock, *The Queen Thanks Sir Howard*, 19.

9 Rosalie Elphinstone to HE, 3 Sept. 1849, family collection.

10 HE Journal, 3 Jan. 1852, transcript in family collection.

11 Rosalie Elphinstone to HE, 22 Sept. 1851, family collection.

12 HE Journal, 29 Aug. 1850, transcript in family collection.

13 Martin, *Life of The Prince Consort*, vol. 2, 316.

14 HE Journal, 30 Aug. 1850, transcript in family collection.

15 *Addresses*, 78.

16 Martin, *Life of The Prince Consort*, vol. 2, 319.

17 HE Journal, 31 Aug. 1850, transcript in family collection.

18 HE Journal, 11 Sept. 1853, transcript in family collection.

19 HE Journal, 16 Sept. 1853, transcript in family collection.

20 HE Journal, 19 Sept. 1853, transcript in family collection.

21 HE Journal, 7 Oct. 1853, transcript in family collection; quoted in McClintock, *The Queen Thanks Sir Howard*, 21.

4

1 *Royal Engineers Journal*, vol. 20, no. 234 (May 1890), 109.

2 *Royal Engineers Journal*, vol. 20, no. 233 (April 1890), 111.

3 *Royal Engineers Journal*, vol. 20, no. 234 (May 1890), 111.

4 Quoted in McClintock, *The Queen Thanks Sir Howard*, 23.

5 Vetch, *Life, Letters and Diaries*, 77.

6 *Royal Engineers Journal*, vol. 24, no. 289 (Dec. 1894).

7 Boulger, *General Gordon's letters*, 46.

8 Connolly, *History*, vol. 2, 350.

9 Quoted in Royle, *Crimea*, 26.

10 Russell, *British Expedition*, 364.

11 HE Journal, 11 May 1857, RA VIC/Add A 25/819.

12 Russell, *British Expedition*, 366.

13 Rosalie Elphinstone to HE, 30 June 1850, family collection.

14 Quoted in Gernsheim and Gernsheim, *Roger Fenton*, 97.

15 Ranken, *Canada and the Crimea*, 34–5.

16 Russell, *British Expedition*, 455.

17 Charles Gordon to his mother, 16 Sept. 1855, British Library, Add MS 33222, fo. 6.
18 Ranken, *Canada and the Crimea*, 54.
19 Ibid., 211.
20 Ibid., 213.

5

1 Victoria, *Leaves from the Journal*, 151.

6

1 Alexander Elphinstone to Andrew Scott, 27 Sept. 1855, National Library of Scotland, MSS ACC 8924/2.
2 Alexander Elphinstone to Andrew Scott, 20 Nov. 1855, National Library of Scotland, MSS ACC 8924/2.
3 HE Journal, 20 Jan. 1857, RA VIC/Add A 25/819.
4 Cambridge to Albert, 16 Nov. 1856, RA VIC/E 37/52.
5 Albert to Cambridge, 20 Nov. 1856, RA VIC/Z 488/25.
6 HE to Lady Frances Elphinstone, 3 May 1857, National Library of Scotland, MSS 8924/8.
7 *The Times*, 16 Oct. 1856.
8 Quoted in Carlton, *Royal Childhoods*, 136.
9 QV to King Leopold of the Belgians, April 1856, RA Y 101/13/16; quoted in Millar, *Victorian Watercolours*, 238.
10 QV to Albert, 7 Oct. 1858, RA VIC/Add A 15/54; quoted in McClintock, *The Queen Thanks Sir Howard*, 25.
11 General Sir Harry Jones to John Cowell, 3 Sept. 1857, RA VIC/Add A 15/31.
12 General Sir Harry Jones to John Cowell, 3 Sept. 1857, RA VIC/Add A 15/32.
13 General Sir Harry Jones to John Cowell, 3 Sept. 1857, RA VIC/Add A 15/31; quoted in McClintock, *The Queen Thanks Sir Howard*, 24.
14 Albert to John Cowell, 8 Sept. 1857, RA VIC/Add A 15/33.
15 Cowell to Albert, 10 Sept. 1857, RA VIC/Add A 15/34.
16 McClintock, *The Queen Thanks Sir Howard*, 24–5.

17 Hansard (House of Commons), 3rd ser., vol. 158 (1860), cols 1859–60, 31 May 1860.

18 HE to John Cowell, 13 Sept. 1857, RA VIC/Add A 15/37.

19 General Sir Harry Jones to HE, 3 Oct. 1857, family collection.

20 Sir William Fraser to Lord Elphinstone, 26 Oct. 1863, National Archives of Scotland, MSS GD 156/7/4.

21 HE to John Cowell, 13 Sept. 1857, RA VIC/Add A 15/37.

22 John Cowell to HE, 15 Sept. 1857, RA VIC/Add A 15/38.

23 Albert to Baron Christian Stockmar, 13 Oct. 1857; quoted in Martin, *Life of The Prince Consort*, vol. 4, 136.

24 General Sir Harry Jones to HE, 3 Oct. 1857, family collection.

25 Sir John Burgoyne to Charles Phipps, 20 Oct. 1857, RA VIC/Add A 15/44.

26 Alice, Countess of Athlone, *For My Grandchildren*, 68.

27 Quoted in Rappaport, *Victoria*, 385.

28 RA QVJ, 6 Nov. 1857.

29 QV to Vicky, 25 Jan. 1859, RA VIC/Add U/32.

30 QV to King Leopold of the Belgians, 18 Jan. 1859, RA VIC/Y 104/3.

31 Draft letter to the Deputy Adjutant General, undated [April 1866], Grey Papers, Durham University Library, GRE/D/III/9/18.

32 Frederick Peel to Cambridge, 22 May 1858, National Archives, PRO WO 32/7308.

33 Cambridge to Frederick Peel, 24 May 1858, National Archives, PRO WO 32/7308.

34 *London Gazette*, 2 June 1858.

35 HE undated annotation to 'Extracts from Col. Tylden's Report on the Capture of the Quarries on the night of 7th June 1855', family collection (emphasis added).

36 *The Times*, 3 Aug. 1858.

37 RA VIC/QVJ, 2 Aug. 1858.

7

1 QV to Albert, 7 Oct. 1858, RA VIC/Add A 15/54.
2 QV to Vicky, 1 Oct. 1858, Fulford, *Dearest Child*, 134.
3 Lady Caroline Barrington to QV, 6 Sept. 1858, RA VIC/M 18/26.
4 QV to Lady Caroline Barrington, 22 Sept. 1858, RA VIC/M 18/34.
5 Lady Caroline Barrington to QV, 6 Sept. 1858, RA VIC/M 18/26.
6 QV to Vicky, 19 Jan. 1859, RA VIC/Add U32.
7 Lady Augusta Bruce to Lady Caroline Barrington, 18 Sept. 1858, RA VIC/M 18/33.
8 Wrottesley, *Burgoyne*, vol. 2, 310.
9 HE Journal, 23 Oct. 1858, RA VIC/Add A 15/819.
10 De La Noy, *Windsor Castle*, 84.
11 HE Journal, 23 Oct. 1858, RA VIC/Add A 15/819.
12 Ibid.
13 QV to Albert, 7 Oct. 1858, RA VIC/Add A 15/54.
14 HE Journal, 23 Oct. 1858, RA VIC/Add A 15/819.
15 Quoted in Martin, *Life of The Prince Consort*, 178. Writing in the Queen's lifetime, Martin qualified Stockmar's remarks by reminding his readers that at least two of George III's sons (including the Queen's father the Duke of Kent) were 'certainly popular' with the public.
16 Quoted in Martin, *Life of The Prince Consort*, 175.
17 Wrottesley, *Burgoyne*, vol. 2, 310.
18 Ibid., 139.
19 Ibid., 140.
20 Anon., *Private Life of the Queen*, 50.
21 Ibid., 82.
22 Ibid., 53.

Notes to Part Two

8

1 QV to Vicky, 15 Jan. 1859, RA VIC/Add U/32.
2 Erskine, *Twenty Years at Court*, 346.
3 QV to Albert, 7 Oct. 1858, RA VIC/Add A 15/54.
4 Anon., *Private Life of the Queen*, 140.
5 QV to King Leopold of the Belgians, 18 Jan. 1859, RA VIC/ Y 104/3.
6 RA QVJ, 17 Jan. 1859.
7 Erskine, *Twenty Years at Court*, 346.
8 RA QVJ, 18 Jan. 1859.
9 Schatzman, *Soul Murder*, 146.
10 Miller, *For Your Own Good*, 5.
11 Ibid., 28.
12 QV to Vicky, 25 Jan. 1859, RA VIC/Add U/32.
13 RA QVJ, 4 Feb. 1859.
14 HE Journal, 6 Feb. 1860, RA VIC/Add A 25/819.
15 Pryce-Jones, *Little Innocents*, 78.
16 QV to Albert, 7 Oct. 1858, RA VIC/Add A 15/54.
17 Bailey, *Diary*, 177.
18 Ponsonby, *Mary Ponsonby*, 13.
19 John Cowell to Charles Grey, 14 May 1859, RA VIC/Add A 20/251.
20 Cartwright, *Journals of Lady Knightly*, 93.
21 Ponsonby, *Mary Ponsonby*, 5.
22 HE Journal, 11 Sept. 1859, RA VIC/Add A 25/819.
23 Fletcher, *Victorian Girls*, 84.
24 Cartwright, *Journals of Lady Knightly*, 65.
25 HE Journal, 19 March 1860, RA VIC Add A 25/819.
26 Family collection.
27 QV to King Leopold of the Belgians, 15 Feb. 1859, RA VIC/ Y 104/6.
28 RA VIC/QVJ, 18 Feb. 1859.
29 RA VIC/QVJ, 7 April 1859.

30 RA QVJ, 1 May 1859.

31 HE Journal, 10 March 1860, RA VIC/Add A 25/819; McClintock, *The Queen Thanks Sir Howard*, 44.

9

1 HE to Albert, 3 Oct. 1860, RA VIC/Add A 15/82.

2 HE Journal, 10 Sept. 1859, RA VIC/Add A 25/819.

3 HE Journal, 26 Nov. 1859, RA VIC/Add A 25/819; McClintock, *The Queen Thanks Sir Howard*, 35.

4 HE Journal, 19 Dec. 1859, RA VIC/Add A 25/819.

5 HE Journal, 27 Dec. 1859, RA VIC/Add A 25/819.

6 QV to Vicky, 25 Jan. 1859, RA VIC/Add U/32.

7 HE Journal, 10 March 1860, RA VIC/Add A 25/819.

8 HE Journal, 26 Nov. 1859, RA VIC/Add A 25/819; McClintock, *The Queen Thanks Sir Howard*, 35.

9 HE Journal, 8 March 1860, RA VIC/Add A 25/819; McClintock, *The Queen Thanks Sir Howard*, 37.

10 HE Journal, 18 Jan. 1860, RA VIC/Add A 25/819.

11 HE Journal, 26 Nov. 1859, RA VIC/Add A 25/819.

12 QV to HE, 4 April 1859, family collection.

13 Whittle, *Victoria and Albert*, 80.

14 HE Journal, 10 Sept. 1859, RA VIC/Add A 25/819; McClintock, *The Queen Thanks Sir Howard*, 31.

15 HE Journal, 21 Sept. 1859, RA VIC/Add A 25/819.

16 RA QVJ, 21 Sept. 1859.

17 Ibid.

18 HE Journal, 21 Sept. 1859, RA VIC/Add A 25/819.

19 RA QVJ, 21 Sept. 1859.

20 Fulford, *Dearest Child*, 211.

21 Notes and Reminiscences dictated by the Duke of Connaught, 3 Nov. 1926, RA VIC/Add A 15/8870.

22 HE Journal, 10 Oct. 1859, RA VIC/Add A 25/819; McClintock, *The Queen Thanks Sir Howard*, 33.

23 HE Journal, 18 Oct. 1859, RA VIC/Add A 25/819; McClintock, *The Queen Thanks Sir Howard*, 33.

24 HE Journal, 26 Nov. 1859, RA VIC/Add A 25/819; McClintock, *The Queen Thanks Sir Howard*, 35.

10

1 QV to HE, 12 Jan. 1873, RA VIC/Add A 25/349; McClintock, *The Queen Thanks Sir Howard*, 146.

2 HE Journal, 27 Nov. 1859, RA VIC/Add A 25/819.

3 HE Journal, 26 Nov. 1859; McClintock, *The Queen Thanks Sir Howard*, 35.

4 HE Journal, 8 Dec. 1859, RA VIC/Add A 25/819.

5 Ibid.

6 HE Journal, 12 Dec. 1859, RA VIC/Add A 25/819; McClintock, *The Queen Thanks Sir Howard*, 36.

7 HE to Albert, 14 Dec. 1859, RA VIC/Add A 15/68.

8 HE Journal, 31 Dec. 1859, RA VIC/Add A 25/819.

9 HE Journal, 20 Jan. 1860, RA VIC/Add A 25/819.

10 HE Journal, 31 Dec. 1859, RA VIC/Add A 25/819.

11 HE to Albert, 14 Dec. 1859, RA VIC/Add A 15/68.

12 HE Journal, 21 Dec. 1859, RA VIC/Add A 25/819.

13 McClintock, *The Queen Thanks Sir Howard*, 38.

14 Erskine, *Twenty Years at Court*, 363–4.

15 Martin, *Life of The Prince Consort*, vol. 4, 510.

16 HE Journal, 26 Dec. 1859, RA VIC/Add A 25/819.

17 HE Journal, 27 Dec. 1859, RA VIC/Add A 25/819.

18 HE Journal, 31 Dec. 1859, RA VIC/Add A 25/819.

19 HE Journal, 31 Dec. 1859, RA VIC/Add A 25/819.

11

1 HE Journal, 4 Jan. 1860, RA VIC/Add A 25/819.

2 Ibid.

3 HE Journal, 6 Feb. 1860, RA VIC/Add A 25/819.

4 HE Journal, 6 Jan. 1860, RA VIC/Add A 25/819.

5 HE Journal, 9 Jan. 1860, RA VIC/Add A 25/819.

6 HE Journal, 11 Jan. 1860, RA VIC/Add A 25/819.

7 Ibid.

8 HE to QV, On Prince Arthur playing at Eton with the College Boys, 20 Nov. 1860, RA VIC/Add A 15/85.

9 QV to HE, 18 Jan. 1860, family collection (transcript at RA VIC/Add A 25/26A); McClintock, *The Queen Thanks Sir Howard*, 40.

10 HE Journal, 18 Jan. 1860, RA VIC/Add A 25/819.

11 HE Journal, 20 Jan. 1860, RA VIC/Add A 25/819.

12 Ibid.

13 Ibid.

14 HE Journal, 6 Jan. 1860, RA VIC/Add A 25/819; McClintock, *The Queen Thanks Sir Howard*, 41. Colonel Bruce hinted at another reason for Bertie's lacklustre progress. He told Elphinstone that Bertie's tutor had revealed that 'though the thought lay there pregnant, the power to express it failed; in fact that his knowledge of English was very imperfect' – a suggestion perhaps of dyslexia or similar learning difficulty.

15 HE Journal, 6 Feb. 1860, RA VIC/Add A 25/819.

16 *The Times*, 26 Jan. 1860.

17 *United Service Magazine* (1860), part I, 118.

18 Luvaas, *Education of an Army*, 84.

19 *United Service Magazine* (1860), part I, 118.

20 HE to Albert, 29 Sept. 1860, RA VIC/Add A 15/80.

21 HE Journal, 29 May 1860, RA VIC/Add A 25/819.

22 HE to Andrew Scott, 30 Aug. 1859, National Library of Scotland, MS 8924/8.

12

1 HE Journal, 7 April 1860, RA VIC/Add A 25/819.

2 Ibid.

3 HE to QV, 2 Jan. 1860, RA VIC/Add A 15/87.

4 Bertie to HE, undated letter [1860], family collection.

5 Family collection.

6 HE Journal, 21 Sept. 1860, RA VIC/Add A 25/819.

7 HE to Albert, 10 Oct. 1860, RA VIC Add A 15/84.

8 HE Journal, 1 Sept. 1860, RA VIC/Add A 25/819.

9   HE Journal, 21 Sept. 1860, RA VIC/Add A 25/819.

10 Albert to HE, 4 Oct. 1860, family collection (transcript at RA VIC/Add A 25/43).

11 Weintraub, *Albert*, 395–6.

12 Ibid., 397.

13 Martin, *Life of The Prince Consort*, vol. 5, 288.

14 Bailey, *Diary*, 200.

15 *Outline of the proposed daily occupation of H.R.H. Prince Leopold*, 29 Jan. 1861, RA VIC/M 18/48.

16 Ibid.

17 QV to HE, 24 March 1861, RA VIC/Add A 25/44.

18 *The Times*, 26 March 1861.

19 St Aubyn, *Queen Victoria*, 318.

20 QV to HE, 15 Oct. 1861, RA VIC/Add A 25/53.

21 QV to Bertie, 2 June 1861, family collection; McClintock, *The Queen Thanks Sir Howard*, 42.

22 Bertie to QV, 4 June 1861, family collection; McClintock, *The Queen Thanks Sir Howard*, 42.

23 Fulford, *Dearest Child*, 334.

24 Ibid., 335.

25 Ibid.

26 Ibid., 340.

27 Zeepvat, *Prince Leopold*, 25.

28 Leopold to HE, 18 Sept. 1861, family collection.

29 Fulford, *Dearest Child*, 362.

30 Cartwright, *Journals of Lady Knightly*, 371.

13

1   QV to Albert, 5 July 1861, RA VIC/Add A 15/96.

2   Fulford, *Dearest Child*, 370.

3   HE to Dr Theodore Günther, 29 Nov. 1861, RA VIC/Add A 30/555.

4   Fulford, *The Prince Consort*, 264.

5   HE to Dr Theodore Günther, 7 Dec. 1861, RA VIC/Add A 30/558.

6 Fulford, *Dearest Child*, 372.

7 Martin, *Life of The Prince Consort*, vol. 5, 433.

8 HE to Dr Theodore Günther, 9 Dec. 1861, RA VIC/Add A 30/559.

9 HE Journal, 14 Dec. 1861, RA VIC/Add A 25/819.

10 Weintraub, *Albert*, 428.

11 HE Journal, 14 Dec. 1861, RA VIC/Add A 25/819.

12 Bloomfield, *Reminiscences*, 290.

13 Baillie and Bolitho, *Letters of Lady Augusta Stanley*, 242.

14 Martin, *Life of The Prince Consort*, vol. 5, 441.

15 Hibbert, *Queen Victoria in her Letters and Journals*, 156.

16 Rhodes James, *Albert*, 273.

17 HE Journal, 14 Dec. 1861, RA VIC/Add A 25/819.

18 Aston, *Duke of Connaught*, 46.

19 HE Journal, 14 Dec. 1861, RA VIC/Add A 25/819; McClintock, *The Queen Thanks Sir Howard*, 46.

20 HE Journal, 14 Dec. 1861, RA VIC/Add A 25/819; McClintock, *The Queen Thanks Sir Howard*, 47.

21 Charles Grey Journal, 14 Dec. 1861, Grey Papers, Durham University Library, GRE/D/5/4, fo. 395.

22 Chomet, *Helena*, 17.

23 Arthur to HE, family collection; McClintock, *The Queen Thanks Sir Howard*, 49.

14

1 Baillie and Bolitho, *Letters of Lady Augusta Stanley*, 246.

2 Fulford, *Dearest Child*, 375.

3 Leopold to HE, 16 Dec. 1861, family collection.

4 HE to Dr Theodore Günther, 15 Dec. 1861, RA VIC/Add A 30/560.

5 HE to Lady Bowater, draft dated 16 Dec. 1861, RA VIC/Add A 25/819.

6 HE to Lord Elphinstone, 9 Dec. 1864, Scottish Record Office, GD156/7/4.

7 Baillie and Bolitho, *Letters of Lady Augusta Stanley*, 247.

8 Charles Grey to Charles Phipps, 27 Dec. 1861, Grey Papers, Durham University Library GRE/D/11/1, fo. 265.

9 Wake, *Princess Louise*, 47.

10 St Aubyn, *Queen Victoria*, 349.

11 *The Times*, 24 Dec. 1861.

12 Wake, *Princess Louise*, 46.

13 Baillie and Bolitho, *Letters of Lady Augusta Stanley*, 251.

14 Quoted in Epton, *Victoria and her Daughters*, 102.

15 QV to HE, 11 March 1862, RA VIC/Add A 25/60; McClintock, *The Queen Thanks Sir Howard*, 48.

16 QV to HE, 26 Jan. 1862, RA VIC/Add A 25/57.

17 Charles Grey to Caroline Grey, 13 March 1862, Grey Papers, Durham University Library, GRE/D/5/3, fo. 30.

18 QV to HE, 11 April 1862, RA VIC/Add A 25/71; McClintock, *The Queen Thanks Sir Howard*, 50.

19 QV to HE, 11 March 1862, RA VIC/Add A 25/60; McClintock, *The Queen Thanks Sir Howard*, 49.

20 QV to Arthur, 10 May 1862, RA VIC/Add A 15/174; McClintock, *The Queen Thanks Sir Howard*, 49.

21 QV to HE, 4 Jan. 1867, RA VIC/Add A 25/193; McClintock, *The Queen Thanks Sir Howard*, 93.

22 Helena to Arthur, 9 March 1862, RA VIC/Add A 15/127.

23 Bailey, *Diary*, 179.

24 HE to QV, 5 March 1862, RA VIC/Add A 15/122.

25 QV to HE, 1 April 1862, RA VIC/Add A 25/66; McClintock, *The Queen Thanks Sir Howard*, 49.

26 HE to QV, 3 April 1862, RA VIC/Add A 15/162.

27 Cartwright, *Journals of Lady Knightly*, 33.

28 HE to QV, 2 Feb. 1863, RA VIC/Add A 15/248.

29 Zeepvat, *Prince Leopold*, 36.

30 RA QVJ, 5 April 1862.

31 QV to HE, 7 April 1862, RA VIC/Add A 25/68.

32 QV to HE, 5 April 1862, RA VIC/Add A 25/67.

33 Chomet, *Helena*, 18.

34 Charles Grey to Charles Phipps, 11 May 1862, Grey Papers,

Durham University Library, GRE/D/11/2, fo. 14.

35 Ponsonby, *Mary Ponsonby*, 6.

36 QV to HE, 8 April 1862, RA VIC/Add A 25/69.

37 QV to Arthur, 10 May 1862, RA VIC/Add A 15/174.

38 QV to HE, 18 May 1862, RA VIC/Add A 25/76.

39 Fulford, *Dearest Mama*, 85.

40 Fulford, *Dearest Child*, 337–8.

41 Hibbert, *Queen Victoria in her Letters and Journals*, 166.

42 HE to QV, 10 Sept. 1862, RA VIC/Add A 15/188.

43 Bertie to HE, 16 Sept. 1862, family collection.

44 Bertie to HE, 13 Nov. 1862, family collection.

45 HE to QV, 28 Sept. 1862, RA VIC/Add A 15/189.

46 HE to QV, 2 Oct. 1862, RA VIC/Add A 15/191; McClintock, *The Queen Thanks Sir Howard*, 62.

47 Ponsonby, *Mary Ponsonby*, 6.

48 QV to HE, 8 Oct. 1862, RA VIC/Add A 25/88; McClintock, *The Queen Thanks Sir Howard*, 63.

49 HE Journal, 8 Oct. 1862, private collection.

50 QV to HE, 4 Oct. 1862, RA VIC/Add A 25/85; McClintock, *The Queen Thanks Sir Howard*, 63.

15

1 Notes and Reminiscences dictated by the Duke of Connaught, 3 Nov. 1926, RA VIC/Add A 15/8870.

2 Bertie to HE, 13 Nov. 1862, family collection.

3 QV to HE, 30 Jan. 1863, RA VIC/Add A 25/100; McClintock, *The Queen Thanks Sir Howard*, 54.

4 HE to QV, 18 Nov. 1863; RA VIC/Add A 15/390.

5 McClintock, *The Queen Thanks Sir Howard*, 55.

6 QV to HE, 18 Aug. 1862, RA VIC/Add A 25/78.

7 QV to HE, 10 Sept. 1862, RA VIC/Add A 25/82.

8 HE to QV, 1 Nov. 1862, RA VIC/Add A 15/194.

9 HE to QV, 25 Nov. 1862, RA VIC/Add A 15/213.

10 HE to QV, 1 Nov. 1862, RA VIC/Add A 15/194.

11 Louise to Arthur, 2 Nov. 1862, RA VIC/Add A 15/195.

12 HE to QV, 4 Nov. 1862, RA VIC/Add A 15/196.

13 HE to QV, 20 Nov. 1862, RA VIC/Add A 15/212.

14 Notes and Reminiscences dictated by the Duke of Connaught, 3 Nov. 1926, RA VIC Add A 15/8870.

15 Ibid.

16 HE to QV, 1 Nov. 1862, RA VIC/Add A 15/194.

17 HE to QV, 7 Dec. 1867, RA VIC/Add A 15/1172.

18 Sir Charles Phipps to QV, 17 Nov. 1862, RA VIC/Add A 15/210.

19 QV to HE, 16 Nov. 1862, RA VIC/Add A 25/93; McClintock, *The Queen Thanks Sir Howard*, 50.

20 HE to QV, 18 Nov. 1862, RA VIC Add A 15/211.

21 Fulford, *Dearest Mama*, 234.

22 Zeepvat, *Prince Leopold*, 38.

23 QV to HE, 30 Jan. 1863, RA VIC/Add A 15/244.

24 Zeepvat, *Prince Leopold*, 194.

25 QV to HE, 14 Jan. 1863, RA VIC/Add A 25/99.

26 Cartwright, *Journals of Lady Knightly*, 69.

27 HE to QV, 1 Nov. 1862, RA VIC/Add A 15/194.

28 HE to QV, 11 July 1863, RA VIC/Add A 15/317.

29 Chomet, *Helena*, 13.

30 Charles Grey to Sir Charles Phipps, 1 June 1863, Grey Papers, Durham University Library, GRE/D/11/2/98.

31 HE to QV, 27 Nov. 1862, RA VIC/Add A 15/214.

32 Bertie to HE, 30 Jan. 1863, family collection.

33 HE to QV, 10 Jan. 1863, RA VIC/Add A 15/227; McClintock, *The Queen Thanks Sir Howard*, 56.

34 QV to HE, 13 Jan. 1863, RA VIC/Add A 25/98; McClintock, *The Queen Thanks Sir Howard*, 56.

16

1 Hudson, *Munby*, 152.

2 Hibbert, *Queen Victoria in her Letters and Journals*, 172.

3 Russell, *Memorial of the Marriage*, 65.

4 Cartwright, *Journals of Lady Knightly*, 48.

5 Russell, *Memorial of the Marriage*, 66.

6 Ibid., 70.

7 Vizetelly, *Glances Back*, vol. 2, 77.

8 *Illustrated London News*, 21 March 1863, 310.

9 Baillie and Bolitho, *Letters of Lady Augusta Stanley*, 307.

10 *Illustrated London News*, 21 March 1863, 310.

11 Vizetelly, *Glances Back*, vol. 2, 77.

12 William II, *My Early Life*, 1.

13 *Illustrated London News*, 21 March 1863, 310.

14 Matthew, *Gladstone Diaries*, vol. 6, 187.

15 *Illustrated London News*, 21 March 1863, 310.

16 *The Times*, 11 March 1863.

17 Baillie and Bolitho, *Letters of Lady Augusta Stanley*, 308.

18 Quoted in Hough, *Edward and Alexandra*, 91.

19 HE to QV, 12 March 1863, RA VIC/Add A 15/263.

20 QV to HE, 20 April 1863, RA VIC/Add A 25/105.

21 QV to HE, 10 Nov. 1863, RA VIC/Add A 25/109.

17

1 Pollock, *Gordon*, 130.

2 Arthur to QV, 28 Jan. 1866, RA VIC/Add A 15/805; McClintock, *The Queen Thanks Sir Howard*, 96.

3 Pollock, *Gordon*, 108.

4 QV to HE, 8 Dec. 1863, RA VIC/Add A 25/111.

5 HE to QV, 19 Jan. 1864, RA VIC/Add A 15/413; McClintock, *The Queen Thanks Sir Howard*, 65.

6 QV to HE, 17 April 1864, RA VIC/Add A 25/118.

7 QV to HE, 16 April 1864, RA VIC/Add A 25/117.

8 QV to HE, 7 Feb. 1864, RA VIC/Add A 25/115; McClintock, *The Queen Thanks Sir Howard*, 65.

9 HE memorandum on Prince Arthur's education, RA VIC/Add A 15/8805.

10 HE to QV, 19 Jan. 1864, RA VIC/Add A 15/413.

11 Ibid.

12 HE to QV, 9 Feb. 1864, RA VIC/Add A 15/427.

13 Quoted in Pakula, *An Uncommon Woman*, 201.

14 QV to HE, 8 Dec. 1863, RA VIC/Add A 25/111.

15 HE to QV, 9 Dec. 1863, RA VIC/Add A 15/402.

16 HE to QV, 4 Feb. 1864, RA VIC/Add A 15/423.

17 QV to HE, 7 Feb. 1864, RA VIC/Add A 25/115.

18 HE to QV, 26 Jan. 1864, RA VIC/Add A 15/419.

19 HE to QV, 11 Feb. 1864, RA VIC/Add A 15/429.

20 HE Journal, 1 July 1864, private collection.

21 HE to Sir Charles Phipps, 13 July 1864, RA VIC/Add A 15/505; McClintock, *The Queen Thanks Sir Howard*, 68.

22 QV to HE, 16 July 1864, RA VIC/Add A 25/125 (copy at RA VIC/Add A 15/50); McClintock, *The Queen Thanks Sir Howard*, 69.

23 QV to HE, 16 July 1864, RA VIC/Add A 25/126; McClintock, *The Queen Thanks Sir Howard*, 71.

24 QV to HE, 16 July 1864, RA VIC/Add A 25/126; McClintock, *The Queen Thanks Sir Howard*, 71.

25 HE to QV, 31 July–1 Aug. 1864, RA VIC/Add A 15/528.

26 HE Journal, 3 Aug. 1864, private collection.

27 QV to HE, 4 Aug. 1864, RA VIC/Add A 25/129; McClintock, *The Queen Thanks Sir Howard*, 72.

28 Colonel Francis Seymour to QV, 11 Aug. 1864, RA VIC/Add A 15/540.

29 Baillie and Bolitho, *Later Letters of Lady Augusta Stanley*, 33.

30 HE Journal, 21 Aug. 1864, private collection.

31 HE to QV, 13 Aug. 1864, RA VIC/Add A 15/542; McClintock, *The Queen Thanks Sir Howard*, 75.

32 HE Journal, 3 Sept. 1864, private collection.

33 HE to QV, 11 Aug. 1864, RA VIC/Add A 15/541.

34 HE to QV, 20 Sept. 1864, RA VIC/Add A 15/575.

35 Colonel Francis Seymour to QV, 11 Aug. 1864, RA VIC/Add A 15/540.

36 Colonel Francis Seymour to QV, 22 Aug. 1864, RA VIC/Add A 15/552.

37 HE to QV, 1 Oct. 1864, RA VIC Add A 15/581.

38 HE to Andrew Scott, 12 Feb. 1862, National Library of

Scotland, MSS 8924/8.
39 HE to QV, 24 Sept. 1864, RA VIC Add A 15/578.
40 QV to HE, 10 Oct. 1864, RA VIC Add A 25/137.

18

1 Charles Grey to Sir Charles Phipps, 5 Jan. 1865, Grey Papers, Durham University Library, GRE/D/11/3, fo. 40.
2 James Clark to Sir Charles Phipps, 30 Dec. 1864, Grey Papers, Durham University Library, GRE/D/11/3, fo. 38.
3 Charles Grey to Sir Charles Phipps, 5 Jan. 1865, Grey Papers, Durham University Library, GRE/D/11/3, fo. 40.
4 Fulford, *Your Dear Letter*, 22.
5 QV to HE, 4 Sept. 1864, RA VIC/Add A 25/134.
6 Zeepvat, *Prince Leopold*, 43.
7 QV to HE, 10 Oct. 1864, RA VIC/Add A 25/137.
8 Ibid.
9 QV to Lord Palmerston, 18 June 1865, RA VIC/Add A 15/700 (draft).
10 Charles Grey to Sir Charles Phipps, 25 Aug. 1865, Grey Papers, Durham University Library, GRE/D/11/3, fos 60–1.
11 QV to HE, 26 June 1865, RA VIC/Add A 25/154.
12 QV to HE, 11 July 1865, RA VIC/Add A 25/156.
13 QV to HE, 15 July 1865, RA VIC/Add A 25/157.
14 Lady Caroline Barrington to Charles Grey, Grey Papers, Durham University Library, GRE/D/I/11, fo. 35.
15 HE to QV, 11 Nov. 1865, RA VIC/Add A 15/776.
16 QV to HE, 8 Jan. 1866, RA VIC/Add A 25/167.
17 Helena to HE, 26 Feb. 1866, family collection.
18 QV to HE, 19 March 1866, RA VIC/Add A 25/168.
19 HE to QV, 21 March 1866, RA VIC/Add A 15/835.
20 QV to HE, 22 March 1866, RA VIC/Add A 25/171.
21 QV to HE, 19 March 1866, RA VIC/Add A 25/168.
22 Quoted in Zeepvat, *Prince Leopold*, 60.
23 Quoted ibid., 46.
24 QV to HE, 28 May 1866, RA VIC/Add A 25/176;

McClintock, *The Queen Thanks Sir Howard*, 85.

25 HE to QV, 10 July 1866, RA VIC/Add A 15/884.

26 QV to HE, 8 July 1866, RA VIC/Add A 25/179.

27 QV to HE, 12 July 1866, RA VIC/Add A 25/180.

28 QV to HE, 8 July 1866, RA Add A 25/179.

29 McClintock, *The Queen Thanks Sir Howard*, 182.

30 Thompson, *Queen Victoria*, 73. Boehm himself later became embroiled in gossip that his relationship with Princess Louise, to whom he taught sculpture, went beyond an appropriately deferential friendship. The artist's sudden death from a heart attack while alone with Louise in his London studio in December 1890 seemed to confirm even the most scurrilous rumours.

31 QV to HE, 12 July 1866, RA VIC/Add A 25/180; McClintock, *The Queen Thanks Sir Howard*, 85.

32 Ibid.

33 QV to HE, 3 Aug. 1866, RA VIC/Add A 25/183.

34 HE to QV, 13 Sept. 1866, RA VIC/Add A 15/923.

35 QV to HE, 10 Sept. 1866, RA VIC/Add A 25/185.

36 Longford, *Darling Loosy*, 98.

37 QV to HE, 7 Sept. 1874, RA VIC/Add A 25/427.

38 Ibid.

39 QV to HE, 2 Oct. 1874, RA VIC Add A 25/430.

40 Zeepvat, *Prince Leopold*, 51.

41 QV to HE, 19 Sept. 1866, RA VIC/Add A 15/186.

42 Zeepvat, *Prince Leopold*, 52.

43 Louise to Louisa Bowater, 22 Dec. 1866, British Library, Add MSS 46361, fo. 61.

Notes to Part Three

19

1 HE Journal, 27 Feb. 1865, private collection; McClintock, *The Queen Thanks Sir Howard*, 76–7.

2 HE Journal, 2 March 1865, private collection; McClintock, *The Queen Thanks Sir Howard*, 77.

3 HE to QV, 3 March 1865, RA VIC/Add A 15/645.

4 Filon, *Memoirs of the Prince Imperial*, 19.

5 HE Journal, 2 March 1865, private collection; McClintock, *The Queen Thanks Sir Howard*, 77.

6 Filon, *Memoirs of the Prince Imperial*, 29.

7 HE Journal, 2 March 1865, private collection; McClintock, *The Queen Thanks Sir Howard*, 77.

8 Journal submitted by HE to QV, 20 April 1865, RA VIC/Add A 15/677.

9 QV to HE, 11 May 1865, RA VIC/Add A 25/149; McClintock, *The Queen Thanks Sir Howard*, 82.

10 HE to Andrew Scott, undated [Sept. 1865], MSS ACC 8924/8.

11 HE to QV, 24 Oct. 1865, RA VIC/Add A 15/770.

12 Sir Charles Phipps to QV, 27 Sept. 1865, RA VIC/Add A 15/765.

13 HE to Lord Elphinstone, 19 Oct. 1866, National Archives of Scotland, GD 156/7/4.

14 HE to the Adjutant General, April 1866, Grey Papers, Durham University Library, GRE/D/3/9, fo. 13.

15 QV to Arthur, 22 April 1866, RA VIC/Add A 15/847 (copy).

16 QV to HE, 1 May 1866, RA VIC Add A 25/174 ('thro' all this tract of years / Wearing the white flower of a blameless life': *The Idylls of the King*, dedication, ll. 23–4).

17 QV to HE, 16 Jan. 1865, RA VIC/Add A 25/144.

18 Louise to Arthur, 10 May 1866, RA VIC/Add A 15/856.

19 HE to QV, 27 June 1866, RA VIC/Add A 15/880.

20 Walker, *Days of a Soldier's Life*, 233.

21 Fulford, *Your Dear Letter*, 79.

22 HE to QV, 25 July 1866, RA VIC/Add A 15/892.

23 Alice to HE, undated [1866]; McClintock, *The Queen Thanks Sir Howard*, 86.

24 HE to QV, 11 Sept. 1866, RA VIC/Add A 15/921.

25 HE to QV, 15 Nov. 1866, RA VIC/Add A 15/944.

26 HE to QV, 24 Nov. 1866, RA VIC/Add A 15/949.

27 HE to QV, 5 Jan. 1867, RA VIC/Add A 15/996.

28 HE to the Reverend Charles Kingsley, 25 Jan. 1867, British Library, Add MSS 41299, fo. 124.
29 HE to QV, 12 Jan. 1867, RA VIC/Add A 15/1011.
30 QV to HE, 23 Sept. 1866, RA VIC/Add A 25/187.
31 Helena to HE, 28 Sept. 1866, family collection.
32 Vicky to HE, 22 Jan. 1867, RA VIC/Add A 15/1025; quoted in McClintock, *The Queen Thanks Sir Howard*, 93.
33 Vicky to Arthur, undated [1867], quoted in McClintock, *The Queen Thanks Sir Howard*, 94.
34 Alice, *Letters to Her Majesty*, 162.
35 QV to HE, 26 Jan. 1867, RA VIC/Add A 25/197; McClintock, *The Queen Thanks Sir Howard*, 94.
36 *Report on Age and Measurement of Prince Arthur on entering Woolwich*, RA VIC/Add A 15/1043.
37 HE to QV, 17 April 1867, RA VIC/Add A 15/1069.
38 HE to QV, 8 June 1867, RA VIC Add A 15/1084.
39 Pollock, *Kitchener*, 19.
40 Ibid., 28.
41 QV to HE, 23 June 1868, RA VIC/Add A 25/229.
42 Ibid.

20

1 HE to QV, 28 June 1867, RA VIC/Add A 15/1093.
2 HE to QV, 25 June 1867, RA VIC/Add A 15/1091; McClintock, *The Queen Thanks Sir Howard*, 97.
3 HE to QV, 28 June 1867, RA VIC/Add A 15/1093.
4 HE to QV, 27 Aug. 1867, RA VIC/Add A 15/1100; McClintock, *The Queen Thanks Sir Howard*, 99.
5 QV to HE, 27 Aug. 1867, RA VIC/Add A 25/204.
6 Charles Grey to Lord Derby, 4 July 1867, Grey Papers, Durham University Library, GRE/D/3/14.
7 Lord Derby to Charles Grey, 27 June 1867, Grey Papers, Durham University Library, GRE/D/3/13.
8 RA QVJ, 4 Aug. 1867.
9 QV to HE, 27 Aug. 1867, RA VIC/Add A 25/204;

McClintock, *The Queen Thanks Sir Howard*, 107.

10 HE to QV, 10 Oct. 1867, RA VIC/Add A 15/1120.

11 *The Times*, 12 Oct. 1867.

12 Alice, *Letters to Her Majesty*, 162.

13 HE to QV, 16 Oct. 1867, RA VIC/Add A 15/1126; McClintock, *The Queen Thanks Sir Howard*, 101.

14 HE to QV, 13 Jan. 1868, RA VIC/Add A 15/1186.

15 Charles Grey to Henry Austin, 16 Dec. 1868, Grey Papers, Durham University Library, GRE/D/2/12, fo. 71.

16 QV to HE, 4 Jan. 1872, RA VIC/Add A 25/324; McClintock, *The Queen Thanks Sir Howard*, 141.

17 HE to QV, 5 Jan. 1872, RA VIC/Add A 15/1843; McClintock, *The Queen Thanks Sir Howard*, 142.

18 Wake, *Princess Louise*, 86.

19 Arthur to HE, 28 Jan. 1868, family collection.

20 Arthur to HE, 1 Feb. 1868, RA VIC/Add A 25/217.

21 Quoted in Zeepvat, *Prince Leopold*, 58.

22 Cambridge to HE, 23 Oct. 1866, family collection.

23 HE to QV, 17 June 1868; RA VIC/Add A 15/1230.

24 QV to Arthur, 19 June 1868, RA VIC/Add A 15/1232.

25 HE to QV, 4 Aug. 1868, RA VIC/Add A 15/1261.

26 Cambridge to HE, 8 Aug. 1868, family collection.

27 Louise to HE, 8 Aug. 1868, family collection; McClintock, *The Queen Thanks Sir Howard*, 108.

28 Arengo-Jones, *Queen Victoria in Switzerland*, 66.

29 QV to HE, undated memorandum [1868], RA VIC/Add A 25/213.

30 HE to QV, 7 Aug. 1868, RA VIC Add A 15/1268.

31 QV to HE, 10 Aug. 1868, RA VIC/Add A 25/234; McClintock, *The Queen Thanks Sir Howard*, 108.

32 Harrison, *Recollections*, 127.

33 HE Journal, 27 March 1854, family collection.

34 See D. A. B. Young, 'Florence Nightingale's Fever', *British Medical Journal*, vol. 311 (23 Dec. 1995), 1697–1700.

35 Louise to HE, 20 June 1868, family collection.

21

1 Baillie and Bolitho, *Later Letters of Lady Augusta Stanley*, 65.

2 Hibbert, *Queen Victoria in her Letters and Journals*, 204.

3 Sir Richard Mayne, Commissioner of the Metropolitan Police, memorandum dated 14 Oct. 1867, Grey Papers, Durham University Library, GRE/D/2/12/2.

4 QV to HE, 22 Dec. 1867, RA VIC/Add A 25/212; McClintock, *The Queen Thanks Sir Howard*, 104.

5 HE to QV, 20 Oct. 1867, RA VIC/Add A 15/1131.

6 HE to QV, 16 Oct. 1867, RA VIC/Add A 15/1126.

7 Louise to HE, undated [Oct. 1867], family collection.

8 Charles Grey to Gathorne Hardy, 19 Oct. 1867, Grey Papers, Durham University Library, GRE/D/2/12/19.

9 Charles Grey to Gathorne Hardy, 19 Oct. 1867; Grey Papers, Durham University Library, GRE/D/2/12/27. The number of police guarding the train was later raised to twenty-four.

10 The Chief Constable of Reading Police to Charles Grey, 12 Nov. 1867, Grey Papers, Durham University Library, GRE/D/2/12/44.

11 HE to QV, 17 Dec. 1867, RA VIC/Add A 15/1175.

12 Gathorne Hardy to Charles Grey, 17 Dec. 1867, Grey Papers, Durham University Library, GRE/D/2/12/57.

13 QV to HE, 22 Dec. 1867, RA VIC/Add A 25/212; McClintock, *The Queen Thanks Sir Howard*, 104.

14 Charles Grey to Lord Derby, 19 Dec. 1867, Grey Papers, Durham University Library, GRE/D/III/3/30.

15 Cullen, *The Empress Brown*, 126.

16 Hibbert, *Queen Victoria in her Letters and Journals*, 202.

17 HE to QV, 26 April 1868, RA VIC/Add A 15/1220.

18 The Duke of Buckingham to HE, undated [April 1868], family collection.

19 Fulford, *Your Dear Letter*, 200.

20 Quoted in Weintraub, *Victoria*, 347.

21 QV to HE, 12 April 1869, RA VIC/Add A 25/251.

22 Earl Spencer to HE, 30 March 1869, family collection.

23 Henry Bruce to QV, 7 April 1869, RA VIC/Add A 15/1380.

24 QV to HE, 2 April 1869, RA VIC/Add A 25/250.

25 Arthur to QV, 5 April 1869, RA VIC/Add A 15/1379.

26 Sir Joseph Napier to Henry Bruce, 20 April 1869, RA VIC/Add A 15/1403.

27 HE to QV, 13 April 1869, RA VIC/Add A 15/1390.

28 HE to Annie, undated [1877], family collection; McClintock, *The Queen Thanks Sir Howard*, 188.

29 HE to QV, 28 April 1869, RA VIC/Add A 15/1415.

30 HE to QV, 29 April 1869, RA VIC/Add A 15/1417.

31 HE to QV, 5 May 1869, RA VIC/Add A 15/1427.

32 Charles Grey to HE, 14 Oct. 1869, RA VIC/Add A 15/1513.

33 Montreal *Evening Star*, 17 Sept. 1869.

34 Sir John Young to Lord Granville, 14 July 1869, RA VIC/Add A 15/1459.

35 Lord Alexander Russell to Lord Granville, 3 June 1869, National Archives, FO 5/1346/122.

36 Edward Thornton to Lord Clarendon, 10 July 1869, National Archives, FO 5/1346/184.

37 Lord Clarendon to QV, 29 July 1869, RA VIC/Add A 15/1461; McClintock, *The Queen Thanks Sir Howard*, 111.

38 William Gladstone to QV, 31 July 1869, RA/VIC Add A 15/1466; McClintock, *The Queen Thanks Sir Howard*, 111.

39 HE to QV, 31 July 1869, RA VIC/Add A 15/1465.

40 QV to William Gladstone, 1 Aug. 1869, RA VIC/Add A 15/1468; McClintock, *The Queen Thanks Sir Howard*, 112.

41 Sir John Macdonald to Charles Coursol, 26 Oct. 1869, National Archives of Canada, MG26A, vol. 13 (516, pt 2), p. 296.

42 *Universal News*, 2 Oct. 1869, National Archives, FO 5/1347/209.

43 Edward Thornton to Sir John Young, 27 Sept. 1869, National Archives, FO 5/1347/162.

44 Charles Coursol to Sir John Macdonald, 30 Oct. 1869, National Archives of Canada, MG26A, vol. 243, 108741.

22

1 QV to HE, 11 Aug. 1869, RA VIC/Add A 25/263; McClintock, *The Queen Thanks Sir Howard*, 113.

2 QV to HE, telegram dated 12 Aug. 1869, RA VIC/Add A 25/264; McClintock, *The Queen Thanks Sir Howard*, 113.

3 QV to HE, 13 Aug. 1869, RA VIC/Add A 25/266.

4 HE to QV, 12 Aug. 1869, RA VIC/Add A 15/1476.

5 HE to QV, 22 Aug. 1869, RA VIC/Add A 15/1478.

6 Longford, *Darling Loosy*, 110.

7 HE to QV, 26 Aug. 1869, RA VIC/Add A 15/1481.

8 Charles Coursol to Sir John Macdonald, 30 Oct. 1869, National Archives of Canada, MG26A, vol. 243, 108741.

9 Walter Page to Gilbert McMicken, 18 Sept. 1869, National Archives of Canada, MG26A, vol. 243, 108683.

10 *Toronto Globe*, 22 Sept. 1869.

11 HE Journal, 24 Sept. 1869, RA VIC/Add A 15/1502.

12 HE to QV, 8 Oct. 1869, RA VIC/Add A 15/1510; McClintock, *The Queen Thanks Sir Howard*, 115.

13 HE Journal, 24 Sept. 1869, RA VIC/Add A 15/1502; McClintock, *The Queen Thanks Sir Howard*, 116.

14 Arthur to QV, 3 Oct. 1869, RA VIC/Add A 15/1505.

15 HE Journal, 24 Sept. 1869, RA VIC/Add A 15/1502; McClintock, *The Queen Thanks Sir Howard*, 116.

16 HE Journal, 27 Sept. 1869, RA VIC/Add A 15/1507.

17 *Buffalo Express* report, quoted in *Toronto Globe*, 30 Sept. 1869.

18 HE Journal, 27 Sept. 1869, RA VIC/Add A 15/1507; McClintock, *The Queen Thanks Sir Howard*, 117.

19 *Buffalo Express* report, quoted in *Toronto Globe*, 30 Sept. 1869.

20 New York *Journal of Commerce*, quoted in *Montreal Evening Star*, 17 Sept. 1869.

21 HE to QV, 5 Nov. 1869, RA VIC/Add A 15/1524; McClintock, *The Queen Thanks Sir Howard*, 117.

22 Blom and Blom, *Canada Home*, 342.

23 HE Journal, 24 Sept. 1869, RA VIC/Add A 15/1502.

24 *Toronto Globe*, 2 Oct. 1869.

25 HE Journal, 1 Oct. 1869, RA VIC/Add A 15/1507.

26 *Montreal Evening Star*, 8 Oct. 1869.

27 HE to QV, 8 Oct. 1869, RA VIC/Add A 15/1510.

28 *Montreal Evening Star*, 8 Oct. 1869.

29 HE Journal, 20 Sept. 1869, RA VIC/Add A 15/1496.

30 Charles Coursol to Sir John Macdonald, 30 Oct. 1869, National Archives of Canada, MG26A, vol. 243, p. 108737.

31 HE to QV, 22 Oct. 1869, RA VIC/Add A 15/1516.

32 HE to QV, 29 Oct. 1869, RA VIC/Add A 15/1521; McClintock, *The Queen Thanks Sir Howard*, 119.

33 Lord Granville to QV, undated [Oct. 1869], RA VIC/Add A 15/1522.

34 QV to HE, 2 Dec. 1869, RA VIC/Add A 25/274.

35 HE to QV, 30 Dec. 1869, RA VIC/Add A 15/1548.

23

1 HE to QV, 29 Oct. 1869, RA VIC/Add A 15/1521.

2 HE to QV, 12 Nov. 1869, RA VIC/Add A 15/1526.

3 HE to QV, 14 Jan. 1870, RA VIC/Add A 15/1554; McClintock, *The Queen Thanks Sir Howard*, 123.

4 QV to HE, 6 Oct. 1869, RA VIC/Add A 25/271.

5 Lord Clarendon to QV, 17 Nov. 1869, RA VIC/Add A 15/1531.

6 Undated newspaper cutting, RA VIC Add A 15/1573.

7 HE to Sir John Cowell, 1 Feb. 1870, McClintock, *The Queen Thanks Sir Howard*, 125.

8 Radforth, *Royal Spectacle*, 336.

9 HE to QV, 24 Jan. 1870, RA VIC/Add A 15/1557.

10 HE to Sir John Cowell, 1 Feb. 1870, McClintock, *The Queen Thanks Sir Howard*, 125.

11 Arthur to QV, 24 Jan. 1870, RA VIC/Add A 15/1558.

12 HE to QV, 24 Jan. 1870, RA VIC/Add A 15/1557.

13 Ibid.

14 Ibid; McClintock, *The Queen Thanks Sir Howard*, 125.

15 HE to QV, 29 Jan. 1870, RA VIC/Add A 15/1562.

16 HE to Sir John Cowell, 1 Feb. 1870, McClintock, *The Queen Thanks Sir Howard*, 124.

17 Ibid.

18 HE to QV, 24 Jan. 1870, RA VIC/Add A 15/1557; McClintock, *The Queen Thanks Sir Howard*, 125.

19 HE to Sir John Cowell, 1 Feb. 1870, McClintock, *The Queen Thanks Sir Howard*, 124.

20 HE to QV, 24 Jan. 1870, RA VIC/Add A 15/1557.

21 Frankland, *Witness of a Century*, 38.

22 Edward Thornton to Lord Clarendon, 8 March 1870, RA VIC/Add A 15/1589.

23 *New York Times*, 29 Jan. 1870, 4, col. 5.

24 Edward Thornton to Lord Clarendon, 1 Feb. 1870, RA VIC/Add A 15/1566.

25 HE to Sir John Cowell, 1 Feb. 1870, McClintock, *The Queen Thanks Sir Howard*, 125.

26 HE to QV, 7–8 Feb. 1870, RA VIC/Add A 15/1571; McClintock, *The Queen Thanks Sir Howard*, 126.

27 Edward Thornton to Lord Clarendon, 7 Feb. 1870, RA VIC/Add A 15/1570.

28 HE to QV, 7–8 Feb. 1870, RA VIC Add A 15/1571; McClintock, *The Queen Thanks Sir Howard*, 126.

29 Edward Thornton to Lord Clarendon, 7 Feb. 1870, RA VIC/Add A 15/1570.

30 *New York Times*, 22 Feb. 1870, 2, col. 6.

31 HE to QV, 7–8 Feb. 1870, RA VIC/Add A 15/1571; McClintock, *The Queen Thanks Sir Howard*, 126.

32 HE to Sir John Cowell, 1 Feb. 1870, McClintock, *The Queen Thanks Sir Howard*, 125.

33 Edward Thornton to QV, 8 March 1870, RA VIC/Add A 15/1589; McClintock, *The Queen Thanks Sir Howard*, 125.

34 Arthur to QV, 30 Jan. 1870, RA VIC/Add A 15/1564.

35 Longford, *Darling Loosy*, 118.

36 HE to QV, 15 April 1870, RA VIC Add A 15/1606; McClintock, *The Queen Thanks Sir Howard*, 129.

37 Quoted in Zeepvat, *Prince Leopold*, 64.

38 HE to Sir John Cowell, 1 Feb. 1870, McClintock, *The Queen Thanks Sir Howard*, 125.

39 HE to Gilbert McMicken, 2 April 1870, National Archives of Canada, MG26A, vol. 244a, p. 109583.

40 HE to QV, 27 May 1870, RA VIC/Add A 15/1621.

41 J. A. Cole, *Prince of Spies*, 64.

42 Arthur to QV, 29 May 1870, RA VIC/Add A 15/1622.

43 QV to HE, 15 June 1870, RA VIC/Add A 25/286.

44 Hibbert, *Queen Victoria: A Personal History*, 331.

45 QV to HE, 24 Feb. 1870, RA VIC/Add A 25/279.

46 QV to HE, 14 April 1870, RA VIC/Add A 25/283; McClintock, *The Queen Thanks Sir Howard*, 128.

47 Charles Grey to Lady Caroline Grey, 24 Oct. 1869, Grey Papers, Durham University Library, GRE/D/V/3/148–9.

48 QV to HE, 15 July 1870, RA VIC/Add A 25/287.

49 McClintock, *The Queen Thanks Sir Howard*, 130.

50 HE to QV, 6 July 1870, RA VIC/Add A 15/1649.

51 HE to QV, 15 June 1870, RA VIC/Add A 15/1633; McClintock, *The Queen Thanks Sir Howard*, 131.

52 Lord Granville to QV, 25 June 1870, RA VIC/Add A 15/1651.

24

1 QV to HE, 4 Aug. 1870, RA VIC/Add A 25/289.

2 *The Times*, 3 Jan. 1871, 3, col. D.

3 Wantage, *Lord Wantage*, 202.

4 HE to QV, 17 Oct. 1870, RA /VIC Add A 15/1666.

5 *The Times*, 16 Jan. 1871, 5, col. E.

6 *The Times*, 6 Feb. 1871, 4, col. A.

7 QV to HE, 16 Feb. 1871, RA VIC/Add A 25/298.

8 QV to HE, 23 July 1871, RA VIC/Add A 15/1794.

9 HE to QV, 14 Feb. 1871, RA VIC/Add A 15/1697.

10 QV to HE, 16 Feb. 1871, RA VIC/Add A 25/298.

11 QV to HE, 15 June 1870, RA VIC/Add A 25/286.

12 Charlotte Zeepvat, 'A Doctor at Court', *Royalty Digest*, vol. 3, no. 7 (Jan. 1998), 194.

13 Louise to HE, 12 April 1870, family collection.

14 Ibid.

15 Louise to HE, 25 May 1870, family collection.

16 Wake, *Princess Louise*, 126.

17 Zeepvat, 'A Doctor at Court', 195.

18 QV to HE, 9 Jan. 1871, RA VIC/Add A 25/296.

19 QV to HE, 6 Nov. 1870, RA VIC/Add A 25/292.

20 Wake, *Princess Louise*, 141.

25

1 QV to HE, 1 May 1871, RA VIC/Add A 25/311.

2 Ibid.

3 QV to HE, 11 May 1871, RA VIC/Add A 25/312.

4 Arthur to QV, 21 April 1871, RA VIC/Add A 15/1730.

5 QV to HE, 21 May 1871, RA VIC/Add A 25/313; McClintock, *The Queen Thanks Sir Howard*, 138.

6 QV to HE, 21 May 1871, RA VIC/Add A 25/313.

7 HE to QV, 14 July 1871; McClintock, *The Queen Thanks Sir Howard*, 110.

8 QV to HE, 17 July 1871, RA VIC/Add A 25/317.

9 QV to HE, 7 April 1871, RA VIC/Add A 25/302; McClintock, *The Queen Thanks Sir Howard*, 134.

10 QV to HE, 7 April 1871, RA VIC/Add A 25/302; McClintock, *The Queen Thanks Sir Howard*, 133.

11 QV to HE, 8 April 1871, RA VIC/Add A 25/304; QV to HE, 7 April 1871, RA VIC/Add A 25/302; McClintock, *The Queen Thanks Sir Howard*, 135.

12 HE to QV, 8 April 1871, RA VIC/Add A 15/1714.

13 HE to QV, 7 April 1871, RA VIC/Add A 15/1710.

14 QV to Arthur, 16 April 1871, RA VIC/Add A 15/1722.

15 Sir Thomas Biddulph to QV, 14 April 1871, RA VIC/Add A 15/1720.

16 Ibid.

17 Henry Ponsonby to QV, 18 June 1871, RA VIC R51/60.

18 Lord Napier to HE, 1 Sept. 1871, family collection.

19 Henry Ponsonby to QV, 18 June 1871, RA VIC R51/60.

20 QV to Henry Ponsonby, 19 June 1871, RA VIC R51/61.

21 QV to HE, 4 July 1871, family collection; McClintock, *The Queen Thanks Sir Howard*, 136.

22 HE to QV, 5 July 1871, RA VIC/Add A 15/1785.

23 QV to HE, 13 Jan. 1872, RA VIC/Add A 25/325; McClintock, *The Queen Thanks Sir Howard*, 153.

24 Ibid.

25 QV to HE, 13 Jan. 1872, RA VIC/Add A 25/325.

26 QV to HE, 14 Feb. 1872, RA VIC/Add A 25/329.

27 QV to Arthur, 30 Dec. 1871, RA VIC/Add A 15/1840.

28 HE to QV, 15 Jan. 1872, RA VIC/Add A 15/1848.

29 HE to QV, 18 Jan. 1872, RA VIC/Add A 15/1849; McClintock, *The Queen Thanks Sir Howard*, 153.

30 HE to QV, 23 Jan. 1872, RA VIC/Add A 15/1856.

31 HE to QV, 21 Jan. 1872, RA VIC/Add A 15/1852.

32 QV to HE, 20 Jan. 1872, RA VIC/Add A 25/326.

33 QV to HE, 23 Jan. 1872, RA VIC/Add A 25/327.

34 HE to QV, 26 Jan. 1872, RA VIC/Add A 15/1858.

35 QV to HE, 24 Feb. 1872, RA VIC/Add A 25/330.

36 QV to HE, 29 Jan. 1872, RA VIC/Add A 25/328.

37 HE to QV, 10 Feb. 1872, RA VIC/Add A 15/1869; McClintock, *The Queen Thanks Sir Howard*, 154.

38 QV to HE, 15 April 1872, RA VIC/Add A 25/335.

39 QV to HE, 14 Feb. 1872, RA VIC/Add A 25/329; McClintock, *The Queen Thanks Sir Howard*, 154.

26

1 QV to HE, 24 Feb. 1872, RA VIC/Add A 25/330; McClintock, *The Queen Thanks Sir Howard*, 146.

2 Fulford, *Darling Child*, 31.

3 Lamont-Brown, *John Brown*, 110.

4 *The Times*, 1 March 1872, 9, col. D.

5   Cullen, *The Empress Brown*, 167.
6   QV to Arthur, 5 March 1872, RA VIC/Add A 15/1877.
7   *The Times*, 11 April 1872, 11, col. A.
8   Cullen, *The Empress Brown*, 166.
9   QV to Arthur, 5 March 1872, RA VIC/Add A 15/1877.
10 Tisdall, *Queen Victoria's John Brown*, 169.
11 Fulford, *Darling Child*, 34.
12 QV to HE, 14 March 1872, RA VIC/Add A 25/331; McClintock, *The Queen Thanks Sir Howard*, 147.
13 QV to HE, 17 March 1872, RA VIC/Add A 25/332; McClintock, *The Queen Thanks Sir Howard*, 147–8.
14 Fulford, *Darling Child*, 38.
15 QV to HE, 31 March 1872, RA VIC/Add A 25/333.
16 HE to QV, 29 July 1873, RA VIC/Add A 15/2056.
17 QV to HE, 9 Aug. 1873, RA VIC/Add A 25/374.
18 QV to HE, 7 Aug. 1873, RA VIC/Add A 25/373; McClintock, *The Queen Thanks Sir Howard*, 157.
19 QV to HE, 1 Sept. 1873, RA VIC/Add A 25/378.
20 QV to HE, 30 Aug. 1873, RA VIC/Add A 25/377.
21 QV to HE, 22 July 1872, RA VIC/Add A 25/344.
22 Fulford, *Darling Child*, 125.
23 HE to QV, 12 Jan. 1874, RA VIC/Add A 15/2126.
24 HE to QV, 15 Jan. 1874, RA VIC/Add A 15/2130; McClintock, *The Queen Thanks Sir Howard*, 170.
25 Baillie and Bolitho, *Later Letters of Lady Augusta Stanley*, 193.
26 Ibid., 196.
27 Ibid., 191.
28 HE to QV, 15 Jan. 1874, RA VIC/Add A 15/2130; McClintock, *The Queen Thanks Sir Howard*, 170.
29 Baillie and Bolitho, *Later Letters of Lady Augusta Stanley*, 200.
30 Ibid., 203.
31 Ibid., 201.
32 Ibid., 212.
33 HE to QV, 25 Jan. 1874, RA VIC/Add A 15/2136.
34 Baillie and Bolitho, *Later Letters of Lady Augusta Stanley*, 203.

35 HE to QV, 18 Jan. 1874, RA VIC/Add A 15/2132; McClintock, *The Queen Thanks Sir Howard*, 171.

36 Baillie and Bolitho, *Later Letters of Lady Augusta Stanley*, 203.

37 Ibid., 215.

38 Loftus, *Diplomatic Reminiscences*, 87.

39 Ibid., 88.

40 Ibid., 89.

41 McClintock, *The Queen Thanks Sir Howard*, 172.

42 Fulford, *Darling Child*, 127.

43 HE to QV, 18 Jan. 1874, RA VIC/Add A 15/2132; McClintock, *The Queen Thanks Sir Howard*, 173.

44 HE to QV, 5 Feb. 1874, RA VIC/Add A 15/2142; McClintock, *The Queen Thanks Sir Howard*, 173.

45 McClintock, *The Queen Thanks Sir Howard*, 174.

Notes to Part Four

27

1 QV to HE, 18 March 1880, RA VIC/Add A 25/551; McClintock, *The Queen Thanks Sir Howard*, 213.

2 QV to HE, 5 July 1875, RA VIC/Add A 25/446; McClintock, *The Queen Thanks Sir Howard*, 161.

3 QV to HE, 12 July 1875, RA VIC/Add A 25/447.

4 QV to HE, 5 July 1875, RA VIC/Add A 25/446; McClintock, *The Queen Thanks Sir Howard*, 161 (the Queen's mention of Colonel Baker by name was marked 'indecipherable' by McClintock).

5 QV to HE, 1 Aug. 1875, RA VIC/Add A 25/452.

6 QV to HE, 3 Aug. 1875, RA VIC/Add A 25/453.

7 HE to QV, 17 July 1875, RA VIC/Add A 15/2306; McClintock, *The Queen Thanks Sir Howard*, 162.

8 Filon, *Memoirs of the Prince Imperial*, 135–6.

9 HE to QV, 17 Aug. 1875, RA VIC/Add A 15/2329.

10 QV to HE, 6 Aug. 1875, RA VIC/Add A 25/454.

11 Vicky to HE, 27 Nov. 1875, RA VIC/Add A 25/463.

12 Vicky to HE, 27 Nov. 1875, RA VIC/Add A 25/463; McClintock, *The Queen Thanks Sir Howard*, 193.

13 Vicky to HE, 18 Dec. 1875, family collection.

14 QV to HE, 31 Aug. 1875, family collection.

15 HE to QV, 21 March 1876, RA VIC/Add A 15/2432.

16 QV to HE, 18 April 1877, RA VIC/Add A 25/521.

17 QV to HE, 1 July 1876, family collection; McClintock, *The Queen Thanks Sir Howard*, 175.

18 HE to Annie, 1 July 1876, family collection; McClintock, *The Queen Thanks Sir Howard*, 176.

19 QV to Arthur, 9 Dec. 1876; RA VIC/Add A 15/2545.

20 Eden, *Juliana Horatia Ewing*, 206.

21 Ewing, *Story of a Short Life*, 47.

22 Carey, *Empress Eugenie*, 137.

23 HE to Annie, 23 July 1877, family collection.

24 Annie Journal, 7 Sept. 1877, family collection.

25 QV to HE, telegram dated 10 Sept. 1877, family collection.

26 Lady Ely to HE, 9 Oct. 1877, family collection.

28

1 QV to HE, 24 July 1877, RA VIC/Add A 25/523.

2 Fulford, *Darling Child*, 285.

3 HE to QV, 3 March 1878, RA VIC/Add A 15/2725.

4 QV to HE, 14 Oct. 1877, family collection (copy at RA VIC/Add A 25/526).

5 Fulford, *Darling Child*, 286.

6 Ibid., 285.

7 HE to Annie, 8 May 1878, family collection; McClintock, *The Queen Thanks Sir Howard*, 189.

8 HE to QV, 8 May 1878, RA VIC/Add A 15/2783; McClintock, *The Queen Thanks Sir Howard*, 190.

9 HE to Annie, 30 Aug. 1878, family collection.

10 HE to Annie, 8 May 1878, family collection; McClintock, *The Queen Thanks Sir Howard*, 189.

11 HE to Annie, 11 May 1878, family collection.

12 HE to QV, 11 May 1878, RA VIC/Add A 15/2791.

13 HE to Annie, 12 May 1878, family collection; McClintock, *The Queen Thanks Sir Howard*, 191.

14 HE to QV, telegram 11 May 1878 (transcript in family collection).

15 HE to Annie, 12 May 1878, family collection.

16 HE to Annie, 12 May 1878, family collection; McClintock, *The Queen Thanks Sir Howard*, 191.

17 Ibid.

18 HE to Annie, 9 May 1878, family collection.

19 HE to Annie, 16 June 1878, family collection; McClintock, *The Queen Thanks Sir Howard*, 192.

20 HE to Annie, 9 May 1878, family collection.

21 Ibid.

22 Lord Salisbury to Henry Ponsonby, 19 May 1878, RA VIC/Add A 15/2841.

23 HE to Annie, 9 June 1878, family collection; McClintock, *The Queen Thanks Sir Howard*, 196.

24 HE to Annie, 9 June 1878, family collection; McClintock, *The Queen Thanks Sir Howard*, 191.

25 HE to Annie, undated letter [June 1878], family collection.

26 HE to Annie, 12 June 1878, family collection.

27 Ibid.; McClintock, *The Queen Thanks Sir Howard*, 192.

28 Arthur to QV, 10 June 1878, RA VIC/Add A 15/2874; McClintock, *The Queen Thanks Sir Howard*, 192.

29 Arthur to QV, 11 June 1878, RA VIC/Add A 15/2875; McClintock, *The Queen Thanks Sir Howard*, 192.

30 HE to Annie, 12 June 1878, family collection.

31 HE to Annie, undated letter [June 1878], family collection; McClintock, *The Queen Thanks Sir Howard*, 192.

32 Longford, *Victoria RI*, 527.

33 HE to QV, 17 June 1878, RA VIC/Add A 15/2881; McClintock, *The Queen Thanks Sir Howard*, 193.

34 HE to QV, 23 June 1869, RA VIC/Add A 15/1448.

35 HE to Annie, 21 Aug. 1878, family collection.

36 Pakula, *An Uncommon Woman*, 390.
37 HE to Annie, 31 Aug. 1878, family collection; McClintock, *The Queen Thanks Sir Howard*, 194.
38 HE to Annie, undated [1878], family collection.
39 Rodd, *Social and Diplomatic Memories*, 50.
40 HE to Annie, 31 Aug. 1878, family collection.
41 Van der Kiste, *Dearest Vicky*, 152.
42 HE to Annie, 31 Aug. 1878, family collection.
43 Röhl, *Young Wilhelm*, 330.
44 Ibid., 333.
45 Pakula, *An Uncommon Woman*, 416.
46 HE to Annie, 6 Sept. 1878, family collection; McClintock, *The Queen Thanks Sir Howard*, 194.

29

1 Hibbert, *Queen Victoria in her Letters and Journals*, 254.
2 HE to Annie, 7 Jan. 1879, family collection.
3 Ibid.
4 HE to Annie, 8 Jan. 1879, family collection.
5 HE to Annie, 7 Jan. 1879, family collection.
6 HE to Annie, 17 Jan. 1879, family collection.
7 HE to Annie, undated letter [Jan. 1879], family collection; McClintock, *The Queen Thanks Sir Howard*, 197.
8 HE to Annie, 12 Jan. 1879, family collection; McClintock, *The Queen Thanks Sir Howard*, 198.
9 HE to Annie, undated [11 Jan. 1879], family collection.
10 HE to Annie, undated [Jan. 1879], family collection; McClintock, *The Queen Thanks Sir Howard*, 197.
11 HE to Annie, 22 Jan. 1879, family collection.
12 HE to Annie, 24 Jan. 1879, family collection; McClintock, *The Queen Thanks Sir Howard*, 201.
13 Pakula, *An Uncommon Woman*, 404.
14 Radziwell, *Those I Remember*, 165.
15 HE to Annie, 11 Jan. 1879, family collection.
16 HE to Annie, 24 Jan. 1879, family collection; McClintock, *The*

Queen Thanks Sir Howard, 199.

17 HE to Annie, 24 Jan. 1879, family collection.

18 HE to Annie, 17 Jan. 1879, family collection; McClintock, *The Queen Thanks Sir Howard*, 198.

19 HE to Annie, 19 Jan. 1879, family collection.

20 HE to Annie, 21 Jan. 1879, family collection.

21 David, *Zulu*, 219.

22 Arthur to QV, 12 Feb. 1879, RA VIC/Add A 15/2975.

23 Filon, *Memoirs of the Prince Imperial*, 188.

24 Ibid., 185.

25 Ibid., 187.

26 Knight, *With his Face to the Foe*, 109.

27 Ibid., 110.

28 HE to Annie, 14 March 1879, family collection.

29 Ibid.; McClintock, *The Queen Thanks Sir Howard*, 203.

30 HE to Annie, 14 March 1879, family collection.

31 McClintock, *The Queen Thanks Sir Howard*, 205.

32 Annie to Jane Cole, family collection; McClintock, *The Queen Thanks Sir Howard*, 207.

33 Annie to Jane Cole, family collection; McClintock, *The Queen Thanks Sir Howard*, 208.

34 HE to QV, 2 April 1879, RA VIC/Add A 15/3074.

35 Knight, *With his Face to the Foe*, 212.

36 Weintraub, *Victoria*, 436.

37 Hibbert, *Queen Victoria in her Letters and Journals*, 257.

38 HE to QV, 20 June 1879, RA VIC/Add A 15/3215.

39 Arthur to QV, 22 June 1879, RA VIC/Add A 15/3217.

40 Harrison, *Recollections*, 177.

41 Knight, *With his Face to the Foe*, 262–3.

42 Arthur to QV, 29 June 1879, RA VIC/Add A 15/3219.

30

1 HE to Charles Gordon, 1 May 1881, British Library, Add MSS 51302, fo. 41.

2 Ibid., fo. 42.

3 HE to A. C. Cooke, 30 April 1881, British Library Add MSS 51302, fo. 48.

4 Quoted in HE to Gordon, 1 May 1881, British Library, Add MSS 51302, fo. 41.

5 HE to Charles Gordon, 1 May 1881, British Library Add MSS 51302, fo. 50.

6 Strachey, *Eminent Victorians*, 241.

7 Henry Ponsonby to QV, 3 May 1881, RA VIC/Add A 15/3418.

8 HE to Charles Gordon, 2 May 1881, British Library Add MSS 51302, fo. 45.

9 Charles Gordon to HE, 24 June 1881, family collection; McClintock, *The Queen Thanks Sir Howard*, 216–17.

10 HE to QV, 30 July 1882, RA VIC/Add A 15/3634; McClintock, *The Queen Thanks Sir Howard*, 221.

11 QV to HE, 10 Aug. 1882, RA VIC/Add A 25/567.

12 HE to QV, 30 July 1882, RA VIC/Add A 15/3631.

13 QV to HE, 10 Sept. 1882, RA VIC/Add A 25/577.

14 Victoria, *More Leaves from the Journal*, 397.

15 HE to QV, 13 Sept. 1882, RA VIC/Add A 15/3699.

16 HE to QV, 13 Sept. 1882, RA VIC/Add A 15/3691.

17 HE to QV, 4 Oct. 1882, RA VIC/Add A 15/3770.

18 Frankland, *Witness of a Century*, 103.

19 Victoria, *More Leaves from the Journal*, 398.

20 Ibid., 401.

21 QV to HE, 15 June 1883, RA VIC/Add A 25/596.

22 QV to HE, 4 March 1884, family collection.

23 Reid, *Ask Sir James*, 40.

24 Lamont-Brown, *John Brown*, 178.

25 HE to Annie, 14 Jan. 1878, family collection; McClintock, *The Queen Thanks Sir Howard*, 215.

26 Hibbert, *Queen Victoria in her Letters and Journals*, 285.

27 HE to QV, 28 May 1884, RA VIC/Add A 15/4246.

28 Arthur to HE, 31 March 1884, RA VIC/Add A 25/607.

31

1 Hibbert, *Queen Victoria in her Letters and Journals*, 278.

2 Wolseley to HE, 24 July 1883, family collection.

3 Pollock, *Gordon*, 275.

4 Hibbert, *Queen Victoria in her Letters and Journals*, 284.

5 HE to Annie, undated [Aug. 1884], family collection; McClintock, *The Queen Thanks Sir Howard*, 227.

6 Van der Kiste, *Dearest Vicky*, 162.

7 Victoria of Prussia, *My Memoirs*, 67.

8 HE to Annie, 28 Aug. 1884, family collection.

9 HE to Annie, undated [Aug. 1884], family collection; McClintock, *The Queen Thanks Sir Howard*, 228.

10 Rodd, *Social and Diplomatic Memories*, 51.

11 HE to QV, 1 Sept. 1884, RA VIC/Add A 15/4306; McClintock, *The Queen Thanks Sir Howard*, 228.

12 HE to Annie, 15 Sept. 1884, family collection.

13 HE to Annie, 16 Sept. 1884, family collection.

14 QV to HE, 10 Sept. 1884, RA VIC/Add A 25/628; McClintock, *The Queen Thanks Sir Howard*, 229.

15 Vassili, *Berlin Society*, v–vi.

16 Sir Edward Malet to Lord Granville, 11 Oct. 1884, National Archives, PRO 30/39/179, fo. 4.

17 Rodd, *Social and Diplomatic Memories*, 71.

18 War Office to Sir Edward Malet, 5 Jan. 1885 and 24 Jan. 1885, National Archives, PRO FO 64/1073.

19 Vassili, *Berlin Society*, 36.

20 HE to QV, 15 Dec. 1884, RA VIC/Add A 15/4365; McClintock, *The Queen Thanks Sir Howard*, 234.

21 QV to HE, 27 Dec. 1884, RA VIC/Add A 25/643.

22 Vassili, *Berlin Society*, 156.

23 Annie to Jane Cole, 25 Dec. 1884, family collection; McClintock, *The Queen Thanks Sir Howard*, 235.

32

1　*The Times*, 23 Jan. 1885, 5, col. A.

2　HE to QV, 22 Jan. 1885, RA VIC/Add A 15/4391.

3　Sir Edward Malet to Lord Granville, 7 Feb. 1885, National Archives PRO 30/29/179, fo. 147.

4　QV to Arthur, 18 April 1885, RA VIC/Add A 15/4454.

5　Fulford, *Beloved Mama*, 181.

6　Corti, *Alexander von Battenberg*, 150.

7　Fulford, *Beloved Mama*, 181.

8　Vicky to HE, 30 Jan. 1885, RA VIC/Add A 25/646; McClintock, *The Queen Thanks Sir Howard*, 236.

9　Vicky to HE, 9/10 April 1885, RA VIC/Add A 25/663; McClintock, *The Queen Thanks Sir Howard*, 237.

10　Annie Journal, 27 February 1885, family collection.

11　Vicky to HE, 14 March 1885, RA VIC/Add A 25/657.

12　Vicky to HE, 24 July 1885, RA VIC/Add A 25/683.

13　Vicky to HE, 9/10 April 1885, RA VIC/Add A 25/663.

14　Vicky to HE, 18 April 1885, RA VIC/Add A 25/665; McClintock, *The Queen Thanks Sir Howard*, 239.

15　Vicky to HE, 18 April 1885, RA VIC/Add A 25/665.

16　Vicky to HE, 1 May 1885, RA VIC/Add A 25/668.

17　McClintock, *The Queen Thanks Sir Howard*, 236.

18　Ibid., 237.

19　Fulford, *Beloved Mama*, 182.

20　Vicky to HE, 24 July 1885, RA VIC/Add A 25/683.

21　Vicky to HE, 21 Sept. 1885, family collection.

22　Vicky to HE, 26 Sept. 1885, RA VIC/Add A 25/699.

23　Corti, *Alexander von Battenberg*, 176.

24　Vicky to HE, 19 Oct. 1885, RA VIC/Add A 25/708.

25　Vicky to HE, 18 Dec. 1885, RA VIC/Add A 25/721.

26　Vicky to HE, 3 Sept. 1886, RA VIC/Add A 25/750.

27　Ramm, *Beloved and Darling Child*, 41.

28　Victoria of Prussia, *My Memoirs*, 72.

29　Vicky to HE, 10 Oct. 1886, family collection; McClintock, *The Queen Thanks Sir Howard*, 241.

30 Annie Journal, 8 Oct. 1886, family collection.
31 Vicky to HE, 7 Nov. 1886; RA VIC/Add A 25/752.
32 Ibid.
33 Vicky to HE, 10 Oct. 1886, family collection; McClintock, *The Queen Thanks Sir Howard*, 241.

33

1 Lant, *Insubstantial Pageant*, 92.
2 Hibbert, *Queen Victoria in her Letters and Journals*, 304.
3 Buckle, *Letters of Queen Victoria*, vol. 1, 317.
4 Victoria of Prussia, *My Memoirs*, 79.
5 McClintock, *The Queen Thanks Sir Howard*, 186.
6 Allingham and Radford, *William Allingham*, 359.
7 Hare, *Story of My Life*, vol. 6, 69.
8 HE to QV, 8 Dec. 1887, RA VIC/Add A 15/5000.
9 HE to QV, 26 March 1888, RA VIC/Add A 15/5063.
10 QV to HE, 21 March 1888, family collection (copy at RA VIC/Add A 25/756); quoted in McClintock, *The Queen Thanks Sir Howard*, 242.
11 Rodd, *Social and Diplomatic Memories*, 133.
12 Ponsonby, *Mary Ponsonby*, 299.
13 Buckle, *Letters of Queen Victoria*, vol. 1, 417.
14 Ibid., 418.
15 HE to Annie, 18 June 1888, family collection; McClintock, *The Queen Thanks Sir Howard*, 243.
16 HE to Annie, 19 June 1888, family collection; McClintock, *The Queen Thanks Sir Howard*, 244.
17 Buckle, *Letters of Queen Victoria*, vol. 1, 420.

34

1 McClintock, *The Queen Thanks Sir Howard*, 257.
2 QV to Arthur, 7 March 1890, RA VIC/Add A 15/5425.
3 Account of Proctor Thomas, a passenger in *Tongariro*, RA VIC/Add A 15/5427.
4 Account of Arthur Pendarves Vivian, RA VIC/Add A 15/5432A.

5 Account of Proctor Thomas, RA VIC/Add A 15/5427.

6 Edith Cole to Sir John Cowell, 11 March 1890; RA VIC/Add A 15/5432.

7 Account of Proctor Thomas, RA VIC/Add A 15/5427.

8 Edith Cole to Sir John Cowell, 11 March 1890, RA VIC/Add A 15/5432.

9 Telegram of Edith Cole to Sir John Cowell, 13 March 1890, RA VIC/Add A 15/5433.

35

1 *The Times*, 21 March 1890, 10, col. C.

2 Annie to QV, 19 March 1890, RA VIC/Add A 15/5468.

3 McClintock, *The Queen Thanks Sir Howard*, 2.

4 Reid, *Ask Sir James*, 40.

5 Pakula, *An Uncommon Woman*, 656.

6 Frankland, *Witness of a Century*, 162.

7 Arthur to Annie, 7 Feb. 1901, RA VIC/Add A 25/840.

8 Family collection.

Index

Page numbers in **bold** refer to pages with illustrations.